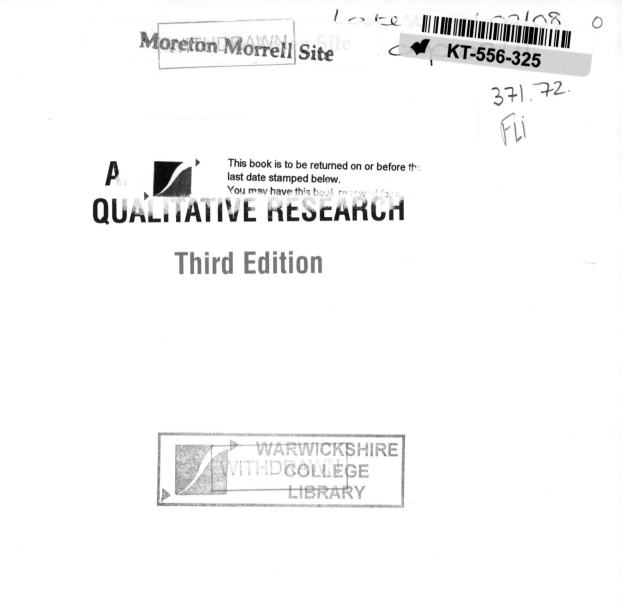

A
QUALITATIVE RESEARCH

Third Edition

AN INTRODUCTION TO QUALITATIVE RESEARCH

Third Edition

UWE FLICK

SAGE Publications

London ● Thousand Oaks ● New Delhi

SAGE Publications Ltd
1 Oliver's Yard
55 City Road
London EC1Y 1SP

SAGE Publications Inc.
2455 Teller Road
Thousand Oaks, California 91320

SAGE Publications India Pvt Ltd
B-42, Panchsheel Enclave
Post Box 4109
New Delhi 110 017

British Library Cataloguing in Publication data

A catalogue record for this book is available from the British Library

ISBN-10 1-4129-1145-0   ISBN-13 978-1-4129-1145-0
ISBN-10 1-4129-1146-X (pbk)   ISBN-13 978-1-4129-1146-7 (pbk)

Library of Congress Control Number 2005927681

Typeset by C&M Digitals (P) Ltd., Chennai, India
Printed on paper from sustainable resources
Printed in Great Britain by The Alden Press, Oxford

CONTENTS

BOXES

FIGURES

TABLES

PREFACE TO THE THIRD EDITION

Qualitative research is in an ongoing process of proliferation with new approaches and methods appearing and it is being taken up by more and more disciplines as a core part of their curriculum. New and older perspectives in qualitative research can be seen in sociology, psychology, anthropology, nursing, engineering, cultural studies and so on. One result of such developments is that the available literature in qualitative research is constantly growing; new books on qualitative research are published, new journals are started and filled with methodological papers on, and results of, qualitative research. Another result is that qualitative research is in danger of falling into different fields of research and methodological discussions and that in the process core principles and ideas of qualitative research across these different fields could be omitted.

Since the publication of the first and second editions of this book, several areas of qualitative research have developed further, which made some revisions necessary again. Research ethics is an issue that attracts a growing attention and has to be developed and specified for qualitative research. The combination of qualitative and quantitative research is *en vogue* as a topic. The Internet has become a field of research and a tool to do research at the same time. Documents are a sort of data in their own right. These are some of the current trends in qualitative research, which made a revision of the book a challenge.

This third edition has been revised, expanded, and complemented compared with earlier editions in several ways:

- Throughout the text, discussions and references have been updated.
- In all chapters, additional features have been integrated including a chapter overview at the beginning, case studies, a list of key points, and a set of exercises at the end.
- Several new chapters have been added:

  - A chapter that is intended to guide you through the book (Chapter 1)
  - A chapter on ethics in qualitative research (Chapter 4)
  - Another chapter explores the uses of literature in qualitative research (Chapter 5)

- An overview chapter concerning research design (Chapter 12)
- A chapter about using documents (Chapter 19)
- Another chapter is about qualitative online research (Chapter 20).

- Some chapters have been moved and integrated in the overall structure of the book – for example, the chapter about qualitative and quantitative research (Chapter 3).
- Several chapters have been extended like the introductory chapter, which has been complemented by a section about the current state of development in qualitative research (Chapter 2), or the chapter about theoretical positions underlying qualitative research (Chapter 6), which now includes sections about feminism, and positivism and constructionism.
- A couple of chapters have been split into more clearly defined and focused chapters. One example is the separation of the chapter about observation (Chapter 17) from that on visual data methods (Chapter 18). In Part 6, the chapter on conversation and discourse analysis (Chapter 24) has been separated from the one on narrative and hermeneutic analysis (Chapter 25).

Berlin

PART 1

FRAMEWORK

Part 1 is set up as a framework for doing qualitative research and for comprehending the later chapters in this book. Chapter 1 serves as a guide for the book, introducing its major parts. Then, it provides an orientation about why qualitative research has become particularly relevant in the last decades of the twentieth century and at the beginning of the twenty-first century. The book begins with an overview of the backgrounds of qualitative research. I will then move on to introduce you to the essential features of qualitative research (in general) and also to the variety of methods and approaches (Chapter 2). Chapter 3 introduces the relations of qualitative and quantitative research as well as the possibilities and pitfalls of combining both approaches. The fourth chapter outlines the ethical issues linked to qualitative researching. Together, these chapters offer background to assist the research and utilization of qualitative methods, which are outlined and discussed in greater detail later in the book.

1

GUIDE TO THIS BOOK

CHAPTER OBJECTIVES
After reading this chapter, you should be able to

✓   understand the organization of this book.
✓   locate various aspects of qualitative research in this book.
✓   identify which chapters to use for various purposes.

Approach of the Book

This book has been written with two groups of readers in mind–the novice and the experienced researcher. First of all, it addresses the novice to qualitative research, maybe even to social research in general. For this group, mostly under-graduate and graduate students, it is conceived as a basic introduction to princi-ples and practices of qualitative research, the theoretical and epistemological background, and the most important methods. Second, the researcher in the field may use this book as a sort of toolkit while facing the practical issues and prob-lems of the day-to-day business of qualitative research. Qualitative research is establishing itself in many social sciences, in psychology, in nursing and the like. As a novice to the field or as an experienced researcher, you can use a great variety of specific methods, each of which starts from different premises and pursues different aims. Each method in qualitative research is based on a specific understanding of its object. However, qualitative methods should not be regarded independently of the research process and the issue under study. They are specifically embedded in the research process and are best understood and described using a process-oriented perspective. Therefore, a presentation of the different steps in the process of qualitative research is the central concern in the book. The most important methods for collecting and interpreting data and for assessing and presenting results are presented and located in the process-oriented framework. This should give you an overview of the field of qualitative research, of concrete methodological alternatives and of their claims, applications, and limits. This should enable you to choose the most appropriate methodological strategy with respect to your research question and issues.

The starting point in this book is that qualitative research, above all, works with text. Methods for collecting information–interviews or observations–produce data, which are transformed into texts by recording and transcription. Methods of interpretation start from these texts. Different routes lead towards the texts at the center of the research and away from them. Very briefly, the qualitative research process can be represented as a path from *theory to text* and another from *text back to theory*. The intersection of the two paths is the collection of verbal or visual data and their interpretation in a specific research design.

Structure of the Book

The book has seven major parts, which aim at unfolding the process of qualitative research in its major stages.

Part 1 sets out the Framework of doing qualitative research as discussed in Chapters 2 through 4.

- *Chapter 2* explores and answers the fundamental questions of qualitative research. For this purpose, the current relevance of qualitative research is outlined against the background of recent trends in society and in social sciences. Qualitative versus quantitative approaches are broached and contextualized in examples of research in the United States and Europe. Finally, the chapter discusses techniques to learn the application of qualitative research.
- *Chapter 3* develops the relation between qualitative and quantitative research. Guiding questions are raised and implemented for assessing the appropriateness of qualitative and quantitative research. This chapter allows you to learn various approaches and then decide which one is best for your research.
- *Chapter 4* focuses on a different framework for qualitative research–research ethics. Ethics of qualitative research deserve special attention, as you will come much closer to privacy issues and the day-to-day life of your participants. Reflection and sensitivity to privacy are essential before launching a

qualitative study. At the same time, general discussions about research ethics often miss the special needs and problems of qualitative research. After reading this chapter, you should know the importance of a code of ethics before beginning your research as well as the need for ethics committees. Whether research is ethical or not depends as much on practical decisions in the field.

After setting out the framework of qualitative research, we can understand the process of a qualitative study. Part 2 takes you From Theory to Text.

- *Chapter 5* introduces the use of literature–theoretical, methodological, and empirical–in a qualitative study. It addresses the use of and the finding of such resources while doing your study and while writing about it. At the end, some suggestions are made how to find literature.
- *Chapter 6* addresses different theoretical positions underlying qualitative research. Symbolic interactionism, ethnomethodology, and structuralist approaches are discussed as paradigmatic approaches for their basic assumptions and recent developments. From these discussions, the list of essential features of qualitative research is completed. In the end, I will address two theoretical debates, which are currently very strong in qualitative research. Feminism and gender studies and the discussion about positivism and constructionism inform a great deal of qualitative research – in how to understand the issues of research, in how to conceive the research process and in how to use qualitative methods.
- *Chapter 7* continues the discussions raised in Chapter 6, as well as outlining the epistemological background of constructionist qualitative research using text as empirical material.

In Part 3, Research Design, we come to the more practical issues of how to plan qualitative research.

- *Chapter 8* outlines the qualitative research process and shows that the single steps are linked much closer with each other than in the clear-cut step-by-step process in quantitative research.
- *Chapter 9* addresses the relevance of a well-defined research question for conducting research and how to arrive at such a research question.
- *Chapter 10* is about how to enter a field and how to get in touch with the participants of your study.
- *Chapter 11* covers the topic of sampling – how to select your participants or groups of participants, situations, and so on.
- *Chapter 12* offers an overview of practical issues of how to design qualitative research. It also covers the basic designs in qualitative research.

Part 4 introduces one of the major strategies of collecting data. Verbal data are produced in interviews, narratives, and focus groups.

- *Chapter 13* presents a range of interviews, which are characterized by using a set of open-ended questions to stimulate the participants' answers. Some of these interviews, like the focused interview, are used for very different purposes, whereas some, like the expert interview, have a more specific field of application.
- *Chapter 14* outlines a different strategy leading to verbal data. Here the central step is the stimulation of narratives (i.e., overall narratives of life histories or more focused narratives of specific situations). These narratives are stimulated in specially designed interviews – the narrative interview in the first and the episodic interview in the second alternative.
- *Chapter 15* explores ways of collecting verbal data in a group of participants. Focus groups are currently very prominent in some areas, while group discussions have a longer tradition. Both are based on the stimulation of discussions whereas group interviews are more about answering questions. Joint narratives want to make a group of people tell a story as a common activity.
- *Chapter 16* summarizes the methods for collecting verbal data. It is intended to support you in making your decision between the different ways outlined in Part 4 by comparing the methods and by developing a checklist for such a decision.

Part 5 examines multi-focus data, such as different communication approaches as well as the use of electronic data.

- *Chapter 17* deals with non-participant or participant observation and ethnography. Other data collection strategies (like interviewing, using documents, etc.) are employed to complement observation itself.
- *Chapter 18* extends the visual part of data to analyzing, studying, and using media like photos, film, and video as data.
- *Chapter 19* goes one step further and explores the use of documents beyond visual data. It explores the construction and process of these documents in qualitative research.
- *Chapter 20* explores the Internet as a field of research and an instrument for conducting research. Here you will meet some methods again, which were dealt with in the chapters before – like interviews, focus groups and ethnography. But here they are described for their use in qualitative online research.
- *Chapter 21* takes comparative and summarizing perspectives on multi-focus data. This overview will help you decide when to choose which method and what the advantages and problems of each method are.

The first parts of the book concentrate on the collection and production of data. Part 6 deals with proceeding from text to theory – how to develop theoretically relevant insights from these data and the text produced with them. For this purpose, qualitative methods for analyzing data are the focus of this part.

- *Chapter 22* discusses how to document data in qualitative research. Field notes and transcriptions are presented in detail in their technical and more general aspects and in examples.
- *Chapter 23* covers methods using coding and categories as tools for analyzing text.
- *Chapter 24* continues with approaches that are more interested in how something is said and not only in what is said. Conversation analysis looks at how a conversation in everyday life or in an institutional context works, which methods people use to communicate any form of context. Discourse and genre analyses have developed this approach further in different directions.
- *Chapter 25* explores narrative analysis and hermeneutics. These approaches examine texts with a combination of content and formal orientations. Here, a narrative is not only analyzed for what is told, but also for how the story is unfolded when it is told and what that reveals about what is told.
- *Chapter 26* discusses the use of computers and especially software for qualitative data analysis. Principles and examples of the most important software are presented. This chapter should help you to decide whether to use software for your analysis and which one.
- *Chapter 27* gives a summarizing overview of the approaches to analyzing text and other material in qualitative research. Again, you will find a comparison of the different approaches and a checklist, which both should help you to select the appropriate method for analyzing your material and advance from your data to theoretically relevant findings.

The final Part 7 goes back to context and methodology and addresses issues of grounding and writing qualitative research.

- *Chapter 28* discusses the use of traditional quality criteria in qualitative research and their limits. It also informs about alternative criteria, which have been developed for qualitative research or for specific approaches. In the end it shows why answering the question of the quality of qualitative research is currently a major expectation from outside of the discipline, and a need for improving the research practice at the same time.
- *Chapter 29* continues with this issue, but explores ways of answering the question of quality in qualitative research beyond the formulation of criteria. Instead strategies of quality management, of answering the question of indication, and triangulation are discussed for this purpose.

- *Chapter 30* finally, addresses issues of writing qualitative research–reporting the results to an audience and the influences of the way of writing on the findings of research. The chapter finishes with a look at the future of qualitative research oscillating between art and method.

Special features of the Book

I have included several features to make this book more useful for learning qualitative research and while conducting a qualitative study. You will find them throughout the following chapters.

- Chapter Objectives

  At the beginning of every chapter, you will find an orientation through the single chapter, which consists of two parts: first there will be an overview of the issues covered in the chapter. Second, you will find a list of chapter objectives, which define what you should have learnt and know after reading the chapter. This should guide you through the chapter and help you to find topics again after reading the chapter or the whole book.

- Boxes

  Major issues are highlighted in boxes. These boxes will have different functions–some summarize central steps of a method, some give practical advice and some list example questions (for interview methods for example). They should structure the text, so that it will be easier to keep an orientation while reading it.

- Case Studies

  Case studies found throughout the text examine methods and prominent researchers' applications of them. The collections of case studies showcase the practice of principles in special occasions. They should help you to think about how things are done in qualitative research, and about which problems or questions come to mind while reading the case studies and the like. Many of the case studies come from published research of key figures in qualitative research. Other case studies come from my own research and in several case studies, you will meet the same research projects, which have been used before to illustrate a different issue.

- Checklists

  Checklists appear in various chapters, particularly in Chapters 16, 21, and 27. Many of the checklists offer a decision-making process for selecting methods and lists for checking the correctness of a decision.

- Tables

  In Chapters 16, 21, and 27, you will also find tables comparing the methods described in detail in the previous chapters. These tables take a comparative perspective on a single method that permits seeing its strengths and weaknesses in the light of other methods. This is a particular feature of this book and is intended again to help you to decide for the "right" method for your research issue.

- Key Questions

  The methods, which are presented here, are evaluated at the end of their presentation by a list of key questions (e.g., What are the limitations of the method?). These key questions come up repeatedly and should make an orientation and assessment of the single method easier.

- Cross-referencing

  Cross-referencing offers the linking of specific methods or methodological problems. This facilitates the placement of information into context.

- Key Points

  At the end of each chapter, you will find a list of key points summarizing the chapter's most important points.

- Exercises

  The exercises at the end of a chapter act as a review in assessing other people's research and planning future research.

- Further Reading

  At the end of a chapter, the list of references offers an opportunity to extend the knowledge presented in the chapter.

How to Use this Book

There are several ways you can use this book, depending on your field specialty and experience in qualitative research. The first way of reading the book is from the beginning to the end, as it guides you through the steps of planning to setting up a research project. These steps lead you from getting the necessary background knowledge to designing and conducting research to issues of quality assessment and writing about your research. In the event that you use this book as a reference tool, the following list highlights areas of interest:

- Theoretical background knowledge about qualitative research is found in Chapters 2 through 7, in which they offer an overview and the philosophical underpinnings.
- Methodological issues of planning and conceiving qualitative research are spelled out in Part 3, where questions of designing qualitative research are discussed. Part 7 retreats to this conceptual level when examining the quality issues in research.
- Issues of how to plan qualitative research are presented on a practical level in Part 3, where you find suggestions for how to sample, how to formulate a research question, or how to enter a field.
- Parts 4 through 7 reveal practical issues relevant for doing qualitative research where a range of methods is described in detail.

2

QUALITATIVE RESEARCH: WHY AND HOW TO DO IT

CHAPTER OBJECTIVES
After reading this chapter, you should be able to

✓ **understand qualitative research in its history and background.**
✓ **discuss current trends in qualitative research.**
✓ **comprehend the common features of qualitative research and the diversity of research perspectives.**
✓ **understand why qualitative research is a timely and necessary approach in social research.**

The Relevance of Qualitative Research

Why use qualitative research; is there a special need for such an approach in the current situation? As a first step, I will outline, why the interest in qualitative research has been growing so much in the last decades. Qualitative research is of specific relevance to the study of social relations, owing to the fact of the pluralization of life worlds. Key expressions for this pluralization are the "new obscurity" (Habermas 1996), the growing "individualisation of ways of living and biographical patterns" (Beck 1992), and the dissolution of "old" social inequalities into the new diversity of milieus, subcultures, lifestyles, and ways of living. This pluralization requires a new sensitivity to the empirical study of issues. Advocates of postmodernism have argued that the era of big narratives and theories is over. Locally, temporally and situationally limited narratives are now required. With regard to the pluralization of lifestyles and patterns of interpretation in modern and post-modern society, Herbert Blumer's statement becomes relevant once again and has new implications. "The initial position of the social scientist and the psychologist is practically always one of lack of familiarity with what is actually taking place in the sphere of life chosen for study" (1969, p. 33). Rapid social change and the resulting diversification of life worlds are increasingly confronting social researchers with new social contexts and perspectives. These are so new for them that their traditional deductive methodologies—deriving research questions and hypotheses from theoretical models and testing them against empirical evidence—are failing due to the differentiation of objects. Thus, research is increasingly forced to make use of inductive strategies. Instead of starting from theories and testing them, "sensitizing concepts" are required for approaching social contexts to be studied. However, contrary to widespread misunderstanding, these concepts are themselves influenced by previous theoretical knowledge. But here, theories are developed from empirical studies. Knowledge and practice are studied as *local* knowledge and practices (Geertz 1983).

Concerning research in psychology in particular, it is argued that it lacks relevance for everyday life because it is not sufficiently dedicated to exactly describing the details of a case in its concrete circumstances. The study of subjective meanings and everyday experience and practice is as essential as the contemplation of narratives (Bruner 1991; Sarbin 1986) and discourses (Harré 1998).

Limits of Quantitative Research as a Starting Point

Beyond these general developments, the limitations of quantitative approaches have always been taken as a starting point to give reasons, why to use qualitative research. Traditionally, psychology and social sciences have taken the natural sciences and their exactness as a model, paying particular attention to developing quantitative and standardized methods. Guiding principles of research and of planning research have been used for the following purposes: to clearly isolate causes and effects, to properly operationalize theoretical relations, to measure and to quantify phenomena, to create research designs allowing the generalization of findings, and to formulate general laws. For example, random samples of populations are selected in order to make a survey representative of that population. *General statements* are made as independently as possible about the concrete cases that have been studied. *Observed phenomena* are classified on their frequency and distribution. In order to classify causal relations and their validity as clearly as possible, the conditions under which the phenomena and relations under study occur are controlled as far as possible. Studies are designed in such a way that the researcher's (as well as interviewer's, observer's, and so on.) influence can be excluded as far as possible. This should guarantee the objectivity of the study, whereby the subjective views of the researcher as well as those of the individuals under study are largely eliminated. General obligatory standards for carrying out and evaluating empirical social research have been formulated. Procedures such as how to construct a questionnaire, how to design an experiment, and how to statistically analyze data have become increasingly refined.

For a long time, psychological research has almost exclusively used experimental designs. These have produced vast quantities of data and results, which demonstrate and test psychological relations of variables and the conditions under which they are valid. For the reasons mentioned above, for a long period empirical social research was mainly based on standardized surveys. The aim was to document and analyze the frequency and distribution of social phenomena in the population (e.g., certain attitudes). To a lesser extent, standards and procedures of quantitative research have been fundamentally examined and analyzed in order to clarify the research objects and questions they are appropriate to or not.

Negative results abound when the targets previously mentioned are balanced. The ideals of objectivity are largely disenchanted; some time ago Max Weber (1919) proclaimed science's task is the "disenchantment of the world". More recently, Bonß and Hartmann (1985) have stated the increasing disenchantment of the sciences–their methods and their findings. In the case of the social sciences, the low degree of applicability of results and the problems of connecting them to theory and societal developments are taken as indicators of this disenchantment. Less widely than expected – and above all in a very different way – have the findings of social research found their way into political and everyday contexts. "Utilization research" (Beck and Bonß 1989) has demonstrated that scientific findings are not carried over into political and institutional practices as much as expected. When they are taken up, they are obviously reinterpreted and picked to pieces: "Science no longer produces 'absolute truths,' which can uncritically be adopted. It furnishes limited offers for interpretation, which reach further than everyday theories but can be used in practice comparatively flexibly" (1989, p. 31).

It has also become clear that social science results are rarely perceived and used in everyday life. In order to fulfil methodological standards, their investigations and findings often remain too far removed from everyday questions and problems. On the other hand, analyses of research practice have demonstrated that the (abstract) ideals of objectivity formulated by methodologists can only be met in parts in conducting concrete research. Despite all the methodological controls, influences from interests, social and cultural backgrounds are difficult to avoid in research and its findings. These factors influence the formulation of research questions and hypotheses as well as the interpretation of data and relations.

Finally, the disenchantment that Bonß and Hartmann discussed has consequences for what kind of knowledge the social sciences or psychology can strive for and above all are able to produce. "On the condition of the disenchantment of ideals of objectivism, we can no longer unreflectively start from the notion of objectively true sentences. What remains is the possibility of statements which are related to subjects and situations, and which a sociologically articulated concept of knowledge would have to establish" (1985, p. 21). To formulate such subject- and situation-related statements, which are empirically well founded, is a goal, which can be attained with qualitative research.

Essential Features of Qualitative Research

The central ideas guiding qualitative research are different from those in quantitative research. The essential features of qualitative research (Box 2.1) are the correct choice of appropriate methods and theories; the recognition and analysis of different perspectives; the researchers' reflections on their research as part of the process of knowledge production; and the variety of approaches and methods.

Box 2.1   A Preliminary List of Qualitative Research Features

- Appropriateness of methods and theories
- Perspectives of the participants and their diversity
- Reflexivity of the researcher and the research
- Variety of approaches and methods in qualitative research

Appropriateness of Methods and Theories

Scientific disciplines used defining methodological standards to distinguish themselves from other disciplines. An example of such includes the use of experiments as the method of psychology or of survey research as the key method of sociology. In this process of establishing as a scientific discipline, the methods become the point of reference for checking the suitability of ideas and issues for empirical investigations. This sometimes leads to suggestions, to refrain from studying those phenomena to which methods like experiment or surveys cannot be applied. Sometimes a clear identification and isolation of variables is not possible, so that they cannot be framed in an experimental design. Or to keep away from phenomena, which can be studied only in very few cases, what makes it difficult to study them in a big enough sample for a representative study and for findings ready for generalization. Of course it makes sense to reflect on whether a research question can be studied empirically or not (see Chapter 9). Most phenomena cannot be explained in isolation, which is a result of its complexity in reality. If all empirical studies were exclusively designed according to the model of clear cause-effect relations, all complex objects would have to be excluded. Not to choose such objects is often suggested for how to treat complex and rare phenomena in social research. A second solution is to take contextual conditions into account in complex quantitative research designs (e.g., multi-level analyses) and to understand complex models empirically and statistically. The necessary methodological abstraction makes it more difficult to reintroduce findings in the everyday situation under study. The basic problem–the study can only show what the underlying model of reality represents–is not solved in this way. Lastly, designing methods open to the complexity of a study's subject is also a way to solve rare issues with qualitative research. Here, the object under study is the determining factor for choosing a method and not the other way round. Objects are not reduced to single variables, but represented in their entirety in their everyday context. Therefore, the fields of study are not artificial situations in the laboratory but the practices and interactions of the subjects in everyday life. Here, in particular, exceptional situations and persons are studied frequently (see Chapter 11). In order to do justice to the diversity of everyday life, methods are characterized by openness towards their objects, which is guaranteed in different ways (see Chapters 13 to 21). The goal of your research then is less to test what is already known (for example, theories already formulated in advance), but to discover and develop the new and to develop empirically grounded theories. Also, the validity of the study is assessed with reference to the object under study and does not exclusively follow abstract academic criteria of science as in quantitative research. Rather, qualitative research's central criteria depend on whether findings are grounded in empirical material or whether the methods are appropriately selected and applied, as well as the relevance of findings and the reflexivity of proceedings (see Chapter 29).

Perspectives of the Participants and Their Diversity

The example of mental disorders allows us to explain another feature of qualitative research. Epidemiological studies show the frequency of schizophrenia in the population and furthermore how its distribution varies: in lower social classes, serious mental disorders like schizophrenia occur much more frequently than in higher classes. Such a correlation was found by Hollingshead and Redlich (1958) in the 1950s and has been confirmed repeatedly since then. However, the direction of the correlation could not be clarified. Do the conditions of living in a lower social class promote the occurrence and outbreak of mental disorders? Or do people with mental problems slide into the lower classes? Moreover, these findings do not tell us anything about what it means to live with mental illness.

Neither is the subjective meaning of this illness (or of health) for those directly concerned made clear nor is the diversity of perspectives on the illness in their context grasped. What is the subjective meaning of schizophrenia for the patient, and what is it for his or her relatives? How do the various people involved deal with the disease in their day-to-day lives? What has led to the outbreak of the disease in the course of the patient's life, and what has made it a chronic disease? What treatments influenced the patient's life? Which ideas, goals, and routines guide their concrete handling of this case?

Qualitative research on a topic like mental illness concentrates on questions like these. It demonstrates the variety of perspectives (those of the patient, of his or her relatives, of professionals) on the object and starts from the subjective and social meanings related to it. Qualitative researchers study participants' knowledge and practices. They analyze interactions about and ways of dealing with mental illness in a particular field. Interrelations are described in the concrete context of the case and explained in relation to it. Qualitative research takes into account that viewpoints and practices in the field are different because of the different subjective perspectives and social backgrounds related to them.

Reflexivity of the Researcher and the Research

Unlike quantitative research, qualitative methods take the researcher's communication as an explicit part of knowledge instead of deeming it an intervening variable. The subjectivity of the researcher *and* of those being studied becomes part of the research process. Researchers' reflections on their actions and observations in the field, their impressions, irritations, feelings and so on, become data in their own right, forming part of the interpretation and are documented in research diaries or context protocols (see Chapter 22).

Variety of Approaches and Methods in Qualitative Research

Qualitative research is not based on a unified theoretical and methodological concept. Various theoretical approaches and their methods characterize the discussions and the research practice. Subjective viewpoints are a first starting point. A second string of research studies the making and course of interactions, while a third seeks to reconstruct the structures of the social field and the latent meaning of practices (see the next chapter for more details). This variety of approaches results from different developmental lines in the history of qualitative research, which evolved partly in parallel and partly in sequence.

A Brief History of Qualitative Research

Here only a brief and rather cursory overview of the history of qualitative research is given. Psychology and social sciences in general have a long tradition of using qualitative methods. In psychology, Wilhelm Wundt (1928) used methods of description and *verstehen* in his folk psychology alongside the experimental methods of his general psychology. Roughly at the same time, an argument between a more monographic conception of science, which was oriented towards induction and case studies, and an empirical and statistical approach began in German sociology (Bonß 1982, p. 106). In American sociology, biographical methods, case studies, and descriptive methods were central for a long time (until the 1940s). This can be demonstrated by the importance of Thomas and Znaniecki's study *The Polish Peasant in Europe and America* (1918–20), and more generally, with the influence of the Chicago School in sociology.

During the further establishment of both sciences, however, increasingly "hard," experimental, standardizing, and quantifying approaches have asserted themselves against "soft" understanding, open, and qualitative descriptive strategies. It was not until the 1960s that in American sociology the critique of standardized, quantifying social research became relevant again (Cicourel 1964; Glaser and Strauss 1967). This critique was taken up in the 1970s in German discussions. Finally, this led to a renaissance of qualitative research in the social sciences and also (with some delay) in psychology (Banister, Burman, Parker, Taylor and Tindall 1994). The developments and discussions in the United States and in Germany not only took place at different times but also are marked by differing phases.

Developments in German-Speaking Areas

In Germany, Jürgen Habermas (1967) first recognized that a "different" tradition and discussion of research was developing in American sociology related to names like Goffman, Garfinkel, and Cicourel. After the translation of Cicourel's (1964) methodological critique, a series of anthologies imported contributions from the American discussions. This has made basic texts on ethnomethodology or symbolic interactionism available for German discussions. From the same period, the model of the research process created by Glaser and Strauss (1967) has attracted a lot of attention. Discussions are motivated by the aim to do more justice to the objects of research than is possible in quantitative research, as Hoffmann-Riem's (1980) claim for the "principle of openness" demonstrates. Kleining (1982, p. 233) has argued that it is necessary to understand the object of research as preliminary until the end of the research, because the object "will present itself in its true colors only at the end". Also the discussions about a "naturalistic sociology" (Schatzmann and Strauss 1973) and appropriate methods are determined by a similar initially implicit and later also explicit assumption. To apply the principle of openness and the rules that Kleining suggests (e.g., to postpone a theoretical formulation of the research object) enables the researcher to avoid constituting the object by the very methods used for studying it. Rather it becomes possible "to take everyday life first and always again in the way it presents itself in each case" (Grathoff 1978; quoted in Hoffmann-Riem 1980, p. 362, who ends her article with this quotation).

At the end of the 1970s, a broader and more original discussion began in Germany, which no longer relied exclusively on the translation of American literature. This discussion deals with interviews, how to apply and how to analyze them, and with methodological questions that have stimulated extensive research (see Flick, Kardorff, and Steinke 2004 for a recent overview). The main question for this period was whether these developments should be seen as a fashion, a trend, or a new beginning.

At the beginning of the 1980s, two original methods were crucial to the development of qualitative research in Germany–the *narrative interview* by Schütze (1977; Rosenthal and Fischer-Rosenthal 2004; see here Chapter 14) and *objective hermeneutics* by Oevermann et al. (1979, see also Reichertz 2004). Both methods were no longer just an import of American developments as was the case in applying participant observation or interviews, with an interview guide oriented towards the focused interview. Both methods have stimulated extensive research practice (mainly in biographical research: for overviews see Bertaux 1981; Rosenthal 2004). But the influence of these methodologies in the general discussion of qualitative methods is at least as crucial as the results obtained from them. In the middle of the 1980s, problems of validity and the generalizability of findings obtained with qualitative methods attracted broader attention. Related questions of presentation and the transparency of results have been discussed. The quantity, and above all, the unstructured nature of the data require the use of computers in qualitative research too (Fielding and Lee 1991; Kelle 1995, 2004; Richards and Richards 1998; Weitzman and Miles 1995). Finally, the first textbooks or introductions have been published on the background of the discussions in the German-speaking area.

Discussions in the United States

Denzin and Lincoln (2000b, pp. 12–18) refer to phases different from those just described for the German-speaking area. They see "seven moments of qualitative research," as follows: The *traditional period* ranges from the early twentieth century to World War II. It is related to the research of Malinowski (1916) in ethnography and the Chicago School in sociology. During this period, qualitative research was interested in the other–the foreign or the strange–and in its more or less objective description and interpretation. For example, foreign cultures interested ethnography and a society's outsiders interested sociology.

The *modernist phase* lasts until the 1970s and is marked by attempts to formalize qualitative research. For this purpose, more and more textbooks were published in the United States. The attitude of this kind of research is still alive in the tradition of Glaser and Strauss (1967), Strauss (1987), and Strauss and Corbin (1990) as well as in Miles and Huberman (1994).

Blurred genres (Geertz 1983) characterize the developments up to the mid 1980s. Various theoretical models and understandings of the objects and methods stand side by side, from which researchers can choose and compare "alternative paradigms," such as symbolic interactionism, ethnomethodology, phenomenology, semiotics, or feminism (see also Guba 1990; Jacob 1987).

In the mid 1980s, the *crisis of representation* discussions in artificial intelligence (Winograd and Flores 1986) and ethnography (Clifford and Marcus 1986) impact qualitative research as a whole. This makes the process of displaying knowledge and findings a substantial part of the research process. The process of displaying knowledge and findings receives more attention as a part of the findings *per se*. Qualitative research becomes a continuous process of constructing versions of reality. The version people present in an interview do not necessarily correspond to the version they would have formulated at the moment when the reported event happened. It does not necessarily correspond to the version they would have given to a different researcher with a different research question. Researchers, who interpret the interview and present it as part of their findings, produce a new version of the whole. Readers of the book, article, or report interpret the researchers' version differently. This means that further versions of the event emerge. Specific interests brought to the reading in each case play a central part. In this context, the evaluation of research and findings becomes a central topic in methodological discussions. This is connected with the question of whether traditional criteria are valid any more and, if not, which other standards should be applied for assessing qualitative research.

The situation in the 1990s is seen by Denzin and Lincoln as the *fifth moment*: narratives have replaced theories, or theories are read as narratives. But here we learn about the end of grand narratives–as in postmodernism in general. The accent is shifted towards theories and narratives that fit specific, delimited, local, historical situations, and problems. The next stage (*sixth moment*) is characterized by post-experimental writing, linking issues of qualitative research to democratic policies, and the *seventh moment* is the future of qualitative research.

If we compare the two lines of development (Table 2.1) in Germany, we find increasing methodological consolidation complemented by a concentration on procedural questions in a growing research practice. In the United States, on the other hand, recent developments are characterized by a trend to question the apparent certainties provided by methods. The role of presentation in the research process, the crisis of representation, and the relativity of what is presented have been stressed, and this has made the attempts to formalize and canonize methods rather secondary. The "correct" application of procedures of interviewing or interpretation counts less than the "practices and politics of interpretation" (Denzin 2000). Qualitative research therefore becomes–or is linked still more strongly with–a specific attitude based on the researcher's openness and reflexivity.

TABLE 2.1 Phases in the History of Qualitative Research

Germany	United States
Early studies (end of nineteenth and early twentieth centuries)	Traditional period (1900 to 1945)
Phase of import (early 1970s)	Modernist phase (1945 to the 1970s)
Beginning of original discussions (late 1970s)	Blurred genres (until the mid 1980s)
Developing original methods (1970s and 1980s)	Crisis of representation (since the mid 1980s)
Consolidation and procedural questions (late 1980s and 1990s)	Fifth moment (the 1990s)
Research practice (since the 1980s)	Sixth moment (post-experimental writing)
	Seventh moment (the future)

Qualitative Research at the Beginning of the Twenty-First Century – State of the Art

What have these developments led to? The following section orients you on a variety of qualitative research and its schools of research. The recent development of qualitative research proceeded in different areas, each of them characterized by specific theoretical backgrounds, specific concepts of reality and their own methodological programs. One example is ethnomethodology as a theoretical program, which first led to the development of conversation analysis (e.g., Bergmann 2004a) and differentiated in new approaches like genre analysis (Knoblauch and Luckmann 2004) and discourse analysis (Parker 2004; Potter and Wetherell 1998). A number of such fields and approaches in qualitative research have developed, which unfold in their own ways with little connection to the discussions and research in other fields of qualitative research. Other examples are objective hermeneutics, narrative based biographical research or, more recently, ethnography or cultural studies. This diversification in qualitative research is intensified by the fact that for example German and Anglo-American discussions are engaged in very different topics and methods and that there is only limited exchange between both.

Research Perspectives in Qualitative Research
Although the various approaches in qualitative research differ in their theoretical assumptions, in their understanding of issues, and in their methodological

focus, three major perspectives summarize them: theoretical points of reference are drawn, first, from traditions of symbolic interactionism and phenomenology. A second main line is anchored theoretically in ethnomethodology and constructionism and interested daily routines and in the making of social reality. Structuralist or psychoanalytic positions assume unconscious psychological structures and mechanisms and latent social configurations and are the third point of reference. These three major perspectives differ in objectives of research and in the methods they employ. Authors like Lüders and Reichertz (1986) juxtapose first approaches highlighting the "viewpoint of the subject" and a second group aiming at describing the processes in the production of existing (mundane, institutional, or more general: social) situations, milieus, and social order (e.g., in ethnomethodological analyses of language). The third approach is characterized by a (mostly hermeneutical) reconstruction of "deep structures generating action and meaning" in the sense of psychoanalytic or objective-hermeneutic conceptions (see Chapter 25).

The available range of methods for collecting and analyzing data can be allocated to these research perspectives as follows: the first perspective is dominated by semi-structured or narrative interviews and procedures of coding and content analyzing. In the second research perspective, data are collected from focus groups, ethnography or (participant) observation, and audio/visual recordings. Then, these data are analyzed by using discourse or conversation analyses. Lastly, the third perspective collects data by recording interactions and using visual material (photos or films) that undergo one of the different versions of hermeneutic analysis (Hitzler and Eberle 2004; Honer 2004).

Table 2.2 summarizes these allocations and complements them with some exemplary fields of research characterizing each of the three perspectives.

Most Important Schools of Research and Recent Developments

All in all, qualitative research in its theoretical and methodological developments and its research practice is characterized by an explicit building of schools, which differ in their influence on the general debates.

GROUNDED THEORY   Research in the tradition of Glaser and Strauss (1967) and their approach of building empirically grounded theories continues to be very attractive for qualitative researchers. The idea of theory development is taken up as a general goal for qualitative research. Some concepts like theoretical sampling (to select cases and material on the background of the state of the empirical analyses in the project–see Chapter 11) or the different methods of coding–open, axial and selective (see Chapter 23)–are employed. A bigger part of the qualitative research refers to one or other part of the program of Strauss and his colleagues (e.g., Chamberlain 1999). The approach has also left its traces in the development of biographical research or is linked to other research programs.

TABLE 2.2   Research Perspectives in Qualitative Research

	Approaches to subjective viewpoints	Description of the making of social situations	Hermeneutic analysis of underlying structures
Theoretical positions	Symbolic interactionism Phenomenology	Ethnomethodology Constructivism	Psychoanalysis Genetic structuralism
Methods of data collection	Semi-structured interviews Narrative interviews	Focus groups Ethnography Participant observation Recording interactions Collecting documents	Recording interactions Photography Film
Methods of interpretation	Theoretical coding Content analysis Narrative analysis Hermeneutic methods	Conversation analysis Discourse analysis Genre analysis Analysis of documents	Objective hermeneutics Deep hermeneutics
Fields of application	Biographical research Analysis of everyday knowledge	Analysis of life worlds and organizations Evaluation Cultural studies	Family research Biographical research Generation research Gender research

ETHNOMETHODOLOGY, CONVERSATION, DISCOURSE, AND GENRE ANALYSIS   Harold Garfinkel's (1967) ethnomethodology is the starting point of the second school. It focuses on the empirical study of mundane practices, through which interactive order is produced in and outside of institutions. For a long time, conversation analysis (Sacks 1992) was the dominant way of making the theoretical project of ethnomethodology empirically work. Conversation analysis studies talk as a process and a form of interaction–which methods are employed to practically organize talk as processes which unfold in a regular way and, beyond this, how specific forms of interaction–conversations at dinner table, gossip, counseling, and assessments– are organized (see Chapter 24). In the meantime, conversation analysis has developed as an independent area out of ethnomethodology. Studies of work designed by ethnomethodologists, like Garfinkel as a second field of research (Bergmann 2004b), have remained less influential. Works extending conversation analytic research questions and analytical principles to bigger entities in genre analysis (Knoblauch and Luckmann 2004) have attracted more attention. Finally, ethnomethodology and conversation analyses have been patrons for formulating at least major parts of the heterogeneous research field of discourse analysis (see Harré 1998; Potter and Wetherell 1998; Parker 2004). Data collection in all these fields is characterized by the attempt to collect natural data (like recording everyday conversations) without using explicit, reconstructing methods like interviews.

NARRATIVE ANALYSIS AND BIOGRAPHICAL RESEARCH Biographical research in German language areas is essentially determined by a specific method used for collecting data and by the diffusion of this method. Here, mainly the narrative interview (see Chapter 14) stands in the foreground. The narrative interview focuses on biographical experiences. This is applied in several areas of sociology, and in recent years, increasingly in education. Through analyzing narratives, bigger topics and contexts are studied (e.g., how people cope with unemployment, experiences of migration, and processes of illness or experiences in families linked to the holocaust). Data are interpreted in narrative analyses (Rosenthal and Fischer-Rosenthal 2004). In recent years, group narratives (see Chapter 15), including multigenerational familial stories (Bude 2004), were an extension of the narrative situation.

ETHNOGRAPHY Ethnographic research has increased since the early 1980s. Ethnography has replaced studies using participant observation (see Chapter 17). It aims less at understanding social events or processes from reports about these events (e.g., in an interview) but at understanding social processes of making these events from the inside by participating in the processes' developments. Extended participation (instead of one spot interviews or observations) and flexible use of different methods (including more or less formalized interviews or analyses of documents) characterize this research. Of central interest since the middle of the 1980s is the part of writing about the observed events. More generally, this interest highlights the relation of the event and its presentation (see Chapter 30). Especially in the United States, "ethnography" (e. g. Denzin 1997) replaces the label "qualitative research" (in all its facets).

CULTURAL STUDIES The new trend of cultural studies has also expanded into the fields of sociology and media studies (Winter 2004). So far, the degree of commitment to elaborate methodology and methodological principles is rather low. The object "cultures" defines the approach; their analysis hinges on media, its orientation on (disadvantaged) subcultures, and on existing relations of power in concrete contexts.

GENDER STUDIES Essential impulses on the development of qualitative research questions and methodologies derived from feminist research and gender studies (Gildemeister 2004). The studies look at the processes of constructing and differentiating gender and of the inequalities. For example, transsexuality is an empirical starting point to demonstrate the social construction of "typical" images of gender (see Chapter 6).

Box 2.2 summarizes the schools of qualitative research briefly mentioned here.

Box 2.2   Schools of Qualitative Research

1. Grounded theory
2. Ethnomethodology, conversation, discourse and genre analysis
3. Narrative analysis and biographical research
4. Ethnography
5. Cultural studies
6. Gender studies

Methodological Developments and Trends

What are the current methodological trends in qualitative research?

Visual and Electronic Data

Visual data are important to the collection of qualitative research beyond the traditional forms of interviews, focus groups, or participant observations. Sociology analyzes video and film just as in media studies (see Denzin 2004a and Harper 2004; see Chapter 18). Using them raises questions like how to edit these data appropriately and whether methods originally created to analyze texts can be applied to these sorts of data. More books are publishing chapters on visual data, a sign of its acceptability. Which new forms of data are available for studying the Internet and electronic communication (like e-mail) and which data have to be collected in order to analyze the processes of construction and communication that are involved? Chapter 20 discusses these topics (also see Bergmann and Meier 2004).

Qualitative Online Research

Several of the existing qualitative methods have been transferred and adapted to research using the Internet as a tool, resource, and issue of research. Such new areas of e-mail interviews, online focus groups, and virtual ethnography raise research questions on ethics and practical problems (see Chapter 20).

Triangulation

The idea of triangulation is widely discussed. Linking different qualitative or qualitative and quantitative methods (Kelle and Erzberger 2004; see Chapter 3) becomes essential. Triangulation goes beyond the limitations of a single method by combining several methods and giving them equal relevance. It is becoming more fruitful, if different theoretical approaches are combined or taken into account in combining methods (see for more details Flick 1992, 2004a and Chapter 29).

Hybridization

Hybridization is evident in many of the research perspectives and schools discussed above, such as ethnography, cultural studies, and grounded theory research. Researchers in the field select methodological and pragmatic approaches. Hybridization is labeled as the pragmatic use of methodological principles and avoidance of a restricting subscription to a specific methodological discourse.

Using Computers

Field practitioners vary in their support for using computers for qualitative research (e.g., Knoblauch 2004). Analyzing texts is the main use of computers. Several computer programs are commercially available (e.g., ATLAS•ti, NUDIST, and MAXQDA).

In the end, are these programs just different ways to achieve a quite similar use and usability? Will they have a sustainable impact on the ways qualitative data are used and analyzed? What are the long-term relations of technical investments and efforts to the resulting facilitation of routines? These issues still have to be assessed (see Chapter 26). These programs support the handling and administration of data material (e. g., matching codes and sources in the text, jointly displaying them, and tracing back categorizations to the single passage in the text they refer to). It is still left to be determined if voice recognition software will lead to computer supported transcription of interviews and whether this will be useful progress or not.

Linking Qualitative and Quantitative Research

Literature identifies several positions linking qualitative and quantitative research. Especially in hermeneutic or phenomenological research, hardly any need is seen for linking with quantitative research and its approaches. This argument is based on the incompatibilities of the two research traditions, epistemologies, and their procedures. At the same time, models and strategies are developed to link qualitative and quantitative research (see Chapter 3). Finally, in the everyday life of research practice beyond methodological discussions, a link of both approaches often is necessary and useful for pragmatic reasons. Therefore, how do you conceptualize triangulation in a way that takes both approaches–their theoretical and methodological peculiarities–into a serious account without any premature subordination of one approach over the other?

Writing Qualitative Research

In the 1980s and 1990s, the discussion about the appropriate ways of presenting qualitative procedures and results had a strong impact, especially in the

United States (Clifford and Marcus 1986). Beyond comparing different strategies of reporting qualitative research, main topics in this discussion include: How can qualitative researchers' writing do justice to the life worlds they studied and to the subjective perspectives they met there? How does the presentation and conceptualization affect the research itself? How does writing influence the assessing and the accessibility of qualitative research? The stress is laid in different ways. Ethnography sees the act of writing about what was studied as at least as important as collecting and analyzing data. In other fields, writing is seen in a rather instrumental way–how do I make my procedures and results in the field transparent and plausible to recipients (i.e., other scientists, readers, the general public, and so on)? All in all, the interest in the discussion about writing has decreased, because of insights like this one: "Apart from a growth in self-reflection these debates yielded little in the way of tangible or useful results for research practice" (Lüders 2004a, p. 228, see Chapter 30).

Quality of Qualitative Research

Assessing the quality of qualitative research still attracts a lot of attention. Several books approach this topic from different angles (e.g., Seale 1999). The basic alternatives, however, are still determining the discussion: Should traditional criteria of validity, reliability and objectivity be applied to qualitative research and how? Or should new, method appropriate criteria be developed for qualitative research? Which are these, and how can they exactly be "operationalized" for assessing the quality of qualitative research? Discussions in the United States exhibit skepticism against using criteria in general. Distinguishing between good and bad research in qualitative research is an internal problem. At the same time, it is a need with regards to the attractiveness and the feasibility of qualitative research on the markets and arenas of teaching, to receive research grants and impact policies in the social sciences (see Chapters 28, 29).

Qualitative Research between Establishing Schools of Research and Research Pragmatics

Methodological purism and research pragmatics cause tension in qualitative research. Further elaborating the pure textbook versions of hermeneutic methods for example leads to further increasing the needs for time, personal, and other resources. This raises the question of how to use such approaches in a research carried out for a ministry or company, or aiming at consulting politicians, in a pragmatic way so that the number of the analyzed cases can be large enough to make results accountable (see Gaskell and Bauer 2000). This leads to the question of what are pragmatic but nevertheless methodologically acceptable short-cut-strategies in collecting, transcribing, and analyzing qualitative data (Lüders 2004b) and in designing qualitative research (see Chapter 12).

Internationalization

So far, there are limited attempts to publish information about the methodological procedures that determine the German-speaking discussion, literature, and research practice, also in English language publications. Accordingly, the resonance of German language qualitative research in the English language discussion is rather modest. An internationalization of qualitative research is needed in several directions. Not only should German language qualitative research pay more attention to what is currently discussed in English–or French–literature, but it should also take it up in its own discourse. Also, it should invest in publishing "home grown" approaches in international, English language journals and at international conferences. And finally, English language discussion needs to open more towards what is going on in other countries' qualitative research.

Indication

A final demand in qualitative research is to further clarify the question of indication. This is similar to how in medicine or psychotherapy the appropriateness of a certain treatment for specific problems and groups of people is checked (see Chapter 29). If this is transferred to qualitative research, the relevant questions include: When are certain qualitative methods appropriate – for which issue, which research question, for which group of people or fields to be studied and so on? When are quantitative methods or a combination of both indicated? This leads to the search for criteria to answer such questions. Finding these criteria can be a contribution to a realist assessment of single qualitative methods and of qualitative research in general. This will finally prevent from falling back into fundamentalist trench fights of the qualitative versus the quantitative research (see Chapter 3).

Box 2.3 summarizes the trends and developments briefly mentioned here.

Box 2.3   Trends and Developments

1. Visual and electronic data
2. Qualitative online research
3. Triangulation
4. Hybridization
5. Using computers
6. Linking qualitative and quantitative research
7. Writing qualitative research
8. Quality of qualitative research
9. Qualitative research between establishing schools of research and research pragmatics
10. Internationalization
11. Indication

How To Learn and How To Teach Qualitative Research

Introductions to qualitative research are facing two basic problems. First, the alternatives summarized under the label of qualitative research are still very heterogeneous. Therefore, such introductions run the risk of giving a unified presentation to an issue, which is and will remain rather diverse. Canonization and codification, which are sometimes called for, may miss the point of creating a unity, which really can be realized. It remains to be asked how desirable such a creation of unity really is. It is instructive to clarify the different theoretical, methodological, and general aims of the various alternatives. Second, introductions to methods might obscure instead of highlight the idea that qualitative research is not merely an application of methods in the sense of technologies. It is not only the tension of technique and art in the methods, but also that qualitative research includes a specific research attitude. This attitude is linked to the primacy of the issue over the methods, to the orientation of the process of research, and to the attitude with which the researchers should meet their "objectives." In addition to the curiosity, openness, and flexibility in handling the methods, part of this attitude is also attributed to a special degree of reflection about the issue, the appropriateness of the research question and methods, and also about his or her own perceptions and blind spots. Two consequences result from this.

There is a need in qualitative methods to find a way between teaching certain techniques (e.g., how to formulate a good question, what is a good code) and teaching the necessary attitude. Curiosity and flexibility cannot be taught in lectures about the history and methods of qualitative research. The appropriate use of qualitative methods often results from experience, problems, failing, and continuing in the field. The pure methodological level should be separated from the level of application as in every research. The concrete field, with its obstructions and necessities, often makes it difficult to apply certain interview techniques in an optimal way. Problems in qualitative methods intensify due to the scope of application and the need for flexibility, which influence decisions on a per situation basis. In the successful case, this flexibility opens a way to the subjective viewpoint of the interviewee. In the case of failure, it makes an orientation in the application more difficult, and the bureaucratic use of the interview guide may be the result. With success, procedures like theoretical coding or objective hermeneutics allow one to find a way into the structure of the text or of the case; when they fail, they leave the researcher in the situation of drowning in texts or data.

An understanding of qualitative research can hardly be produced only on a theoretical level. Beyond that, the learning and teaching should include practical experience in applying methods and in the contact with concrete research subjects. Introduce qualitative researching by combining teaching and research, allowing students to work continuously for a longer period of time on a research question using one method (or several methods). Learning by doing may provide a framework for practical experiences that are necessary to obtain an understanding of the options and limits of qualitative methods (see Flick and Bauer 2004 for examples). Teach and understand the procedures of interviewing and interpreting data from an applications perspective.

Failure of qualitative research is rarely discussed. The impression arises sometimes that validated knowledge and correct application are the bases of qualitative methods. Analyzing failures in qualitative research strategies (see examples in Borman, LeCompte, and Goetz 1986; or focus on entering the research field and failures in this process in Wolff 2004a and in Chapter 10) can provide insights of how these strategies work in contact with concrete fields, institutions, or human beings.

Qualitative Research at the End of Modernity

At the beginning of this chapter, some changes to the potential objects were mentioned in order to show the relevance of qualitative research. Recent diagnoses in the sciences result in more reasons to turn to qualitative research. In his discussion of the "hidden agenda of modernity," Stephen Toulmin (1990) explains in great detail why he believes modern science is dysfunctional. He sees four tendencies for empirical social research in philosophy and science as a way forward:

- the return to the oral traditions–carried out empirical studies in philosophy, linguistics, literature and social sciences by studying narratives, language, and communication;
- the return to the particular–carried out empirical studies with the aim "not only to concentrate on abstract and universal questions but to treat again specific, concrete problems which do not arise generally but occur in specific types of situations" (1990, p. 190);
- the return to the local–studied systems of knowledge, practices, and experiences in the context of those (local) traditions and ways of living in which they are embedded, instead of assuming and attempting to test their universal validity;
- the return to the timely–placed problems to be studied and solutions to be developed in their temporal or historical context and to describe them in this context and explain them from it.

Qualitative research is oriented towards analyzing concrete cases in their temporal and local particularity and starting from people's expressions and activities in their local contexts. Therefore, qualitative research is in a position to design ways for social sciences, psychology, and other fields to make concrete the tendencies that Toulmin mentions, to transform them into research programs and to maintain the necessary flexibility towards their objects and tasks:

> Like buildings on a human scale, our intellectual and social procedures will do what we need in the years ahead, only if we take care to avoid irrelevant or excessive stability, and keep them operating in ways that are adaptable to unforeseen–or even unforeseeable–situations and functions. (1990, p. 186)

Concrete suggestions and methods for realizing such programs of research will be outlined in the following chapters.

KEY POINTS

- Qualitative research has for several reasons a special relevance for contemporary research in many fields.
- Quantitative methods and qualitative methods both have limitations to their research.
- Qualitative research has a variety of approaches.
- There are common features among the different approaches in qualitative research. Also, different schools and trends distinguish its research perspectives.
- The best way to teach and learn qualitative research is learning by doing – working in the field and on material is most fruitful.

Exercise 2.1

Look for a qualitative study, read it, and answer the following questions:

1. How are essential features listed at the beginning of this chapter relevant to the example you chose?
2. Are the methods and approaches applied in this study appropriate to the issue under study?
3. Which research perspective does this study belong to?
4. Is it an example for one of the schools of qualitative research mentioned in this chapter?

Exercise 2.2

1. If you plan your own study, reflect why qualitative research is adequate for the study.
2. Discuss the reasons for or against using quantitative methods in your study.

FURTHER READING

Overviews of Qualitative Research
The first two references extend the short overview given here of the German and United States discussions, while Strauss's book represents the research attitude behind this book and qualitative research in general.

Denzin, N. and Lincoln, Y.S. (eds) (2000) *Handbook of Qualitative Research* (2nd edn). London: SAGE.
Flick, U., Kardorff, E.v. and Steinke, I. (eds) (2004) *A Companion to Qualitative Research*. London: SAGE.
Strauss, A.L. (1987) *Qualitative Analysis for Social Scientists*. Cambridge: Cambridge University Press.

Learning and Teaching Qualitative Methods
Find examples of teaching qualitative research by doing concrete research in this source.

Flick, U. and Bauer, M. (2004) "Teaching Qualitative Research," in U. Flick, E.v. Kardorff and I. Steinke (eds) *A Companion to Qualitative Research*. London: SAGE. pp. 340–348.

3

QUALITATIVE AND QUANTITATIVE RESEARCH

CHAPTER OBJECTIVES

After reading this chapter, you should be able to

✓   **understand the distinctiveness of qualitative and quantitative research.**
✓   **distinguish which alternatives exist if you want to combine both.**
✓   **recognize what to take into account when alternative research methods are combined.**

The Current Discussions about Qualitative and Quantitative Research

In the last few years, you will find quite a lot of publications addressing the relations, the combination, or the distinctiveness of qualitative research. Before we focus on the special aspects of qualitative research and methods in the following chapters, here I want to give a brief overview of the qualitative-quantitative debates and versions of combining both. This should help you to locate qualitative research in this broader field and also to get a clearer picture of the strengths and features of qualitative research.

Bryman (1992) identifies eleven ways of integrating quantitative and qualitative research. The logic of triangulation (1) means for him to check for examples of qualitative against quantitative results. Qualitative research can support quantitative research (2) and vice versa (3); both are combined in or to provide a more general picture of the issue under study (4). Structural features are analyzed with quantitative methods and processual aspects with qualitative approaches (5). The perspective of the researchers drives quantitative approaches, while qualitative research emphasizes the viewpoints of the subjective (6). According to Bryman, the problem of generality (7) can be solved for qualitative research by adding quantitative findings, whereas qualitative findings (8) may facilitate the interpretation of relationships between variables in quantitative data sets. The relationship between micro and macro levels in a substantial area (9) can be clarified by combining qualitative and quantitative research, which can be appropriate in different stages of the research process (10). Finally, there are hybrid forms (11) that use qualitative research in quasi-experimental designs (see Bryman 1992, p. 59–61).

Beyond that there are publications on the integration of qualitative and quantitative methods about "mixed methodologies" (Tashakkori and Teddlie 2003a), but also about triangulation of qualitative and quantitative methods (Kelle and Erzberger 2004; Flick 2004c). The terms already show that different claims are made with these approaches. Mixed methodology approaches are interested in a pragmatic combination of qualitative and quantitative research. This shall end the paradigm wars of earlier times. The approach is declared to be "a third methodological movement" (Tashakkori and Teddlie 2003b: ix). Quantitative research and methods are seen as the first, qualitative research as the second movement. The goals of a methodological discussion here are to clarify the "nomenclature," questions of design and applications of mixed-methodologies-research and of inferences in this context. From a methodological point of view, a paradigmatic foundation of mixed-methodologies-research is the aim. Using the concept of paradigms in this context, however, shows that the authors start from two closed approaches, which can be differentiated, combined, or rejected, without reflecting the concrete methodological problems of combining them.

The claims for mixed-methodologies research are outlined as follows:

> We proposed that a truly mixed approach methodology (a) would incorporate multiple approaches in all stages of the study (i.e., problem identification, data collection, data analysis, and final inferences) and (b) would include a transformation of the data and their analysis through another approach. (Tashakkori and Teddlie 2003b, p. xi)

These claims are very strong, especially if you take the transformation of data and analyses (qualitative in quantitative and vice versa) into account (see below).

Relations of Qualitative and Quantitative Research

In many cases, qualitative methods were developed in the context of a critique of quantitative methods and research strategies (for example Cicourel 1964). The debates about the "right" understanding of science are not settled yet (see Becker 1996), but in both domains, a broad research practice has developed which speaks for itself, independent of the fact that there is good and bad research on both sides. An indicator that qualitative research has become independent of quantitative research and of old trench fights against quantitative research is that Denzin and Lincoln (2000a) provide no extra chapter about relations to quantitative research and their index lists few references to quantitative research. However, the combination of both strategies has crystallized as a perspective, which is discussed and practiced in various forms. The relations of qualitative and quantitative research are discussed and established on different levels:

- epistemology (and epistemological incompatibilities) and methodology;
- research designs combining or integrating the use of qualitative and quantitative data and/or methods;
- research methods that are both qualitative and quantitative;
- linking findings of qualitative and quantitative research;
- generalization of findings;
- assessing the quality of research–applying quantitative criteria to qualitative research or vice versa.

Stressing the Incompatibilities
On the level of epistemology and methodology, discussions often center around the different ways of relating qualitative and quantitative research. A first relation is to stress the incompatibilities of qualitative and quantitative research in epistemological and methodological principles (e.g., Becker 1996) or of goals and aims to pursue with research in general. This is often linked to different theoretical positions like positivism versus constructionism or post-positivism. Sometimes these incompatibilities are mentioned as different paradigms and both camps are seen as involved in paradigm wars (e.g., Lincoln and Guba 1985).

Defining Fields of Application
One solution to this discussion aims to see the research strategies separately but side-by-side, depending on the issue and the research question. The researcher, who wants to know something about subjective experience of a chronic mental illness, should conduct biographic interviews with some patients and analyze them in great detail. The researcher, who wants to find out something about the frequency and distribution of such diseases in the population, should run an

epidemiological study on this topic. For the first question, qualitative methods are appropriate, for the second quantitative methods are suitable; each method refrains from entering the territory of the other.

Dominance of Quantitative over Qualitative Research

This approach still dominates quantitative research textbooks and research practice. This is the case for example, where an exploratory study with open interviews precedes the collection of data with questionnaires, but the first step and its results are only seen as preliminary. Arguments such as using a representative sample are often used for substantiating the claim that only the quantitative data lead to results in the actual sense of the word, whereas qualitative data play a more illustrative part. Statements in the open interviews are then tested and "explained" by their confirmation and frequency in the questionnaire data.

Superiority of Qualitative over Quantitative Research

This position is taken more seldom but more radically. Oevermann et al. (1979, p. 352) for example stated that quantitative methods are only research economic short cuts of the data generating process, whereas only qualitative methods, particularly the objective hermeneutics Oevermann developed (see Chapter 25) are able to provide the actual scientific explanations of facts. Kleining (1982) holds that qualitative methods can live very well without the later use of quantitative methods, whereas quantitative methods need qualitative methods for explaining the relations they find. Cicourel (1981) sees qualitative methods as being especially appropriate in answering micro sociological questions and quantitative methods for answering macro sociological questions. McKinlay (1995), however, makes it clear that in public health qualitative methods rather than quantitative methods lead to relevant results at the level of socio-political topics and relations due to their complexity. Thus, reasons for the superiority of qualitative research are found both on the level of research program and at the level of the appropriateness to the issue under study.

Linking Qualitative and Quantitative Research in One Design

Qualitative and quantitative methods can link in the design of one study in different ways.

Integration of Qualitative and Quantitative Research

Miles and Huberman (1994, p. 41) outline four types of designs for integrating both approaches in one design as in Figure 3.1.

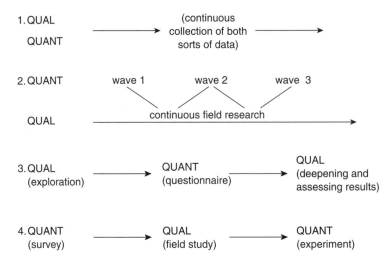

FIGURE 3.1 Research Designs for the Integration of Qualitative and Quantitative Research
Source: Adapted from Miles and Huberman 1994, p. 41

   In the first design, both strategies are pursued in parallel. Continuous observation of the field provides a basis on which in a survey, the several waves are related or from which these waves are derived and shaped in the second design. The third combination begins with a qualitative method, a semi-structured interview that is followed by a questionnaire study as an intermediate step before the results from both steps are deepened and assessed in a second qualitative phase. In the fourth design, a complementary field study adds more depth to the results of a survey in the first step and is followed by an experimental intervention in the field for testing the results of the first two steps. (See Creswell 2003 or Patton 2002 for similar suggestions of mixed designs.)

Sequencing Qualitative and Quantitative Research
Not necessarily focused on reducing one of the approaches to being inferior or defining the other as the real research, a study may include qualitative and quantitative approaches in different phases of the research process. Barton and Lazarsfeld (1955), for example, suggest using qualitative research for developing hypotheses, which afterwards will be tested by quantitative approaches. In their argumentation, they do not focus only on the limits of qualitative research (compared to quantitative) but they explicitly see the strength of qualitative research in the exploration of the phenomenon under study. Following this argumentation, both areas of research are located at different stages of the research process.

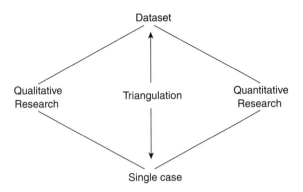

FIGURE 3.2   Levels of Triangulation of Qualitative and Quantitative Research

Triangulation of Qualitative and Quantitative Research

Triangulation (see Chapter 29) means combining several qualitative methods (see Flick 1992; 2004a), but it also means combining qualitative and quantitative methods. Here, the different methodological perspectives complement each other in the study of an issue, and this is conceived as the complementary compensation of the weaknesses and blind spots of each single method. The slowly establishing insight "that qualitative and quantitative methods should be viewed as complementary rather than as rival camps" (Jick 1983, p. 135) is the background of such a conception. But the different methods remain autonomous, operating side-by-side, and their meeting point is the issue under study. And finally, none of the methods combined is seen as superior or preliminary. Whether or not the methods are used at the same time or one after the other is less relevant compared to when they are seen as equal in their role in the project.

Some practical issues are linked to these combinations of different methods in the design of one study (e.g., on which level the triangulation is concretely applied). Two alternatives distinguish triangulation. Triangulation of qualitative and quantitative research can focus the single case. The same people are interviewed and fill in a questionnaire. Their answers in both are compared with each other, put together, and referred to each other in the analysis. Sampling decisions are taken in two steps (see Chapter 11). The same people are included in both parts of the study, but in a second step, it has to be decided which participants of the survey study are selected for the interviews. Establish a link on the level of the data set as well. The answers to the questionnaires are analyzed for their frequency and distribution across the whole sample. Then the answers in the interviews are analyzed and compared, and, for example, a typology is developed. Then the distribution of the questionnaire answers and the typology are linked and compared (see Figure 3.2 and Flick 2004c).

Case Study: Burdens and Achievements of Cancer Patients' Relatives

I selected the following example, since the authors combined qualitative and quantitative methods to study a currently relevant issue in the health area. Both authors work in the area of rehabilitation.

Schönberger and Kardorff (2004) study the challenges, burdens, and achievements of cancer patients' relatives in a combination of a questionnaire study with two waves of surveys (189 and 148 relatives and 192 patients) and a number of case studies (17, of which 7 are presented in more detail). The research questions for both parts of the study are characterized as follows: "On the background of the existing research, we have focused on the experience of burdens, on individual and partnership coping, on integration in networks, and the evaluation of the services in the system of rehabilitation. The social scientific hermeneutic part of the study aimed at discovering structure-theoretical generalizations" (2004, p. 25). In addition, the authors conducted 25 expert interviews in the hospitals involved in the study and 8 expert interviews in after-care institutions. The participants for the case studies were selected from the sample for the survey. Criteria for selecting a couple for a case study were: they shared a flat, the partner should not suffer from a severe illness and the ill partner should be in a rehabilitation clinic or after-care center at the time of the first data collection (p. 95). Furthermore, contrasting cases to this sample were included–people living by themselves, couples with both partners being ill or cases in which the patient's partner had died more than a year ago. The quantitative data were first analyzed using several factor analyses and then in relation to the research question. In the presentation of the questionnaire results, "a link to the case studies is made, if their structural features match findings from the questionnaire" (p. 87) or, "if they show exceptions or a deviance." All in all, the authors highlight the gains of differentiation due to the combination of survey and case studies: "Thus, the case studies not only allow for a differentiation and a deeper understanding of the relatives' response patterns to the questionnaire. Their special relevance is that analyzing them made it possible to discover the links between subjective meaning making (in the illness narratives) as well as the decisions and coping strategies that were reported and the latent meaning structures. Going beyond the psychological coping concepts, it became clear that it were less the personality traits or single factors, which make it easy or difficult to stabilize a critical life situation. Above all, the structural moments and the learned capacities to integrate the situational elements in one's own biography and in the one shared with the partner were important" (2004, p. 202).

This study can be seen as an example for combining qualitative and quantitative methods (and data), in which both approaches were applied consequently and in their own logic. They provide different aspects in the findings. The authors also show, how the case studies can add substantial dimensions to the questionnaire study. Unfortunately, the authors do not refer to which findings from the questionnaires were helpful for understanding the single cases or what the relevance of the quantitative finding was for the qualitative results.

Combining Qualitative and Quantitative Data

Data may be oriented to transforming qualitative data into quantitative data and vice versa. Here are a few examples.

Transformation of Qualitative Data into Quantitative Data

Repeatedly, there have been attempts to quantify statements of open or narrative interviews. Observations can also be analyzed in terms of their frequency. The frequencies in each category can be specified and compared. Several statistical methods for calculating such data are available. Hopf (1982) criticizes a tendency in qualitative researchers to try to convince their audiences by an argumentation based on a quantitative logic (e.g. "five of seven interviewees have said . . ."; "the majority of the answers focused . . .") instead of looking for a theoretically grounded interpretation and presentation of findings. This can be seen as an implicit transformation of qualitative data into quasi-quantitative findings.

Transformation of Quantitative Data into Qualitative Data

The inverse transformation is normally more difficult. It is difficult to disclose each answer's context on a questionnaire. If this task is attempted then it is achieved by the explicit use of additional methods such as complementary interviews for a part of the sample. Whereas analyzing the frequency of certain answers in interviews may provide additional insights for these interviews, the additional explanation for why certain patterns of answering can be found in large numbers in questionnaires requires the collection and involvement of new sorts of data (e.g., interviews and field observations).

Combining Qualitative and Quantitative Methods

There are only a few examples in which methodological procedures are constructed that really integrate qualitative and quantitative strategies in one method. Many questionnaires include open ended or free text questions. This is, in some contexts, already defined as qualitative research, although hardly any methodological principle of qualitative research is taken aboard with these questions. Again, this is not an explicit combination of both forms of research but an attempt to pick up a trend.

For the realm of analyzing qualitative data, Kuckartz (1995) describes a procedure of first and second order coding in which dimensional analyses lead to the definition of variables and values, which can be used for a classification and quantification. Roller et al. (1995) present a method called *hermeneutic classificatory content analysis*, which integrates ideas and procedures of objective hermeneutic (see Chapter 25) into basically a quantitative content analysis. In a similar direction goes the transfer of data analyzed with a program like ATLAS•ti into

SPSS and statistical analyses. In these attempts, the relation of classification and interpretation remains rather unclear. To develop really integrated qualitative/quantitative methods of data collection or data analysis remains an unsolved problem.

Linking Qualitative and Quantitative Results

More often combinations of both approaches are established by linking the results of qualitative and quantitative research in the same project or different projects, one after the other or at the same time. An example can be combining the results of a survey and an interview study. This combination can be pursued with different aims:

- to obtain knowledge about the issue of the study which is broader than a single approach provided;
- or to mutually validate the findings of both approaches.

Basically, three sorts of outcomes of this combination (see Kelle and Erzberger 2004) may result:

1. qualitative and quantitative results converge, mutually confirm, and support the same conclusions;
2. both results focus different aspects of an issue (e.g., subjective meanings of a specific illness and its social distribution in the population), but are complementary to each other and lead to a fuller picture;
3. qualitative and quantitative results are divergent or contradictory.

The outcomes are helpful if the interest in combining qualitative and quantitative research has a focus to know more about the issue. The third case (and maybe the second) needs a theoretical interpretation or explanation of the divergence and contradictions. Combining both approaches in the third case (and maybe the second) offers both valid findings and their limits. For a greater discussion on the problematic notion of validation through different methodologies, consult literature on triangulation (see Chapter 29 and Flick 1992, 2004a).

Research Evaluation and Generalization

A common form of implicitly combining qualitative and quantitative research is given when the research model of quantitative research (see Chapter 8) is applied to qualitative research. For example, the question of sampling (see Chapter 11) is seen as basically a numeric problem, as in the following question, often asked by students: "How many cases do I need to be able to make a scientific statement?" Here a quantitative logic is applied to qualitative research.

Another implicit combination of qualitative and quantitative research is to apply the quality criteria of one area to the other. Qualitative research is often criticized for not meeting the quality standards of quantitative research (see Chapter 28), without taking into account that these criteria do not fit qualitative research's principles and practices. In the other direction, the same problem is given, but this is relatively seldom the case.

With respect to the problem of generalization of qualitative research, you will find quite often a third form of implicit combination of qualitative and quantitative research. Then it is forgotten that to generalize findings of a study based on a limited number of interviews in a representative survey is just one form of generalization. This numerical generalization is not necessarily the right one, as many qualitative studies aim at developing new insights and theories. The more relevant question is how to generalize qualitative findings on a solid theoretical background. It is less the number of cases that are studied, but rather the quality of sampling decisions on which the generalization depends. Relevant questions here are "which cases?" rather than "how many?" and "what do the cases represent or what were they selected for?" Thus, the question of generalization in qualitative research is less closely linked to quantification than it is sometimes assumed.

Appropriateness of the Methods as a Point of Reference

The debate about qualitative and quantitative research, which was originally oriented to epistemological and philosophical standpoints, has increasingly moved towards questions of research practice such as the appropriateness of each approach. Wilson (1982) states that for the relation of both methodological traditions: "qualitative and quantitative approaches are complementary rather than competitive methods [and the] use of a particular method [. . .] rather must be based on the nature of the actual research problem at hand" (p. 501). Authors like McKinlay (1993, 1995) and Baum (1995) argue in a similar direction in the field of public health research. The suggestion is that rather than fundamental considerations determining the decision for or against qualitative or for or against quantitative methods, this decision should be determined by the appropriateness of the method for the issue under study and the research questions. Bauer and Gaskell (2000), for example, stress that it is more the degree of formalization and standardization, which distinguishes the two approaches than the juxtaposition of words and numbers.

The problems in combining qualitative and quantitative research nevertheless have not yet been solved in a satisfying way. Attempts to integrate both approaches often end up in a one-after-the-other (with different preferences), a side-by-side (with various degrees of independence of both strategies) or dominance (also with different preferences). The integration is often restricted to the level of the research design – a combination of various methods with different degrees of interrelations among each other. However, the differences of research concerning appropriate designs (see Chapter 8) and appropriate forms of assessing the procedures, data, and results (see Chapter 28) continue to exist. The question–how to take these differences into account in the combination of both strategies–needs further discussion.

There are some guiding questions for assessing examples of combining qualitative and quantitative research:

- Are both approaches given equal weight (in the plan of the project, in the relevance of the results, and in judging the quality of the research for example)?
- Are both approaches just applied separately or are they really related to each other? For example, many studies use qualitative and quantitative methods rather independently, and in the end, the integration of both parts refer to comparing the results of both.
- What is the logical relation of both? Are they only sequenced, and how? Or are they really integrated in a multi-methods design?
- What are the criteria used for evaluating the research all in all? Is there a domination of a traditional view of validation or are both forms of research evaluated by appropriate criteria?

Answering these questions and taking their implications into account allows the development of sensitive designs of using qualitative and quantitative research in a pragmatic and reflexive way.

KEY POINTS

- Linking qualitative and quantitative research is a topic that attracts a lot of attention.
- The combination is realized on different levels.
- In this context it is very important that the combination is not only an issue of pragmatics but that it is adequately reflected.
- The central point of reference is the appropriateness of the methods or of the combination to the issue under study.

Exercise 3.1

1. Reflect on the different ways of combining qualitative and quantitative research.
2. Find an example of research in which both approaches were combined; apply to this study what you learned in this chapter.
3. Why was the combination of qualitative and quantitative methods adequate for this study?

Exercise 3.2

1. Think about an issue in your own research in which a combination of qualitative and quantitative research could be helpful.
2. Think about problems you might face in applying a combination of qualitative and quantitative approaches in your research.

FURTHER READING

Here are some pragmatic and thoughtful works about ways and problems in linking both kinds of research.

Flick, U. (1992) "Triangulation Revisited: Strategy of or Alternative to Validation of Qualitative Data," *Journal for the Theory of Social Behavior*, 22: 175–197.
Kelle, U. and Erzberger, C. (2004) "Quantitative and Qualitative Methods: No Confrontation," in U. Flick, E.v. Kardorff and I. Steinke (eds), *A Companion to Qualitative Research*. London: SAGE. pp. 172–177.
Miles, M.B. and Huberman, A.M. (1994) *Qualitative Data Analysis: A Sourcebook of New Methods* (2nd edn). Newbury Park: SAGE.
Tashakkori, A. and Teddlie, Ch. (eds) (2003) *Handbook of Mixed Methods in Social & Behavioral Research*. Thousand Oaks: SAGE.

4

ETHICS OF QUALITATIVE RESEARCH

CHAPTER OBJECTIVES
After reading this chapter, you should be able to

✓ understand the ethical issues linked to qualitative research.
✓ develop a sensitivity for the ethics in qualitative research.
✓ recognize that there is no simple solution to these issues.
✓ construct (qualitative) research in an ethical framework.

In many domains, research has become an issue of ethics. Questions of how to protect the interests of those who are ready to take part in a study or scandals referring to manipulated data have repeatedly drawn research ethics to the foreground. Codes of ethics have been developed in several disciplines and in several countries for the same discipline. Ethics committees have been established especially in medical research, but also in other contexts. Sometimes, their focus is more generally on protecting all participants in the research process. In some countries, it is more the sensitivity of the research for ethnic diversity, which is in the focus of the ethics committee. In this chapter, I want to address some of the problems linked with research ethics if you intend to do qualitative research.

A Need for Ethics in Research and the Ethical Dilemmas of Qualitative Research

In the wider public, a sensitivity for ethical issues in research is growing due to scandals. The misuse of captives for research and experiments by doctors during the Nazi period in Germany are particularly horrifying examples, which led to the development of ethical codes for research. Past and recent cases of research have lead the German research council to develop rules of good practice, which have to be accepted and enacted by every university or institute applying for research funding. The growing sensitivity for ethical issues in research over the years has led to the formulation of a large number of codes of ethics and the establishment of ethics committees in many areas. As often in ethics, the tension is between formulating general rules (as in codes of ethics, for example) and establishing institutions of control (like ethics committees, for example) and the taking into account of principles in day-to-day practices in the field and in the process of research. As we will see, ethics here, as well as in other contexts, are often difficult to put into clear-cut solutions and clarifications. Rather, researchers face ethical issues in every stage of the research process as a sort of dilemma.

Codes of Ethics – An Answer to all Questions?

Codes of ethics are formulated to regulate the relations of researchers to the people and fields they intend to study. Principles of research ethics ask that researchers avoid harming participants involved in the process by respecting and taking into account their needs and interests. Here are a few examples of codes of ethics found on the Internet:

- The British Psychological Society (BPS) has published a Code of Conduct, Ethical Principles, and Guidelines (www.bps.org.uk/the-society/ethics-rules-charter-code-of-conduct/ethics-rules-charter-code-of-conduct_home.cfm).
- The British Sociological Association (BSA) has formulated a Statement of Ethical Practice (www.britsoc.co.uk).
- The American Sociological Association (ASA) refers to its Code of Ethics (www.asanet.org/members/ecoderev.html).
- The Social Research Association (SRA) has formulated Ethical Guidelines (www.the-sra.org.uk/Ethicals.htm).
- The German Sociological Association (GSA) has developed a Code of Ethics (www.soziologie.de/index_english.htm).

These codes of ethics require that research should be based on informed consent (i.e., the study's participants have agreed to partake on the basis of information given to them by the researchers). They also require that the research should avoid harming the participants, including not invading their privacy and not deceiving them about the research's aims.

Murphy and Dingwall speak of "ethical theory" in this context, which they see linked to four issues:

> *Non-maleficence*–researchers should avoid harming participants.
> *Beneficence*–research on human subjects should produce some positive and identifiable benefit rather than simply be carried out for its own sake.
> *Autonomy or self-determination*–research participants' values and decisions should be respected.
> *Justice*–all people should be treated equally. (2001, p. 339)

For example, in the code of ethics of the GSA, the need to reduce the risk to participants of having any damage or disadvantage is formulated:

> Persons, who are observed, questioned or who are involved in some other way in investigations, for example in connection with the analysis of personal documents, shall not be subject to any disadvantages or dangers as a result of the research. All risks that exceed what is normal in everyday life must be explained to the parties concerned. The anonymity of interviewees or informants must be protected. (Ethik-Kodex 1993: I B 5)

The principles of informed consent and of voluntary participation in studies are fixed as follows:

> A general rule for participation in sociological investigations is that it is voluntary and that it takes place on the basis of the fullest possible information about the goals and methods of the particular piece of research. The principle of informed consent cannot always be applied in practice, for instance if comprehensive pre-information would distort the results of the research in an unjustifiable way. In such cases an attempt must be made to use other possible modes of informed consent. (Ethik-Kodex 1993: I B2)

At the level of abstraction given in such general rules, Murphy and Dingwall see a consensus in the application of the ethical principles. They acknowledge the problems on the level of the research practice. From their background of ethnographic research (see Chapter 17), Murphy and Dingwall identify two major problems mentioned in the literature about experiences with such codes and principles in the research practice.

> First, ethical codes that are not method-sensitive may constrain research unnecessarily and inappropriately. Secondly and just as importantly, the ritualistic observation of these codes may not give real protection to research participants but actually increase the risk of harm by blunting ethnographers' sensitivities to the method-specific issues which do arise. (2001, p. 340)

As these authors show in many examples, a strict orientation in general rules of research is difficult in areas like ethnographic research and does not necessarily solve the ethical dilemmas in this field. In other examples, the special ethical problems in action research (Williamson and Prosser 2002), qualitative online research (see Chapter 20 and Mann and Stewart 2000, Ch. 3), or in feminist research (Mauthner, Birch, Jessop and Miller (2002) are discussed in detail.

Case Study: Covert Observation of Homosexual Practices

In the 1960s, Humphreys (1975) conducted an observational study of the sexual behavior of homosexuals. This study led to a debate on the ethical problems of observations in this and comparable fields which continued for a long time, because it made visible the dilemmas of non-participant observation (see Chapter 17). Humphreys observed in public toilets, which were meeting places in the homosexual subculture. As homosexuality was still illegal at that time, toilets offered one of the few possibilities for clandestine meetings. This study is an example of observation without participation, because Humphreys conducted his observation explicitly from the position of sociological voyeur, not as a member of the observed events and not accepted as an observer. In order to do this Humphreys took the role of somebody (the "watch queen") whose job it was to ensure that no strangers approached the events. In this role, he could observe all that was happening without being perceived as interfering and without having to take part in the events:

> Outwardly I took on the role of a voyeur, a role which is excellently suitable for sociologists and which is the only role of a watchdog, which is not of a manifest sexual nature. . . . In the role of the watch-queen-voyeur, I could freely move in the room, walk from window to window and observe everything without my subjects becoming suspicious and without disturbing the activities in any other way. (Humphreys 1973, p. 258)

After covertly observing the practices in the field, Humphreys then went on by collecting participant's car license numbers and using this information to obtain their name and address. He used this information to invite a sample of these members to take part in an interview survey.

Humphreys used unethical strategies to disclose participants' personal information in what was originally an anonymous event. At the same time, he did a lot to keep his own identity and role as a researcher concealed by conducting covert observation in his watch-queen role. Each part of this is unethical in itself–keeping the research participants uninformed about the research and lifting the privacy and secrecy of the participants. The ethical dilemmas of observation are described here in three respects. Researchers must find a way into the field of interest. They want to observe in a way that influences the flow of events as little as possible; and in sanctioned, forbidden,

(Continued)

(Continued)

criminal, or dangerous activities in particular, the problem arises of how to observe them without the researcher becoming an accomplice. Therefore, this example was and is still discussed with some emphasis in the context of research ethics. This example is prominent in particular for the ethical issues linked to it and which can be demonstrated with it. But at the same time, it shows the dilemmas of finding and taking a role in observation.

Ethics Committees – A Solution?

Ethics committees have been established in many areas. In order to ensure ethical standards, the committees examine the research design and methods before they can be applied. In these fields, good ethical practice in research is then based on two conditions–that the researcher will conduct their research in accordance with ethical codes and that research proposals have been reviewed by ethics committees for their ethical soundness. Reviews of ethical soundness will focus on three aspects (see Allmark 2002, p. 9): scientific quality, the welfare of participants and respect for the dignity, and rights of participants.

Scientific Quality

According to this, any research, which is only duplicating existing research or which does not have the quality to contribute new knowledge to the existing knowledge, can be seen as unethical (see for example: Department of Health 2001). In such a notion, there is already a source for conflict. For judging the quality of research, the members of the ethics committee should have the necessary knowledge for assessing a research proposal on a methodological level. This often means the members of the committees should be researchers themselves or at least some of the members. If you talk for a while with researchers about their experiences with ethics committees and with proposals submitted to them, you will come across many stories about how a research proposal was rejected because the members did not understand its premise. Or because they had a methodological background different from that of the applicant or that they simply disliked the research and rejected it for scientific rather than ethical reasons. These stories show a dilemma of ethics committees; there are a variety of reasons why a committee may decide to reject or block a research proposal, not always based on ethical reasons.

Welfare of Participants

Welfare in this context is often linked to weighing the risks (for the participants) against the benefits (of new knowledge and insights about a problem or of finding a new solution to an existing problem). Again, we find a dilemma here–weighing the risks and benefits rather than what is absolute and clear.

Dignity and Rights of the Participants

Dignity and rights of the participants are linked to consent given by the participant, to a sufficient and adequate information provided as a basis for giving that consent and that the consent is given voluntarily (Allmark 2002, p. 13). Beyond this researchers need to guarantee participants complete confidentiality that the information about them is only used in a way which makes it impossible for other persons to identify the participants or for any institution to use them against the interest of the participant.

The ethics committees review and canonize these general principles (for a detailed discussion of such principles see Hopf 2004b and Murphy and Dingwall 2001). I will discuss in the next section why these principles are not necessarily a solution to ethical dilemmas but more an orientation about how to act ethically in the research process especially in qualitative research.

How to Act Ethically in Your Qualitative Research

Northway (2002, p. 3) outlines the overall ethical involvement of any research: "However, all aspects of the research process, from deciding upon the topic through to identifying a sample, conducting the research and disseminating the findings, have ethical implications." You will be confronted with ethical issues at every step of the research. The way you enter a field and address and select your participants raises the issue of how you inform your participants and whom you inform about your research, its purposes, and your expectations.

Informed Consent

When we take the principle of informed consent as a precondition for participation, you will find some criteria in the literature:

* The consent should be given by someone competent to do so;
* The person giving the consent should be adequately informed;
* The consent is given voluntarily (Allmark 2002, p. 13).

This should not be too difficult to realize if you, for example, want to interview middle class, middle age people with a similar educational level as your researchers have. Then you can inform them, they may reflect and decide to consent or not. But what if you want to study people who are not (seen as) competent to understand and decide—say younger children (as in the case of Allmark 2002) or very old people with dementia or people with mental health problems? These people are referred to in this context as "vulnerable people." Then you may ask another person to give you the consent as a substitute—children's parents, family members or responsible medical personnel in the case of an elderly or ill person. Does this meet the criterion of informed consent? You could easily find other examples in which you have to decide how far you can deviate from the general principle without ignoring it.

Avoiding Harm in Collecting Data

Collecting your data may confront you with another ethical problem. If you are interested in how people live and cope with a chronic illness, for example, the planned interview questions may confront people with the severity of the illness or the lack of prospects in their future life. This may in some cases produce an internal crisis for these people. Is it ethically correct to take this risk for the sake of your research?

Doing Justice to Participants in Analyzing Data

In analyzing and writing about your data, you will come to certain judgements (e.g., a specific person can be allocated to specific coping behaviors while other persons are allocated other types of coping skills). If your participants read this result, they may find it embarrassing to be compared with other people and they may also see themselves in a different way.

Confidentiality in Writing about Your Research

The issue of confidentiality or anonymity may become problematic when you do research with several members of a specific setting. When you interview several people in the same company, or several members of a family, the need for confidentiality is not only in relation to a public outside this setting. Readers of your report should not be able to identify which company or which persons took part in your research. For this purpose, change the specific details to protect identities. Try to guarantee that colleagues cannot identify participants from their information. For example when interviewing children, you may often find that parents want to know what their children said in the interview. To avoid this problem, you should inform the parents right in the beginning of your research that this is not possible (see Allmark 2002, p. 17). Finally, it is very important, that you store your data (i.e., recordings and transcripts in a safe, completely secure container, so that no one will be able to access these data who is not meant to (see Lüders 2004b).

The Problems of Context in Qualitative Data and Research

Generally, the data of qualitative research produces more context information about a single participant than quantitative research. Usually it is impossible to identify a participant from a survey and the statistical/numerical data published across numerous cases. When you study a single case or a limited number of cases in well-defined fields and use excerpts from life histories in your publication, it is much easier to identify the "real" person from the context information included in such a quotation.

Case study: Interaction as an Ethically Sensitive Subject of Research

This example will show that also a specific research topic can require a specific ethical sensitiveness. Maijalla, Astedt-Kurki, and Paavilainen (2002) completed a study using grounded theory (see Chapter 8 and 23) with families. They studied the interaction between the caregiver and a family expecting a child with an abnormality. The families involved in the study were in a situation of crisis after receiving the information that their child might be born with a malformation or might not survive. Doing research with families in such a situation first of all comes with the ethical dilemma, whether it is justified to additionally confront them with their situation by asking questions about it. Thus, the participation in the study may cause some harm for the family or single members. The authors did interviews with parents from 18 families in that situation and with 22 caregivers who interacted with these families. The interviews were tape-recorded and due to ethical reasons, there was no videotaping used for documenting the data. Potential participants received a letter stating the study's intentions and modalities of confidentiality. As this research was carried out in the context of nursing research, an ethical issue was how to separate the roles of researcher and caregiver. It had to be clarified that the purpose of the interview was to collect data, not to work with the participants on the situation and the ways of coping with it. However, it was necessary to keep an eye on the participants' well being during and after the interview, as the issue produced a distressing situation. Thus, the role of the caregiver became part of the arrangement again in some cases. Researchers gave justice to the participants' viewpoints during the analysis period. To support this, each researcher wrote research diaries, and research supervision was given. The transcription of the interviews was done by a professional "who signed a written commitment to secrecy and who was experienced in dealing with confidential data" (p. 30). In reporting their findings, the authors took care that the formulations were general enough to protect the anonymity of their informants (p. 31).

This example showed how during the different stages of the research process ethical issues came up and also how the authors tried to cope with them. Maybe the problems were more urgent here as the families were in a crisis and became part of this study due to this crisis. But most of the ethical issues can be transferred to other issues of qualitative research.

Qualitative Research Ethics – Necessary for Better Research

Qualitative research is often planned as very open and adapted to what happens in the field. Methods here are less canonized than in quantitative research. This makes reviews by ethics committees more difficult as it is, for example, difficult to foresee what sorts of data will be collected in an ethnographic study. It also makes it sometimes difficult to ask for the consent of those being researched, when observations are done in open spaces like market places, train stations, and the like. The openness sometimes leads to a rather comprehensive approach in data collection ("Please tell me the story of your life and everything maybe important for my research…") instead of a clearly focused (and limited) set of questions or things to observe. Therefore, it may be helpful to reflect about a rather economic approach to the field, which means only to collect those data and aspects that are really necessary to answer the research question. Research ethics is an important issue in planning and doing your research. It is often not possible to find easy and very general solutions to the problems and dilemmas. It has a lot to do with reflection and sensitiveness. Thinking about ethical dilemmas, however, should not prevent you from doing your research, but should help you do it in a more reflective way and to take your participants' perspective on a different level. Try to take the participants' role and think from their perspective, how would it be for you to do what you expect them to do in your research. This may be a good starting point for reflecting on the ethical issues linked to your specific research.

KEY POINTS

- Finding solutions to ethical dilemmas is essential to legitimate research.
- In qualitative research, ethical dilemmas are sometimes more difficult to solve than in quantitative research.
- Codes of ethics regulate the treatment of ethical issues generally. Ethic committees can be an important instrument to assess research proposals and the rights and interests of its participants.
- The dynamics of ethical dilemmas unfold their dynamics in the field and in the contact with persons or institutions.
- Many ethical dilemmas come from the need to weigh the research interest (better knowledge, new solutions for existing problems, and the like) against the interest of participants (confidentiality, avoidance of any harm, and the like).

Exercise 4.1

Find a qualitative study, and determine if the authors addressed ethical issues. How did they deal with them? Try to imagine which other issues of research ethics you expect in such a study.

Exercise 4.2

In your own course of study, contemplate the ethical issues, establish guidelines, and create a plan for participants.

FURTHER READING

The following two texts give a good overview of the discussion of ethical issues for qualitative research.

Hopf, C. (2004b) "Research Ethics and Qualitative Research," in U. Flick, E.v. Kardorff and I. Steinke (eds), *A Companion to Qualitative Research.* London: SAGE. pp. 334–339.

Murphy, E. and Dingwall, R. (2001) "The Ethics of Ethnography," in P. Atkinson, A. Coffey, S. Delamont, J. Lofland, and L. Lofland (eds), *Handbook of Ethnography.* London: SAGE. pp. 339–351.

PART 2

FROM THEORY TO TEXT

In Part 1, we looked for a framework for doing qualitative research or a qualitative study. As we saw in Chapter 2, qualitative research is a lot about producing and analyzing texts, such as transcripts of interviews or field notes and other analytic materials. I will turn now to the first part of the overall journey of a qualitative research project. We will start this with the stage leading us from theory to text before going back from text to theory (Part 6). Here, I will first address the ways in which to use theories in qualitative research. This is in order to dispel the prejudice that qualitative researchers should stay away from reading the existing body of research literature and from reading the methodology literature and theories about the research topic (Chapter 5). I will then discuss the major theoretical positions undepinning qualitative research. These theoretical positions can be seen as the background theories of qualitative research, each of them coming along with assumptions about the nature of realities, how to address an issue conceptually, and how to plan research (Chapter 6). In this chapter, we will also address two influential discussions in qualitative research. The first is about positivism and constructivism as a basic epistemological assumption; the second focuses on the impact of feminist positions on qualitative research in general. The first discussion will be unfolded a little more in the final chapter of this part (Chapter 7). Here, I will discuss the epistemological background of using text in qualitative research and address the basic processes in constructing and understanding texts. This part as a whole sets the epistemological and theoretical ground for the more practical parts of the book in which you will learn more about how to do qualitative research.

5
MAKING USE OF LITERATURE IN QUALITATIVE RESEARCH

CHAPTER OBJECTIVES
After reading this chapter, you should be able to

✓   comprehend the relevance of existing literature for planning your own research.
✓   understand the necessity to rely on methodological literature as well as the existing research in your area in qualitative research.
✓   familiarize yourself with finding the relevant literature for your research.

How and When to Use Literature in Qualitative Research

Most textbooks in qualitative research do not include an extra chapter on the use of existing literature in the field of a study. Sometimes you find the idea that qualitative research does not need to start from reviewing the existing literature or should even avoid that step at the beginning. This is because qualitative research is closely linked to the idea of discovering new fields and exploring areas that are new to the world of science and to research.

However, it is rather naive to think there are still new fields to explore, where nothing ever has been published before. This may have been the case at the beginning of qualitative research, when an anthropologist sailed off to explore uncharted islands. Maybe this was the case when social research (as a systematic enterprise) started to do the first studies among immigrant subcultures. But at the start of the twenty-first century, after more than a century of social research and decades of rediscovering qualitative research, you will have more and more trouble to find a completely undiscovered field. Not everything has been researched, but almost everything you want to research will probably connect with an existing, neighboring field. One reason for this lack of chapters devoted to the use of literature may come from a very early statement about grounded theory research. In their introduction to the *Discovery of Grounded Theory* Glaser and Strauss (1967) suggested (see Chapter 8) that the researchers should start collecting and analyzing data without looking for existing literature in the field. *Tabula rasa* was the keyword, which has often been used later on as an argument against scientific claims linked to qualitative research. Strauss revised this standpoint a long time ago, but this notion is still present in many images of qualitative research.

In this chapter, I will suggest that you should use several forms of literature in a qualitative study including:

- theoretical literature about the topic of your study;
- empirical literature about earlier research in the field of your study or similar fields;
- methodological literature about how to do your research and how to use the methods you chose;
- theoretical and empirical literature to contextualize, compare, and generalize your findings.

How to Use Theoretical Literature about the Topic of your Study

As in any other field of research, I suggest you familiarize yourself with the literature in your field. What are the existing writings about the social situation in a field in which you want to do interviews or observations? What is known about the people that you want to interview for example? If you want to do a study with cancer patients for example, this does not mean so much what is known about the (concrete) persons that you want to interview? Rather, what is known about people living in a similar situation; what is a regular career for persons with that specific cancer; how often does it occur, and so on? Are there any explanatory models about the causes and consequences of this specific disease?

Different from a quantitative study, you would not take the existing literature about the issue of your study to derive hypotheses from it, which you then basically test. In qualitative research, you use insights and information coming from existing literature as context knowledge, which you use to see statements and observations in your research in their context. Or you use it to understand the differences in your study before and after its initial discovery process. Reviewing the theoretical literature in your area of research should help you answer questions such as:

- What is already known about this issue in particular, or the area in general?
- Which theories are used and discussed in this area?
- What concepts are used or disputed about?
- What are the theoretical or methodological debates or controversies in this field?
- What are still open questions?
- What has not been studied yet?

When Glaser and Strauss wrote their book in the 1960s, there was widespread dissatisfaction with the development of theory in the social sciences. Social Scientists wanted to find overall grand theories, like the systems theories of Talcott Parsons (e.g., Parsons and Shils 1951), which were originally meant to explain more or less everything, but ended up explaining almost nothing on the level of everyday phenomena. In this situation, a need for theories closer to mundane or practically relevant issues arose, which should be answered by the empirically based theories developed in the research of grounded theory researchers. Currently, the situation is quite different. The era of the overall grand theories has ended, and there is a wide variety of models and explanatory approaches for detailed problems. The trend is more towards diversification than to unification and a lot of these rather limited theories and models might be helpful for analyzing empirical material in related areas.

The Use of Theories in Qualitative Research

Let us take an example to illustrate this. For example, you want to study the social representations of skin cancer in middle-class women in a certain segment of the United Kingdom. In the context of such a research question, we can distinguish different forms of relevant theories. First, there are theories explaining the issue under study (take for instance medical or psychological theories of skin cancer in our example). They may inform you about the state of the art of scientific knowledge and about the forms of skin cancer and their reoccurrences. These theories may also inform you about possible reasons for such a disease, about ways of treating it, and finally about ways of dealing with it (e.g., treatment, coping, the likelihood of success of treatments, and so on).

This is a theoretical context, which you should read literature about. When your focus is especially on people and this disease in the United Kingdom, it might be interesting again, to know how the issue of skin cancer is specifically relevant in the United Kingdom. So, you might try to find press coverage of this disease, the normal or special distribution and frequency of the disease in this country, and so on. To find this information, you will read theoretical literature. The theories subject to this literature are called substantial theories.

The second form of theory that is relevant for your research in this example is the theory of social representations (see also Chapter 6). It gives you an idea that there are different forms of knowledge among lay people in different groups. It also provides you with ideas about how such knowledge is developed, transformed, and transmitted. This will give you a theoretical framework for conceptualizing your study.

When you focus on the middle class in your study, you probably start from a notion of social classes, social inequality, and the distribution of privileges and disadvantages in society. This is again a background theory for conceiving your study. When you focus on women as the target group of your study, you may also have a gender focus in your study, starting from the idea of gender differences in experience, ways of living, or knowing. Maybe you have an explicitly feminist perspective in your study (see also Chapter 6). Call these theories context theories for your research.

Finally, you may decide to use a specific methodology—say episodic interviews (see Chapter 14)—to show how social representations have developed along the life course of your interviewees. This method comes with a specific theoretical conception of the issues that can be studied with it. This theory focuses, for example, on biographical information— what is a normal biography, what makes an individual life course a deviation or a special case. It also starts from an assumption about how memory is organized. Conceptual or semantic and biographical or episodic memory and knowledge are distinguished (see Chapter 14 for details). This method comes with a lot of theoretical knowledge about how to design the situation of data collection, so that the data are as rich as possible and so on. Here again, theory, which will be helpful to know, becomes relevant.

How to Use Empirical Literature about Earlier Research in the Same Field or Similar Fields

Before you start your own empirical research, it might be very helpful to find out whether there has been any other research in that or a similar area. You should systematically search for other studies in your field. They can be fruitful in inspiring you – what to do in your own research, how to design your research, what to ask in an interview and so on. If the research is a good example, you can use it as an orientation of how to do your own research; if it is a bad example, you can use as an orientation for how not to proceed or which mistakes to avoid.

But mainly, you should read empirical literature to see how other people in your area work, what has been studied, what has been focused on, and what has been left out. If it is an area where much research is going on, it might be helpful to know on which level the research concentrates and its results.

Reviewing the empirical literature in your area of research should help you to answer questions like:

- What are the methodological traditions or controversies here?
- Are there any contradictory results and findings which you could take as a starting point?

In a similar way, Strauss and Corbin (1998, pp. 49–52) list several ways of using literature: (1) Concepts from the literature can be a source for making comparisons in data you have collected. (2) To be familiar with relevant literature can enhance the sensitivity to subtle nuances in data. (3) Published descriptive materials can give accurate descriptions of reality helpful for understanding your own material. (4) Existing philosophical and theoretical knowledge can inspire you and give you an orientation in the field and material. (5) Literature can be a secondary source of data–for example, quotations from interviews in articles may complement your own materials. (6) Literature can be used beforehand to formulate questions that help you as a springboard in early interviews and observations. (7) Literature may stimulate questions while you analyze your material. (8) Areas for theoretical sampling (see Chapter 11) can be suggested by the literature. (9) Literature can be used for confirming findings or can be overcome by your findings. These nine points refer to publications from scientific writing, research, and methodology (what is called technical literature by Strauss and Corbin). Non-technical literature, like letters, biographies, and all sorts of documents (see Chapter 20) can be used as primary data of their own quality or for supplementing other forms of data (like interviews).

How to Use Methodological Literature about the Methods of Your Study

Before you decide to use a specific method for your study, I suggest that you read the relevant methodological literature. If you want to use focus groups (see Chapter 15) in a qualitative study, familiarize yourself with a detailed overview of the current state of qualitative research. You can obtain this overview by reading a textbook or an introduction to the field. Also look through some of the relevant journals and see what has been published there in the last couple of years. Then you should identify the relevant publications about your method of choice by reading a special book, some chapters about it, and prior research examples using this method. The first step will allow you to take your decision for a specific method in the context of existing alternatives and of knowledge about them. The second step will prepare you for the more technical steps of planning to use the method and to avoid problems and mistakes mentioned in the literature. Both will help you give a detailed and concise account of why and how you used your method in your study, when you write your report later on, and so on.

Reviewing the methodological literature in your area of research should help you to answer questions like:

- What are the methodological traditions, alternatives, or controversies here?
- Are there any contradictory ways of using the methods, which you could take as a starting point?

For example, if you decide to use a grounded theory approach (see Chapters 8 and 23) for your research, it may be helpful to read about the two versions developed by Strauss and Corbin (1998) and Glaser (1992) over time. If you want to use discourse analysis, it may be necessary to read about the different versions (e.g., Parker 2004, Potter and Wetherall 1998, or Willig 2003; see Chapter 24) to see the distinctions, alternatives, and strengths or weaknesses of one approach over the other.

In reading and writing about your method, to review the methodological literature in that area will help you and the readers of your research report to see your approach and findings in a wider context.

How to Use Literature when Writing about Your Study

As in the above list suggested by Strauss and Corbin and elsewhere in the earlier parts of this chapter, an important part of using literature is during writing about your study (see Chapter 30). Here, existing literature becomes relevant for grounding your argumentation, for showing that your findings are in concordance with the existing research, that your findings go beyond or contradict existing research. Part of more extensive reports – or a thesis for example – should be a literature review. Hart gives a concise definition about a literature review's contents:

> The selection of available documents (both published and unpublished) on the topic, which contain information, ideas, data, and evidence written from a particular standpoint to fulfill certain aims or express certain views on the nature of the topic and how it is to be investigated, and the effective evaluation of these documents in relation to the research being proposed. (1998, p. 13)

You should demonstrate in the way you present the literature you used in your study that you did a skilful search into the existing literature. Also it should be evident that you have a good command of the subject area and that you understand the issue, the methods you use, the state of the art of research in your field, and so on.

How and Where to Find Literature

In general, it depends on your topic where to search and find the relevant literature. If you want to find out whether your usual library holds the literature you are looking for, you can simply go to the library and check the catalogue. This can be time consuming and frustrating if the book is not in stock. If you find out which library holds the book (or journal) you are looking for, you can try to find an Internet access to the library's OPAC. Therefore, you should go to the home page of one or more libraries. Or use a link to several libraries at the same time. Examples are copac.ac.uk for 24 of the major university libraries and the British Library or www.ubka.uni-karlsruhe.de/hylib/en/kvk.html for most of the German but also many UK or US university libraries. There you can find an exhaustive overview of the existing books or the information for completing your reference lists. To get a book, you still have to go to the library, but you will know where to go and whether it is available or has to be ordered first.

For journal articles, you can use search engines like: wok.mimas.ac.uk. This will lead you to the *Social Sciences Citation Index*, which you can search for authors, titles, keywords, and the like. If you want to read the whole article, you need to be registered or you can buy the right to download it.

The same applies with some online publication services organized by publishing houses like SAGE. At online.sagepub.com you can search all the journals published by this publisher, read the abstracts, and get the exact reference dates for free. If you need to read the whole article, you have to be a subscriber to the service or the journal, or buy the article from the homepage or see whether your library has subscribed to the journal that published the article.

Also in a qualitative study, you should make use of the theoretical, methodological, and empirical literature referring to your topic, area, and approach. This will help you to see what your material has to offer in a wider context, will inform you about how to do your research, and what problems to avoid. The Internet offers a lot of supporting services helping you along on the way to finding the literature. In the end, a good review of the literature will be a substantial part of your research report.

KEY POINTS

- In qualitative research, the use of existing literature has become increasingly relevant.
- There are several points in the research process, where the use of literature can be helpful and necessary.
- In planning research, in analyzing materials, in writing about findings, you should make use of existing literature about other research, about theories and the methods you use in your study.

Exercise 5.1

Look for a qualitative study, read it, and answer the following questions:

1. How much did the authors deal with existing literature about their field of research?
2. At which points in the publication did the authors use and refer to existing literature about their study?

Exercise 5.2

If you plan your own study, use the ways of finding literature mentioned above, and try to find the relevant literature for planning and doing your study.

FURTHER READING

Literature Search
The following book is the most comprehensive overview of how to do a literature search for your research, where to look, and how to proceed.

Hart, C. (2001) *Doing a Literature Search.* London: SAGE.

Literature Reviews
Here you will find the most comprehensive overview of how to do a literature review for your study, which pitfalls to avoid, and how to write about what you found.

Hart, C. (1998) *Doing a Literature Review.* London: SAGE.

6

THEORETICAL POSITIONS UNDERLYING QUALITATIVE RESEARCH

CHAPTER OBJECTIVES
After reading this chapter, you should be able to

✓   know the major background theories in qualitative research.
✓   acknowledge the common and distinctive features of these theories.
✓   understand the difference between positivism and constructivism.
✓   consider the contribution of feminist theories to qualitative research.

Research Perspectives in the Field of Qualitative Research

As you will have learned from reading Chapter 2, various research approaches are summarized under the umbrella heading of qualitative research. These are different in their theoretical assumptions, in the way they understand their object, and in their methodological focus. Generally speaking, these approaches orient towards three basic positions. The tradition of symbolic interactionism is concerned with studying subjective meanings and individual meaning making. Ethnomethodology is interested in routines of everyday life and their production. Structuralist or psychoanalytic positions are starting from processes of psychological or social unconsciousness. It is possible to differentiate those approaches foregrounding the "subject's viewpoint" from those seeking descriptions of given (everyday, institutional, or more generally social) milieus. Additionally, you can find strategies interested in how social order is produced (e.g., ethnomethodological analyses of language) or oriented towards reconstructing deep structures that generate action and meaning from psychoanalysis or objective hermeneutics.

Each of these positions conceptualizes how the subjects under study–their experiences, actions and interactions–relate to the context in which they are studied in different ways.

Subjective Meaning: Symbolic Interactionism

In the first perspective, the empirical starting point is the subjective meaning individuals attribute to their activities and their environments. These research approaches refer to the tradition of symbolic interactionism:

> The name of this line of sociological and sociopsychological research was coined in 1938 by Herbert Blumer (1938). Its focus is processes of interaction–social action that is characterised by an immediately reciprocal orientation–and the investigations of these processes are based on a particular concept of interaction, which stresses the symbolic character of social actions. (Joas 1987, p. 84)

As Joas shows, this position has been developed from the philosophical tradition of American pragmatism. Generally, it represents the understanding of theory and method in the Chicago School (W.I. Thomas, Robert Park, Charles Horton Cooley or George Herbert Mead) in American sociology. In general, this approach plays a central role in qualitative research both recently and historically. Sociologists such as Anselm Strauss, Barney Glaser, Norman K. Denzin, Howard Becker, and others directly refer to this position; Blumer's (1969) work on the "methodological position of symbolic interactionism" had a big influence on the methodological discussions of the 1970s.

Basic Assumptions

What are the basic assumptions of this approach? Blumer summarizes the starting points of symbolic interactionism as "three simple premises":

> The first premise is that human beings act toward things on the basis of the meanings that the things have for them . . . The second premise is that the meaning of such things is derived from, or arises out of, the social interaction that one has with one's fellows. The third premise is that these meanings are handled in, and modified through, an interpretative process used by the person in dealing with the things he encounters. (1969, p. 2)

What does this mean for the research situation? The consequence is that the different ways in which individuals invest objects, events, experiences, and so on with meaning form the central starting point for research in this approach. The reconstruction of such subjective viewpoints becomes the instrument for analyzing social worlds. Another central assumption is formulated in the so-called Thomas theorem, further grounding the methodological principle[1] just mentioned. Thomas's theorem:

> …claim[s] that when a person defines a situation as real, this situation is real in its consequences, leads directly to the fundamental methodological principle of symbolic interactionism: researchers have to see the world from the angle of the subjects they study. (Stryker 1976, p. 259)

From this basic assumption, the methodological imperative is drawn to reconstruct the subject's viewpoint in different respects. The first is in the form of subjective theories, used by people to explain the world–or at least a certain area of objects as part of this world–for themselves. Thus, there is a voluminous research literature on subjective theories of health and illness (for overviews see e.g., Flick 2003), on subjective theories in pedagogy, and in counseling actions. The second is in the form of autobiographical narratives, biographical trajectories that are reconstructed from the perspective of the subjects. But it is important that these should give access to the temporal and local contexts, reconstructed from the narrator's point of view.

Recent Developments in Sociology: Interpretive Interactionism

In recent years, Denzin has argued from a position, which starts from symbolic interactionism but integrates several alternative and more recent streams. Here we find phenomenological considerations (following Heidegger), structuralist ways of thinking (Foucault), feminist and post-modern critiques of science, the approach of "thick descriptions" (Geertz 1973), and that of concepts from literature.[2] Denzin specifies or limits this approach in two respects. It "should only be used when the researcher wants to examine the relationship between personal troubles (e.g., wife-battering or alcoholism), and the public policies and public institutions that have been created to address those personal problems" (1989a, p. 10). Furthermore, Denzin restricts the perspective taken when he repeatedly emphasizes that the processes being studied should be understood biographically and necessarily interpreted from this angle (e.g., 1989a, pp. 19–24).

Recent Developments in Psychology:
Subjective Theories as Research Program

The aim of analyzing subjective viewpoints is pursued in a most consistent way in the framework of research on subjective theories. Here, the starting point is that individuals in everyday life–like scientists–develop theories on how the world and their own activities function. They apply and test these theories in their activities and revise them if necessary. Assumptions in such theories are organized in an interdependent way and with an argumentative structure corresponding to the structure of statements in scientific theories. This type of research seeks to reconstruct these subjective theories. For this purpose, a specific interview method has been developed (see Chapter 13 for the semi-standardized interview). In order to reconstruct subjective theories as close as possible to the subject's point of view, special methods for a (communicative) validation of the reconstructed theory have been created (see Chapter 28).

The concentration on the subjects' points of view and on the meaning they attribute to experiences and events, as well as the orientation towards the meaning of objects, activities and events, informs a large part of qualitative research. Combining subject-oriented research with symbolic interactionism, as has been done here, certainly cannot take place without reservations. For example, the reference to symbolic interactionism in recent research on subjective theories usually remains rather implicit. Also, other research perspectives arise out of the traditions of Blumer and Denzin, which are more interested in interactions than in subjective viewpoints (e.g., the contributions to Denzin 1993). For such interactionist studies, however, it remains essential to focus the subjective meanings of objects for the participants in interactions. With regard to methods, this approach mainly uses different forms of interviews (see Chapters 13 and 14) and participant observation (see Chapter 17). These two positions–the study of subjective viewpoints and the theoretical background of symbolic interactionism–mark one pole in the field of qualitative research.

The Making of Social Realities: Ethnomethodology

The limitations of interactionism's concern with the subjects' viewpoints are exceeded theoretically and methodologically in the framework of ethnomethodology. Harold Garfinkel (1967) is the founder of this school. It addresses the question of how people produce social reality in and through interactive processes. Its central concern is with the study of the methods used by members to produce reality in everyday life.[3] Garfinkel defines the research interests related to ethnomethodology:

> Ethnomethodological studies analyze everyday activities as members' methods for making those same activities visibly-rational-and-reportable-for- all-practical-purposes, i.e. "accountable", as organizations of commonplace everyday activities. The reflexivity of that phenomenon is a singular feature of practical actions, of practical circumstances, of common sense knowledge of social structures, and of practical sociological reasoning. (1967, p. vii)

The interest in everyday activities, in their execution and beyond–in the constitution of a locally oriented context of interaction in which activities are carried out–characterize the ethnomethodological research program in general. This research program has been realized mainly in the empirical researches of conversation analysis (see Chapter 24).

Basic Assumptions

What are the basic assumptions of this approach? The premises of ethnomethodology and conversation analysis are encapsulated in three basic assumptions by Heritage:

> (1) Interaction is structurally organized; (2) contributions of interaction are both context shaped and context renewing; and (3) thus two properties inhere in the *details* of interaction so that no order of detail in conversational interaction can be dismissed *a priori* as disorderly, accidental, or irrelevant. (1985, p. 1)

Interaction is produced in a well-ordered way. The context is the framework of interaction that is produced in and through the interaction at the same time. Decisions as to what is relevant to members in social interaction can only be made through an analysis of that interaction and not *a priori* taken for granted. The focus is not the subjective meaning for the participants of an interaction and its contents but how this interaction is organized. The research topic becomes the study of the routines of everyday life rather than the outstanding events consciously perceived and invested with meaning.

In order to uncover the methods through which interaction is organized, researchers seek to adopt an attitude of *ethnomethodological indifference* (Garfinkel and Sacks 1970). They should abstain from any *a priori* interpretation as well as from adopting the perspectives of the actors or one of the actors. To understand the perspective of ethnomethodology, context plays a key role where interaction takes place. An empirical study shows this relevance to its participants. Wolff et al. illustrate that very clearly:

> The fundamental starting point of an ethnomethodological . . . proceeding is to regard any event as constituted through the production efforts of the members on the spot. This is the case not only for the actual facts in the interaction, as for example the unwinding of question–answer sequences, but also for realizing so-called macro-facts, like the institutional context of a conversation. (1988, p. 10)

Let us take an example to illustrate this a little more. According to such a notion, a counseling conversation becomes what it is (different from other types of conversation) through the members' efforts in creating this situation. Thus, we are concerned not with the researcher's *a priori* definition of the situation. Rather, we are interested in the members' conversational contributions, as it is through the turn-by-turn organization of the talk that the conversation is constituted as a consultation. The institutional context, however, is also made relevant in the conversation and constituted in and through the members' contributions. Only the specific practices of the counselor and the client turn a conversation into a consultation and turn a consultation into a consultation in a specific context (e.g., in a "sociopsychiatric service").

Recent Developments of Ethnomethodology in the Social Sciences: Studies of Work

Ethnomethodological research has focused and narrowed more and more on the increasingly formal analysis of conversations. Since the 1980s the second main focus on the "studies of work" has been the analysis of work processes (see Bergmann 2004a; Garfinkel 1986). Here, processes of work are studied in a broad sense and particularly in the context of scientific work in laboratories or, for example, how mathematicians construct proofs (Livingston 1986). In these studies various methods for describing work processes as exactly as possible are used, among which conversation analysis is just one approach. The scope is enlarged from studying interactive practices to a concern with "embodied knowledge," materializing in such practices as well as in their results (Bergmann 2004a). These studies contribute to the wider context of recent research on the sociology of scientific knowledge (see Knorr-Cetina and Mulkay 1983). In general, the sociology of scientific knowledge has been developed from the tradition of ethnomethodology.

Recent Developments in Psychology: Discursive Psychology

Starting from conversation analysis and laboratory studies, a program of "discursive psychology" has been developed in British social psychology (see Harré 1998; Potter and Wetherell 1998). Here psychological phenomena such as cognition or memory are studied by analyzing relevant discourses concerned with certain topics. These discourses range from everyday conversations to texts in media. The stress lies on communicative and constructive processes in interactions. The methodological starting point is to analyze the "interpretive repertoires" that the participants of certain discourses use to produce a specific version of reality and to assert it: "Interpretive repertoires are broadly discernible clusters of terms, descriptions, and figures of speech often assembled around metaphors or vivid images. They can be thought of as the building blocks used for manufacturing versions of actions, self, and social structures in talk" (Potter and Wetherell 1998, pp. 146–147). The contents and procedures of cognitive processes are reconstructed from such discourses as well as the ways in which social or collective memories referring to certain events are constructed and mediated.

In these approaches, the perspective remains restricted to describing the *how* in the making of social reality. Ethnomethodological analyses often provide impressively exact descriptions of how social interaction is organized and are able to develop typologies of conversational forms in this way. However, the aspect of subjective ascription of meaning remains rather neglected, as does the question of what role pre-existing contexts such as specific cultures play in the construction of social practices.

Cultural Framing of Social and Subjective Reality: Structuralist Models

Qualitative research is based on a third type of theoretical approach. A common feature of this is–although with various degrees of emphasis–that cultural systems of meaning are assumed to somehow frame the perception and making of subjective and social reality.

Basic Assumptions

Here a distinction is made between the surface of experience and activity on the one hand and the deep structures of activities on the other. While the surface is accessible to the participant subject, the deep structures are not accessible to everyday individual reflections. The surface is associated with intentions and the subjective meaning related to actions, whereas deep structures are understood as generating activities. Deep structures like these are contained in cultural models (D'Andrade 1987), in interpretive patterns and latent structures of meaning (Reichertz 2004), and finally in those latent structures that remain unconscious according to psychoanalysis (König 2004). Psychoanalysis attempts to reveal the unconscious both in society and in the research process. Analyzing this process and the relation of the researcher to those who are interviewed or observed becomes a resource for discovering how the "societal production of unconsciousness" (Erdheim 1984) works. For these analyses, the implicit and explicit rules of action are of special importance. For objective hermeneutics, which is taken here as an example of the other approaches mentioned, it is argued:

> On the basis of rules, which may be reconstructed, texts of interaction constitute the *objective meaning structures*. These objective meaning structures represent the *latent structures* of sense of the interaction itself. These objective meaning structures of texts of interaction, prototypes of objective social structures in general, are reality (and exist) analytically (even if not empirically) independent of the concrete intentional representation of the meanings of the interaction on the part of the subjects participating in the interaction. (Oevermann et al. 1979, p. 379)

In order to reconstruct rules and structures, various methodological procedures for analyzing "objective" (i.e., non-subjective) meanings are applied. You will find linguistic analyses to extrapolate cultural models, strictly sequential analyses of expressions and activities to uncover their objective structure of meanings, and the researcher's "evenly suspended attention" in the psychoanalytical process of interpretation.

In particular, objective hermeneutics following Oevermann et al. (1979) has attracted wide attention and stimulated voluminous research in German-speaking areas (see Chapter 25). However, there is an unsolved problem in the theoretical basics of the approach, which is the unclear relation of acting subjects to the structures to be extrapolated. Lüders and Reichertz (1986, p. 95), for example, criticize the "metaphysics of structures" which are almost studied as "autonomously acting structures". Other problems are the naive equation of text and world ("the world as text") and the assumption that, if analyses were pursued far enough, they would lead to the structures that generate the activities of the case under study. This assumption is based on the structuralist background of Oevermann's approach.

Recent Developments in Social Sciences: Poststructuralism

After Derrida (1990/1967), such structuralist assumptions have been questioned in qualitative research as well. Lincoln and Denzin (2000, p. 1051), for example, ask whether the text produced for the purposes of interpretation, as well as the text formulated as a result of the interpretation, corresponds not only to the interests (of research or whatever) of the interpreter. How far does it correspond also to the interests of those being studied and forming a topic in the text? According to this view, texts are neither the world per se nor an objective representation of parts of this world. Rather they result from the interests of those who produced the text as well as of those who read it. Different readers resolve the vagueness and ambiguity every text contains in different ways, depending on the perspectives they bring to the particular text. On the basis of this background, the reservations formulated about the objective hermeneutics concept of structure—that "between the surface and deep structures of language use . . . in objective hermeneutics there is a methodological 'hiatus', which at best can be closed by teaching and treating the method as art" (Bonß 1995, p. 38)—become yet more relevant.

Recent Developments in Psychology: Social Representations

What remains unclear in structuralist approaches is the relation between implicit social knowledge and individual knowledge and actions. To answer this question, one might take up a research program in social psychology, which was engaged in studying the "social representation" of objects (e.g., scientific theories on cultural objects and processes of change: for an overview see Flick 1998). Such a program would address the problem of how such socially and culturally shared knowledge influences individual ways of perception, experience, and action. A social representation is understood as a system of values, ideas and practices with a twofold function: first to establish an order which will enable individuals to orient themselves in their material and social world and to master it; and secondly to enable communication to take place among the members of a community by providing them with a code for social exchange and a code for naming and classifying unambiguously the various aspects of their world and their individual and group history. (Moscovici 1973, p. xvii)

This approach is increasingly used as a theoretical framework for qualitative studies dealing with the social construction of phenomena such as health and illness, madness or technological change in everyday life. Here again, social rules deriving from social knowledge about each topic are studied without being conceived as a reality *sui generis*. From a methodological point of view, different forms of interviews (see Chapter 13) and participant observation (see Chapter 17) are used.

Rivalry of Paradigms or Triangulation of Perspectives

The different perspectives in qualitative research and their specific starting points may be put in a scheme as in Figure 6.1. In the first perspective, you would start from the subjects involved in a situation under study and from the meanings that this situation has for them. You would then reconstruct the situational context, the interactions with other members and–as far as possible–the social and cultural meanings step-by-step from these subjective meanings. As the example of counseling shows, in this perspective the meaning and the course of the event "counseling" is reconstructed from the subjective viewpoint (e.g., a subjective theory of counseling). If possible, the cultural meaning of the situation "counseling" is disclosed on this path.

In the second perspective, you would start from the interaction in counseling, and study the discourse (of helping, on certain problems, and so on.). Here you would treat participants' subjective meanings as less interesting than the way in which the conversation is formally organized as a consultation and how participants mutually allocate their roles as members. Cultural and social contexts outside the interaction only become relevant in the context of how they are produced or continued in the conversation.

In the third perspective you would ask which implicit or unconscious rules govern the explicit actions in the situation and which latent or unconscious structures generate activities. Focus on the relevant culture and the structures and rules it offers the individuals in and for situations. Subjective views and interactive perspectives are especially relevant as means to expose or reconstruct structures.

Beyond such juxtapositions for clarifying the perspectives, there are two ways of responding to different perspectives of research. First, you could adopt a

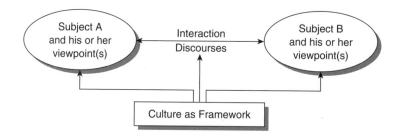

FIGURE 6.1   Research Perspectives in Qualitative Research

single position and its perspective on the phenomenon under study as the "one and only" and critically reject the other perspectives. This kind of demarcation has determined methodological discussion for a long time. In the American discussion, different positions have been formalized into paradigms and then juxtaposed in terms of competing paradigms or even "paradigm wars" (see Guba and Lincoln 1998, p. 218).

Alternatively, you can understand different theoretical perspectives as different ways of accessing the phenomenon under study. Any perspective may be examined as to which part of the phenomenon it discloses and which part remains excluded. Starting from this understanding, different research perspectives may be combined and supplemented. Such a triangulation of perspectives (Flick 1992; 2004a) enlarges the focus on the phenomenon under study, for example by reconstructing the participants' viewpoints and analyzing afterwards the unfolding of shared situations in interactions.

Common Features of the Different Positions

Despite differences of perspective, we can summarize the following points as common features across these different theoretical positions:

- *Verstehen as epistemological principle.* Qualitative research aims at understanding the phenomenon or event under study from the interior. It is the view of one subject or of different subjects, the course of social situations (conversations, discourse, processes of work), or the cultural or social rules relevant for a situation, which you would try to understand. How you put this understanding into methodological terms and which in particular of the above aspects you focus on, depends on the theoretical position underpinning your research.
- *Reconstructing cases as starting point.* A second feature common to the different positions is that the single case is analyzed more or less consistently before comparative or general statements are made. For instance, first, the single

subjective theory, the single conversation, and its course or the single case is reconstructed. Later other case studies and their results are used in comparison to develop a typology (of the different subjective theories, of the different courses of conversations, of the different case structures). What you will understand in each case as "case"–an individual and their viewpoints, a locally and temporally delimited interaction, or a specific social or cultural context in which an event unfolds–depends on the theoretical position you use to study the material.

- *Construction of reality as basis.* The reconstructed cases or typologies contain various levels of construction of reality. Subjects with their views on a certain phenomenon construe a part of their reality; in conversations and discourses, phenomena are interactively produced and thus reality is constructed; latent structures of sense and related rules contribute to the construction of social situations with the activities they generate. Therefore, the reality studied by qualitative research is not a given reality, but is constructed by different "actors": which actor is regarded as crucial for this construction depends on the theoretical position taken to study this process of construction.

- *Text as empirical material.* In the process of reconstructing a case, you will produce texts on which you make your actual empirical analyses. The view of the subjects is reconstructed as their subjective theories or is formulated this way; the course of an interaction is recorded and transcribed; reconstruction of latent structures of meaning can only be formulated from texts given in the necessary detail. In all these cases, texts are the basis of reconstruction and interpretation. What status the text is given depends on the theoretical position of the study.

TABLE 6.1 Theoretical Positions in Qualitative Research

	Subjects' points of view	Making of social realities	Cultural framing of social realities
Traditional theoretical background	Symbolic interactionism	Ethnomethodology	Structuralism, psychoanalysis
Recent developments in social sciences	Interpretive interactionism	Studies of work	Poststructuralism
Recent developments in psychology	Research program "subjective theories"	Discursive psychology	Social representations
Common features	• *Verstehen* as epistemological principle • Reconstructing cases as starting point • Construction of reality as basis • Text as empirical material		

Thus, the list of features of qualitative research discussed in Chapter 2 may now be completed as in Box 6.1.

Box 6.1   Features of Qualitative Research: Completed List

- Appropriateness of methods and theories
- Perspectives of the participants and their diversity
- Reflexivity of the researcher and the research
- Variety of approaches and methods in qualitative research
- *Verstehen* as epistemological principle
- Reconstructing cases as starting point
- Construction of reality as basis
- Text as empirical material

So far, I have outlined the major research perspectives I see in the current qualitative research for their theoretical background assumptions. In the remaining part of this chapter, I will address two major points of reference for theoretical discussions in qualitative research.

Feminism and Gender Studies

More than a research perspective, feminist research started out as a fundamental critique of social science and research in general. The research focused on the ignorance of women's life situation and of male dominance. Feminist research and qualitative research were often synonymous due to the methods opening up more to women's voices and needs in general. Mies (1983) outlines reasons why feminist research is more linked to qualitative than quantitative research. Quantitative research often ignores the voices of women, turns them into objects, and they are studied in a value-neutral way rather than researched specifically as women. Qualitative research allows women's voices be heard and goals realized. According to Ussher (1999, p. 99), feminist research is focused on a "critical analysis of gender relationships in research and theory ... an appreciation of the moral and political dimensions of research ... and the recognition of the need for social change to improve the lives of women." This leads not only to defining an issue of research (gender inequalities for example) but to challenging the way research is done on different levels. Skeggs (2001) and Smith (2002) outline a feminist understanding of ethnography on the level of data collection as well as analysis and representation of findings (and the voices of the participants).

Ussher (1999) uses health psychology to address specific issues within feminist qualitative research. Kitzinger (2004) presents an approach of feminist conversation analysis in order to analyze voices in their interactional context. Wilkinson (1999) discusses focus groups as a feminist methodology. Maynard (1998) again challenges the close link of feminist and qualitative research, asking why, for example, a combination of qualitative and quantitative research should be incompatible with the framework of feminist research. Gildemeister (2004) more recently discusses gender studies as a step beyond feminist and women's studies as a program. Here, "it is consistently pointed out ... that gender is a *social* category, and that it is always, in some fundamental way, a question of social *relationships*. For this reason the focus is no longer made to deal with difference as a matter of substance or essence, but on analyzing gender relationships under aspects of their hierarchical arrangement and social inequality" (p. 123). Gender in this context is seen either as a structural category or as gender as a social construct. The first is more interested in social inequality resulting from gender (differences), the latter more in doing gender (West and Zimmermann 1991) and how social distinctions of genders are constructed in everyday and institutional practices. For example, the study of transsexuality has become a special approach to show how normality is constructed interactionally and can be deconstructed by analyzing the breakdown of such normality:

> The *interactional* deep structure in the social construction of gender has been particularly well illustrated by trans-sexual research.... This type of research investigates, at the breakdown point of normality, how bi-sexuality is constructed in everyday practice and methodologically, because in the change from one gender to the other the processes involved in "doing gender" can be analyzed as if in slow motion. (Gildemeister 2004, p. 126)

Feminist researchers have contributed to reflection on qualitative methods by developing a research program for studying issues of gender, gender relations, inequality, and neglect of diversity. This program is developed on levels of epistemology, methodology, and research methods at the same time and has a valuable influence on qualitative research in general.

Positivism and Constructionism

This distinction underlies the epistemological discussion of qualitative research quite widely. As Oakley (1999) shows, it is often linked to the context of feminism in qualitative research, too. Positivism as an epistemological program originally comes from natural sciences, and therefore, is used more as a negative foil to distinguish one's own research from that spelt out in social science discussions.

Bryman (2004, p.11) summarizes several assumptions of positivism: only phenomenal knowledge confirmed by the sense can be warranted as knowledge (phenomenalism); theories are used to generate hypotheses that can be tested and allow explanations of laws to be assessed (deductivism); knowledge can be produced by collecting facts that provide the basis for laws (inductivism); science must and can be conducted in a way that is value free and thus objective; and, finally, a clear distinction between scientific and normative statements is seen. Positivism is often associated with realism. Both assume that natural and social sciences should and can apply the same principles to collecting and analyzing data and that there is a world out there (an external reality) separate from our descriptions of it. The use of the word "positivism" is often criticized: Hammersley (1995, p. 2) notes, "all one can reasonably infer from unexplicated usage of the word 'positivism' in the social research literature is that the writer disapproves of whatever he or she is referring to."

To this position, social constructionism (or constructivism) is juxtaposed (see also Flick 2004b). A number of programs with different starting points are subsumed under these labels. What is common to all constructionist approaches is that they examine the relationship to reality by dealing with constructive processes in approaching it. Examples of constructions can be found on different levels:

1. In the tradition of Piaget, cognition, perception of the world and knowledge about it are seen as constructs. Radical constructivism (Glasersfeld 1995) takes this thought to the point where every form of cognition–because of the neurobiological processes involved–has direct access only to images of the world and of reality, but not of both.
2. Social constructivism in the tradition of Schütz (1962), Berger and Luckmann (1966), and Gergen (1985, 1999) inquires after the social conventionalizations, perception, and knowledge in everyday life.
3. Constructivist sociology of science in the tradition of Fleck et al. (1979), the present-day "laboratory-constructivist" research (Knorr-Certina 1981), seeks to establish how social, historical, local, pragmatic, and other factors influence scientific discovery in such a way that scientific facts may be regarded as social constructs ("local products").

Constructionism is not a unified program, but is developing in parallel fashion in a number of disciplines: psychology, sociology, philosophy, neurobiology, psychiatry, and information science. It informs a lot of qualitative research programs with the approach that the realities we study are social products of the actors, of interactions, and institutions.

Construction of Knowledge

Taking three main authors, we may clarify how the genesis of knowledge and its functions may be described from a constructionist viewpoint. Schütz (1962, p. 5) starts from the following premise: "All our knowledge of the world, in common-sense as well as in scientific thinking, involves constructs, i.e., a set of abstractions, generalizations, formalizations and idealizations, specific to the relevant level of thought organization." Schütz sees every form of knowledge as constructed by selection and structuring. The individual forms differ according to the degree of structuring and idealization, and this depends on their functions. The constructions will be more concrete as the basis of everyday action or more abstract as a model in the construction of scientific theories. Schütz enumerates different processes which have in common that the formation of knowledge of the world is not to be understood as the simple portrayal of given facts, but that the contents are constructed in a process of active production. This interpretation is developed further in radical constructivism whose "core theses" are formulated by Glasersfeld (1992, p. 30) as follows:

1. What we call "knowledge" in no sense represents a world that presumably exists beyond our contact with it. … Constructivism, like pragmatism, leads to a modified concept of cognition/knowledge. Accordingly, knowledge is related to the way in which we organize our experiential world.
2. Radical constructivism in *no sense* denies an external reality. …
3. Radical constructivism agrees with Berkeley that it would be unreasonable to confirm the existence of something that can/could not (at some point) be perceived. …
4. Radical constructivism adopts Vico's fundamental idea that human knowledge is a human construct. …
5. Constructivism abandons the claim that cognition is "true" in the sense that it reflects objective reality. Instead, it only requires that knowledge be *viable* in the sense that it should *fit* into the experiential world of the one who knows ….

Seen in this way, knowledge organizes experiences, which first permit cognition of the world beyond the experiencing subject or organism. Experiences are structured and understood through concepts and contexts, which are constructed by this subject. Whether the picture that is formed in this way is true or correct cannot be determined. But its quality may be assessed through its *viability*, that is, the extent to which the picture or model permits the subject to find its way and to act in the world. Here an important point of orientation is the question of how the "construction of concepts" functions (Glasersfeld 1995, pp. 76–88).

For social constructionism, the processes of social interchange in the genesis of knowledge take on a special significance, and in particular, the concepts that are used. Accordingly, Gergen formulates the following:

> assumptions for a social constructionism: The terms by which we account for the world and ourselves are not dictated by the stipulated objects of such accounts … . The terms and forms by which we achieve understanding of the world and ourselves are social artifacts, products of historically and culturally situated interchanges among people … . The degree to which a given account of the world or self is sustained across time is not dependent on the objective validity of the account but on the vicissitudes of social processes … . Language derives its significance in human affairs from the way in which it functions within patterns of relationship … . To appraise existing forms of discourse is to evaluate patterns of cultural life; such evaluations give voice to other cultural enclaves. (Gergen 1994, pp. 49–50)

Knowledge is constructed in processes of social interchange, it is based on the role of language in such relationships, and above all it has social functions. The eventualities of the social processes involved have an influence on what will survive as a valid or useful explanation. Research acts are also part of the social construction of what we can address and find in social research. And the acts of writing contribute to this social construction of worlds under study. These issues will be spelled out in more detail for qualitative research in the next chapter.

KEY POINTS

- Three research perspectives with different consequences for the methods used to pursue these perspectives in empirical research summarize the theoretical positions in qualitative research.
- Basic assumptions and recent developments describe these perspectives.
- We can draw some common features from these research perspectives.
- Going across these research perspectives, we find two contributions challenging the research practice on the background of a theoretical framework: feminism challenges normalities and routines in everyday lives that we study as well as in the research practice.
- The distinction of positivism and constructionism highlights the differences of qualitative research from natural sciences (and those social sciences, which are created according to the model of natural sciences).

Exercise 6.1

1. Look for a published study and identify which of the research perspectives discussed in this chapter was an orientation for the researcher.
2. Reflect for your own study. Which of the issues in this chapter are relevant for it?

Notes

1   One starting point is the symbolic interactionist assumption: "One has to get inside of the defining process of the actor in order to understand his action" (Blumer 1969, p. 16).
2   "Epiphany" in the sense of James Joyce as "a moment of problematic experience that illuminates personal characteristics, and often signifies a turning point in a person's life" (Denzin 1989a, p. 141).
3   Bergmann holds for the general approach and the research interests linked to it: "Ethnomethodology characterizes the methodology used by members of a society for proceeding activities, which simply makes the social reality and order which is taken as given and for granted for the actors. Social reality is understood by Garfinkel as a procedural reality, i.e., a reality which is produced locally (there and then, in the course of the action), endogenously (i.e., from the interior of the situation), audio visually (i.e., in hearing and speaking, perceiving and acting) in the interaction by the participants. The aim of ethnomethodology is to grasp the 'how,' i.e., the methods of this production of social reality in detail. It asks, for example, how the members of a family interact in such a way that they can be perceived as a family" (1980, p. 39).

FURTHER READING

The first two references give overviews of the more traditional positions discussed here, while the latter four represent more recent developments.

Blumer, H. (1969) *Symbolic Interactionism: Perspective and Method.* Berkeley, CA: University of California.
Garfinkel, H. (1967) *Studies in Ethnomethodology.* Englewood Cliffs, NJ: Prentice-Hall.
Denzin, N.K. (1989a) *Interpretative Interactionism.* London: SAGE.
Denzin, N.K. (2004b) "Symbolic Interactionism," in U. Flick, E.v. Kardorff and I. Steinke (eds), *A Companion to Qualitative Research.* London: SAGE, pp. 81–87
Flick, U. (ed.) (1998) *Psychology of the Social.* Cambridge: Cambridge University Press.
Reichertz, J. (2004) "Objective Hermeneutics and Hermeneutic Sociology of Knowledge," in U. Flick, E.v. Kardorff and I. Steinke (eds), *A Companion to Qualitative Research.* London: SAGE. pp. 290–295.

Feminism and Gender Studies

Gildemeister, R. (2004) "Gender studies," in U. Flick, E.v. Kardorff and I. Steinke (eds), *A Companion to Qualitative Research.* London: SAGE. pp. 123–128

Positivism and Constructionism

Flick, U. (2004b) "Constructivism," in U. Flick, E.v. Kardorff and I. Steinke, (eds), *A Companion to Qualitative Research.* London: SAGE. pp. 88–94.

7

EPISTEMOLOGICAL BACKGROUND: CONSTRUCTION AND UNDERSTANDING OF TEXTS

CHAPTER OBJECTIVES
After reading this chapter, you should be able to

✓   understand that the relation of social realities under study and the representation in texts used for studying them is not a simple one-to-one relation.
✓   acknowledge that there are different processes of social construction involved.
✓   identify mimesis as a useful concept for describing these processes.
✓   apply this to a prominent form of qualitative research.

In the previous chapter, I argued that *verstehen,* reference to cases, construction of reality, and using texts as empirical material are common features of qualitative research across different theoretical positions. From these features, various questions emerge. How can you understand the process of constructing social reality in the phenomenon under study but also in the process of studying it? How is reality represented or produced in the case that is (re)constructed for investigative purposes? What is the relation between text and realities? This chapter will outline these relations and answer these questions.

Text and Realities

Texts serve three purposes in the process of qualitative research: not only are they the essential data on which findings are based, but also the basis of interpretations and the central medium for presenting and communicating findings. This is the case not only for objective hermeneutics, which has made the textualization of the world a program, but more generally, for the current methods in qualitative research. Either interviews comprise the data, which are transformed into transcripts (i.e., texts), and interpretations of them are produced afterwards (in observations, field notes are often the textual database); or research starts from recording natural conversations and situations to arrive at transcriptions and interpretations. In each case, you will find text as the result of the data collection and as the instrument for interpretation. If qualitative research relies on understanding social realities through the interpretation of texts, two questions become especially relevant: what happens in the translation of reality into text, and what happens in the re-translation of texts into reality or in inferring from texts to realities?

In this process, text is substituted for what is studied. As soon as the researcher has collected the data and made a text out of them, this text is used as a substitute for the reality under study in the further process. Originally biographies were studied but now the narrative produced in the interview is available for interpretation. From this narrative there remains only what the recording has "caught" and what is documented by the chosen method of transcription. The text produced in this way is the basis of further interpretations and the findings so derived–checking back to the acoustic recordings is as unusual as checking back to the subjects interviewed (or observed). It is difficult to establish control of how much and what this text contains and reproduces of the original issue (e.g., of a biography). The social sciences, which have necessarily turned into a textual science and rely on texts as ways of fixing and objectifying their findings, should pay more attention to these kinds of questions. The rarely mentioned question of producing *new* realities (e.g., life as narrative) in generating and interpreting data as texts and texts as data has to be further discussed.

Text as World Making: First-Degree and Second-Degree Constructions

That the relation of text and reality cannot be reduced to a simple representation of given facts has been discussed for quite a while in different contexts as a "crisis of representation." In the discussion around the question of how far the world can be represented in computer systems or cognitive systems, Winograd and Flores (1986) express heavy doubts about this simple idea of representation, while Paul Ricoeur sees such discussions as a general topic of modern philosophy. Starting from debates in ethnography (e.g., Clifford and Marcus 1986), this crisis is discussed for qualitative research as a double crisis of representation and of legitimation. In terms of the crisis of representation, and as a consequence of the linguistic turn in the social sciences, it is doubted that social researchers can "directly capture lived experience. Such experience, it is now argued, is created in the social text written by the researcher. This is the crisis of representation . . . It . . . makes the direct link between experience and text problematic" (Denzin and Lincoln 2000b, p. 17). The second crisis is the crisis of legitimation in which the classic criteria for assessing research are rejected for qualitative research or–following postmodernism–the possibility of legitimizing scientific knowledge is rejected in general (see Chapter 30).

The crucial point in these discussions is how far, especially in social research, we are still able to suppose a reality existing outside subjective or socially shared viewpoints and on which we can validate its "representation" in texts or other products of research. The several varieties of social constructivism or constructionism (see Flick 2004b for a short overview) reject such suppositions. Rather, they start from the idea that the participants through the meanings ascribed to certain events actively produce realities and objects and that social research cannot escape this ascription of meanings if it wants to deal with social realities. Questions that are asked and have to be asked in this context are: What do the social subjects take for real themselves and *how*? What are the conditions of such a holding-for-real? Under which conditions do researchers hold the things they observe this way for real?

Thus, the points of departure for research are the ideas of social events, of things or facts which we meet in a social field under study, and the way in which these ideas communicate with one another (i.e., compete, conflict, and succeed are shared and taken for real).

Social Constructions as Starting Points

Alfred Schütz has already stated that facts only become relevant through their selection and interpretation:

> Strictly speaking, there are no such things as facts, pure and simple. All facts are from the outset facts selected from a universal context by the activities of our mind. They are, therefore, always interpreted facts, either facts looked at as detached from their context by an artificial abstraction or facts considered in their particular setting. In either case, they carry their interpretational inner and outer horizons. (1962, p. 5)

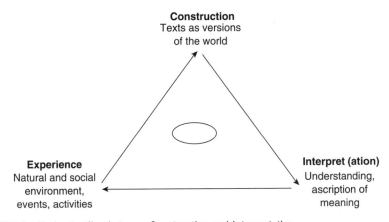

FIGURE 7.1 Understanding between Construction and Interpretation

Here we can draw parallels with Goodman (1978). For Goodman, the world is socially constructed through different forms of knowledge–from everyday knowledge to science and art as different "ways of world making." According to Goodman–(and Schütz)–social research is an analysis of such ways of world making and the constructive efforts of the participants in their everyday lives. A central idea in this context is the distinction Schütz makes between first-degree and second-degree constructions. According to Schütz "the constructs of the social sciences are, so to speak, constructs of the second degree, that is, constructs of the constructs made by the actors on the social scene." In this sense, Schütz holds that "the exploration of the general principles according to which man in daily life organizes his experiences, and especially those of the social world, is the first task of the methodology of the social sciences" (1962, p. 59).

According to this, everyday perception and knowledge are the basis for social scientists to develop a more formalized and generalized "version of the world" (Goodman 1978). Correspondingly, Schütz (1962, pp. 208–210) assumes "multiple realities" of which the world of science is only one and is organized partly according to the same principles of everyday life and other principles.

In particular, social science research is confronted with the problem that it encounters the world it wants to study always and only in those versions of this world interacting subjects construct of it commonly or concurrently. Scientific knowledge and presentations of interrelations include different processes of constructing reality. Everyday subjective constructions on the part of those who are studied and scientific (i.e., more or less codified) constructions on the part of the researchers in collecting, treating, and interpreting data and in the presentation of findings are involved (see Figure 7.1).

In these constructions, taken-for-granted relations are translated: everyday experience into knowledge by those who are studied, reports of those experiences or events, and activities into texts by the researchers. How can these processes of translation be made more concrete?

World Making in the Text: Mimesis

To answer this question, the concept of mimesis will be taken from aesthetics and literary sciences (see Iser 1993), which can offer insights for social science based on texts. Mimesis refers to the transformation of (originally, for example, in Aristotle, natural) worlds into symbolic worlds. It was first understood as "imitation of nature"; however, this concept has been discussed more extensively (Gebauer and Wulf 1995). A succinct example of mimesis, and one repeatedly used, would be the presentation of natural or social relations in literary or dramatic texts or on the stage: "In this interpretation, mimesis characterizes the act of producing a symbolic world, which encompasses both practical and theoretical elements" (1995, p. 3). However, the interest in this concept now goes beyond presentations in literary texts or in the theater. Recent discussions treat mimesis as a general principle with which to map out understanding of the world and of texts:

> The individual "assimilates" himself or herself to the world via mimetic processes. Mimesis makes it possible for individuals to step out of themselves, to draw the outer world into their inner world, and to lend expression to their interiority. It produces an otherwise unattainable proximity to objects and is thus a necessary condition of understanding. (Gebauer and Wulf 1995, pp. 2–3)

In applying these considerations to qualitative research and to the texts used within such research, mimetic elements can be identified in the following respects:

- in the transformation of experience into narratives, reports, and so on regarding the part of the persons being studied;
- in the construction of texts on this basis and in the interpretation of such constructions on the part of the researchers;
- finally, when such interpretations are fed back into everyday contexts, for example in reading the presentations of these findings.

To analyze the mimetic processes in the construction and interpretation of social science texts, the considerations of Ricoeur (1981; 1984) offer a fruitful starting point. For literary texts, Ricoeur has separated the mimetic process "playfully yet seriously" into the three steps of mimesis$_1$, mimesis$_2$ and mimesis$_3$:

> Hermeneutics, however, is concerned with reconstructing the entire arc of operations by which practical experience provides itself with works, authors, and readers . . . It will appear as a corollary, at the end of this analysis, that the reader is that operator *par excellence* who takes up through doing something–the act of reading–the unity of the traversal from mimesisis$_1$ to mimesis$_3$ by way of mimesis$_2$. (1984, p. 53)

Reading and understanding texts becomes an active process of producing reality, which involves not only the author of (in our case social science) texts, but also the person for whom they are written and who reads them. Transferred to qualitative research, this means that in the production of texts (on a certain subject, an interaction, or an event) the person who reads and interprets the written text is as involved in the construction of reality as the person who writes the text. According to Ricoeur's understanding of mimesis, three forms of mimesis may be distinguished in a social science based on texts:

- Everyday and scientific interpretations are always based on a preconception of human activity and of social or natural events, *mimesis$_1$*. "Whatever may be the status of these stories which somehow are prior to the narration we may give them, our mere use of the word 'story' (taken in this pre-narrative sense) testifies to our pre-understanding that action is human to the extent it characterizes a life story that deserves to be told. Mimesis$_1$ is that pre-understanding of what human action is, of its semantics, its symbolism, its temporality. From this pre-understanding, which is common to poets and their readers, arises fiction, and with fiction comes the second form of mimesis which is textual and literary" (Ricoeur 1981, p. 20).
- The mimetic transformation in "processing" experiences of social or natural environments into texts–whether in everyday narratives recounted for other people, in certain documents, or in producing texts for research purposes– should be understood as a process of construction, *mimesis$_2$*: "Such is the realm of mimesis$_2$ between the antecedence and the descendance of the text. At this level mimesis may be defined as the configuration of action" (1981, p. 25).
- The mimetic transformation of texts in understanding occurs through processes of interpretation, *mimesis$_3$*–in the everyday understanding of narratives, documents, books, newspapers, and so on just as in the scientific interpretations of such narratives, research documents (protocols, transcripts, and so on), or scientific texts: "Mimesis$_3$ marks the intersection of the world of text and the world of the hearer or reader" (1981, p. 26).

According to this view, which has been formulated by Ricoeur in dealing with literary texts, mimetic processes can be located in social science understanding as

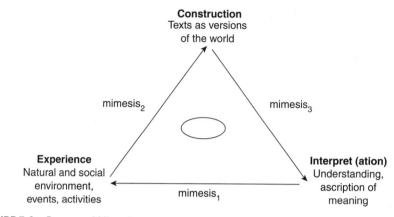

FIGURE 7.2   Process of Mimesis

the interplay of construction and interpretation of experiences (Figure 7.2). Mimesis includes the passage from pre-understanding across the text to interpretation. The process is executed in the act of construction and interpretation as well as in the act of understanding. Understanding, as an active process of construction, involves the one who understands. According to this conception of mimesis, this process is not limited to access to literary texts but extends to understanding as a whole and thus also to understanding as a concept of knowledge in the framework of social science research. Gebauer and Wulf (1995) clarified this in their more general discussion of mimesis. They refer to Goodman's (1978) theory of the different ways of world making and the resulting versions of the world as outcome of knowledge:

> Knowing in terms of this model is a matter of invention: modes of organisation "are not found in the world but *built into a world*". Understanding is creative. With the aid of Goodman's theory of world making, mimesis can be rehabilitated in opposition to a tradition that rigidly deprived it of the creative element – and that itself rests on false presuppositions. The isolated object of knowledge, the assumption of a world existing outside codification systems, the idea that truth is the correspondence between statements and an extralinguistic world, the postulate that thought can be traced back to an origin. Nothing of this theory remains intact after Goodman's critique: worlds are made "*from other worlds*". (1995, p. 17)

Thus, Gebauer and Wulf discuss mimesis in terms of the construction of knowledge in general. Ricoeur uses it to analyze processes of understanding literature in a particular way, without invoking the narrow and strict idea of representation of given worlds in texts and without the narrow concept of reality and truth.[1]

Mimesis in the Relation of Biography and Narrative

For further clarification, we can now apply this idea of the mimetic process to a common procedure in qualitative research. A big part of research practice concentrates on reconstructing life stories or biographies in interviews (see Chapter 14). The starting point is to assume that a narrative is the appropriate form of presenting biographical experience (for more details see Chapters 14, 15, and 16). In this context, Ricoeur maintains "the thesis of a narrative or pre-narrative quality of experience as such" (1981, p. 20). For the mimetic relation between life stories and narratives, Bruner highlights

> that the mimesis between life so-called and narrative is a two-way affair . . . Narrative imitates life, life imitates narrative. "Life" in this sense is the same kind of construction of the human imagination as "a narrative" is. It is constructed by human beings through active ratiocination, by the same kind of ratiocination through which we construct narratives. When someone tells you his life . . . it is always a cognitive achievement rather than a through the clear-crystal recital of something univocally given. In the end, it is a narrative achievement. There is no such thing psychologically as "life itself". At very least, it is a selective achievement of memory recall; beyond that, recounting one's life is an interpretive feat. (1987, pp. 12–13)

This means that a biographical narrative of one's own life is not a representation of factual processes. It becomes a mimetic presentation of experiences, which are constructed in the form of a narrative for this purpose—in the interview. The narrative, in general, provides a framework in which experiences may be located, presented, and evaluated—in short, in which they are lived. The issue studied by qualitative research (here) is already constructed and interpreted in everyday life in the form in which it wants to study it (i.e., as a narrative). In the situation of the interview, this everyday way of interpreting and constructing is used to transform these experiences into a symbolic world—social science and its texts. The experiences are then reinterpreted from this world: "In mimetic reference, an interpretation is made from the perspective of a symbolically produced world of a prior (but not necessarily existing) world, which itself has already been subject to interpretation. Mimesis construes anew already construed worlds" (Gebauer and Wulf 1995, p. 317).

In the reconstruction of a life from a specific research question, a version of the experiences is constructed and interpreted. To what extent life and experiences really have taken place in the reported form cannot be verified in this way. But it is possible to ascertain which constructions the narrating subject presents of both and which versions evolve in the research situation. When it comes to the presentation of the findings of this reconstruction, these experiences and the world in which they have been made will be presented and seen in a specific way—for example, in (new) theory with claims to validity. "Mimetic action involves the intention of displaying a symbolically produced world in such a way that it will be perceived as a specific world" (1995, p. 317). Mimesis becomes relevant at the intersections of the world symbolically generated in research and the world of everyday life or the contexts that research is empirically investigating: "Mimesis is by nature intermediary, stretched between a symbolically produced world and another one" (1995, p. 317).

Following the views of several of the authors mentioned here, mimesis avoids those problems, which led to the concept of representation ending up in a crisis and becoming an illusion.[2] Mimesis can be released from the context of literary presentation and understanding and used as a concept in the social sciences, which takes into account that the things to be understood are always presented on different levels. Mimetic processes can be identified in the processing of experiences in everyday practices, in interviews, and through these in the construction of versions of the world that are textualized and textualizable (i.e., accessible for social science, as well as in the production of texts for research purposes). In mimetic processes, versions of the world are produced which may be understood and interpreted in social research. Ricoeur's differentiation of various forms of mimesis and Schütz's distinction between everyday and scientific constructions may further contribute to the framework claimed by Goodman with the assumption of different versions of the world constructed in everyday, artistic, and scientific ways. This allows the researcher to avoid the illusions and crises, which are characteristic of the idea of representation, whilst not disregarding the constructive elements in the process of representation (or better presentation) as well as in the process of understanding.

Case Study: Mimesis in the Social Construction of Self and Technology

I have studied the social representation of technology and how it became integrated into everyday life and how it changed it (see Flick 1995). The study included several groups (information engineers, social scientists and teachers) in three contexts (France, East and West Germany). Individuals from these groups were asked to tell stories about the first encounter with technology they remember. These stories were not only representations of events, but also revealed ways in which the storytellers see themselves in relation to technology. In these stories, mimetic processes of constructing reality, self, and technology can be found. For example, information engineers tell a story showing successful ways of managing technical activities (e.g., successfully mending a broken HiFi) or their *active mastering* of machines (e.g., learning to drive a big truck as a little boy). Social scientists' stories deal with *failures because of the device* or using *toys* as more or less passive experiences, while teachers tell how they *observed relatives handling technologies* (e.g., grandfather chopping wood or uncle working with a circular saw). In all groups, we find narratives of situations showing the role of technology in the family. While these narratives are related to a *decision for a technical profession* in the case of the information engineers, consequences are contrary in the case of the other groups. For example, a female information engineer tells how she decided to become an information engineer against her father's wishes and the climate in the family that she felt to be anti-technology, while a teacher talks about his father's expectations that he should choose a technical profession, which he had to disappoint.

The topics that are common for interviewees from West Germany may be located along the dimension of *acting* with technology *versus observing* others doing this, while stories of East-German interviewees move along the dimension of *mastering and failure* and around the background topic of *family and technology*. Together with this last topic, French interviewees tell stories that can be filled in the dimension of *success versus failure*. As general topical lines for all the stories, we can note the dimension *success-activity-failure* and the background topic of *family* and *technology*.

To use this concept in describing the process of social construction of objects, processes and so on, researchers could look at what people tell and when they are asked to tell their first encounter with technology, for example. The relevant questions then are: What kind of version of that encounter do they construct? In what kind of context do they put this experience? What kinds of social processes or changes do they mention at that occasion or try to explain for the researcher or for themselves by this encounter of human beings and technology? Referring again to the narratives presented above, mimetic aspects can be found on one hand in the interviewees' retrospective interpretations of their own relations to technology as actively shaping, successfully acting or failing. On the other hand, relations to their families are interpreted and used to re-construct and contextualize one's own access to technology. Technology becomes here an interpretative instrument for the own self-image (for or against technology) as well as for a specific social relation—one's own family background. At first glance, this may seem circular, but should rather be understood as two sides of the same coin. Contexts are used for embedding specific objects or experiences, and these objects or experiences are also used to understand and interpret these contexts. Both self-image and social relation become instruments to interpret one's own relation to technology at least in situations of first experience. Technology serves for interpreting and constructing a part of one's own experiences and social contacts, as these are used to interpret one's own encounter with technology. Mimetic interpretations are twofold: on one hand, embedding technology-related experiences in social and self-related contexts underlines the subjective construction of technology as social phenomenon; on the other hand, technology is used to interpret or to anchor social and autobiographic experiences (mimesis₁ according to Ricoeur). Technology here is the topic or medium through which these situations are retrospectively reconstructed. The situations are starting points for retrospectively anchoring the new aspects of technology as phenomenon. In this retrospective anchoring, as well as in the social distribution and differentiation between the social groups and cultural contexts, the social representation of technology becomes evident.

Qualitative research, which takes as its epistemological principle the understanding realized in different methodological procedures, is already confronted with the construction of reality on the part of its "object." Experiences are not simply mirrored in narratives or in the social science texts produced about them. The idea of mirroring reality in presentation, research, and text has ended in crisis. It may be replaced by the multistage circle of mimesis according to Ricoeur in a way that takes into account the constructions of those who take part in the scientific understanding (i.e., the individual being studied, the author of the texts on him or her, and their reader). The difference between everyday and scientific understanding in qualitative research lies in its methodological organization in the research process, which the following chapters will deal with in greater detail.

KEY POINTS

- Texts are the basic material of most of qualitative research.
- Producing texts in the research process is a special case of the social construction of reality.
- World making and mimesis are two concepts for describing the process of social construction of text and realities.
- Ricoeur's model of three forms of mimesis describes the process of social construction step-by-step.
- Narratives about biographies are examples of such construction in which mimesis plays a central role.

Exercise 7.1

1. Explain the difference between first-degree and second-degree construction of a biographical interview.
2. Describe the three forms of mimesis for the same example.

Notes

1 "Mimesis in this sense is ahead of our concepts of reference, the real and truth. It engenders a need as yet unfilled to think more" (Ricoeur 1981, p. 31).
2 "Mimesis, which seems to me less shut in, less locked up, and richer in polysemy, hence more mobile and more mobilizing for a sortie out of the representative illusion" (Ricoeur 1981, p. 15).

FURTHER READING

The epistemological position that is briefly outlined here is based on the last four references and is detailed further and put into empirical terms in the first.

Flick, U. (1995) "Social Representations," in R. Harré, J. Smith and L. Van Langenhove (eds), *Rethinking Psychology*. London: SAGE. pp. 70–96.

Gebauer, G. and Wulf, C. (1995) *Mimesis: Culture, Art, Society*. Berkeley, CA: University of California Press.

Goodman, N. (1978) *Ways of Worldmaking*. Indianapolis: Hackett.

Ricoeur, P. (1984) *Time and Narrative*, Vol. 1. Chicago: University of Chicago Press.

Schütz, A. (1962) *Collected Papers, Vol. 1. Den Haag: Nijhoff.*

PART 3

RESEARCH DESIGN

Part 3 will introduce you to different aspects of the research process, which can be summarized under research planning and creating a research design. I will focus on stages of the research process prior to collecting and analyzing data. We will compare the different models of the research process used in quantitative and in qualitative research (Chapter 8) before we address the relevance and practical problems of formulating a good research question (Chapter 9). As you will see, entering the research field is not only a technical problem for which simple solutions are available. Problems and strategies for this step are outlined in Chapter 10. Sampling in qualitative research again is different from standard practices in quantitative research. Models and pitfalls for this are discussed next (Chapter 11). In the last chapter of this part, the discussion of research designs is rounded up (Chapter 12), so that you should be prepared for the next stage–encountering fields, people, and the collection of data.

8

THE QUALITATIVE RESEARCH PROCESS

CHAPTER OBJECTIVES
After reading this chapter, you should be able to

✓ understand the research process in qualitative research is often different from the clear-
   cut stages of the research process in quantitative research.
✓ explain the different functions of theory in the qualitative research process.
✓ utilize a case study to understand how both works–the use of theory in qualitative
   research and the research process.

Qualitative research cannot be characterized by its choice of certain methods
over and above others. Qualitative and quantitative research are not incompatible opposites that should not be combined (see Chapter 3); old and unfruitful methodological debates on fundamental questions are not reopened here.
However, qualitative research does presuppose a different understanding of
research in general, which goes beyond the decision to use a narrative interview
or a questionnaire, for example. Qualitative research comprises a specific understanding of the relation between issue and method (see Becker 1996). Furthermore,
only in a very restricted way is it compatible with the logic of research familiar from
experimental or quantitative research. In this type of research, the process of research
can be neatly arranged in a linear sequence of conceptual, methodological, and
empirical steps. Each step can be taken and treated one after the other and separately. If you want to do qualitative research, there is a mutual interdependence
of the single stages of the research process and you should take this into account
much more. Most clearly, Glaser and Strauss (1967) developed this idea of the

research process in their approach of grounded theory research (see also Strauss and Corbin 1990 and Strauss 1987).

Research as Linear Process

But first, we should look at the traditional concept of the research process. The traditional version of quantitative social sciences starts from building a model: before entering the field to be studied, and while still sitting at their desks, the researchers construct a model of the assumed conditions and relations. The researcher's starting point is the theoretical knowledge taken from the literature or earlier empirical findings. From this, hypotheses are derived, which are operationalized and tested against empirical conditions. The concrete or empirical "objects" of research, like a certain field or real persons, have the status of the exemplary against which assumed general relations (in the form of hypotheses) are tested. The aim is that you want to guarantee that your study is representative in its data and findings (e.g., because random samples of the persons that are studied are drawn). A further aim is the break down of complex relations into distinct variables, which allows the researcher to isolate and test their effects. Theories and methods are prior to the object of research. Theories are tested and perhaps falsified on the way. If they are enlarged, it is through additional hypotheses, which are again tested empirically and so on.

The Concept of Process in Grounded Theory Research

In contrast to this theory-driven and linear model of the research process, the grounded theory approach gives priority to the data and the field under study over theoretical assumptions. Theories should not be applied to the subject being studied but are "discovered" and formulated in working with the field and the empirical data to be found in it. Studied subjects are selected on their relevance to the research topic. They are not selected for constructing a (statistically) representative sample of a general population. The aim is not to reduce complexity by breaking it down into variables but rather to increase complexity by including context. Methods too have to be appropriate to the issue under study and have to be chosen accordingly. The relation of theory to empirical work in this type of research is outlined as follows: "The principle of openness implies, that the theoretical structuring of the issue under study is postponed until the structuring of the issue under study by the persons being studied has 'emerged'" (Hoffmann-Riem 1980, p. 343). Here it is postulated that researchers should at least suspend the *a priori* theoretical knowledge that they bring into the field. However, in contrast to a widespread misunderstanding, this is postulated above all for the way to treat hypotheses and less for the decision concerning the research question (see the following chapter): "The delay in structuring implies the abandonment of the *ex ante* formulation of hypotheses. In fact, the research question is outlined under theoretical aspects . . . But the elaboration does not culminate in . . . the set of hypotheses" (1980, p. 345).

This understanding of qualitative research suggests that the researcher should adopt an attitude of what, in a different context, has been termed "evenly suspended attention." According to Freud, this allows one to avoid the ensuing problems:

> For as soon as anyone deliberately concentrates his attention to a certain degree, he begins to select from the material before him; one point will be fixed in his mind with particular clearness and some other will be correspondingly disregarded, and in making this selection he will be following his expectations or inclinations. This, however, is precisely what must not be done. In making this selection, if he follows his expectations he is in danger of never finding anything but what he already knows; and if he follows his inclinations, he will certainly falsify what he may perceive. (1958, p. 112)

Applied to qualitative research, this means that researchers—partly because of their own theoretical assumptions and structures, which direct their attention to concrete aspects, but also because of their own fears—might remain blind to the structures in the field or person under study. This makes them and their research lose the discovery of the actual "new."

The model of the process in grounded theory research mainly includes the following aspects: theoretical sampling (see Chapter 11), theoretical coding (see Chapter 23), and writing the theory (see Chapter 30). This approach strongly focuses on the interpretation of data no matter how they were collected. Here the question of which method to use for collecting data becomes minor. Decisions on data to be integrated and methods to be used for this are based on the state of the developing theory after analyzing the data already at hand at that moment.

Various aspects of Glaser and Strauss's model have become relevant in their own right in methodological discussions and qualitative research practice. Theoretical sampling in particular, as a strategy of defining a sample step-by-step, is also applied in research in which methods of interpretation are used that are completely different from those Glaser and Strauss suggest or in which the claim for developing a theory is not made. Theoretical coding as a method of analyzing texts has also gained its own relevance. The idea of developing theories by analyzing empirical material has become essential in its own right to the discussions of qualitative research, quite independently from using the methods of the approach at the same time. Researchers often ignore the consistency with which the approach of Strauss interrelates its individual components. Theoretical sampling, for example, actually is only feasible as a strategy if the consequence is appreciated that not all interviews are completed in the first stage and the interpretation of the data starts only after interviewing is finished. It is rather the immediate interpretation of collected data, which is the basis for sampling decisions. These decisions are not limited to selecting cases, but also comprise the decisions about the type of data to integrate next and–in extreme cases–about changing the method.

Linearity and Circularity of the Process

This circularity of the parts of the research process in the model of grounded theory research is a central feature of the approach. It was the force behind a multitude of approaches starting from case analyses (e.g., Ragin and Becker 1992). However, this circularity causes problems where the general linear model of research (theory, hypotheses, operationalization, sampling, collecting data, interpreting data, validation) is used to evaluate research. In general, this is the case in two respects: in proposing a research project or in applying for a grant, and in the evaluation of this research and its results by the use of traditional quality indicators (see Chapter 28).

However, notwithstanding that problem, this circularity is one of the strengths of the approach, because it forces the researcher to permanently reflect on the whole research process and on particular steps in the light of the other steps–at least when it is applied consistently. The close (also temporal) link between collecting and interpreting data and the selection of empirical material on the other, unlike in the traditional linear method of proceeding, allows the researcher not only to ask the following question repeatedly but also to answer it: How far do the methods, categories, and theories that are used do justice to the subject and the data?

Theories in the Research Process as Versions of the World

Now, what is the function of theories[1] in a research process in the style of Glaser and Strauss? There are two starting points for answering this question. The first is Goodman's (1978) concept that theories–similar to other forms of presenting empirical relations–are versions of the world. These versions undergo a continuous revision, evaluation, construction, and reconstruction. According to this, theories are not (right or wrong) representations of given facts, but versions or perspectives through which the world is seen. By the formulation of a version and by the perspective on the world hidden in it, the perception of the world is determined in a way that feeds back into the social construction of this perspective, and thus, the world around us (see Chapter 7). Thus, theories as versions of the world become preliminary and relative. Further developing the version (e.g., by additional interpretations of new materials) leads to an increased empirical grounding in the object that is studied. But here the research process, too, does not start as a *tabula rasa*. The starting point is rather a pre-understanding of the subject or field under study.

Accordingly, the second point of reference for defining the role of theories in the model of grounded theory research is the first rule that Kleining formulates for qualitative research: "The initial understanding of the facts under study should be regarded as preliminary and should be exceeded with new, non-congruent information" (1982, p. 231).

Theoretical assumptions become relevant as preliminary versions of the understanding of and the perspective on the object being studied, which are reformulated, and above all, are further elaborated in the course of the research process. These revisions of versions on the basis of the empirical material thrust the construction of the subject under study. The researcher's methodological decisions, as designed in the model of Glaser and Strauss, contribute to this construction.

Case Study: Awareness of Dying

The following example represents one of the first and major studies using this form of research process and the goal of developing theories from qualitative research in the field. Barney Glaser and Anselm Strauss worked from the 1960s as pioneers of qualitative research and of grounded theory in the context of medical sociology. They did this study in several hospitals in the United States around San Francisco. Their research question was what influenced the various persons' interaction with dying people and how the knowledge—that the person will die soon—determines the interaction with that person. More concretely, they studied which forms of interaction between the dying person and the clinical staff in the hospital, between the staff and the relatives, and between relatives and the dying person could be noted.

The starting point of the research was the observation when the researchers' relatives were in the hospital that the staff in hospitals (at that time) seemed not to inform the patients with a terminal disease and their relatives about the state and the life expectancy of the patient. Rather the possibility that the patient might die or die soon was treated like a taboo. This general observation and the questions it raised were taken as a starting point for a more systematic observation and interviews in one hospital. These data were analyzed and used to develop categories. That was also the background for deciding to include another hospital and to continue the data collection and analysis there. Both hospitals—as cases—were immediately compared for similarities and differences. Results of such comparison were used to decide which hospital to use next and until finally six hospitals were included in the study. These included a teaching hospital, a VA hospital, two county hospitals, a private Catholic hospital, and a state hospital. Wards included among others geriatrics, cancer, intensive care, pediatrics, and neurosurgery in which the fieldworkers stayed two to four weeks each. The data from

(Continued)

(Continued)

each of these units (different wards in one hospital, similar wards in different hospitals, hospitals amongst each other) were contrasted and compared in order to show similarities and differences. At the end of the study, comparable situations and contexts outside hospitals and health care were included as another dimension of comparison.

Analyzing and comparing the data allowed developing a theoretical model, which then was transferred to other fields in order to develop it further. The result of this study was a theory of awareness contexts as ways of dealing with the information and with the patients' needs to know more about their situation. Details of the results and ways of analyzing the data will be discussed in more detail in Chapter 23.

This study is a good example for making the research process outlined in this chapter work in order to develop theoretically relevant insights from a series of case studies and their comparison (see Glaser and Strauss 1965a for details). Here theory was not a starting point, as there was no theory available at that time to explain the initial experiences of the researchers with their own relatives in hospital. Theory was the end product of the research, and it was developed out of empirical material and the analysis of this material.

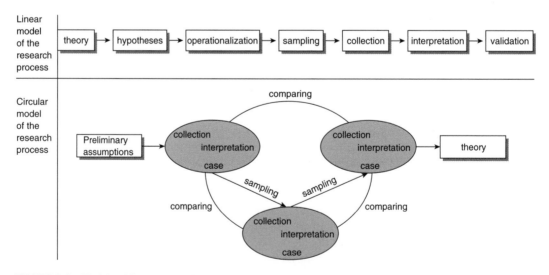

FIGURE 8.1 Models of Process and Theory

Qualitative research fits the traditional, linear logic of research only in a limited way. Rather, the circular inter-linking of empirical steps, as the model of Glaser and Strauss suggests (see Figure 8.1), does justice to the character of discovery in qualitative research. The context of this model of the research process should be referred to when single parts–like theoretical sampling–are taken from it and used in isolation. This process–oriented understanding allows one to realize the epistemological principle of *verstehen* with a greater degree of sensitivity than in linear designs. The relative relevance of theories as versions of the object to be reformulated takes the construction of reality in the research process into account more seriously. The central part reserved for the interpretation of data (compared with their collection or the *a priori* construction of elaborated designs) takes into account the fact that text is the actual empirical material and the ultimate basis for developing the theory.

KEY POINTS

- The research process in qualitative research is often difficult to cut into clearly separated phases.
- Qualitative research unfolds its real potential when important parts of the research process are interlinked.
- This understanding originally comes from grounded theory research but is also fruitful for other approaches.
- Theories are seen as versions of the world, which change and are further developed through the research.

Exercise 8.1

1. Take a qualitative study and identify the steps of the research process in it.
2. Decide if this study was planned along the linear or circular model of the research process.

Exercise 8.2

Think about your own research project and plan it step-by-step. Then imagine how your research should be planned according to the circular model.

Note

1 Here "theories" means assumptions about the subject under study, whereas the notion "theoretical positions" in Chapter 6 refers to differing assumptions about the methods and goals of research.

FURTHER READING

The epistemological positions of qualitative research are outlined in the first text, whereas the others give both classical and more recent versions of the process model of grounded theory research.

Becker, H.S. (1996) "The Epistemology of Qualitative Research," in R. Jessor, A. Colby, and R.A. Shweder (eds), *Ethnography and Human Development*. Chicago: University of Chicago Press. pp. 53–72.
Glaser, B.G. and Strauss, A.L. (1967) *The Discovery of Grounded Theory: Strategies for Qualitative Research*. New York: Aldine.
Strauss, A.L. (1987) *Qualitative Analysis for Social Scientists*. Cambridge: Cambridge University Press.

9
RESEARCH QUESTIONS

CHAPTER OBJECTIVES

After reading this chapter, you should be able to

✓ understand why research questions are so important for running a successful study.
✓ explain why it is important to carefully formulate and focus the research question.
✓ articulate the different types of research questions from which you should choose one for your project.

If you want to start your qualitative study, a first and central step, and one that essentially determines success in qualitative research but tends to be ignored in most presentations of methods,[1] is how to formulate the research question(s). However, you are confronted with this problem not only at the beginning when you conceptualize your study or your project but you also have to deal with formulating the research question at several stages of the process: when you conceptualize the research design, when you enter the field, when you select the cases, and when you collect the data. Reflecting and reformulating the research question are central points of reference for assessing the appropriateness of the decisions you take at several points. It becomes relevant, when you decide about the method(s) of collecting data, when you conceptualize interview schedules, but also when you conceptualize the interpretation, which method you use and which material you select. You should formulate research questions in concrete terms with the aim of clarifying what the field contacts are supposed to reveal.

The less clearly you formulate your research question, the greater is the danger that you will find yourself in the end confronted with mountains of data helplessly trying to analyze them. Although the quoted "principle of openness" questions the *a priori* formulation of hypotheses, it by no means implies you should abandon attempts to define and formulate research questions. It is important that you develop a clear idea of your research question but remain open to new and perhaps surprising results. Clear ideas about the nature of the research questions that are pursued are also necessary for checking the appropriateness of methodological decisions in the following respects: which methods are necessary to answer the questions? Is it possible to study the research question with the chosen methods at all? Is qualitative research the appropriate strategy to answer these questions?[2] More generally, the elaboration of the research question in the research process may be characterized in Figure 9.1.

Cutting Questions to Size

Research questions do not come from nowhere. In many cases, their origin lies in the researchers' personal biographies and their social contexts. The decision about a specific question mostly depends on the researchers' practical interests and their involvement in certain social and historical contexts. Everyday and scientific contexts both play a part here. Recent research studying scientific processes has demonstrated how much traditions and styles of thinking influence the formulation of research questions in scientific laboratories and in work groups in social sciences.

If you decide upon a concrete research question, this is always linked to reducing variety, and thus, to structuring the field under study: certain aspects are brought to the fore, others are regarded as less important, and (at least for the time being) left in the background or excluded. For instance in collecting data, such a decision is particularly crucial when you want to use single interviews (see Chapters 13 to 16). However, if you the collect your data in a processual manner, as for example in participant observation (see Chapter 17) or with repeated interviews, you can change the consequences of such a decision more easily.

Specifying an Area of Interest and Delimiting the Issue

The result of formulating research questions is that it helps you to circumscribe a specific area of a more or less complex field which you regard as essential, although the field would allow various research definitions of this kind. For studying "counseling," for example, you could specify any of the following as areas of interest:

- interactive processes between counselor and client;
- organization of the administration of clients as "cases";

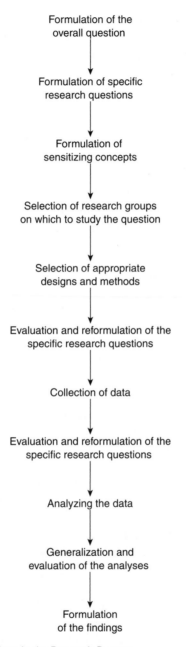

Formulation of the
overall question

Formulation of specific
research questions

Formulation of
sensitizing concepts

Selection of research groups
on which to study the question

Selection of appropriate
designs and methods

Evaluation and reformulation of the
specific research questions

Collection of data

Evaluation and reformulation of the
specific research questions

Analyzing the data

Generalization and
evaluation of the analyses

Formulation
of the findings

FIGURE 9.1   Research Questions in the Research Process

- organization and maintenance of a specific professional identity (e.g., to be a helper under unfavorable circumstances);
- subjective or objective manifestations of the patient's "career."

All these areas are relevant aspects of the complexity of everyday life in an institution (counseling service, socio-psychiatric service). You can focus on each of these areas in a study and embody it in a research question. For example, you could approach a complex (e.g., institutional) field with the aim of focusing on gaining an understanding of the viewpoint of one person or of several persons acting in this field. You could also focus on describing a life world. Similarly, you could be dedicated to reconstructing subjective or objective reasons for activities and thus to explaining human behavior. Alternatively, you can concentrate on the relation between subjective interpretations and the structural features of activity environments that can be described objectively. Only in very rare cases in qualitative research does it make sense and is it realistic to include this multitude of aspects. Rather it is crucial that you define the field and the research question in such a way that the latter can be answered with the available resources and a sound research design can be derived. This also calls for the formulation of a research question in such a way that it does not implicitly raise a lot of other questions at the same time, which would result in too indistinct an orientation to the empirical activities.

Key Concepts and the Triangulation of Perspectives

At this stage, you will face the problem of which aspects you want to include (the essential, the manageable, the relevant perspective, and so on) in your research and which to exclude (the secondary, the less relevant, and so on). How should you shape this decision in order to ensure the least "frictional loss" possible (i.e., ensure that the loss of authenticity remains limited and justifiable through an acceptable [degree of] neglect of certain aspects)?

Key concepts that give you wide access to a spectrum of processes relevant in a field may be the starting point of your research. Glaser and Strauss call these "analytical and sensitizing concepts" (1967, p. 38). For instance, when I studied the institutional everyday life of counseling, a concept like "trust" has proved to be useful. This concept could be applied, for example, to aspects of interactions between counselor and client. I could also use it to study the counselor's task, the clients' impressions of the institution and their perceptions of the counselor's competence, to the problematic of how to make a conversation a consultation, and so on.

The frictional loss in decisions between research perspectives can be reduced by the approach of systematic triangulation of perspectives. This refers to the combination of appropriate research perspectives and methods that are suitable for taking into account as many different aspects of a problem as possible. An example of this would be the combination of attempts at understanding persons' points of view with attempts at describing the life world in which they act. According to Fielding and Fielding (1986, p. 34), structural aspects of a problem should be linked with reconstructing its meaning for the people involved (see Chapter 29 for triangulation). In the previous example, I realized this by linking the reconstruction of counselors' subjective theories on trust with a description of the process of producing trust in a conversation in the special world of "counseling."

If you use key concepts to gain access to the relevant processes and triangulation of perspectives to disclose as many different aspects as possible, you can increase the degree of proximity to the object in the way you explore cases and fields. This process may also enable the opening up of new fields of knowledge.

Generally speaking, the precise formulation of the research question is a central step when you conceptualize your research design. Research questions should be examined critically as to their origins (what has led to the actual research question?). They are points of reference for checking the soundness of your research design and the appropriateness of methods you intend to use for collecting and interpreting your data. This is relevant for evaluating any generalizations: the level of generalization that is appropriate and obtainable depends on the research questions pursued.

Types of Research Questions

There are different types of research questions, which may be located in a schema comprising (according to Lofland and Lofland 1984, p. 94) the components displayed in Table 9.1. This includes links to the "coding paradigm" that Strauss (1987, p. 27) suggests for formulating questions on text to be interpreted (for more details see Chapter 23).

Generally speaking, we can differentiate between research questions oriented towards describing states and those describing processes. In the first case, you should describe how a certain given state (which type, how often) has come about (causes, strategies) and how this state is maintained (structure). In the second case, the aim is to describe how something develops or changes (causes, processes, consequences, strategies).

The description of states and the description of processes as the two main types of research question may be classified in terms of the increasingly complex "units" (Lofland and Lofland 1984) in the left-hand column of Table 9.1. This schema can be used for locating research questions in this space of possibilities and also for checking the selected research question for additional questions raised.

Finally, you can assess or classify research questions as to how far they are suitable for confirming existing assumptions (like hypotheses) or how far they aim at discovering new ones, or at least allow this. Strauss calls the latter "generative questions" and defines them as follows: "Questions that stimulate the line of investigation in profitable directions; they lead to hypotheses, useful comparisons, the collection of certain classes of data, even to general lines of attack on potentially important problems" (1987, p. 22).

TABLE 9.1 Types of Research Questions

Units	What type is it?	What is its structure	How frequent is it?	What are the causes?	What are its processes?	What are its consequences?	What are people's strategies?
			QUESTIONS				
Meanings							
Practices							
Episodes							
Encounters							
Roles							
Relationships							
Groups							
Organizations							
Settlements							
Worlds							
Lifestyles							

Source: Lofland and Lofland © 1984, p. 94. (Reprinted with kind permission of Wadsworth, Inc. Belmont, CA)

Case Study: Adoption of a Public Health Orientation by Doctors and Nurses

In a recent project (Flick et al. 2002), we were generally interested in whether and how far a public health orientation had reached some of the key institutions of home care services in the health field. This is of course not yet a research question, which you can use for starting an empirical study. So, we had to pin down this general interest to a more focused perspective. Therefore, we focused on health concepts held by home care nurses and general practitioners. Then we focused on the attitude held towards prevention and health promotion as parts of their work, and more concretely, with a specific part of their clientele–the elderly. Against this background, we developed a set of questions we wanted to pursue in a study using interviews:

- What are the concepts of health held by doctors and nurses?
- Which dimensions of health representations are relevant for professional work with the elderly?
- What is the attitude of professionals towards prevention and health promotion for the elderly?

(Continued)

(Continued)

- What are the concepts of ageing held by general practitioners and home-care nurses? What is the relation of these concepts with those of health?
- What relevance do professionals ascribe to their own concepts of health and ageing for their own professional practice?
- Are there any relations between the concepts of health and ageing and professional training and experience?

We took these research questions as a starting point for developing an instrument for episodic interviews (see Chapter 14) with doctors and nurses. Looking back on this project, we thought critically about the number of different research questions included in the above list. Particularly, if you are a novice to qualitative research, I suggest that you concentrate on one or two such questions in planning a similar project to the one we did.

Research questions are like a door to the research field under study. Whether empirical activities produce answers or not depends on the formulation of such questions. Also dependent on this is the decision as to which methods are appropriate and who (i.e., which persons, groups, or institutions) or what (i.e. what processes, activities, or lifestyles) you should include in your study. The essential criteria for evaluating research questions include their soundness and clarity, but also whether they can be answered in the framework of given and limited resources (time, money, etc., see Chapter 12). You should take into account that formulating a research question means to define the overall guiding question for your entire project and not to formulate the concrete questions you will ask in your interviews for example.

KEY POINTS

- It is absolutely essential to formulate a clear research question.
- Most issues of research can be pinned down to several research questions, but it is important to decide which one to pursue (first).
- Research questions are refined and reformulated along the way through the empirical research project.

Exercise 9.1

1. Look for a qualitative study in the literature. Identify the study's guiding research question.
2. Assess this research question: Was it clear and well formulated?
3. Formulate a better research question for this study.

Exercise 9.2

1. Decide on an issue you want to study and then formulate different research questions.
2. Decide which one you want to pursue.
3. Refine the research question so that it is one which you can answer with your research project.

Notes

1 Almost no textbook dedicates a separate chapter to this topic. In most subject indexes, one looks for it in vain. Exceptions can be found in Silverman (1985, Chapter 1; 1993), Strauss (1987, p. 17) and Strauss and Corbin (1990, pp. 37–40).
2 If the research question in a study implicitly or explicitly leads to the determination of the frequencies of a phenomenon, quantitative methods are not only more appropriate but generally also simpler to apply.

FURTHER READING

The first two texts deal with linking perspectives in research questions in some detail, whereas the other two give classical and more elaborate information about how to deal with research questions in qualitative research.

Fielding, N.G. and Fielding, J.L. (1986) *Linking Data*. Beverly Hills, CA: SAGE.
Flick, U. (2004a) "Triangulation in Qualitative Research," in U. Flick, E.v. Kardorff and I. Steinke (eds), *A Companion to Qualitative Research*. London, SAGE. pp. 178–183.
Lofland, J. and Lofland, L.H. (1984) *Analyzing Social Settings* (2nd edn). Belmont, CA: Wadsworth.
Strauss, A.L. (1987) *Qualitative Analysis for Social Scientists*. Cambridge: Cambridge University Press.

10
ENTERING THE FIELD

CHAPTER OBJECTIVES
After reading this chapter, you should be able to

✓ develop a sensitiveness to this key step in the research process.
✓ understand that you as researcher will have to locate yourself in the field.
✓ learn the strategies which institutions use to deal with researchers and sometimes to keep them out.
✓ comprehend the dialectics of strangeness and familiarity in this context.

Expectations of Qualitative Researchers and the Problem of Access

The question of how to gain access to the field under study is more crucial in qualitative research than in quantitative research. Here, the contact that researchers look for is either closer or more intense, and this can briefly be demonstrated in terms of the expectations linked to some of the current qualitative methods. For example, if you want to do open interviews, they require that the interviewed person and you get more closely involved than would be necessary for simply handing over a questionnaire. If you want to record everyday conversations, you expect from participants a degree of disclosing of their own everyday life, which they cannot easily control in advance. As a participant observer, you normally come to the field for longer periods. From a methodological point of view, research does more justice to its object through these procedures. From the perspective of everyday practicability, these procedures produce a much more extensive demand on the persons who are involved. This is why the question of how to find access to a field and to those persons and processes in it that are of particular interest deserves special attention. The general term "field" may mean a certain institution, a subculture, a family, a specific group of persons with a special biography, decision makers in administrations or enterprises, and so on. In each of these cases, you will face the same problems: how can you secure the collaboration of the potential participants in your study? How do you achieve not only that people express their willingness, but that this also leads to concrete interviews or other data?

Role Definitions in Entering an Open Field

In qualitative research, you as the researcher and your respondent have a special importance. You as a researcher and your respondent and your communicative competencies are the main "instruments" of collecting data and of recognition. Because of this, you cannot adopt a neutral role in the field and in your contacts with the persons to be interviewed or observed. Rather you will have to take—or you will be allocated—certain roles and positions (sometimes vicariously and/or unwillingly). Which information in your research you will have access to and which you will remain debarred from depends essentially on the successful adoption of an appropriate role or position. You should see taking or being assigned a role as a process of negotiation between researcher and participants, which runs through several stages. "Participants" here refers to those persons to be interviewed or observed. For research in institutions, it also refers to those who have to authorize or facilitate access. The growing insight into the importance of the interactive process of negotiating and allocating roles to the researchers in the field finds its expression in the metaphors used to describe it.

Using the example of participant observation in ethnographic field research (see Chapter 17), Adler and Adler (1987) have presented a system of membership roles in the field (see Figure 10.1). They show how this problem has been differently treated in the history of qualitative research. At one pole, they position the studies of the Chicago School (see Chapter 2) and their use of pure observation of the members in a field of open and well-directed interaction with them and of active participation in their everyday life. The dilemma of participation and observation becomes relevant in questions of necessary distancing (how much participation is needed for a good observation, how much participation is permissible in the context of scientific distancing?). For Douglas's (1976) "existential sociology," in an intermediate position, Adler and Adler see the problem solved in participation aiming at revealing the secrets of the field. At the other pole, the concern of

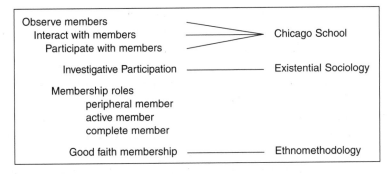

FIGURE 10.1   Membership Roles in the Field (Adler and Adler 1987, p. 33)

recent ethnomethodology (see Chapter 6) is with describing members' methods rather than their perspectives in order to describe the process under study from the inside. Here the problem of access is managed by immersion in the work process observed and by membership in the researched field.

For Adler and Adler, the Chicago School's handling of this problem is too committed to scientific distancing from the "object" of research. On the other hand, they are rather critical of the types of access obtained by ethnomethodology as well as by existential sociology (although positioned at different poles in their systematic). In both cases, access is obtained by completely fusing with the research object. Their concept of membership roles seems to them to be a more realistic solution located between these two poles. They work out the types of "membership roles: the peripheral, the active, and the complete member." For studying delicate fields (in their case, drug dealers), they suggest a combination of "overt and covert roles" (1987, p. 21). This means that they do not disclose their actual role (as researchers) to all the members in a field in order to gain insights that are as open as possible.

Access to Institutions

When you want to do your research in institutions (e.g., counseling services), this problem becomes more complicated. In general, different levels are involved in the regulation of access. First, there is the level of the persons responsible for authorizing the research. In case of difficulties, they are held responsible for this authorization by external authorities. Second, we find the level of those to be interviewed or observed, who will be investing their time and willingness.

For research in administrations, Lau and Wolff (1983, p. 419) have outlined the process as follows. In an institution like social administration, researchers with their research interest are defined as clients. Like a client, the researcher has to make his request in formal terms. This request, its implications (research question, methods, time needed), and the person of the researcher have to undergo an "official examination." The treatment of a researcher's request is "pre-structured" by the fact that the researcher has been sent by other authorities. This means that the authorization or support for the request by a higher authority in the first instance may produce distrust in the people to be interviewed (why is this higher authority in favor of this research?). Being endorsed by other people (e.g., colleagues from another institution), however, may facilitate access at the same time. In the end, the researcher's request can be fitted into administrative routines and treated using institutionally familiar procedures. This process, termed "work of agreement," is a "joint product, in some cases an explicit working problem for both sides." For instance, the main task is the negotiation of common linguistic rules between researchers and practitioners. The analysis of this entry as a constructive process, and more importantly, the analysis of failures in this process allow the researcher to reveal central processes of negotiation and routinization in the field in an exemplary manner (for example, with "real" clients).

Wolff (2004a) summarizes the problems of entering institutions as a research field as follows:

1. Research is always an intervention into a social system.
2. Research is a disruptive factor for the system to be studied to which it reacts defensively.
3. A mutual opacity exists between the research project and the social system to be researched.
4. To exchange a whole mass of information on entering the research field does not reduce the opacity. Rather, it leads to increasing complexity in the process of agreement and may lead to increased "immune reactions." On both sides, myths are produced, which are fed by increased exchange of information.
5. Instead of mutual understanding at the moment of entry, one should strive for an agreement as a process.
6. Data protection is necessary, but may contribute to increased complexity in the process of agreement.
7. The field discovers itself when the research project enters the scene (e.g., the limits of a social system are perceived).
8. The research project cannot offer anything to the social system. At most, it can be functional. The researcher should take care not to make promises about the usefulness of the research for the social system.
9. The social system has no real reasons for rejecting the research.

These nine points already contain within themselves various reasons for a possible failure in the agreement about the purpose and necessity of the research. A research project is an intrusion into the life of the institution to be studied. Research is a disturbance, and it disrupts routines, with no perceptible immediate or long-term pay off for the institution and its members. Research unsettles the institution with three implications: that the limitations of its own activities are to be disclosed; that the ulterior motives of the "research" are and remain unclear for the institution; and finally, that there are no sound reasons for refusing research requests. Thus, reasons have to be invented and sustained if research is to be prevented. Here the part played by irrationality in the ongoing process of agreement is situated. Finally, providing more information on the background, intentions, procedure, and results of the planned research does not necessarily lead to more clarity, but rather may lead to more confusion and produce the opposite of understanding. That is, if you negotiate entry to an institution, this is less a problem of providing information than one of how to establish a relationship. In this relationship, enough trust must be developed in the researchers as persons, and in their request, that the institution–despite all reservations–gets by being involved in the research. However, it remains necessary to underline that the discrepancies of interests and perspectives between researchers and the institutions under study cannot in principle be removed. However, you can minimize them if you manage to develop trust on the side of the participants and institutions far enough to forge a working alliance in which research becomes possible.

Access to Individuals

Once you have gained access to the field or the institution in general, you will face the problem of how to reach those persons within it, who are the most interesting (see Chapter 11) participants. For example, how can you recruit experienced and practicing counselors for participation in the study and not simply trainees without practical experience who are not yet allowed to work with the relevant cases, but have–for that reason–more time for participating in the research? How can you access the central figures in a setting and not merely the minor figures? Here again, processes of negotiation, strategies of reference in the sense of snowballing, and above all, competencies in establishing relationships play a major part. Often the reservations in the field caused by certain methods are different in each case.

Case Study: Reservations against Research Methods

These different reservations against various methods may be demonstrated by examining various methods which I used to study the question of trust in counseling. In this study I employed interviews and conversation analyses. I approached the individual counselors with two requests: I asked for permission to interview them for one to two hours and for permission to record one or more consultations with clients (who had also agreed beforehand). After they had agreed in general to participate in the

(Continued)

(Continued)

study, some of the counselors had reservations about being interviewed (time, fear of "indiscreet" questions), whereas they saw the recording of a counseling session as routine. Other counselors had no problem with being interviewed, but big reservations about allowing someone to delve into their concrete work with clients. Precautions guaranteeing anonymity may dispel such reservations only up to a point. This example shows that various methods may produce different problems, suspicions, and fears in different persons.

With regard to access to persons in institutions and specific situations, you will face in your research the problem of willingness above all else. However, with regard to access to individuals, the problem of how to find them proves just as difficult. In the framework of studying individuals who cannot be approached as employees or clients in an institution or as being present in a particular setting, the main problem is how to find them. We can take the biographical study of the course and subjective evaluation of professional careers as an example. In such a study, for example, it would be necessary to interview men living alone after retirement. The question then is how and where you find this kind of person. Strategies could be to use the media (advertisements in papers, announcements in radio programs) or to post notices in institutions (education centers, meeting points) that these persons might frequent. Another route to selecting interviewees is for the researcher to snowball from one case to the next. In using this strategy, often friends of friends are chosen and thus you would look for persons from your own broader environment. Hildenbrand warns of the problems linked to this strategy:

> While it is often assumed that access to the field would be facilitated by studying persons well known to the researcher and accordingly finding cases from one's own circle of acquaintances, exactly the opposite is true: the stranger the field, the more easily may researchers appear as strangers, whom the people in the study have something to tell which is new for the researcher. (1995, p. 258)

Strangeness and Familiarity

The question of how to find access (to persons, institutions or fields) raises a problem, which can be expressed by the metaphor of the researcher as professional stranger (Agar 1980) (Box 10.1). The need to orient oneself in the field and to find your way around it gives the researcher a glimpse into routines and self-evidence. These have been familiar to the members for a long time and have become routines and unquestioned and taken for granted by them. The individuals no longer reflect on such routines, because they are often no longer accessible for them. A potential way of gaining further knowledge is to take and (at least temporarily) maintain the perspective of an outsider and to take an attitude of doubt towards any sort of social self-evidence. This status of a stranger can be differentiated–depending on the strategy of the research–into the roles of the "visitor" and the "initiate." As a visitor you appear in the field–in the extreme case–only once for a single interview, but you will be able to receive knowledge through questioning the routines mentioned above. In the case of the initiate, it is precisely the process of giving up the outsider's perspective step-by-step in the course of the participant observation, which is fruitful. Above all, the detailed description of this process from the subjective perspective of the researcher can become a fruitful source of knowledge and you should see entering the field as a process of learning.

Certain activities in the field, however, remain hidden from the view of the researcher as stranger. In the context of social groups, Adler and Adler mention "two sets of realities about their activities: one presented to outsiders and the other reserved for insiders" (1987, p. 21). Qualitative research is normally not simply interested in the exterior presentation of social groups. Rather, you want to become involved in a different world or subculture and first to understand it as far as possible from inside and from its own logic. A source of knowledge in this context is that you gradually take an insider's perspective–to understand the individual's viewpoint or the organizational principles of social groups from a member's perspective. The limits of this strategy become relevant in Adler and Adler's (1987) example mentioned above–dealing drugs. Here, aspects of reality remain hidden and are not disclosed to you as a researcher–even if you are integrated in the field and the group as a person. These areas will only be accessible if researchers conceal from certain members in the field their role as researchers. Fears of passing on information and of negative sanctions by third parties for the people researched are here trenchantly revealed as well as ethical problems in the contact with the people under study. But they play a part in all research. Issues are raised here of how to protect the trust and interests of the people researched, of data protection, and of how the researchers deal with their own aims.

Box 10.1 Roles in the Field

- Stranger
- Visitor
- Initiant
- Refused

Case Study: Street Corner Society

The following example comes from one of the classical studies of qualitative research using participant observation and ethnography (see Chapter 17) in a field. William F. Whyte was one of the most influential researchers in the sociology of the 1940s. He lived for three and half years with the community he studied. His classic ethnographic study of a street gang in a major city in the eastern United States in the 1940s offers, on the basis of individual observations, personal notes and other sources, a comprehensive picture of a dynamic local culture. Through the mediation of a key figure, Whyte (1955) had gained access to a group of young second-generation Italian migrants. Whyte gives detailed descriptions of how he negotiated his access to the area he studied, how he used his key person to find access, and to get accepted by the social group. He also describes the needs to keep the distance to the field to avoid becoming a member of the group and going native in the group and the field. As a result of a two-year period of participant observation, he was able to obtain information about the motives, values, and life awareness and also about the social organization, friendships, and loyalties of this local culture

These were condensed in theoretically important statements such as:

> Whyte's gangs can be seen simply as an example of a temporary non-adjustment of young people. They withdraw from the norms of the parental home … and at the same time see themselves as excluded from the predominant norms of American society. Deviant behavior is to be noted both towards the norms of the parental home and towards the prevailing norms of the country of immigration. Deviant behavior, even as far as criminality, may be seen as a transient faulty adaptation that bears within itself both the option of adaptation and of permanent non-adaptation. (Atteslander 1996: XIII)

This is a paradigmatic example for how a researcher sought and found access to a community and studied their rituals and routines making up a special form of daily life.

In summary, researchers face the problem of negotiating proximity and distance in relation to the person(s) studied. The problems of disclosure, transparency, and negotiation of mutual expectations, aims, and interest are also relevant. Finally, you will have to make the decision between adopting the perspective of either an insider or an outsider with regard to the object of the research. Being an insider and/or an outsider with regard to the field of research may be analyzed in terms of the strangeness and familiarity of the researcher. Where you as researcher locate yourself in this area of conflict between strangeness and familiarity will determine in the continuation of the research which concrete methods are chosen and also which part of the field under study will be accessible and inaccessible for your research. A specific role again is played by the partly unconscious fears that prevent the researcher from meddling in a certain field. For researchers, it depends on the form of access permitted by the field, and on their personality, how instructive descriptions of the cases will be and how far the knowledge obtained remains limited to confirming what was known in advance.

KEY POINTS

- Entering the field includes more than just being there. It is a complex process of locating yourself and being located in the field.
- It has to do with taking and being allocated to a role in the field.
- In institutions, there are often no good reasons to reject research in general. Therefore, representatives of institutions introduce substitutional reasons for rejecting a research project if they do not want to let it enter. This makes negotiations more complex for the researcher.
- Access to individuals inside and outside of institutions is another important step. Here you should try to win people you do not know personally for your research in order to receive fruitful insights.

Exercise 10.1

1. Choose a study with qualitative methods from the literature. Try to identify in the text which problems of access the researcher mentions. And try to imagine which problems arose when they attempted to enter the field.
2. Think about your own study and plan how to access the field you want to study. Whom do you have to ask for permission? How will you approach those people you want to include in your study?

FURTHER READING

These texts deal with concrete problems and examples of entering a field and taking a role and position in it. Schütz's paper is a good sociological description of the qualities of being a stranger, which allows insights into what is familiar to members of a field.

Adler, P.A. and Adler, P. (1987) *Membership Roles in Field Research*. Beverly Hills, CA: SAGE.

Schütz, A. (1962) "The Stranger," in A. Schütz, *Collected Papers*, Vol. II. Den Haag: Nijhoff. pp. 91–105.

Wolff, S. (2004a) "Ways into the Field and their Variants," in U. Flick, E.v. Kardorff and I. Steinke (eds), *A Companion to Qualitative Research*. London: SAGE. pp. 195–202.

11

SAMPLING

CHAPTER OBJECTIVES
After reading this chapter, you should be able to

✓ understand the role and importance of sampling in qualitative research.
✓ identify the differences of theoretical and statistical sampling.
✓ distinguish different forms of sampling in qualitative research.
✓ comprehend how a case is constituted in qualitative research.

Sampling Decisions in the Research Process

You will encounter the issue of sampling at different stages in the research process (Table 11.1). In an interview study, it is connected to the decision about which persons you will interview (case sampling) and from which groups these should come (sampling groups of cases). Furthermore, it emerges with the decision about which of the interviews should be further treated, i.e., transcribed and analyzed (material sampling). During interpretation of the data, the question again arises when you decide which parts of a text you should select for interpretation in general or for particular detailed interpretations (sampling within the material). Finally, it arises when presenting the findings: which cases or parts of text are best to demonstrate your findings (presentational sampling)?

TABLE 11.1 Sampling Decisions in the Research Process

Stage in research	Sampling methods
While collecting data	Case sampling Sampling groups of cases
While interpreting data	Material sampling Sampling within the material
While presenting the findings	Presentational sampling

In the literature, various suggestions have been made for the problem of sampling. But quite unambiguously, they are located at two poles–on more or less abstract or concrete criteria.

A Priori Determination of the Sample Structure

At one pole, criteria are abstract insofar as they start from an idea of the researched object's typicality and distribution. This should be represented in the sample of the material, which you study (i.e., collect and analyze) in a way that allows you to draw the inference of the relations in the object. This is the logic of statistical sampling in which material is put together according to certain (e.g., demographic) criteria. For example, you draw a sample that is homogeneous in age or social situation (women with a certain profession at a specific biographical stage) or a sample representing a certain distribution of such criteria in the population. These criteria are abstract, because they have been developed independently of the concrete material analyzed and before its collection and analysis, as the following examples show.

Case study: Sampling with Social Groups Defined in Advance

In my study on the social representation of technological change in everyday life, I took three starting points. One was that the perceptions and evaluations of technological change in everyday life are dependent upon the profession of the interviewee. The second was that they depend on gender as well, and thirdly that they are influenced by cultural and political contexts. In order to take these factors into account, I defined several dimensions of the sample. The professions of information engineers (as developers of technology), social scientists (as professional users of technology), and

(Continued)

(Continued)

teachers in human disciplines (as everyday users of technology) should be represented in the sample by cases with a certain minimum of professional experience. Male and female persons should be integrated. I took the different cultural backgrounds into account by selecting cases from the contexts of West Germany, East Germany, and France. This led to a sample structure of nine fields (Table 11.2), which I filled as evenly as possible with cases representing each group. The number of cases per field depended on the resources (how many interviews could be conducted, transcribed, and interpreted in the time available?) and on the goals of my study (what do the individual cases or the totality of the cases stand for?).

This example shows how you can work with comparative groups in qualitative research that have been defined in advance, not during the research process or the sampling process.

Sampling cases for data collection is oriented towards filling the cells of the sample structure as evenly as possible or towards filling all cells sufficiently. Inside the groups or fields, theoretical sampling (see below) may be used in the decision as to which case to integrate next.

Complete Collection in Qualitative Research

Gerhardt applied an alternative method of sampling. She used the strategy of complete collection (1986, p. 67): "In order to learn more about events and courses of patients' careers in chronic renal failure, we decided to do a complete collection of all patients (male, married, 30 to 50 years at the beginning of the treatment) of the five major hospitals (renal units) serving the south-east of Britain." The sampling is limited in advance by certain criteria: a specific disease, a specific age, a specific region, a limited period, and a particular marital status characterize the relevant cases. These criteria delimit the totality of possible cases in such a way that all the cases may be integrated in the study. But here, as well, sampling is carried out because virtual cases, which do not meet one or more of these criteria, are excluded in advance. It is possible to use such methods of sampling mainly in regional studies.

In research designs using *a priori* definitions of the sample structure, you take sampling decisions with a view to selecting cases or groups of cases. In complete collection, the exclusion of interviews already done will be less likely in that data collection and analysis is aimed at the keeping and the integration of all cases available in the sample. Thus whilst the sampling *of* materials is less relevant, questions about sampling *in* the material (which parts of the interview are interpreted more intensely, which cases are contrasted?) and about sampling *in* presentation are as relevant as in the method of gradual definition of the sampling structure.

TABLE 11.2   Example of a Sampling Structure with Dimensions Given in Advance

| | CONTEXT AND GENDER | | | | | | |
| | West Germany | | East Germany | | France | | |
PROFESSION	Female	Male	Female	Male	Female	Male	Total
Information engineers							
Social scientists							
Teachers							
Total							

What are the Limitations of the Method?

In this strategy, the structure of the groups taken into account is defined before data collection. This restricts the range variation in the possible comparison. At least on this level, there will be no real new findings. If the development of theory is the aim of your study, this form of sampling restricts the developmental space of the theory in an essential dimension. Thus, this procedure is suitable for further analyzing, differentiating, and perhaps testing assumptions about common features and differences between specific groups.

Gradual Definition of the Sample Structure in the Research Process: Theoretical Sampling

Gradual strategies of sampling are mostly based on "theoretical sampling" developed by Glaser and Strauss (1967). Decisions about choosing and putting together empirical material (cases, groups, institutions, etc.) are made in the process of collecting and interpreting data. Glaser and Strauss describe this strategy as follows:

> Theoretical sampling is the process of data collection for generating theory whereby the analyst jointly collects, codes and analyses his data and decides what data to collect next and where to find them, in order to develop his theory as it emerges. This process of data collection is controlled by the emerging theory. (1967, p. 45)

Sampling decisions in theoretical sampling may start from either of two levels: They may be made on the level of the groups to be compared or they may directly focus on specific persons. In both cases, the sampling of concrete individuals, groups, or fields is not based on the usual criteria and techniques of statistical sampling. A representative sample is guaranteed neither by random sampling nor by stratification. Rather, you select individuals, groups, and so on according to their (expected) level of new insights for the developing theory in relation to the state of theory elaboration so far. Sampling decisions aim at that material that promises the greatest insights, viewed in the light of the material already used, and the knowledge drawn from it. The main question for selecting data is: "*What* groups or subgroups does one turn to *next* in data collection? And for *what* theoretical purpose? The possibilities of multiple comparisons are infinite, and so groups must be chosen according to theoretical criteria" (1967, p. 47).

Given the theoretically unlimited possibilities of integrating further persons, groups, cases, and so on it is necessary to define criteria for a well-founded limitation of the sampling. These criteria are defined here in relation to the theory. The theory developing from the empirical material is the point of reference. Examples of such criteria are how promising the next case is and how relevant it might be for developing the theory.

An example of applying this form of sampling is found in Glaser and Strauss's (1965a) study on awareness of dying in hospitals. In this study, the authors did participant observation in different hospitals and institutions in order to develop a theory about how dying in hospital is organized as a social process (see also Chapter 23 for more details). The memo in the following case study describes the decision and sampling process.

Case Study: Example of Theoretical Sampling

The pioneers of grounded theory research, Glaser and Strauss, developed theoretical sampling during their research in medical sociology in the 1960s. They describe in the following passage how they proceeded in theoretical sampling:

Visits to the various medical services were scheduled as follows. I wished first to look at services that minimized patient awareness (and so first looked at a premature baby service and then at a neurosurgical service where patients were frequently comatose). Next I wished to look at the dying in a situation where expectancy of staff and often of patients was great and dying was quick, so I observed on an Intensive Care Unit. Then I wished to observe on a service where staff expectations of terminality were great but where the patient's might or might not be, and where dying tended to be slow. So I looked next at a cancer service. I wished then to look at conditions where death was unexpected and rapid, and so looked at an emergency service. While we were looking at some different types of services, we also observed the above types of services at other types of hospitals. So our scheduling of types of service was directed by a general conceptual scheme—which included hypotheses about awareness, expectedness, and rate of dying—as well as by a developing conceptual structure including matters not at first envisioned. Sometimes we returned to services after the initial two or three or four weeks of continuous observation, in order to

(Continued)

(Continued)

check upon items which needed checking or had been missed in the initial period. (Glaser and Strauss 1967, p. 59)

This example is instructive as it shows how the researchers went step-by-step in constructing their sample in the contact with the field while they collected their data.

A second question, as crucial as the first, is how to decide when to stop integrating further cases. Glaser and Strauss suggest the criterion of "theoretical saturation" (of a category etc): "The criterion for judging when to stop sampling the different groups pertinent to a category is the category's theoretical saturation. Saturation means that no additional data are being found whereby the sociologist can develop properties of the category" (1967, p. 61). Sampling and integrating further material is finished when the "theoretical saturation" of a category or group of cases has been reached (i.e., nothing new emerges any more).

Table 11.3 highlights the theoretical sampling in the comparison with statistical sampling.

Case Study: Gradual Integration of Groups and Cases

In my study of the role of trust in therapy and counseling, I included cases coming from specific professional groups, institutions, and fields of work. I selected them step-by-step in order to fill the blanks in the database that became clear according to the successive interpretation of the data incorporated at each stage. First, I collected and compared cases from two different fields of work (prison versus therapy in private practice). After that I integrated a third field of work (sociopsychiatric services) to increase the meaningfulness of the comparisons on this level. When I interpreted the collected material, sampling on a further dimension promised additional insights. I extended the range of professions in the study up to that point (psychologists and social workers) by a third one (physicians) to further elaborate the differences of viewpoints in one field of work (sociopsychiatric services). Finally, it became clear that the epistemological potential of this field was so big that it seemed less instructive for me to contrast this field with other fields than to systematically compare different institutions within this field. Therefore, I integrated further cases from other sociopsychiatric services (see Table 11.4, in which the sequence and order of the decisions in the selection are indicated by the letters A to C).

This example illustrates how you can develop a sample and a sample structure step-by-step in the field while collecting your data.

In the end, you can see that the use of this method leads to a structured sample as well as the use of the method of statistical sampling does. However, you will not

TABLE 11.3   Theoretical versus Statistical Sampling

Theoretical sampling	Statistical sampling
Extension of the basic population is not known in advance	Extension of the basic population is known in advance
Features of the basic population are not known in advance	Distribution of features in the basic population can be estimated
Repeated drawing of sampling elements with criteria to be defined again in each step	One-shot drawing of a sample following a plan defined in advance
Sample size is not defined in advance	Sample size is defined in advance
Sampling is finished when theoretical saturation has been reached	Sampling is finished when the whole sample has been studied

Source: Wiedemann 1995, p. 441

TABLE 11.4   Example of a Sample Structure Resulting from the Process

	Prison	Private practice	Sociopsychiatric services
Psychologists	A	A	B
Social workers	A	A	B
Physicians			C

define the structure of the sample here before you collect and analyze your data. You will develop it step-by-step while you collect data and analyze them and complete it by new dimensions or limited to certain dimensions and fields.

Gradual Selection as a General Principle in Qualitative Research

If we compare different conceptions of qualitative research in this respect, we can see that this principle of selecting cases and material has also been applied beyond Glaser and Strauss. The basic principle of theoretical sampling is to select cases or case groups according to concrete criteria concerning their content instead of using abstract methodological criteria. Sampling proceeds according to the relevance of cases instead of their representativeness. This principle is also characteristic of related strategies of collecting data in qualitative research.

On the one hand, parallels can be drawn with the concept of "data triangulation" in Denzin (1989b), which refers to the integration of various data sources, differentiated by time, place, and person (see Chapter 29). Denzin suggests studying "the same phenomenon" at different times and places and with different persons. He also claims to have applied the strategy of theoretical sampling in his own way as a purposive and systematic selection and integration of persons and groups of persons, and temporal and local settings. The extension of the sampling procedure to temporal and local settings is an advantage of the system of access in Denzin's method compared with that of Glaser and Strauss. In the example just mentioned, I took this idea into account by purposively integrating different institutions (as local settings) and professions and by using different sorts of data.

Znaniecki (1934) (see Chapter 29) put forward "analytic induction" as a way of making concrete and further developing theoretical sampling. But here attention is focused less on the question of which cases to integrate in the study in general. Rather this concept starts from developing a theory (pattern, model, and so on) at a given moment and state and then specifically looking for and analyzing deviant cases (or even case groups). Whereas theoretical sampling mainly aims to enrich the developing theory, analytic induction is concerned with securing it by analyzing or integrating deviant cases. Whereas theoretical sampling wants to control the process of selecting data by the emerging theory, analytic induction uses the deviant case to control the developing theory. The deviant case here is a complement to the criterion of theoretical saturation. This criterion remains rather indeterminate but is used for continuing and assessing the collection of data. In the example mentioned above, cases were minimally and maximally contrasted in a purposeful way instead of applying such strategies starting from deviant cases (see Chapter 29).

This brief comparison of different conceptions of qualitative research may demonstrate that the basic principle of theoretical sampling is the genuine and typical form of selecting material in qualitative research. This assumption may be supported by reference to Kleining's (1982) idea of a typology of social science methods. According to this idea, all research methods have the same source in everyday techniques; qualitative methods are the first and quantitative methods are the second level of abstraction from these everyday techniques. If this is applied analogously to strategies for selecting empirical material, theoretical sampling (and basically related strategies as mentioned before) is the more concrete strategy and is closer to everyday life. Criteria of sampling like being representative for a population and so on are the second level of abstraction. This analogy of levels of abstraction may support the thesis that theoretical sampling is the more appropriate sampling strategy in qualitative research, whereas classical sampling procedures remain oriented to the logic of quantitative research. To what extent the latter should be imported into qualitative research has to be checked in every case. Here we can draw parallels with the discussion about the appropriateness of quality indicators (see Chapter 28).

Recent Concepts of Gradual Selection

Gradual selection is not merely the original principle of sampling in various traditional approaches in qualitative research. More recent discussions, which describe strategies for how to proceed with selecting cases and empirical material, take it up again repeatedly. In the framework of evaluation research, Patton (2002) contrasts random sampling in general with purposive sampling and makes some concrete suggestions:

- One is to integrate purposively *extreme* or deviant cases. In order to study the functioning of a reform program, particularly successful examples of realizing it are chosen and analyzed. Or cases of failure in the program are selected and analyzed for the reasons for this failure. Here the field under study is disclosed from its extremities to arrive at an understanding of the field as a whole.
- Another suggestion is to select particularly *typical* cases (i.e., those cases in which success and failure are particularly typical for the average or the majority of the cases). Here the field is disclosed from inside and from its center.
- A further suggestion aims at the *maximal variation* in the sample–to integrate only a few cases, but those which are as different as possible, to disclose the range of variation and differentiation in the field.
- Additionally, cases may be selected according to the *intensity* with which the interesting features, processes, experiences, and so on are given or assumed in them. Either cases with the greatest intensity are chosen or cases with different intensities are systematically integrated and compared.
- The selection of *critical cases* aims at those cases in which the relations to be studied become especially clear (e.g., in the opinion of experts in the field) or which are particularly important for the functioning of a program to be evaluated.
- It may be appropriate to select a politically important or *sensitive case* in order to present positive findings in evaluation most effectively, which is an argument for integrating them. However, where these may endanger the program as a whole, owing to their explosive force, they should rather be excluded.
- Finally, Patton mentions the criterion of *convenience,* which refers to the selection of those cases that are the easiest to access under given conditions. This may simply be to reduce the effort. However, from time to time it may be the only way to do an evaluation with limited resources of time and people.

In the end, it depends on these strategies of selection and how you can generalize your results. In random sampling this may be greatest, whereas in the strategy of least effort, mentioned last, it will be most restricted. However, it must be noted that generalization is not in every case the goal of a qualitative study, whereas the problem of access may be one of the crucial barriers.

Correspondingly, Morse (1998, p. 73) defines several general criteria for a "good informant." These may serve more generally as criteria for selecting meaningful cases (especially for interviewees). They should have the necessary knowledge and experience of the issue or object at their disposal for answering the questions in the interview or–in observational studies–for performing the actions of interest. They should also have the capability to reflect and articulate, should have time to be asked (or observed), and should be ready to participate in the study. If all these conditions are fulfilled, this case is most likely to be integrated into the study. Integrating such cases is characterized by Morse as *primary selection*, which she contrasts with *secondary selection*. The latter refers to those cases that do not fulfil all the criteria previously mentioned (particularly of knowledge and experience), but are willing to give their time for an interview. Morse suggests that you should not invest too many resources in these cases (e.g., for transcription or interpretation). Rather, one should only work with them further if it is clear that there really are not enough cases of the primary selection to be found.

Box 11.1 summarizes the sampling strategies discussed.

Box 11.1   Sampling Strategies in Qualitative Research

- *A priori* determination
- Complete collection
- Theoretical sampling
- Extreme case sampling
- Typical case sampling
- Maximal variation sampling
- Intensity sampling
- Critical case sampling
- Sensitive case sampling
- Convenience sampling
- Primary selection
- Secondary selection

Width or Depth as Aims of Sampling

What is decisive when you choose one of the sampling strategies just outlined, and for your success in putting together the sample as a whole, is whether it is rich in relevant information. Sampling decisions always fluctuate between the aims of covering as wide a field as possible and of doing analyses, which are as deep as possible. The former strategy seeks to represent the field in its diversity by using as many different cases as possible in order to be able to present evidence on the distribution of ways of seeing or experiencing certain things. The latter strategy seeks to further permeate the field and its structure by concentrating on single examples or certain sectors of the field. Considering limited resources (people, money, time, etc.) you should see these aims as alternatives rather than projects to combine. In the example mentioned above, the decision to deal more intensively with one type of institution (sociopsychiatric services) and, owing to limited resources, not to collect or analyze any further data in the other institutions, was the result of weighing width (to study trust in counseling in as many different forms of institutions) against depth (to proceed with the analyses in one type of institution as far as possible).

Case Constitution in the Sample

In this context, the question arises of what is the case that is considered in a sample and—more concretely—what this case represents. In the studies of trust in counseling and technological change that I have already mentioned several times, I treated the *case as a case*: sampling as well as collecting and interpreting data proceeded as a sequence of case studies. For the constitution of the sample in the end, each case was representative in five respects:

- The case represents itself. According to Hildenbrand, the "single case dialectically can be understood as an individualized universal" (1987, p. 161). Thus, the single case is initially seen as the result of specific individual socialization against a general background (e.g., as physician or psychologist with a specific individual biography against the background of the changes in psychiatry and in the understanding of psychiatric disorders in the 1970s and 1980s). This also applies to the socialization of an information engineer against the background of the changes in information science and in the cultural context of each case. This socialization has led to different, subjective opinions, attitudes, and viewpoints, which can be found in the actual interview situation.
- In order to find out what the "individualized universal" here concretely means, it proved to be necessary to also conceptualize the case as follows. The case represents a specific institutional context in which the individual acts and which he or she also has to represent to others. Thus, the viewpoints in subjective theories on trust in counseling are influenced by the fact that the case (e.g., as doctor or social worker) orients his or her practices and perceptions to the goals of the institution of "sociopsychiatric services." Or he or she may even transform these viewpoints into activities with clients or statements in the interview, perhaps in critically dealing with these goals.
- The case represents a specific professionalization (as doctor, psychologist, social worker, information engineer, etc.), which he or she has attained and which is represented in his or her concepts and ways of acting. Thus, despite the

existence of teamwork and co-operation in the institution, it was possible to identify differences in the ways professionals from the same sociopsychiatric services presented clients, disorders, and starting points for treating them.

- The case represents a developed subjectivity as a result of acquiring certain stocks of knowledge and of evolving specific ways of acting and perceiving.
- The case represents an interactively made and make-able context of activity (e.g., counseling, developing technology).

Sampling decisions cannot be made in isolation. There is no decision or strategy, which is right *per se*. The appropriateness of the structure and contents of the sample, and thus the appropriateness of the strategy chosen for obtaining both, can only be assessed with respect to the research question of the study: which and how many cases are necessary to answer the questions of the study? The appropriateness of the selected sample can be assessed in terms of the degree of possible generalization, which is striven for. It may be difficult to make generally valid statements based only on a single case study. However, it is also difficult to give deep descriptions and explanations of a case, which was found by applying the principle of random sampling. Sampling strategies describe ways of disclosing a field. This can start from extreme, negative, critical, or deviant cases and thus from the extremities of the field. It may be disclosed from the inside, starting from particularly typical or developed cases. It can be tapped by starting from its supposed structure—by integrating cases as different as possible in their variation. The structure of the sample may be defined in advance and filled in through collecting data, or it may be developed and further differentiated step-by-step during selection, collection, and interpretation of material. Here, in addition, the research question and the degree of generalization one is seeking should determine the decision between defining in advance and gradually developing the sample.

The characteristics of qualitative research mentioned in Chapter 6 also apply to sampling strategies. Implicit in the selection made in sampling decisions resides a specific approach to understanding the field and the selected cases. In a different strategy of selection, the understanding would be different in its results. As sampling decisions start from integrating concrete cases, the origin of reconstructing cases is concretely realized. In sampling decisions, the reality under study is constructed in a specific way: certain parts and aspects are highlighted and others are phased out. Sampling decisions determine substantially what becomes empirical material in the form of text, and what is taken from available texts concretely and how it is used.

KEY POINTS

- In qualitative research sampling is a very important step.
- Sampling decision (who or which group next?) is often taken during and as a result of data collection and analysis.

- Sampling decisions in qualitative research are often taken on a substantial, concrete level rather than on an abstract and formal level: purposeful decisions for a specific case rather than random sampling.
- In sampling, you will constitute cases as cases and the case of your research.

Exercise 11.1

1. Take a qualitative study from the literature. Describe how the authors did their sampling, and define the rationale or plan visible in the presentation of the study.
2. Think about your own research. How would you plan your sampling? How would you proceed?
3. What are the limits of the alternatives of sampling discussed in this chapter?

FURTHER READING

The first text is the classical text about theoretical sampling. The other three texts offer recent concepts for refining this strategy.

Glaser, B.G. and Strauss, A.L. (1967) *The Discovery of Grounded Theory: Strategies for Qualitative Research.* New York: Aldine.

Merkens, H. (2004) "Selection Procedures, Sampling, Case Construction," in U. Flick, E.v. Kardorff and I. Steinke (eds), *A Companion to Qualitative Research.* London: SAGE. pp. 165–171.

Morse, J.M. (1998) "Designing Funded Qualitative Research," in N. Denzin and Y.S. Lincoln (eds), *Strategies of Qualitative Research*, London: SAGE. pp. 56–85.

Patton, M.Q. (2002) *Qualitative Research and Evaluation Methods* (3rd edn). London: SAGE.

12

HOW TO DESIGN QUALITATIVE RESEARCH: AN OVERVIEW

CHAPTER OBJECTIVES
After reading this chapter, you should be able to

✓ know the basic components that influence the construction of a research design.
✓ recognize the most important basic designs in qualitative research.
✓ understand that you can combine some of these basic designs in your own study.
✓ learn from an example how this works.

How to Plan and Construct Designs in Qualitative Research

Generally speaking, the keywords "research design" address the questions of how to plan a study. In the previous chapters, you were given information about issues of entering a field or of sampling and first of all of formulating a research question. In this chapter, I will round out this point. Further issues of designing qualitative research are: How should you set up the data collection and analysis? How should you select empirical "material" (situations, cases, persons, etc.), so that you can answer your research questions and that you can achieve this within the time available for you using the available means? Ragin (1994, p. 191) gave a comprehensive definition of research design: "Research design is a plan for collecting and analyzing evidence that will make it possible for the investigator to answer whatever questions he or she has posed. The design of an investigation touches almost all aspects of the research, from the minute details of data collection to the selection of the techniques of data analysis."

Mostly the issue of research design in qualitative research is addressed in two respects. Basic models of qualitative research designs are defined and the researcher may choose between these for his or her concrete study (e.g., Cresswell 2003). Or else the components from which a concrete research design is put together are listed and discussed (e.g., Maxwell 1996).

If you construct a concrete research design for your study, you should consider the following components:

- The goals of the study;
- The theoretical framework;
- Its concrete questions;
- The selection of empirical material;
- The methodological procedures;
- The degree of standardization and control;
- The generalization goals; and
- The temporal, personal, and material resources available.

The process of qualitative research may be described as a sequence of decisions. When you start your research and to propel your project, you can make a choice between a number of alternatives at various points in the process–from questions to data collection and analysis and ultimately to presentation of results. In these decisions, you will set up the design of your study in a dual sense. A design you planned in advance is translated into concrete procedures or else, while in process, the design is constituted and modified by virtue of the decisions in favor of particular alternatives.

Goals of the Study

You can use a qualitative study to pursue a number of different goals. The approach of grounded theory development in accordance with the model of Glaser and Strauss (1967; see Chapter 8) gives often a general orientation. In this context, I suggest bearing in mind that the requirement of theory development is an excessive burden for many types of qualitative studies. In a graduation thesis with a very limited time budget, this goal can be as unrealistic as it is incompatible with the intentions of many of those who commission qualitative research projects. Here what is required are detailed descriptions or evaluations of current practice. In the case of a stage that seeks to provide an exact description of sequences of events in institutional or everyday practice, some of the methodological tools of Glaser and Strauss (e.g., theoretical sampling) may be applied, but do not necessarily have to be. There are different types of objectives for qualitative studies you can pursue: description, sometimes testing of hypotheses, theory-development. At the level of objectives, Maxwell (1996: 16) makes a further distinction. He distinguishes between studies that pursue primarily personal goals (e.g., a graduation thesis or dissertation), those that pursue practical goals (discovering if and how a particular program or product functions) and those that pursue research goals (and are more concerned with developing general knowledge of a particular subject).

Formulation of the Research Questions

The research question of a qualitative investigation is one of the decisive factors in its success or failure, as you should already know from Chapter 9. The way in which they are formulated exerts a strong influence on the design of the study. Questions must be formulated as clearly and unambiguously as possible, and this must happen as early as possible in the life of the project. In the course of the project, however, questions become more and more concrete, more focused, and they are also narrowed and revised. Maxwell (1996: 49) holds a different viewpoint and sees that questions should be less the starting point but the result of the formulation of a research design. Consequently, questions may be viewed or classified according to the extent to which they are suited to the confirmation of existing assumptions (for instance in the sense of hypotheses) or whether they aim at new discoveries or permit this.

Research questions may be kept too broad, which means that they would provide almost no guidance in the planning and implementation of a study. But they may also be kept too narrow and thereby miss the target of investigation or block rather than promote new discoveries. Questions should be formulated in such a way that (in the context of the planned study and using the available resources) they are capable of being answered. Maxwell (1996), with an eye on research design, distinguishes between generalizing and particularizing questions, together with questions that focus on distinctions, and those that focus on the description of processes.

Goals of Generalization and Representation

If you set up a research design, I would advise you taking into account what your goals of generalization are in your study. Is your goal of detailed analysis with as many facets as possible, or is it a comparison or a typology of different cases, situations, and individuals, and so on? In comparative studies, the question of the principal dimensions, according to which particular phenomena are to be compared arises. If your study is restricted to one or very few comparative dimensions based on some theory or on the research questions, this will avoid the possible compulsion to consider all possible dimensions and include cases from a large number of groups and contexts. In my experience, it is important to check critically the extent to which classic demographic dimensions need to be considered in every study. Do the phenomenon being studied and the research question really require a comparison according to gender, age, town or country, east or west, and so on? If you have to consider all these dimensions, then you have to include a number of cases for each of the manifestations. Then very soon you will need such a large number of cases that you can no longer handle them within a project that is limited in time and personnel. Therefore, in my experience it is preferable to clarify which of these dimensions is the decisive one for your study. Studies with a sensibly limited claim to generalization are not only easier to manage but also, as a rule, more meaningful.

In qualitative research, a distinction must be made between numerical and theoretical generalization. A very small number of projects claim either to want or to be able to draw conclusions from the cases investigated about a particular population. What is more informative is the question of the theoretical generalization of the results. Here the number of individuals or situations studied is less decisive than the differences between cases involved (maximal variation) or the theoretical scope of the case interpretations. To increase the theoretical generalization, the use of different methods (triangulation) for the investigation of a small number of cases is often more informative than the use of one method for the largest possible number of cases. If you intend to develop a typology, for example, it is necessary not only to use the target selection of cases, but also to include counterexamples and to undertake case contrasts in addition to case comparisons.

Finally, you should consider what presentation goals you have with a qualitative study: Is your empirical material the basis for the writing of an essay or rather for a narrative presentation that would give it more of an illustrative function? Or is it a matter of providing a systematization of the variation found in the cases investigated?

Degree of Standardization and Control

Miles and Huberman (1994, pp. 16–18) distinguish between tight and loose research design. They see indications for both variations in concrete cases according to the research question and conditions. Narrowly restricted questions and strictly determined selection procedures determine tight research designs. The degree of openness in the field of investigation and the empirical material remains relatively limited. The authors see these designs as appropriate when researchers lack experience of qualitative research, when the research operates on the basis of narrowly defined constructs, and when it is restricted to the investigation of particular relationships in familiar contexts. In such cases, they see loose designs as a roundabout route to the desired result. Tighter designs make it easier to decide what data or data extractions are relevant and irrelevant to the investigation, and they also make it easier, for example, to compare and summarize data from different interviews or observations.

Loose designs are characterized by somewhat broadly defined concepts and have, in the first instance, little in the way of fixed methodological procedures.

Miles and Huberman see this type of design as appropriate when a large measure of experience is available of research in different fields, when new fields are being investigated and the theoretical constructs and concepts are relatively undeveloped. This second variant is clearly oriented to the methodological suggestions of Glaser and Strauss (1967) that are characterized, for example, in their handling of theoretical sampling by great openness and flexibility.

Even though qualitative research often sees itself as indebted to the principle of openness, I think it is sensible for many questions and projects to consider what degree of control is necessary. To what extent must there be constancy in the contextual conditions in which the comparative differences between two groups are manifested (see above)? What degree of control or comparability should be provided in conditions under which the various interviews in a study are carried out?

Selection: Sampling and Formation of Groups for Comparison

Selection decisions in qualitative research focus on persons or situations, from which data is collected, and on extracts from the material collected, from which novel interpretations are made or results are presented as examples. This theoretical sampling is considered the royal way for qualitative studies. Frequently, however, other selection strategies are more appropriate if the goal is not to develop a theory but rather the evaluation of institutional practice.

One essential component of the decision about data selection (in comparative investigations) is the formation of groups for comparison. Here you should clarify at what level the comparisons are to be made: between individuals, situations, institutions, or phenomena? Accordingly, the selection should be made in such as way that several cases are always included in a single group for comparison.

Resources

One factor is frequently undervalued in the development of a research design. The available resources like time, personnel, technical support, competencies, experience, and so on are very important factors. Research proposals are frequently based on an unrealistic relationship between the planned tasks and the personnel resources (realistically) requested. For realistic project planning, I advise making a calculation of the activities involved which assumes, for example, that an interview of around 90 minutes will need as much time again for locating interview partners, organizing appointments, and travel. With regard to the calculation of time for transcribing interviews, the estimates will diverge depending on the precision of the system of transcription in place. Morse (1998, pp. 81–82) suggests that for fast-writing transcribers, the length of the tape containing the interview recording be multiplied by a factor of four. If checking the finished transcript against the tape is also included, the length of the tape should be multiplied by a total of six. For the complete calculation of the project she advises doubling the time allowed for unforeseen difficulties and "catastrophes." If you plan a project that will work with transcribed interviews, you should use a high quality tape recorder for the recordings. A special player with a foot-operated switch is essential for transcription. Marshall and Rossman (1995, pp. 123–125) offer sample plans of how to calculate the time parameters of empirical projects. The time you will need for data interpretation is difficult to calculate. If you decide to use computers and programs such as ATLAS•ti and NUDIST (see Chapter 24) for data interpretation, then you have to include sufficient time for technical preparation (installation, removal of errors, induction of team members in the use of the program, and so on) in your project plan. In the process of approving a project, the equipment asked for is sometimes reduced and additional methodological stages, such as an additional group for comparison or phase of data collection may be required. At this stage, if not before, it becomes essential that you check the relationship between tasks and resources, and you should consider short-cut strategies in the methodological procedures, if necessary.

Short-cut strategies

Many of the qualitative methods in current use are connected with a high degree of precision and an equally high investment of time. In data collection, I mention the narrative interview (see Chapter 14). Transcription (see Chapter 22) and interpretation (e.g., the procedures of objective hermeneutics and theoretical coding) both require a great deal of time (see Chapter 24 and 25). In externally funded projects and commissioned research, but also in graduation theses, this need for time is often confronted with a very tight deadline within which the research questions have to be answered. "Short-cut strategies" refers to (justifiable) deviations from the maximum requirements of precision and completeness of such methods. For instance, for interviews with experts, you will have to consider that your interviewees will be under considerable pressure for time and you should take that into account when planning your interview. Sometimes (see Strauss 1987, p. 266) it is suggested that only parts of interviews should be transcribed, and only as precisely as is actually required by the questions of the particular investigation. The non-transcribed sections of interviews can be kept within the research process, for instance by means of summaries or lists of topics to be transcribed if necessary. Open coding (see Chapter 21) often leads to an excessive quantity of codes or categories. It has often proved useful to draw up lists of priorities related to the research questions that make it possible to select and reduce the categories. The same may be said of the selection of textual contexts, based on the research question, which are required to undergo a process of intensive interpretation.

Research designs may ultimately be described as the means of achieving the goals of the research. They link theoretical frameworks, questions, research,

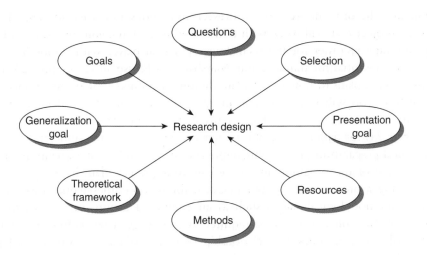

Figure 12.1   Components of Qualitative Research Design

generalization, and presentational goals with the methods used and resources available under the focus of goal achievement. Their realization is the result of decisions reached in the research process. Figure 12.1 summarizes again the influential factors and decisions, which determine the concrete formulation of the research design.

Basic Designs in Qualitative Research

You can distinguish the following basic designs in qualitative research (cf. also Cresswell 1998):

- Case studies;
- Comparative studies;
- Retrospective studies;
- Snapshots: analyses of state and process at the time of the research; and
- Longitudinal studies.

Case Studies

The aim of case studies is the precise description or reconstruction of a case (for more detail cf. Ragin and Becker 1992). The term "case" is rather broadly understood here. You can take persons, social communities (e.g., families), organizations, and institutions (e.g., a nursing home) as the subject of a case analysis. Your main problem then will be to identify a case that would be significant for your research question and to clarify what else belongs to the case and what methodological approaches its reconstruction requires. If your case study is concerned with school problems of a child you have to clarify, for instance, whether it is enough to observe the child in the school environment. Or do you need to interview the teachers and/or fellow pupils? To what extent should the family and its everyday life be observed as part of the analysis? Finally, you should clarify what this case represents (see Chapter 11).

Comparative Studies

In a comparative study, you will not observe the case as a whole and in its complexity, but rather a multiplicity of cases with regard to particular excerpts. For example, you might compare the specific content of the expert knowledge of a number of people or biographies in respect of a concrete experience of illness and the subsequent course of life are compared with each other. Here arises the question about the selection of cases in the groups to be compared. A further problem is what degree of standardization or constancy you need in the remaining conditions that are not the subject of the comparison. To be able to show cultural differences in the views of health among Portuguese and German women, we selected interview partners from both cultures. They had to live in as many respects as possible (big city life, comparable professions, income and level of education) under at least very similar conditions in order to be able to relate differences to the comparative dimension of "culture" (cf. Flick 2000b).

So we see the dimension of single case–comparative study as one axis according to which we can classify the basic design of qualitative research. An interim stage consists of the interrelation of a number of case analyses, which can initially be carried out as such and then compared or contrasted with each other. A second axis for categorizing qualitative design follows the dimension of time, from retrospective analyses to snapshots and then to longitudinal studies.

Snapshots: Analysis of State and Process at the Time of the Investigation

A major part of qualitative research focuses on snapshots. For example, you might collect different manifestations of the expertise, which exists in a particular field at the time of the research in interviews and compare them to one another. Even if certain examples from earlier periods of time affect the interviews, your research does not aim primarily at the retrospective reconstruction of a process. It is concerned rather with giving a description of circumstances at the time of the research.

A range of process-oriented procedures are also strongly related to the present and are therefore not interested in the reconstruction of past events from the point of view of (any of) them but in the course of currents from a parallel temporal perspective. In ethnographic studies, researchers participate in the development of some event over an extended period in order to record and analyze this in parallel to its actual occurrence. In conversation analyses (see Chapter 24), a conversation is recorded and then analyzed in terms of its sequencing, while in objective hermeneutics (see Chapter 25) a protocol is interpreted in a strictly sequential manner "from beginning to end."

In these approaches from the design point of view, there arises the question of how to limit the empirical material: how can your selection guarantee that the phenomenon that is relevant to the research question actually comes up in empirically documented extracts from conversations and processes? Where should the beginning and end (of a conversation or observation) be located? According to what criteria should you select and contrast material for comparison—what conversations or conversational extracts and what observational protocols should you compare exactly?

Retrospective Studies

The principle of case reconstruction is characteristic of a great number of biographical investigations that operate with a series of case analyses in a comparative, typologizing, or contrastive manner. Biographical research is an example of a retrospective research design in which retrospectively from the point in time when the research is carried out, certain events and processes are analyzed in respect of their meaning for individual or collective life histories. Design questions in relation to retrospective research involve the selection of informants who will be meaningful for the process to be investigated. They also involve defining appropriate groups for comparison, justifying the boundaries of the time to be investigated, checking the research question, deciding which (historical) sources, and documents should be used in addition to interviews. Another issue is how to consider the influences of present views on the perception and evaluation of earlier experiences.

Longitudinal Studies

The final variant of a basic design in qualitative research consists of longitudinal studies, in which you analyze an interesting process or state again at later times of data collection. This strategy has rarely been used, at least explicitly, in qualitative research. In most qualitative methods, you will find little guidance on how they could be applied in longitudinal studies with several periods of data collection. Implicitly a longitudinal perspective within a temporally limited framework is realized in ethnography by virtue of the researchers' extended participation in the field of study, and also—with a retrospective focus—in biographical research, which considers an extended section of a life history. The great strength of a longitudinal study—of being able to document changes of view or action through repeated collection cycles, where the initial state of a process of change can be recorded without any influence from its final state—cannot therefore be fully realized.

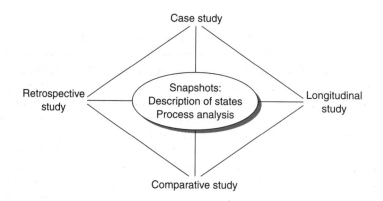

Figure 12.2 Basic Designs in Qualitative Research

Figure 12.2 arranges the basic designs in qualitative research that we have discussed according to the two dimensions time and comparison.

Case Study: Health Concepts of Women in Portugal and Germany

In this project, we were interested in whether the representation of health and illness is a cultural phenomenon or not. To answer this question, we tried to show cultural differences in the views of health among Portuguese and German women. Therefore, we selected interview partners from both cultures. To be able to trace differences in the interviewees' health concepts, we kept as many other conditions in the case as constant as possible. Therefore, the women we included in the study had to live in as many respects as possible (big city life, professions, income and education) under at least very similar conditions in order to be able to relate differences to the comparative dimension of "culture" (cf. Flick 2000b). The study was planned as an exploratory study, so that we could limit the number of cases in each subgroup. The design of the study was a comparative design–two groups of women were compared for a specific feature, their health and illness concepts. In the planning of the interviews, we kept a focus on the development of the current health and illness concept in the interviewees' biographies. Therefore, the study was a retrospective study, too. We found different core concepts in the representations of health, which focus on culture-specific topics. The central phenomenon, which reappeared in the interview with Portuguese women again and again, is "lack of awareness" (in Portuguese: "*falta de cuidado*"). This term is difficult to translate into other languages but means "not to take care of one self, not to be cautious for oneself." It seems to be a general problem in Portugal that people do not care for themselves and was named by different interviewees as the main source of illness. For the women we interviewed, Portuguese people "let things simply run." They know that there are things they should do for their health (eating, little stress, sport, prevention), but they see themselves as not having enough initiative.

(Continued)

(Continued)

So many interviewees attribute this lack of awareness to themselves or to the people in Portugal in general. But they also mentioned many reasons for this lack of awareness as coming from the Portuguese health system. One interviewee says: "Who depends on the public health system might die in the meantime." Waiting two or three months for an appointment with the doctor, waiting years for operations and five to six hours at the health center despite a fixed appointment are seen as quite normal.

In the German interviews, the central phenomenon was the feeling of being "forced to health." Interviewees linked it to their feeling that they have to be healthy. They see how the society and the media make ill people outsiders rather than integrating them in society. The interviewees repeatedly stressed the importance of sport and healthy eating for their health. The knowledge mediated to them has become anchored in their social representations. The women did not only link negative impressions to "being forced to health," but also positive ones. The information offered by media and health insurance was also evaluated positively. The women feel informed and have developed a critical awareness towards traditional medicine. Rules of when and how often certain forms of prevention should be used were experienced as a relief.

What you can see in this brief case study is how to create a comparative, retrospective design by keeping other dimensions constant in order to analyze differences on one dimension. This was only an explanatory study indeed, but it does show this special aspect of how to plan such a study.

These designs are discussed as the basic designs in qualitative research, and I group them here along two dimensions. In research practice, you will often find combinations of these basic designs (e.g., a case study with a retrospective focus or a comparative, longitudinal study).

KEY POINTS

- Designing a qualitative study is the result of a series of decisions.
- It is not only the knowledge interest of a study, but also the context conditions that influence the shaping of a study, such as resources, aims, and expectations from others and the like.
- You can find a list of basic designs in qualitative research.
- Design in qualitative research has a lot to do with planning research. It has less to do with control than in quantitative research, but of course, this plays a role here, too.

Exercise 12.1

1. Select a qualitative study from the literature, and describe the design the study is based on.
2. Think about the components of the design of your own study, and plan your research with this background.

FURTHER READING

These three texts address the issue of research design in qualitative research in a systematic way.

Creswell, J.W. (2003) *Research Design – Qualitative, Quantitative, and Mixed Methods Approaches*. Thousand Oaks, London, New Delhi: SAGE.

Marshall, C. and Rossman, G.B. (1995) *Designing Qualitative Research* (2nd edn). Thousand Oaks, London, New Delhi: SAGE.

Maxwell, J.A. (1996) *Qualitative Research Design – An Interactive Approach*. Thousand Oaks, London, New Delhi: SAGE.

PART 4

VERBAL DATA

Part 4 will introduce you to the variety of methods that are used to collect data, mainly focusing on the spoken word. Here you will find three basic strategies. You can use interviews based on questions, and the answers that are elicited by them. This approach is outlined in more detail in Chapter 13. Alternatively, you can use people's stories as collectable data for your research. Using narratives is embedded again in special forms of interviews, which are based on making the interviewees tell the story of their lives–in the narrative interview–or of more specific situations with the issue that you want to study. These narrative methods are described in Chapter 14. The third alternative is not to interview a single person, but to collect data from groups by making them discuss the issue you want to study in your research. Here you can use group discussions and the more trendy approach of focus groups. A similar strategy is to make a group, say a family, tell its joint story (joint narratives). These group oriented strategies are outlined in Chapter 15. The final chapter in this part summarizes and compares the three approaches to collecting verbal data.

13

INTERVIEWS

CHAPTER OBJECTIVES

After reading this chapter, you should be able to

✓ **understand the various types of interviews.**
✓ **acknowledge the principles and pitfalls of interviewing.**
✓ **construct an interview guide.**
✓ **select the appropriate interview technique among the different versions.**

In the United States and particularly in earlier periods of qualitative research, methodological discussion has revolved for a long time around observation as the main method for collecting data. Open interviews are more dominant in the German-speaking areas (e.g., Hopf 2004a) and now attract more attention in the Anglo-Saxon areas as well (see e.g., Gubrium and Holstein 2001). Semi-structured interviews, in particular, have attracted interest and are widely used. This interest is linked to the expectation that the interviewed subjects' viewpoints are more likely to be expressed in an openly designed interview situation than in a standardized interview or a questionnaire. Several types of interviews can be distinguished. Some of them I will present and discuss here both in terms of their own logic and also in terms of their contribution to further developing the interview as a method in general.

The Focused Interview

Robert Merton was one of the most influential sociologists in the United States. He has worked over a long period in fields like media research. He and his colleagues (Merton and Kendall 1946) developed the focused interview in the 1940s. I will describe this method in some detail, as you can learn from Merton and Kendall quite a lot about how to plan and conduct interviews in qualitative research.

In the focused interview, you proceed as follows: After a uniform stimulus (a film, a radio broadcast, etc.) is presented, its impact on the interviewee is studied using an interview guide. The original aim of the interview was to provide a basis for interpreting statistically significant findings (from a parallel or later quantified study) on the impact of media in mass communication. The stimulus presented is content analyzed beforehand. This enables a distinction to be made between the "objective" facts of the situation and the interviewees' subjective definitions of the situation with a view to comparing them.

During the design of the interview guide and the conducting of the interview itself, use the following four criteria: non-direction, specificity, range, and the depth and personal context shown by the interviewee. The different elements of the method will serve to meet these criteria.

What are the Elements of the Focused Interview?

Non-direction is achieved by using several forms of questions.[1] The first is unstructured questions (e.g., "What impressed you most in this film?"). In the second form, semi-structured questions, either the concrete issue (e.g., a certain scene in a film) is defined and the response is left open (e.g., "How did you feel about the part describing Jo's discharge from the army as a psychoneurotic?"). Or, the reaction is defined and the concrete issue is left open (e.g., "What did you learn from this pamphlet which you hadn't known before?"). In the third form of questioning, structured questions, both are defined (e.g., "As you listened to Chamberlain's speech, did you feel it was propagandistic or informative?"). You should ask unstructured questions first and introduce increased structuring only later during the interview to prevent the interviewer's frame of reference being imposed on the interviewee's viewpoints (Box 13.1). In this respect, Merton and Kendall call for the flexible use of the interview schedule. The interviewer should refrain as far as possible from making early evaluations and should perform a non-directive style of conversation. Problems may arise if questions are asked at the wrong moment and interviewees are thus prevented from rather than supported in presenting their views, or if the wrong type of question is used at the wrong time.

The criterion of *specificity* means that the interview should bring out the specific elements, which determine the impact or meaning of an event for the

---

Box 13.1   Example Questions from the Focused Interview

- What impressed you most in this film?
- How did you feel about the part describing Jo's discharge from the army as a psychoneurotic?
- What did you learn from this pamphlet, which you hadn't known before?
- Judging from the film, do you think that the German fighting equipment was better, as good as, or poorer than the equipment used by the Americans?
- Now that you think back, what were your reactions to that part of the film?
- As you listened to Chamberlain's speech, did you feel it was propagandistic or informative?

Source: Merton and Kendall 1946

interviewees in order to prevent the interview from remaining on the level of general statements. For this purpose, the most appropriate forms of questions are those that handicap the interviewee as little as possible. To increase specificity, you should encourage *retrospective inspection*. You can support the interviewees in recalling a specific situation by using materials (e.g., an excerpt of a text, a picture) and corresponding questions ("Now that you think back, what were your reactions to that part of the film?"). Alternatively, you may achieve this criterion by "explicit reference to the stimulus situation" (e.g., "Was there anything in the film that gave you that impression?"). As a general rule, Merton and Kendall suggest that "specifying questions should be explicit enough to aid the subject in relating his responses to determinate aspects of the stimulus situation and yet general enough to avoid having the interviewer structure it" (1946, p. 552).

The criterion of *range* aims at securing that all aspects and topics relevant to the research question are mentioned during the interview. The interviewees must be given the chance to introduce new topics of their own in the interview. The interviewer's double task is mentioned here at the same time: step-by-step to cover the topical range (contained in the interview guide) by introducing new topics or initiating changes in the topic. This means as well that they should lead back to topics that have already been mentioned but not detailed deeply enough, especially if they have the impression that the interviewee led the conversation away from a topic in order to avoid it. Here interviewers should reintroduce the earlier topic again with "reversional transitions" (1946, p. 553). However, in realizing this criterion, Merton and Kendall see the danger of "confusing range with superficiality" (1946, p. 554). To what extent this becomes a problem depends on the way the interviewers introduce the topical range of the interview guide and whether they become too dependent on the interview guide. Therefore, interviewers should only mention topics if they really want to ensure that they are treated in detail.

Depth and *personal context* shown by the interviewees mean that the interviewers should ensure that emotional responses in the interview go beyond simple assessments like "pleasant" or "unpleasant." The goal is rather "a maximum of self-revelatory comments concerning how the stimulus material was experienced" by the interviewee (1946, pp. 554–555). A concrete task for interviewers resulting from this goal is to continuously diagnose the current level of depth in order to "shift that level toward whichever end of the 'depth continuum' he finds appropriate to the given case." Strategies for raising the degree of depth are for example to "focus on feelings," "restatement of implied or expressed feelings," and "referring to comparative situations." Here reference to the nondirective style of conducting a conversation can also be seen.

The application of this method in other fields of research is mainly oriented to the general principles of the method. Focusing in the interview is understood as related to the topic of study rather than to the use of stimuli such as films.

Case Study: Persons' Concepts of Human Nature

Based on Merton and Kendall's method, cultural psychologist Rolf Oerter (1995; see also Oerter et al. 1996, pp. 43–47) developed the "adulthood interview" for studying concepts of human nature and adulthood in different cultures (United States, West Germany, Indonesia, Japan and Korea) (Box 13.2).

The interview is divided into four main parts. In the first part, general questions about adulthood are asked; for example, what should an adult look like, what is appropriate for adulthood. The second part deals with the three main roles of adulthood: the family, occupational, and political. The third part draws attention to the past of the interviewee, asking for developmental changes during the previous two or three years. The last part of the interview deals with the near future of the interviewee, asking for his or her goals in life and his or her further development (1995, p. 213).

> The interviewee is then confronted with dilemma stories, which are followed again by a focused interview: The subject is asked to describe the situation [in the story] and to find a solution. The interviewer is asking questions and tries to reach the highest possible level the subject can achieve. Again, the interviewer must be trained in understanding and assessing the actual level of the individual in order to ask questions at the level proximal to the individual's point of view. (1995, p. 213)

In order to focus the interview more on the subject's point of view, the interview guide includes "general suggestions" like "Please encourage the subject as often as necessary: Can you explain this in more detail? What do you mean by . . .?" (Oerter et al. 1996, pp. 43–47). This is a good example of how the focused interview was taken as a starting point for developing a form of interview, which is tailor-made for a specific issue of research.

Box 13.2   Example Questions from the Adulthood Interview

---

1   *General Questions about Adulthood*

    (a)   How should an adult behave? Which abilities/capabilities should he or she have? What is your idea of an adult?

    (b)   How would you define real adults? How do real adults differ from ideal adults? Why are they as they are?

    (c)   Can the differences between the ideal and the real adult (between how an adult should behave and how an adult actually does behave) be narrowed down? How? (If the answer is "no," then why not?)

    (d)   Many people consider responsibility to be an important criterion of adulthood. What does responsibility mean to you?

    (e)   Striving for happiness (being happy) is often viewed as the most important goal for human beings. Do you agree? What is happiness, and what is being happy in your opinion?

    (f)   What is the meaning of life in your opinion? Why are we alive?

2   *Further Explanations about the Three Leading Roles of an Adult*

    (a)   Conceptions about one's professional role
        What do you think you need to get a job?
        Are work and a job really necessary? Are they part of being an adult or not?

    (b)   Conceptions about one's future family
        Should an adult have a family of his or her own?
        How should he or she behave in his or her family? How far should he or she be involved in it?

    (c)   Political role
        What about an adult's political role? Does he or she have political tasks? Would he or she engage in political activities?
        Should he or she care about public affairs? Should he or she take on responsibilities for the community?

Source: Oerter et al. 1996, pp. 43–47

What are the Problems in Conducting the Interview?

The criteria Merton and Kendall (1946) suggest for conducting the interview incorporate some targets, which cannot be matched in every situation (e.g., specificity and depth versus range). Fulfilling these criteria cannot be realized in advance (e.g., in designing the interview guide). How far they are really met in an actual interview depends to a great extent on the actual interview situation and how it goes off. These criteria highlight the decisions that the interviewers have to make and the necessary priorities they have to establish *ad hoc* in the interview situation. They also mention there is no "right" behavior for the interviewer in the focused (or any other semi-structured) interview. The successful carrying out of such interviews depends essentially on the interviewer's situational competence. This competence may be increased by practical experience of making decisions necessary in interview situations, in rehearsal interviews, and in interview training. In such training, interview situations are simulated and analyzed afterwards with a view to providing trainee interviewers with some experience. Some examples are given of typical needs for decisions between more depth (obtained by probing) and guaranteeing the range (by introducing new topics or the next question of the interview guide) and with the different solutions at each point. This makes the dilemmas of contradictory targets easier to handle, although they cannot be completely resolved.

What is the Contribution to the General Methodological Discussion?

The four criteria and the problems linked to them can be applied to other types of interviews without using an advance stimulus and pursuing other research questions. They have become general criteria for designing and conducting interviews and a starting point for describing dilemmas in this method (e.g., in Hopf 2004a). Altogether, the concrete suggestions Merton and Kendall made for realizing the criteria and for formulating questions may be used as an orientation for conceptualizing and conducting interviews more generally. To focus on a specific object and its meaning as far as possible has become a general aim of interviews. The same is the case for the strategies Merton and Kendall have suggested for realizing these aims– mainly to give the interviewees as much scope as possible to introduce their views.

How is the Method Fitting into the Research Process?

With this method, you can study subjective viewpoints in different social groups. The aim may be to generate hypotheses for later quantitative studies, but also the deeper interpretation of experimental findings. The groups investigated are normally defined in advance and the research process is linear in design (see Chapter 11). Research questions focus on the impact of concrete events or the subjective handling of the conditions of one's own activities. Interpretation is not fixed to a specific method. But coding procedures (see Chapter 23) seem to be most appropriate.

What are Limitations of the Method?

The specific feature of the focused interview–the use of a stimulus like a film in the interview–is a variation of the standard situation of the semi-structured interview, which is hardly ever used but which nevertheless gives rise to some specific problems that need consideration. Merton and Kendall are concerned less with how interviewees perceive and assess the concrete material and more with general relations in the reception of filmed material. In this context, they are interested in subjective views on concrete material. It may be doubted that they obtain the "objective facts of the case" (1946, p. 541) by analyzing this material that can be distinguished from the "subjective definitions of the situation." However, they receive a second version of the object in this way. They can relate subjective views of the single interviewee as well as the range of perspectives of the different interviewees to this second version. Furthermore, they have a basis for answering questions like, which elements of the interviewee's presentations have a counterpart in the result of the content analysis of the film. Which parts have been left out on his or her side, although they are in the film according to the content analysis? Which topics has the interviewee introduced or added?

A further problem with this method is that it is hardly ever used in its pure and complete form. Its current relevance is defined rather by its impetus for conceptualizing and conducting other forms of interviews, which have been developed from it and are often used. Furthermore, the suggestion to combine open interviews with other methodological approaches to the object under study may be noted. These might provide a point of reference for interpreting subjective viewpoints in the interview. This idea is discussed more generally under the headline of "triangulation" (see Chapter 29).

The Semi-Standardized Interview

In their method for reconstructing subjective theories, Scheele and Groeben (1988) suggest a specific elaboration of the semi-structured interview (see also Groeben 1990). Brigitte Scheele and Norbert Groeben are psychologists, who have developed the approach of studying subjective theories as a special model for studying everyday knowledge. They developed their approach in the 1980s and 1990s to study subjective theories in fields like school and other areas of professional work. I have chosen this method here, because it is a special form of developing the method of interviewing quite a bit further and it might be interesting for designing other forms of interviews. The term "subjective theory" refers to the fact that the interviewees have a complex stock of knowledge about the topic under study. For example, people have a subjective theory of cancer—what is cancer, what are different types of cancer, why they think people fall ill with cancer, what the possible consequences of cancer will be, how it might be treated, and so on. This knowledge includes assumptions that are explicit and immediate and which interviewees can express spontaneously in answering an open question. These are complemented by implicit assumptions. In order to articulate these, the interviewees must be supported by methodological aids, which is why different types of questions (see below) are applied here. They are used to reconstruct the interviewee's subjective theory about the issue under study (e.g., the subjective theories of trust used by counselors in activities with their clients). The actual interview is complemented by a graphic representation technique called the "structure laying technique." By applying it together with the interviewees, their statements from the preceding interview are turned into a structure. Also, this allows their communicative validation (i.e., the interviewee's consent to these statements is obtained).

What are the Elements of the Semi-Standardized Interview?

During the interviews, the contents of the subjective theory are reconstructed. The interview guide mentions several topical areas. Each of these is introduced by an open question and ended by a confrontational question. The following examples come from my study about subjective theories of trust held by professionals in the health system. *Open questions* ("what do you think, and why are people in general ready to trust each other?") may be answered on the basis of the knowledge that the interviewee has immediately at hand.

Additionally, *theory-driven, hypotheses-directed questions* are asked. These are oriented to the scientific literature about the topic or are based on the researcher's theoretical presuppositions ("Is trust possible among strangers, or do the people involved have to know each other?"). In the interview, the relations formulated in these questions serve the purpose of making the interviewees' implicit knowledge more explicit. The assumptions in these questions are

---

Box 13.3   Example Questions from the Semi-Standardized Interview

- Briefly, could you please tell me what you relate to the term "trust" if you think of your professional practice?
- Could you tell me what are the essential and the decisive features of trust between client and counselor?
- There is a proverb: "Trust is good, control is better." If you think of your work and relations to clients, is this your attitude when you approach them?
- Can counselors and clients reach their goals without trusting each other?
- Will they be ready to trust each other without a minimum of control?
- How do people that are ready to trust differ from people who are not willing to trust?
- Are there people who are more easily trusted than others? How do those trustworthy people differ from the others?
- Are there activities in your work, which you can practice without trust between you and your client?
- If you think of the institution you work in, what are the factors, which facilitate the development of trust between you and your clients? What are the factors that make it more difficult?
- Does the way people come to your institution influence the development of trust?
- Do you feel more responsible for a client if you see that he or she trusts you?

designed as an offer to the interviewees, which they might take up or refuse according to whether they correspond to their subjective theories or not.

The third type of questions–*confrontational questions*– respond to the theories and relations the interviewee has presented up to that point in order to critically re-examine these notions in the light of competing alternatives. It is stressed that these alternatives have to stand in "real thematic opposition" to the interviewee's statements in order to avoid the possibility of their integration into the interviewee's subjective theory. Therefore, the interview guide includes several alternative versions of such confrontational questions. Which one is used concretely depends on the view of the issue developed in the interview up to that point.

Conducting the interview here is characterized by introducing topical areas and by the purposive formulation of questions based on scientific theories on the topic (in the hypotheses-directed questions) (Box 13.3).

The Structure Laying Technique (SLT)

In a second meeting with the interviewee, no more than one or two weeks after the first interview, the structure laying technique (SLT) is applied. In the meantime, the interview just outlined has been transcribed and roughly content analyzed. In the second meeting, the interviewee's essential statements are presented to him or her as concepts on small cards for two purposes. The first is to assess the contents: the interviewees are asked to recall the interview and check if its contents are correctly represented on the cards. If this is not the case, they may reformulate, eliminate, and/or replace statements with other more appropriate statements. This assessment regarding the contents (i.e., the communicative validation of the statements by the interviewees) is finished for the moment. The second purpose is to structure the remaining concepts in a form similar to scientific theories by applying the SLT rules. For this purpose, the interviewees are given a short paper introducing the SLT, in order to familiarize them with the rules for applying it and–as far as necessary and possible–with the way of thinking it is based on. Also, given in the paper is a set of examples. Figure 13.1 shows an excerpt from an example of applying the technique and some of the possible rules for representing causal relations among concepts, such as "A is a precondition for B" or "C is a promoting condition of D."

The result of such a structuring process using the SLT is a graphic representation of a subjective theory. At the end, the interviewee compares his or her structure with the version the interviewer has prepared between the two meetings. This comparison–similar to the confrontational questions–serves the purpose of making the interviewee reflect again on his or her views in the light of competing alternatives.

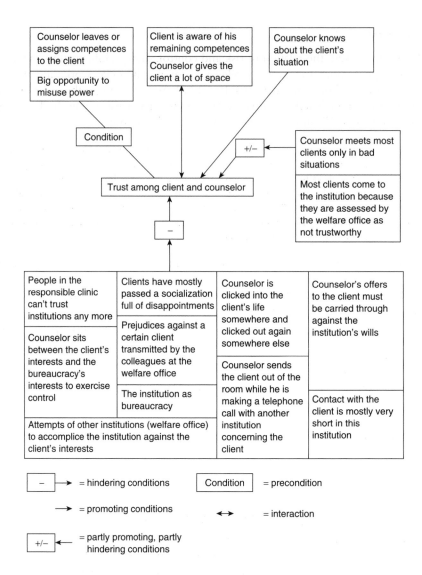

FIGURE 13.1   Excerpt from a Subjective Theory on Trust in Counseling

Case Study: Subjective Theories on Trust in Counseling

In my study of trust in counseling, I used this method to interview fifteen counselors with different professional backgrounds (e.g., psychologists, social workers, and physicians). The interview schedule included topics like the

(Continued)

(Continued)

definition of trust, the relation of risk and control, strategy, information and preceding knowledge, reasons for trust, its relevance for psychosocial work, and institutional framework conditions and trust (see Box 13.3). As a response to the question– "Could you please tell me briefly what you relate to the term 'trust,' if you think of your professional practice?"–an inter viewee gave as her definition:

> If I think of my professional practice–well . . . very many people ask me at the beginning whether they can trust me in the relationship, and–because I am a representing a public agency–whether I really keep confidential what they will be telling me. Trust for me is to say at this point quite honestly how I might handle this, that I can keep it all confidential up to a certain point, but if they tell me any jeopardizing facts that I have difficulties with then I will tell them at that point. Well, this is trust for me: to be frank about this and the point of the oath of secrecy, that actually is the main point.

The interviews showed how subjective theories consisted of stocks of knowledge in store for identifying different types of opening a counseling situation, target representations of ideal types of counseling situations and their conditions, and ideas of how at least to approximately produce such conditions in the current situation. Analyzing counseling activities showed how counselors act according to these stocks of knowledge and use them for coping with current and new situations.

This study showed the content and the structure of the individual subjective theories and differences in the subjective theories of counselors working in the same field but coming from different professional backgrounds. The structuration of the questions as part of the interview guide and coming from using the SLT later on allowed the context of single statements to be shown.

What are the Problems in Applying the Method?

The main problem in both parts of the method is how far the interviewers manage to make the procedure plausible to interviewees and deal with irritations, which may be caused by confrontational questions. If you carefully introduce alternative viewpoints (e.g., "One could perhaps see the problem you just mentioned in the following way: . . .") this could be a way of handling such annoyances. The rules of the SLT and the way of thinking they are based on can produce irritations, because it is not always standard procedure for people to put concepts into formalized relations in order to visualize their interconnections. Therefore, I suggest that you make clear to the interviewee that applying the SLT and its rules by no means should be understood as a performance test, but that they should rather be used playfully. After initial inhibitions have been overcome, in most cases it is possible to produce in the interviewee the necessary confidence in applying the method.

What Is the Contribution to the General Methodological Discussion?

The general relevance of this approach is that the different types of questions allow the researchers to deal more explicitly with the presuppositions they bring to the interview in relation to aspects of the interviewee. The "principle of openness" in qualitative research has often been misunderstood as encouraging a diffuse attitude. Here this principle is transformed into a dialogue between positions as a result of the various degrees of explicit confrontation with topics. In this dialogue, the interviewee's position is made more explicit and may also be further developed. The different types of questions, which represent different approaches to making implicit knowledge explicit may point the way to the solution of a more general problem of qualitative research. A goal of interviews in general is to reveal existing knowledge in a way that can be expressed in the form of answers and so become accessible to interpretation. The structure laying technique also offers a model for structuring the contents of interviews in which different forms of questions have been used. That this structure is developed with the interviewee during data collection, and not merely by the researcher in the interpretation makes it an element of the data. Whether the shape Scheele and Groeben suggest for this structure, and the suggested relations, correspond with the research issue can only be decided in an individual case. In summary, a methodological concept has been proposed here, which explicitly takes into account the reconstruction of the object of research (here a subjective theory) in the interview situation instead of propagating a more or less unconditional approach to a given object.

How is the Method Fitting into the Research Process?

The theoretical background to this approach is the reconstruction of subjective viewpoints. Presuppositions about their structure and possible contents are made. But the scope of this method for shaping the contents of the subjective theory remains wide enough for the general target of formulating grounded theories to be realized as well as the use of case-oriented sampling strategies. Research questions that are pursued with this method concentrate partly on the content of subjective theories (e.g., psychiatric patients' subjective theories of illness) and partly on how they are applied in (e.g., professional) activities.

What are Limitations of the Method?

The fastidious details of the method (types of questions, rules of the SLT) need to be adapted to the research question and the potential interviewees. One way is to reduce or modify the rules suggested by Scheele and Groeben. Another way is to perhaps also abandon confrontational questions (e.g., in interviews with patients on their subjective theories of illness). In the major part of the research on subjective theories, only a short version of the method is applied. Another problem is the interpretation of the data collected with it, because there are no explicit suggestions for how to proceed. Experience shows that coding procedures fit best (see Chapter 23). Owing to the complex structure of the single case, attempts at generalization face the problem of how to summarize different subjective theories to groups. For research questions related to (e.g., biographical) processes or unconscious parts of actions, this method is not suitable.

The Problem-Centered Interview

The problem-centered interview suggested by Witzel (see 2000) has attracted some interest and been applied mainly in German psychology. Andreas Witzel has developed it in the context of biographical research interested in professional biographies of different groups of people. We will look at it in some detail here, as it includes some suggestions of how to formulate questions and of how to probe during the interview itself. In particular, by using an interview guide incorporating questions and narrative stimuli it is possible to collect biographical data with regard to a certain problem. This interview is characterized by three central criteria: *problem centering* (i.e., the researcher's orientation to a relevant social problem); *object orientation* (i.e., that methods are developed or modified with respect to an object of research); and finally *process orientation* in the research process and in the understanding of the object of research.

What are the Elements of the Problem-Centered Interview?

Witzel originally names four "partial elements" for the interview he has conceptualized: "qualitative interview," "biographical method," "case analysis," and "group discussion." His conception of a qualitative interview comprises a preceding short questionnaire, the interview guide, the tape recording, and the postscript (an interview protocol). The interview guide is designed to support the narrative string developed by the interviewee. But above all, it is used as a basis for giving the interview a new turn "in the case of a stagnating conversation or an unproductive topic." The interviewer has to decide on the basis of the interview guide "when to bring in his or her problem-centered interest in the form of exmanent [i.e. directed] questions in order to further differentiate the topic" (Box 13.4). Four central communicative strategies in the problem-centered interview are mentioned: the conversational entry, general and specific prompting, and *ad hoc* questions. In a study on how adolescents found their occupation, Witzel used as a conversational entry: "You want to become [a car mechanic, etc.], how did you arrive at this decision? Please, just tell me that!" General probing provides further "material" and details of what has so far been presented. For this purpose, additional questions like "What happened there in detail?" or "Where do you know that from?" are used. Specific probing deepens the understanding on the part of the interviewer by mirroring (summarizing, feedback, interpretation by the interviewer) what has been said, by questions of comprehension, and by confronting the interviewee with contradictions and inconsistencies in his statements. Here, it is seen as important that the interviewer makes clear his or her substantial interest and is able to maintain a good atmosphere in the conversation.

Case Study: Subjective Theories of Illness in Pseudo-croup

The following example shows how this method can be applied, if you concentrate on its core elements. The example comes from an area of health problems. The study is a typical example for using interviews in a qualitative study. The issue under study was a relatively new issue, with little research available at that time. The research focused on lay knowledge and the perspective of the participants on the issue under study. Therefore, this example was selected to show what you can do with problem-centered or similar interviews. In his study about the subjective theories of illness[2] of 32 children with pseudo-croup (a strong cough in children caused by environmental pollution), Ruff (1998) conducted problem-centered interviews with the subjects' parents. The interview guide included the following key questions (see also Box 13.4):

- How did the first illness episode occur, and how did the parents deal with it?
- What do the parents see as the cause of their children's illness?
- What are the consequences of the parents' view of the problem for their everyday life and further planning of their life?
- According to the parents' judgement, which environmental pollutants carry risks for their children's health? How do they deal with them? (1998, p. 287)

As a main finding, it was stated that about two-thirds of the interviewed parents assumed a relation between their children's illness of the respiratory tract and the air pollution in their subjective theories of illness. Although they saw air pollution mostly as only one reason among possible others and linked the causal assumptions with high uncertainty, the majority of these parents had adapted their everyday lives and also partly the planning of their further lives to that new view of the problem (1998, pp. 292–294).

This example shows how some of the basic ideas of the problem-centered interview were taken up by the author and adapted to his specific research question.

Box 13.4   Example Questions from the Problem-Centered Interview

1. What comes spontaneously to your mind when you hear the key words "health risks or dangers"?
2. Which health risks do you see for yourself?
3. Do you do anything to keep yourself healthy?

(Continued)

Box 13.4   *(Continued)*

---

4. Many people say that poisons in air, water, and food impair our health.

    (a) How do you estimate that problem?
    (b) Do you feel environmental pollutants endanger your health? By which ones?
    (c) What made you concern yourself with the health consequences of environmental pollutants?

    . . .

11 (a) How do you inform yourself about the topic "environment and health"?
    (b) How do you perceive the information in the media?
    (c) How credible are scientific statements in this context? What about the credibility of politicians?

Source: Ruff 1990

What Is the Contribution to the General Methodological Discussion?

For a general discussion beyond his own approach, Witzel's suggestion to use a short questionnaire together with the interview is fruitful. Using this questionnaire will allow you to collect the data (e.g., demographic data), which are less relevant than the topics of the interview itself before the actual interview. This permits you to reduce the number of questions and–what is particularly valuable in a tight time schedule–to use the short time of the interview for more essential topics. Contrary to Witzel's suggestion to use this questionnaire before the interview, I think it makes more sense to use it at the end in order to prevent its structure of questions and answers from imposing itself on the dialogue in the interview.

As a second suggestion, the postscript may be carried over from Witzel's approach into other forms of interviews. Immediately after the end of the interview the interviewer should note his or her impressions of the communication, of the interviewee as a person, of himself or herself and his or her behavior in the situation, external influences, the room in which the interview took place, and so on. Thus, context information that might be instructive is documented. This may be helpful for the later interpretation of the statements in the interview and allow the comparison of different interview situations. With regard to the tape recording of interviews suggested by Witzel for being able to better take the context of statements into account, this has already been established for a long time in using interviews. The different strategies for probing the interviewee's answers that Witzel suggests (general and specific probing) are another suggestion, which might be carried over to other interview forms.

How is the Method Fitting into the Research Process?

The theoretical background of the method is the interest in subjective viewpoints. The research is based on a process model with the aim of developing theories (see Chapter 8). Research questions are oriented to knowledge about facts or socialization processes. The selection of interviewees should proceed gradually (see Chapter 11) in order to make the process orientation of the method work. This approach is not committed to any special method of interpretation but mostly to coding procedures and qualitative content analysis (see Chapter 23) is mainly used (see also Witzel 2000 for suggestions how to analyze this form of interviews).

What are the Limitations of the Method?

The combination of narratives and questions suggested by Witzel is aimed at focusing the interviewee's view of the problem around which the interview is centered. At some points, Witzel's suggestions of how to use the interview guide give the impression of an over-pragmatic understanding of how to handle the interview situation. So he suggests introducing questions to shortcut narratives about an unproductive topic. Witzel includes group discussions and "biographical method" with the aim of integrating the different approaches. As the author discusses these parts under the headline of elements of the problem-centered interview, the role of the group discussion, for example, remains unclear here: it might be added as a second or additional step, but a group discussion cannot be part of an interview with one person. There have been reservations about the criterion of problem centering. This criterion is not very useful in distinguishing this method from others as most interviews are focusing on special problems. However, the name and the concept of the method make the implicit promise that it is—perhaps more than other interviews—centered on a given problem. This makes the method often especially attractive for beginners in qualitative research. Witzel's suggestions for the interview guide stress that it should comprise areas of interest but does not mention concrete types of questions to include. Although instructions about how to shape deeper inquiries to interviewee's answers are given to the interviewer with the "general and specific probing," applications of the method, however, have shown that these instructions do not prevent the interviewers from the dilemmas between depth and range mentioned above for the focused interview.

The interviews discussed up to now have been presented in greater detail with regard to methodological aspects. The focused interview has been described because it was the driving force behind such methods in general and because it offers some suggestions for how to realize interviews in general. The semi-standardized interview includes different types of questions and is complemented by ideas about how to structure its contents during data collection. The problem-centered interview offers additional suggestions about how to document the context and how to deal with secondary information. In what follows some other types of semi-structured interviews, which have been developed for specific fields of application in qualitative research, are briefly discussed.

The Expert Interview

Meuser and Nagel (2002) discuss expert interviews as a specific form of apply-ing semi-structured interviews. In contrast to biographical interviews, here the interviewees are of less interest as a (whole) person than their capacities of being an expert for a certain field of activity. They are integrated into the study not as a single case but as representing a group (of specific experts; see also Chapter 11). The range of potentially relevant information provided by the interviewee is restricted much more than in other interviews. Therefore, the interview guide here has a much stronger directive function with regard to excluding unproduc-tive topics. Corresponding to this peculiarity, Meuser and Nagel discuss a series of problems and sources of failing in expert interviews. The main question is whether or not the interviewer manages to restrict and determine the interview and the interviewee to the expertise of interest. Meuser and Nagel (2002, pp. 77–79) name as versions of failing:

- The expert blocks the interview in its course, because he or she proves not to be an expert for this topic as previously assumed.
- The expert tries to involve the interviewer in ongoing conflicts in the field and talks about internal matters and intrigues in his or her work field instead of talking about the topic of the interview.
- He or she often changes between the roles of expert and private person, so that more information results about him or her as a person than about his or her expert knowledge.
- As an intermediate form between success and failure, the "rhetoric inter-view" is mentioned. In this, the expert gives a lecture on his or her know-ledge instead of joining the question–answer game of the interview. If the lecture hits the topic of the interview, the latter may nevertheless be useful. If the expert misses the topic, this form of interaction makes it more difficult to return to the actual relevant topic.

Interview guides have a double function here: "The work, which goes into developing an interview guide, ensures that researchers do not present themselves as incompetent interlocutors. . . . The orientation to an interview guide also ensures that the interview does not get lost in topics that are of no relevance and permits the expert to extemporize his or her issue and view on matters" (2002, p. 77).

In this field of application, you will find the highlights of various interview problems. Problems of directing arise here more intensely, because the intervie-wee is less interesting as a person than in a certain capacity. The need for the interviewer to make clear in the interview that they are also familiar with its topic is in general a condition for successfully conducting such interviews. The interpretation of expert interviews mainly aims at analyzing and comparing the content of the expert knowledge. Cases are integrated into the study according to the pattern of gradual sampling.

The Ethnographic Interview

In the context of ethnographic field research, participant observation is mainly used. In applying it, however, interviews also play a part. A particular problem is how to shape conversations arising in the field into interviews in which the unfolding of the other's specific experiences is aligned with the issue of the research in a systematic way. The local and temporal framework is less clearly delimited than in other interview situations. There time and place are arranged exclusively for the interview. Here opportunities for an interview often arise spontaneously and surprisingly from regular field contacts. Explicit suggestions for conducting such an ethnographic interview are made by Spradley:

> It is best to think of ethnographic interviews as a series of friendly conversations into which the researcher slowly introduces new elements to assist informants to respond as informants. Exclusive use of these new ethnographic elements, or introducing them too quickly, will make interviews become like a formal interrogation. Rapport will evaporate, and informants may discontinue their co-operation. (1979, pp. 58–59)

According to Spradley (1979, pp. 59–60), ethnographic interviews include the following elements that distinguish them from such "friendly conversations":

- a specific request to hold the interview (resulting from the research question);
- ethnographic explanations in which the interviewer explains the project (why an interview at all) or the noting of certain statements (why he or she notes what); these are completed by everyday language explanations (with the aim that informants present relations in their language), interview explanations (making clear why this specific form of talking is chosen, with the aim that the informant gets involved), and explanations for certain (types of) questions, introducing the way of asking explicitly;
- ethnographic questions, that is descriptive questions, structural questions (answering them should show how informants organize their knowledge about the issue), and contrast questions (they should provide information about the meaning dimensions used by informants to differentiate objects and events in their world).

With this method, the general problem of making and maintaining interview situations arises in an emphasized way because of the open framework. The characteristics Spradley mentions for designing and explicitly defining interview situations apply also to other contexts in which interviews are used. In these, some of the clarifications may be made outside the actual interview situation. Nonetheless, the explicit clarifications outlined by Spradley are helpful in any case for producing a reliable working agreement for the interview, which guarantees that the interviewee really joins in. The method is mainly used in combination with field research and observational strategies (see Chapter 17).

You can find a more recent overview of using ethnographic interviews in Heyl (2001). Following Kvale (1996), a stronger focus is on the interview as a co-construction by the interviewer and the interviewee. Heyl links the field of ethnographic interviewing, with current works concerning how to shape interviews in general (like Bourdieu 1996; Gubrium and Holstein 1995; Kvale 1996, Mishler 1986 and others), but is not developing a specific approach in ethnographic interviewing.

Conducting Interviews: Problems of Mediation and Steering

So far, various versions of the interview as one of the methodological bases of qualitative research have been discussed. It is characteristic of these interviews that you will bring more or less open questions to the interview situation in the form of an interview guide. You will hope that the interviewee will answer these questions freely. If you want to check your instruments before conducting your interviews, you can use a list of key points for checking the way you constructed your interview guide and how you formulated your questions. This list was suggested by Ulrich (1999 – see Box 13.5).

Box 13.5   Key Points for Evaluating Questions in Interviews

1. Why do you ask this specific question?

   - What is its theoretical relevance?
   - What is the link to the research question?

2. For what reason do you ask in this question?

   - What is the substantial dimension of this question?

3. Why did you formulate the question in this way (and not differently)?

   - Is the question easy to understand?
   - Is the question unambiguous?
   - Is the question productive?

4. Why did you position this question (or block of questions) at this specific place in the interview guide?

   - How does it fit into the rough and detailed structure of the interview guide?
   - How is the distribution of types of question spread across the interview guide?
   - What is the relation between single questions?

The starting point of the method is the assumption that inputs are character-istic for standardized interviews or questionnaires and are restricting when the sequence of topics dealt with obscure rather than illuminate the subject's view-point. Problems also arise when trying to secure topically relevant subjective perspectives in an interview: problems of mediating between the input of the interview guide and the aims of the research question on the one hand, and the interviewee's style of presentation on the other. Thus, the interviewer can and must decide during the interview when and in which sequence to ask the ques-tions. Whether a question has already been answered *en passant* and may be left out can only be decided *ad hoc*. As interviewer, you will also face the question of if and when to probe in greater detail and to support the interviewee if rov-ing far afield or when to return to the interview guide when the interviewee is digressing. The term "semi-standardized interview" is also used with respect to choice in the actual conduct of the interview. You will have to choose between trying to mention certain topics given in the interview guide and at the same time being open to the interviewee's individual way of talking about these top-ics and other topics relevant for them. These decisions, which can only be taken in the interview situation itself, require a high degree of sensitivity to the con-crete course of the interview and the interviewee. Additionally, they require a great deal of overview of what has already been said and its relevance for the research question in the study. Here a permanent mediation between the course of the interview and the interview guide is necessary. Hopf (1978) warns against applying the interview guide too bureaucratically. This might restrict the benefits of openness and contextual information because the interviewer is sticking too rigidly to the interview guide. This might encourage him or her to interrupt the interviewee's accounts at the wrong moment in order to turn to the next ques-tion instead of taking up the topic and trying to get deeper into it. According to Hopf (1978, p. 101), there may be several reasons for this:

- the protective function of the interview guide for coping with the uncer-tainty due to the open and indeterminate conversational situation;
- the interviewer's fear of being disloyal to the targets of the research (e.g., because of skipping a question);
- finally, the dilemma between pressure of time (due to the interviewee's limited time) and the researcher's interest in information.

Therefore, detailed interview training has proved to be necessary in which the application of the interview guide is taught in role-plays. These simulated inter-view situations are recorded (if possible on videotape). Afterwards they are eval-uated by all the interviewers taking part in the study–for interview mistakes, for how the interview guide was used, for procedures and problems in introducing and changing topics, the interviewer's non-verbal behavior, and their reactions to the interviewee. This evaluation is made in order to make different interviewers' interventions and steering in the interviews more comparable. This allows one to take up so-called "technical" problems (how to design and conduct interviews) and to discuss solutions to them in order to further back up the use of interviews.

For preparing and conducting the interview itself, you will find some helpful suggestions in Hermanns (2004). He sees the interview interaction as an evolving drama and the interviewer's task in facilitating that this drama can evolve. He also warns interviewers not to be too anxious about using tape recording during the interview. Hermanns emphasizes that most interviewees have no problems with the recording of an interview and that it is often the interviewers who project their own uneasiness of being recorded onto the interviewee. In his stage directions for interviewing (2004, p. 212–213), you will find suggestions such as, to carefully explain to the interviewees what you expect from them during the interview, how to create a good atmosphere in the interview, and to give room to your interviewees to open up. Most crucial in his suggestions in my experience is that during the interview you should not try to discover theoretical concepts but the life world of the interviewees. Of similar importance is that you should be aware of the fact that research questions are not the same as interview questions and that you should try to use everyday language instead of scientific concepts in the questions. Discovering theoretical concepts and using scientific concepts is something for analyzing the data, and using concrete everyday wordings is what should happen in your questions and the interview.[3]

The advantage of this method is that the consistent use of an interview guide increases the comparability of the data and that they will be more structured as a result of the questions in the guide. If concrete statements about an issue are the aim of the data collection, a semi-structured interview is the more economic way. If the course of a single case and the context of experiences are the central aim of your research, you should consider narratives of the development of experiences as the preferable alternative.

KEY POINTS

- The interview forms in this chapter go different ways to reach a similar goal. The interviewees shall be given as much scope as possible to unfold their views. At the same time, they shall be given a structure for what to talk about in their answers.
- The interview forms can be applied in themselves, but most often they are an orientation for how to shape and design an interview and a list of questions to cover the research issue.
- A very important step is the planning for probing. What will you ask if the interviewee's answers remain too general or if they miss the point that you intended?
- Interviews can be extended to a second meeting aiming at a communicative validation and at producing a structure of the statements with the interviewee.

Exercise 13.1

1. Look in a journal for a qualitative study based in interviews. Use it to identify the methods presented in this chapter or decide its orientation in relation to the study.
2. Consider the study's questions and then improve them by using one or more of the interviewing methods presented in this chapter.
3. Think of your own study and develop an interview guide for your research question according to one of the interview forms presented here.

Notes

1 The examples are taken from Merton and Kendall (1946).
2 Whereas the method described before was developed especially for reconstructing subjective theories, the problem-centered interview is used for this purpose as well. Thus, it is rather coincidental that subjective theories are the object in both examples.
3 For more recent developments in the field of online interviewing see Chapter 20.

FURTHER READING

The Focused Interview
The first text is the classic text on the focused interview. The other two texts offer recent developments and applications of this strategy.

Merton, R.K. and Kendall, P.L. (1946) "The Focused Interview," *American Journal of Sociology*, 51: 541–557.

Merton, R.K. (1987) "The Focused Interview and Focus Groups: Continuities and Discontinuities," *Public Opinion Quarterly*, 51: 550–556.

Oerter, R., Oerter, R., Agostiani, H., Kim, H.O. and Wibowo, S. (1996) "The Concept of Human Nature in East Asia: Etic and Emic Characteristics," *Culture & Psychology*, 2: 9–51.

The Semi-Standardized Interview
The first two texts outline methodological strategies for realizing the aims of this kind of method, whereas the third gives an introduction to the theoretical background and assumptions they are based on.

Flick, U. (1992) "Triangulation Revisited: Strategy of or Alternative to Validation of Qualitative Data," *Journal For the Theory of Social Behavior*, 22: 175–197.

Groeben, N. (1990) "Subjective Theories and the Explanation of Human Action," in G.R. Semin and K.J. Gergen (eds), *Everyday Understanding: Social and Scientific Implications*. London: SAGE. pp. 19–44.

(Continued)

The Problem-Centered Interview
This text outlines the method and the problems of applying it.

Witzel, A. (2000, January). The problem-centered interview [27 paragraphs]. Forum: Qualitative Social Research. (www.qualitative-research.net/fqs-texte/1-00/1-00witzel-e.htm) [Dec., 10th, 2004].

The Expert Interview
This text outlines the methods and the problems of applying it.

Meuser, M. and Nagel, U. (2002) "ExpertInneninterviews – vielfach erprobt, wenig bedacht. Ein Beitrag zur qualitativen Methodendiskussion," in A. Bogner, B. Littig and W. Menz (eds), *Das Experteninterview*. Qpladen: Leske & Budrich. pp. 71–95.

The Ethnographic Interview
The first text is an outline of the method and the second puts it in the framework of participant observation.

Heyl, B.S. (2001). "Ethnographic Interviewing," in P. Atkinson, A. Coffey, S. Delamont, J. Lofland, and L.Lofland (eds) *Handbook of Ethnography*. London: SAGE. pp. 369–383.
Spradley, J.P. (1979) *The Ethnographic Interview*. New York: Holt, Rinehart and Winston.
Spradley, J.P. (1980) *Participant Observation*. New York: Holt, Rinehart and Winston.

Mediation and Steering
The first text is typical for a more attitudinal approach to interviewing, whereas the others treat more concrete and also technical problems.

Fontana, A. and Frey, J.H. (2000) "The Interview: From Structural Questions to Negotiated Texts," in N. Denzin and Y.S. Lincoln (eds), *Handbook of Qualitative Research*. London: SAGE. pp. 645–672.
Hermanns, H. (2004) "Interviewing as An Activity," in U. Flick, E.v. Kardorff and I. Steinke (eds), *A Companion to Qualitative Research*. London: SAGE. pp. 209–213.
Kvale, S. (1996) *Interviews: An Introduction to Qualitative Research Interviewing*. London: SAGE.
Mason, J. (2002) "Qualitative Interviewing: Asking, Listening and Interpreting," in T. May (ed.), *Qualitative Research in Action*. London: SAGE. pp.225–241.
Smith, J.A. (1995) "Semi-Structured Interview and Qualitative Analysis," in J.A. Smith, R. Harré and L.v. Langenhove (eds), *Rethinking Methods in Psychology*. London: SAGE. pp. 9–26.
Wengraf, T. (2001) *Qualitative Research Interviewing: Biographic Narrative and Semi-Structured Methods*. London: SAGE.

14

NARRATIVES

CHAPTER OBJECTIVES
After reading this chapter, you should be able to

✓ understand how to use narratives in qualitative research.
✓ identify the difference between life histories and episodes as a basis for narratives.
✓ distinguish the advantages and problems of using the different forms of narratives in interviews.

You can use narratives[1] produced by interviewees as a form of data as an alternative to semi-structured interviews. The basic skepticism about how far subjective experiences may be tapped in the question–answer scheme of traditional interviews, even if this is handled in a flexible way, is the methodological starting point for the propagation of using narratives. Narratives allow the researcher to approach the interviewee's experiential yet structured world in a comprehensive way. A narrative is characterized as follows:

> First the initial situation is outlined ("how everything started"), then the events relevant to the narrative are selected from the whole host of experiences and presented as a coherent progression of events ("how things developed"), and finally the situation at the end of the development is presented ("what became"). (Hermanns 1995, p. 183)

As a special method for collecting this form of data, the narrative interview introduced by Schütze (see Riemann and Schütze 1987; Rosenthal 2004) is a particularly good example of this type of approach. With the attention it attracted (especially in the German-speaking areas) it has intensified the interest in qualitative methods as a whole. Narratives as a mode of knowledge and of presenting experiences are also increasingly analyzed in psychology (e.g., Bruner 1990; 1991; Flick 1996; Murray 2000; Sarbin 1986). Two methods, which use narratives in this way, are discussed in this chapter.

The Narrative Interview

The narrative interview is mainly used in the context of biographical research (for overview see Bertaux 1981; Rosenthal 2004). The method was developed in the context of a project on local power structures and decision processes. Its basic principle of collecting data is described as follows:

> In the narrative interview, the informant is asked to present the history of an area of interest, in which the interviewee participated, in an extempore narrative . . . The interviewer's task is to make the informant tell the story of the area of interest in question as a consistent story of all relevant events from its beginning to its end. (Hermanns 1995, p. 183)

Elements of the Narrative Interview

The narrative interview is begun using a "generative narrative question" (Riemann and Schütze 1987, p. 353), which refers to the topic of the study and is intended to stimulate the interviewee's main narrative. The latter is followed by the stage of narrative probing in which narrative fragments that were not exhaustively detailed before are completed. The last stage of the interview is the "balancing phase, in which the interviewee may also be asked questions that aim at theoretical accounts of what happened and at balancing the story, reducing the 'meaning' of the whole to its common denominator" (Hermanns 1995, p. 184). At this stage, the interviewees are taken as experts and theoreticians of themselves.

If you want to elicit a narrative, which is relevant to your research question, you must formulate the generative narrative question broadly but at the same time sufficiently specifically for the interesting experiential domain to be taken up as a central theme. The interest may refer to the informant's life history in general. In this case, the generative narrative question is rather unspecified, for example: Then, I would like to ask you to begin with your life history. Or it may aim at a specific, temporal, and topical aspect of the informant's biography, e.g., a phase of professional reorientation and its consequences. An example of such a generative question is shown in Box 14.1.

It is important that you check whether the generative question really is a narrative question. Clear hints on the course of events told are given in the example by Hermanns in Box 14.1. These refer to several stages and include the explicit request for a narration and for detailing it.

If the interviewee begins a narrative after this question, it is crucial for the quality of the data in this narrative that it is not interrupted or obstructed by the interviewer. For example, you should not ask questions in this part (e.g., "Who is this about?") or interrupt with directive interventions (e.g., "Could this problem not have been managed in a different way?") or evaluations ("That was a good idea of yours!"). Instead, as interviewer, as an active listener, you should signal (e.g., by reinforcing "*hm's*") that you empathize with the narrated story and the perspective of the narrator. Thus, you will support and encourage the narrators to continue their narratives until their ends.

Box 14.1   Example of a Generative Narrative Question in the Narrative Interview

This is a typical example for a good generative narrative question:

"I want to ask you to tell me how the story of your life occurred. The best way to do this would be for you to start from your birth, with the little child that you once were, and then tell all the things that happened one after the other until today. You can take your time in doing this, and also give details, because for me everything is of interest that is important for you."

Source: Hermanns 1995, p. 182

The end of the story is indicated by a "coda," e.g., "I think I've taken you through my whole life" (Riemann and Schütze 1987, p. 353) or "That was pretty well it by and large. I hope that has meant something to you" (Hermanns 1995, p. 184). In the next stage—the questioning period—the story's fragments that have not been further carried out are readdressed or the interviewer with another generative narrative question takes up those passages that had been unclear. For example: "You told me before how it came about that you moved from X to Y. I did not quite understand how your disease went on after that. Could you please tell me that part of the story in a little more detail?" In the balancing phase, more and more abstract questions are asked, which aim for description and argumentation. Here, it is suggested first to ask "how" questions and then only afterwards to complement them with "why" questions aiming at explanations.

A main criterion for the validity of the information is whether the interviewee's account is primarily a narrative. Although to some extent descriptions of situations and routines or argumentation may be incorporated in order to explain reasons or goals, the dominant form of presentation should be a narrative of the course of events (if possible from the beginning to the end) and of developmental processes.

This distinction is clarified by Hermanns (1995, p. 184) who uses the following example:

> My attitude towards nuclear plants cannot be narrated, but I could tell the story about how my present attitude came about. "Well, I walked, it must have been 1972, across the site at Whyl, all those huts there and I thought, well that is great, what these people have got going here, but with their concern about nuclear energy they are kind of mad. I was strongly M/L at that time."[2]

That this method works and the main narrative provides a richer version of the events and experiences than the other forms of presentation that are argued as consequences to one main reason that the narrators become entangled in certain constraints ("threefold narrative zugzwangs"). This entangling starts as soon as they have got involved in the situation of the narrative interview and started the narrative. The constraints are the *constraint of closing gestalt*, the *constraint of condensing*, and the *constraint of detailing*. The first makes narrators bring to an end a narrative once they have started it. The second requires that only what is necessary for understanding the process in the story becomes part of the presentation. The story is condensed not only because of limited time but also so that the listener is able to understand and follow it. The narrative provides background details and relationships necessary for understanding the story. Through these narrative constraints, the narrator's control, which dominates in other forms of oral presentation, is minimized to such an extent that awkward topics and areas are also mentioned:

> Narrators of unprepared extempore narratives of their own experiences are driven to talk also about events and action orientations, which they prefer to keep silent about in normal conversations and conventional interviews owing to their awareness of guilt or shame or their entanglements of interests. (Schütze 1976, p. 225)

Thus, there was the creation of a technique for eliciting narratives of topically relevant stories. This technique provides data that you cannot produce in other forms of interviewing for three reasons. First, the narrative takes on some independence during its recounting. Second, "people 'know' and are able to present a lot more of their lives than they have integrated in their theories of themselves and of their lives. This knowledge is available to informants at the level of narrative presentation but not at the level of theories" (Hermanns 1995, p. 185). Finally, an analogous relationship between the narrative presentation and the narrated experience is assumed: "In the retrospective narrative of experiences, events in the life history (whether actions or natural phenomena) are reported on principle in the way they were experienced by the narrator as actor" (Schütze 1976, p. 197).

Case Study: Excerpt from a Narrative Interview

As an illustration, the following is taken from the beginning of a biographical main narrative of a mental patient (E). Gerd Riemann is one of the protagonists of biographical research with narrative interviews. This example comes from a typical study of biographies using the narrative interview (1987, pp. 66–68). While reading it, look for when the interviewee comes to the topic of the interview (mental illness). References to villages and areas are replaced by general words in double brackets ((. . .)). Words in italics are strongly emphasized; a slash indicates the interruption of a word by another; and the interviewer's reinforcing signals ("hmh," "Oh yes") are represented exactly at the position they occurred:

1	E	Well, I was born in ((area in the Former East Germany))
2	I	hmh
3	E	actually in ((. . .)) which is a purely Catholic, purely/mainly.
4		Catholic district of ((area, western part)
5	I	Oh yes
6	E	((town))
7	I	hmh
8	E	My Father uh . . . was captain
9	l	hmh
10	E	and . . . uh was already county court judge . . .
11		and then was killed in the war.
12	I	hmh
13	E	My mother got stuck alone with my elder brother/he is three years
14		older than me and uh–fled with us.
15	I	hmh
16	E	About the journey I don't know anything in detail, I only remember–
17		as a memory that I once uh sat in a train and felt terrible/uh
18		terrible thirst or anyhow hunger
19	I	hmh
20	E	and that then somebody came with a pitcher and a cup for us
21		uh poured coffee and that I felt that to be very refresh-
22	I	hmh
23	E	-ing.
24		But other memories are also related to that train which
25		maybe point uh to very much later, well, when
26	I	hmh
27	E	came into psychiatry, see.
28		Namely, uh–that comes up again as an image from time to time.
29		And we had laid down in that train to go to sleep
30		and I was somehow raised . . . uh to be put to sleep
31	I	hmh
32	E	And I must have fallen down in the night without waking

(Continued)

(Continued)

33		up.
34	I	hmh
35	E	And there I rem/remember that a uh female, not my
36		mother, a female person took me in her arms and smiled
37		at me.
38	I	hmh
39	E	Those are my earliest memories.
40	I	hmh.

This narrative continues over another 17 pages of transcript. The interview is continued in a second meeting. A detailed case analysis is presented by Riemann (1987, pp. 66–200).

In this example, you can see how a narrative interview begins, how the interviewee's life history is unfolded in it, and how the interview slowly approaches issues directly relevant for the research question but also provides a lot of information that might look less relevant at a first glance. The latter unfold their relevance maybe during the analysis of the interview.

In the narrative interview, on the one hand, the expectation is that factual processes will become evident in it, that "how it really was" will be revealed, and this is linked to the nature of narrative data. On the other hand, analyzing such narrated life histories should lead to a general theory of processes. Schütze (1983) calls this "process structures of the individual life course." In some areas, such typical courses have been demonstrated empirically, as in the following.

Case Study: Professional Biographies of Engineers

Harry Hermanns is another of the main protagonists in developing and using the narrative interview in this case in the context of professional biographies. Hermanns (1984) has applied this method to around 25 engineers in order to elaborate the patterns of their life histories–patterns of successful professional courses and patterns of courses characterized by crises. The case studies showed that at the beginning of his or her professional career, an engineer should go through a phase of seeking to acquire professional competencies. The central theme of the professional work of the following years should result from this phase. If one fails with this, the professional start turns into a dead-end. From the analyses, a series of typical fields for the engineer's further specialization resulted. A decisive stage is to build up "substance" (i.e., experience and knowledge), for example by becoming an expert in a technical domain. Other types

(Continued)

(Continued)

of building up substance are presented by Hermanns. The next stage of engineers' careers is to develop a biographical line in the occupation (i.e., to link themselves to a professional topic for a longer time and construct a basis from which they can act). Lines can be accelerated by successes, but also may "die" (e.g., by losing the basis because the competence for securing the line is missing, because the topic loses its meaning in some crisis, or because a new line emerges). Professional careers fail when one does not succeed in constructing a basis, developing and securing a line, building up competence and substance when one of the central professional tasks distilled from the analysis of professional biographies is not managed successfully.

This example shows how patterns of biographical courses can be elaborated from case studies of professional biographies. These patterns and the stages of the biographical processes contained in them can be taken as points of reference for explaining success and failure in managing the tasks of successful biographies.

What are Some Problems in Conducting the Interview?

One problem in conducting narrative interviews is the systematic violation of the role expectations of both participants. First, expectations relating to the situation of an "interview" are violated, because (at least for the most part) questions in the usual sense of the word are not asked. Second, rarely is an interviewee's narrative of everyday life given. These violations of situational expectations often produce irritations in both parties, which prevent them from settling down into the interview situation. Furthermore, although being able to narrate may be an everyday competence, it is mastered to varying degrees. Therefore, it is not always the most appropriate social science method: "We must assume that not all interviewees are capable of giving narrative presentations of their lives. We meet reticent, shy, uncommunicative, or excessively reserved people not only in everyday social life but also in biographical interviews" (Fuchs 1984, p. 249). Additionally, some authors see problems in applying this method in foreign cultures, because the validity of the narrative schema dominant in Western culture cannot simply be presumed for other, non-western cultures.

Because of these problems, interview training that focuses on active listening (i.e, signaling interest without intervention and on how to maintain the relationship with the interviewee) is necessary in this case, too. This training should be tailor-made for the concrete research question and the specific target group whose narratives are sought. For this, role-plays and rehearsal interviews are recommended here as well. The recordings of these should be systematically evaluated by a group of researchers for problems in conducting the interview and with the interviewer's role behavior. A precondition for successfully conducting the interview is to explain the specific character of the interview situation to the interviewee. For this purpose, I suggest paying special attention to explaining, in detail, targets and procedures during the phase of recruiting interviewees.

What Is the Contribution to the General Methodological Discussion?

The narrative interview and its attached methodology highlight a qualitative interview's making of the responsive structure and experiences. A model that reconstructs the internal logic of processes stresses the narrative as a gestalt loaded with more than statements and reported "facts." This also provides a solution to the dilemma of the semi-structured interview–how to mediate between freedom to unfold subjective viewpoints and the thematic direction and limitation of what is mentioned. This solution includes three elements:

- The primary orientation is to provide the interviewees with the scope to tell their story (if necessary, for several hours) and to require them to do so.
- Concrete, structuring, or thematically deepening interventions in the interview are postponed until its final part in which the interviewer may take up topics broached before and ask more direct questions. The restriction of the structuring role of the interviewer to the end of the interview and to the beginning is linked to this.
- The generative narrative question serves not only to stimulate the production of a narrative, but also to focus the narrative on the topical area and the period of the biography with which the interview is concerned.

The methodological discussion so far has dealt mainly with questions of how interviewers should behave to keep a narrative going once it is stimulated and to enable it to be finished with the least disturbance possible. But the argument that a good generative narrative question highly structures the following narrative has not yet fully been taken into account. Imprecise and ambiguous generative narrative questions often lead to narratives, which remain general, disjointed, and topically irrelevant. Therefore, this method is not the completely open interview that it is often erroneously presented as being in some textbooks. However, the structuring interventions by the interviewer are more clearly localized than in other methods–in their limitation to the beginning and the end of the interview. In the framework thus produced, the interviewees are allowed to unfold their views unobstructed by the interviewer as far as possible. Thus, this method has become a way of employing the potential of narratives as a source of data for social research.

How is the Method Fitting into the Research Process?

Although dependent on the method used for interpretation, the theoretical background of studies using narrative interviews is mainly the analysis of subjective views and activities. Research questions pursued from within this perspective focus biographical processes against the background and in the context of concrete and general circumstances (e.g., life situations such as a phase of professional orientation and a certain social context and biographical period–the post-war period in Germany). The procedure is mainly suitable for developing grounded theories (see Chapter 8). A gradual sampling strategy according to the concept of theoretical sampling (see Chapter 11) seems to be most useful. Special suggestions for interpreting narrative data gathered using this method have been made that take into account their formal characteristics as well as their structure (see Chapter 25). The goal of analysis is often to develop typologies of biographical courses as an intermediate step on the way to theory building (see Chapter 28).

What are the Limitations of the Method?

One problem linked to the narrative interview is the following assumption: that it allows the researcher to gain access to factual experiences and events. This assumption is expressed in putting narrative and experience in an analogous relationship. However, what is presented in a narrative is constructed in a specific form during the process of narrating, and memories of earlier events may be influenced by the situation in which they are told. These are further problems, which obstruct the realization of some of the claims to the validity of the data, which are linked to the narrative interview. Furthermore, it is necessary to critically ask another question before applying the method. Is it as appropriate for your own research question, and above all for the interviewees, to rely on the effectiveness of narrative constraints and entanglements in a narrative, as it was during the developmental context of the method? The local politicians Schütze originally interviewed with this method probably had different reasons for and better skills at concealing awkward relations than other potential interviewees. In the latter case, using this kind of strategy for eliciting biographical details also raises questions of research ethics.

A more practical problem is the sheer amount of textual material in the transcripts of narrative interviews. Additionally, these are less obviously structured (by topical areas, by the interviewer's questions) than semi-structured interviews. At the very least, it is more difficult to recognize their structure. The sheer mass of unstructured texts produces problems in interpreting them. The consequence is often that only a few but extremely voluminous case studies result from applying this method. Therefore, before choosing this method you should decide beforehand whether it is really the course (of a life, a patient's career, a professional career), which is central to your research question. If it is not, the purposive topical steering allowed by a semi-structured interview may be the more effective way to achieve the desired data and findings.

Critical discussions provoked by this method have clarified the limits of narratives as a data source. These limits may be based on the issue of the interview in each case: "It is always only 'the story of' that can be narrated, not a state or an always recurring routine" (Hermanns 1995, p. 183). In the face of these limits of narratives it should be settled, before applying this method, whether narratives are appropriate as the only approach to the research question and the potential interviewees, and whether and with which other sorts of data they should be combined.

The Episodic Interview

The starting point for the episodic interview (Flick 2000a) is the assumption that subjects' experiences of a certain domain are stored and remembered in forms of narrative-episodic and semantic knowledge. Whereas episodic knowledge is organized closer to experiences and linked to concrete situations and circumstances, semantic knowledge is based on assumptions and relations, which are abstracted from these and generalized. For the former, the course of the situation in its context is the main unit around which knowledge is organized. In the latter, concepts and their relation among each other are the central units (Figure 14.1).

To access both forms of knowledge about a domain, I have designed a method to collect and analyze narrative-episodic knowledge using narratives, whilst semantic knowledge is made accessible by concrete pointed questions. However, it is not so much a time-saving, pragmatic jumping between the data types "narrative" and "answer," which is intended but rather the systematic link

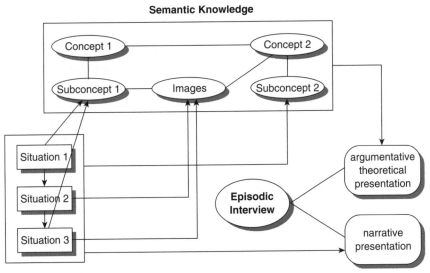

FIGURE 14.1   Forms of Knowledge in the Episodic Interview

between forms of knowledge that both types of data can make accessible. The episodic interview yields context-related presentations in the form of a narrative, because these are closer to experiences and their generative context than other presentational forms. They make the processes of constructing realities more readily accessible than approaches, which aim at abstract concepts and answers in a strict sense. But the episodic interview is not an attempt to artificially stylize experiences as a "narrate-able whole." Rather it starts from episodic-situational forms of experiential knowledge. Special attention is paid in the interview to situations or episodes in which the interviewee has had experiences that seem to be relevant to the question of the study. Both the form of the presentation (description or narrative) of the situation and the selection of other situations can be chosen by the interviewee according to aspects of subjective relevance. In several domains, the episodic interview facilitates the presentation of experiences in a general, comparative form and at the same time, it ensures that those situations and episodes are told in their specificity. Therefore, it includes a combination of narratives oriented to situational or episodic contexts and argumentation that peel off such contexts in favor of conceptual and rule-oriented knowledge. The interviewee's narrative competence is used without relying on zugzwangs and without forcing the interviewee to finish a narrative against his or her intentions.

Which are the Elements of the Episodic Interview?

The central element of this form of interview is that you recurrently ask the interviewee to present narratives of situations (e.g., "If you look back, what was your first encounter with television? Could you please recount that situation for me?"). Also, you will mention chains of situations. ("Please, could you recount how your day yesterday went off, and where and when technology played a part in it?") You will prepare an interview guide in order to orient the interview to the topical domains for which such a narrative is required. In order to familiarize the interviewee with this form of interview its basic principle is first explained (e.g., "In this interview, I will ask you repeatedly to recount situations in which you have had certain experiences with technology in general or with specific technologies"). A further aspect is the interviewee's imaginations of expected or feared changes ("Which developments do you expect in the area of computers in the near future? Please imagine, and tell me a situation which would make this evolution clear for me!"). Such narrative incentives are complemented by questions, in which you ask for the interviewee's subjective definitions ("What do you link to the word 'television' today?"). Also, you will ask for abstractive relations ("In your opinion, who should be responsible for change due to technology, who is able to, or should take the responsibility?"). This is the second large complex of questions aimed at accessing semantic parts of everyday knowledge.

Case Study: Technological Change in Everyday Life

In a comparative study, I conducted 27 episodic interviews on the perception and evaluation of technological change in everyday life. In order to be able to analyze different perspectives on this issue, I interviewed information engineers, social scientists, and teachers as members of professions dealing with technology in different degrees (as developers of technology, as professional and everyday users of technology). The interview mentioned the following topical fields. The interviewees' "technology biographies" (their first encounter with technology they remember, their most important experiences linked to technology) were one point of reference. The interviewees' technological everyday life (how yesterday went off with regard to where and when technology played a part in it; domains of everyday life like work, leisure, household, and technology) was the second.

As a response to the narrative incentive "If you try to recall, what was your first encounter with technology? Could you please recount that situation?" e.g., the following situation was recounted:

> I was a girl, I am a girl, let's say, but I was always interested in technology, I have to say, or and, well I was given puppets as usual. And then sometime, my big dream, a train set, and uh yeah that train. I wound it up and put it on the back of my sister's head, and then the little wheels turned. And the hair got caught up in the train wheels. And then it was over with the technology, because then my sister had to go to the hairdresser. The train had to be taken to pieces, it was most complicated, she had no more hair on her head, everybody said, "Oh how awful," I cried because my train was taken to pieces. That was already the end of the technology. Of course, I did not know at all what had happened, I did not realize at all what would happen. I don't know what drove me, why I had the devil in me. She was sitting around and I thought, "put the train on her head." How long I actually played with the train before, don't really know. Probably not very long, and it was a great train. Yeah, then it was over for a while. That was an experience, not a very positive experience.

Another example is the following situation, which is remembered as a first encounter with technology:

> Yes, electric lights on the Christmas tree. I knew that already from that time, yeah and that has impressed me deeply. I saw those candles at other children's houses and actually, nowadays would say that this is much more romantic, much more beautiful. But at that time, of course, it was impressive, if I turned a candle, all the lights went off, yes, and when I wanted. And that was just the case on the first Christmas holiday, it's a holiday, the parents sleep longer. And the children, of course, are finished with sleeping very early. They go out to the Christmas tree to continue playing with the gifts, which had had to be stopped on Christmas Eve. And I could then turn on the candles again and everything shone again, and with wax candles, this was not the case.

A large part of the interview focused on the use of various exemplary technologies, which determine changes in everyday life in an extraordinary way (computer,

(Continued)

(Continued)

television). For these examples, definitions and experiences were mentioned. As a response to the question, "What do you link to the word 'computer' today?" a female information engineer gave the following definition:

> Computer, of course I must have an absolutely exact conception of that . . . Computer, well, uh, must have a processor, must have a memory, can be reduced to a Turing machine. These are very technical details. That means a computer can't do anything except go left, go right and write on a tape, that is a model of the computer. And I don't link more to it at all at first. This means, for me, a computer is a completely dull machine.

Consequences of technological change in different areas (e.g., family life, children's life, etc.) were focused across the different technologies. In each of these areas, narrative incentives were complemented by conceptual-argumentative questions (Box 14.2). A context protocol was written for every interview. The interviews showed the common aspects of the different views, so that in the end an everyday theory of technological change could be formulated across all cases. They also showed group-specific differences in the views, so that every group-specific accentuation of this everyday theory could be documented.

In this example, you can see how the episodic interview is applied to study a social psychological issue. Here, narratives of specific situations are given and concepts and definitions are mentioned.

Box 14.2   Example Questions from the Episodic Interview

- What does "technology" mean for you? What do you associate with the word "technology"?
- When you look back, what was your first experience with technology? Could you please tell me about this situation?
- If you look at your household, what part does technology play in it, and what has changed in it? Please tell me a situation typical for that.
- On which occasion did you first have contact with a computer? Could you please tell me about that situation?
- Have your relations with other people changed due to technologies? Please tell me a typical situation.
- Please recount how your day yesterday went off and when technologies played a part in it.
- Which parts of your life are free of technology? Please tell me about a typical situation.
- What would life without technology look like for you? Please tell me about a situation of this type, or a typical day.
- If you consider the life of (your) children today and compare it with your life as a child, what is the part played by technology in each case? Please tell me a about situation typical for that which makes this clear for you and me.

Box 14.2   (Continued)

- What do you link to the word television today? Which device is relevant for that?
- What part does TV play in your life today? Please tell me about a typical situation.
- What determines if and when you watch TV? Please tell me a situation typical for that.
- If you look back, what was your first encounter with TV? Please tell me about that situation.
- On which occasion did TV play its most important role in your life? Please tell me about that situation.
- Are there areas in your life in which you feel fear when technology enters? Please tell me about a situation typical for that.
- What gives you the impression that a certain technology or a device is outdated? Please tell me about a typical situation.

What are the Problems in Conducting the Interview?

The general problem of interviews generating narratives—that some people have greater problems with narrating than others—is also the case here. But it is qualified here, because you will not request a single overall narrative—as in the narrative interview—but rather stimulate several delimited narratives. The problem of how to mediate the principle of recounting certain situations to the interviewee has to be handled carefully in order to prevent situations (in which certain experiences have been made) from being mentioned but not recounted. As in other forms of interviews, it is an essential precondition that you as the interviewer have really internalized the principle of the interview. Therefore, I suggest careful interview training using concrete examples here as well. This should focus on how to handle the interview guide and, above all, how to stimulate narratives and—where necessary—how to probe.

What is the Contribution to the General Methodological Discussion?

In episodic interviews, you try to employ the advantages of both the narrative interview and the semi-structured interview. These interviews use the interviewee's competence to present experiences in their course and context as narratives. Episodes as an object of such narratives and as an approach to the experiences relevant for the subject under study allow a more concrete approach than does the narrative of the life history. In contrast to the narrative interview, routines and normal everyday phenomena are analyzed with this procedure. For a topic like technological change, these routines may be as instructive as the particulars of the interviewee's history with technology. In the episodic interview, the range of experiences is not confined to those parts that can be presented in a narrative. As the interviewer you have more options to intervene and direct it through a series of key questions concerning a subject recounting and defining situations. Thus, the extremely one-sided and artificial situation given in the narrative interview here is replaced by a more open dialogue in which narratives are used as only one form of data. By linking narratives and question–answer sequences, this method realizes the triangulation of different approaches as the basis of data collection.

How is the Method Fitting into the Research Process?

The theoretical background of studies using the episodic interview is the social construction of reality during the presentation of experiences. The method was developed as an approach to social representations. Therefore, research questions have mainly up to now focused on group-specific differences in experiences and everyday knowledge. The comparison between certain groups is the goal of sampling cases (see Chapter 11). The connection between a linear and a circular understanding of the research process underlies its application. The data from episodic interviews should be analyzed with the methods of thematic and theoretic coding (see Chapter 22).

Limitations of the Method

Apart from the problems already mentioned in conducting episodic interviews, their application is limited to the analysis of everyday knowledge of certain objects and topics and interviewees' own history with them. As with other interviews, it gives access neither to activities nor to interactions. However, these can be reconstructed from the participants' viewpoints and group-specific differences in such experiences may be clarified.

Narratives Between Biography and Episode

Interviews primarily aiming at interviewees' narratives collect data in the form of a more or less comprehensive and structured whole—as a narrative of life histories or of concrete situations in which interviewees have made certain experiences. Thus, these interviews are more sensitive and responsive to interviewees' viewpoints than other interviews in which concrete topics and the way these should be treated are prestructured very much by the questions that are asked. Procedures generating narratives, however, are also based on interviewers' inputs and ways of structuring the situation of collecting data. Which form of narrative you should prefer as a source of data—the comprehensive biographical narrative in the narrative interview or the narrative of details that are linked to situations in the episodic interview—you should decide with regard to the research question and the issue under study. Such decisions should not be made on the basis of the fundamentally postulated strength of one method compared with all other methods of collecting data, as the programmatic discussions around the narrative interview sometimes suggest. An alternative to creating a myth about narratives in such a programmatic way is to reintroduce a dialogue between the interviewer and the interviewee in the episodic interview. A second alternative is to stimulate this dialogue among the members in a family in joint narratives of family histories. These will be discussed in the second part of the next chapter.

KEY POINTS

- Narratives can be used in interviews to receive a more comprehensive and contextualized version of events and experiences.
- This can be achieved with overall life histories–biographical narratives–or situation-oriented narratives.
- There are different ways of conceiving narratives in interviews as the main form standing alone or embedded in different forms of questions.
- Not everything can be an issue for a narrative presentation, so that sometimes other forms of accessing experiences are needed complementary to or instead of narratives.

Exercise 14.1

1. When would you use a narrative interview, when would you prefer the episodic interview, and when a different type of interview?
2. If you have a research question in your own research project, for which the narrative interview is adequate, develop a narrative generative question.
3. Develop an interview guide for an episodic interview for a research question of your own.

Notes

1   Sometimes also in semi-structured interviews, narratives are integrated as an element (e.g., in the problem-centered interview). In case of doubt, if they are unproductive, they are subordinated to the interview guide. More generally, Mishler (1986, p. 235) has studied what happens when interviewees in the semi-structured interview start to narrate, how these narratives are treated, and how they are suppressed rather than taken up.

2   Whyl is a place where a nuclear power plant was planned and built and where big anti-nuclear demonstrations took place in the 1970s, with lots of people camping on the site of the planned plant. M/L was a quite influential Marxist-Leninist political group at that time, which was not supporting this kind of demonstration.

FURTHER READING

The Narrative Interview
The first two texts deal with the topic of biographical research, whereas the third introduces the method into English language.

Bertaux, D. (ed.) (1981) *Biography and History: The Life History Approach in Social Sciences.* Beverly Hills, CA: SAGE.
Denzin, N.K. (1988) *Interpretive Biography.* London: SAGE.
Rosenthal, G. (2004) "Biographical Research," in C. Seale, G. Gobo, J. Gubrium and D. Silverman (eds), *Qualitative Research Practice.* London: SAGE. pp. 48–65.

The Episodic Interview
In these texts, some applications and the methodological background of the episodic interview can be found.

Flick, U. (1994) "Social Representations and the Social Construction of Everyday Knowledge: Theoretical and Methodological Queries," *Social Science Information*, 33: 179–197.
Flick, U. (1995) "Social Representations," in R. Harré, J. Smith and L.v. Langenhove (eds), *Rethinking Psychology.* London: SAGE. pp. 70–96.
Flick, U. (2000a) "Episodic Interviewing," in M. Bauer and G. Gaskell (eds), *Qualitative Researching with Text, Image and Sound: A Practical Handbook.* London: SAGE. pp. 75–92.

Narratives between Biography and Episode
To enter into a discussion of these questions more deeply, these two works of Bruner are very instructive.

Bruner, J. (1987) "Life as Narrative," *Social Research*, 54: 11–32.
Bruner, J. (1991) "The Narrative Construction of Reality," *Critical Inquiry*, 18: 1–21.

15

FOCUS GROUPS

CHAPTER OBJECTIVES

After reading this chapter, you should be able to

✓ familiarize yourself with the different ways of collecting data in a group.
✓ understand the differences between group interview, group discussion, and focus group.
✓ identify the problems linked to using groups for collecting qualitative data.

In the last chapters, I have presented several forms of open-ended interviews as a way to collect qualitative data. Semi-structured and narrative interviews were developed starting from a critique of standardized interview situations. The skepticism about this type of interview situation was partly based on the argument of its artificiality, because the interviewee is separated from all everyday relations during the interview. Also, the interaction in the standardized interview is not comparable in any way with everyday interactions. Particularly when studying opinions and attitudes about taboo subjects it was repeatedly suggested to use the dynamics of a group discussing such topics, because this is more appropriate than a clear and well-ordered single interview situation. These methods have been discussed as group interviews, group discussions, or focus groups. In contrast to narration produced as a monologue in the narrative interview, processes of constructing social reality are referred to that take place in joint narratives of family members for example. By thus extending the scope of data collection, it is attempted to collect the data in context and to create a situation of interaction that comes closer to everyday life than the (often one-off) encounter of interviewer and interviewee or narrator permits.

Group Interviews

One suggestion of how you can extend the interview situation is to interview a group of people. Beginning with Merton et al. (1956), group interviews have been conducted in a number of studies (Fontana and Frey 2000; Merton 1987). Patton, for example, defines the group interview as follows:

> A focus group interview is an interview with a small group of people on a specific topic. Groups are typically six to eight people who participate in the interview for one-half to two hours. (2002, p. 385)

Several procedures are differentiated, which are more or less structured and moderated by an interviewer. In general, the interviewer should be "flexible, objective, empathic, persuasive, a good listener" (Fontana and Frey 2000, p. 652). Objectivity here mainly means the mediation between the different participants. The interviewer's main task is to prevent single participants or partial groups from dominating the interview and thus the whole group with their contributions. Furthermore, the interviewer should encourage reserved members to become involved in the interview and give their views and should try to obtain answers from the whole group in order to cover the topic as far as possible. Finally, interviewers must balance their behavior between (directively) steering the group and (non-directively) moderating it.

Patton sees the focus group interview as a highly efficient qualitative data-collection technique, which provides some quality controls on data collection: "Participants tend to provide checks and balances on each other which weeds out false or extreme views. The extent to which there is a relatively consistent, shared view can be quickly assessed" (2002, p. 386). He also discusses some weaknesses of the method such as the limited number of questions you can address and the problems of taking notes during the interview. Therefore, he suggests the employment of pairs of interviewers, one of whom is free to document the responses while the other manages the interview and the group. In contrast to other authors Patton underlines the fact that: "The focus group interview is, first and foremost, an interview. It is not a problem-solving session. It is not a decision-making group. It is not primarily a discussion, although direct interactions among participants often occur. It is an *interview*" (2002, p. 385–386).

In summary, the main advantages of group interviews include that they are low cost and rich in data, that they stimulate the respondents and support them in remembering events, and that they can lead beyond the answers of the single interviewee.

Group Discussions

Apart from the saving of time and money made by interviewing a group of people at the same time instead of interviewing different individuals at different times, the elements of group dynamics and of discussion among the participants are highlighted when group discussions are conducted. Blumer, for example, holds that:

> A small number of individuals, brought together as a discussion or resource group, is more valuable many times over than any representative sample. Such a group, discussing collectively their sphere of life and probing into it as they meet one another's disagreements, will do more to lift the veils covering the sphere of life than any other device that I know of. (1969, p. 41)

Although they have a similar critique of standardized interviews as a background, group discussions have been used as an explicit alternative to open interviews in the German-speaking area. They have been proposed as a method of interrogation since the studies of the Frankfurt Institute for Social Research (Pollock 1955). Unlike the group interview, the group discussion stimulates a discussion and uses its dynamic of developing conversation in the discussion as the central sources of knowledge. The method attracted a lot of interest and isn't usually left out of any textbook, although marketing research and other fields use it often now (see also Bohnsack 2004 for a more general overview). People have different reasons for using this method. In methodological debates about group discussions, there is also the problem of contradictory understandings of what an appropriate group is like. However, it is up to the researcher actually using the method to decide on the "right" conception (i.e. the one, which is best fitted to the research object). The alternatives to be found in the literature will be discussed here briefly.

Reasons for Using Group Discussions

Group discussions are used for various reasons. Pollock prefers them to single interviews because "studying the attitudes, opinions and practices of human beings in artificial isolation from the contexts in which they occur should be avoided" (1955, p. 34). The starting point here is that opinions, which are presented to the interviewer in interviews and surveys, are detached from everyday forms of communication and relations. Group discussions on the other hand correspond to the way in which opinions are produced, expressed, and exchanged in everyday life. Another feature of group discussions is that corrections by the group concerning views that are not correct, not socially shared, or extreme are available as means for validating statements and views. The group becomes a tool for reconstructing individual opinions more appropriately. However, some researchers studied the group opinion (i.e., the participants' consensus negotiated in the discussion about a certain issue). Mangold (1973) takes the group opinion as an empirical issue, which is expressed in the discussion but exists independently of the situation and applies for the group outside the situation. Another aim of group discussions is the analysis of common processes of problem solving in the group. Therefore, a concrete problem is introduced and the group's task is to discover, through discussion of alternatives, the best strategy for solving it. Thus, approaches that take group discussions as a medium for better analyzing individual opinions can be differentiated from those that understand group discussions as a medium for a shared group opinion, which goes beyond individuals. However, studying processes of negotiating or solving problems in groups should be separated from analyzing states like a given group opinion which is only expressed in the discussion.

Forms of Groups

A brief look at the history of and the methodological discussion about this procedure shows that there have been different ideas about what a group is. A common feature of the varieties of group discussions is to use as a data source the discussion on a specific topic in a natural group (i.e., existing in everyday life) or an artificial group (i.e., put together for the research purpose according to certain criteria). Sometimes it is even suggested to use real groups, which means groups that are concerned by the issue of the group discussion also independently of the discussion and as a real group including the same members as in the research situation. A reason for this is that real groups start from a history of shared interactions in relation to the issue under discussion and thus have already developed forms of common activities and underlying patterns of meaning.

Furthermore, there is a distinction between homogeneous and heterogeneous groups. In homogeneous groups, members are comparable in the essential dimensions related to the research question and have a similar background. In heterogeneous groups, members should be different in the characteristics that are relevant for the research question. This is intended to increase the dynamics of the discussion in order that many different perspectives will be expressed and also that the reserve of individual participants' will be broken down by the confrontation between these perspectives.

Case Study: Student Dropouts: How to Set Up a Group

In a study of the conditions and the subjective experience of students dropping out of teaching programs, a homogeneous group would consist of students of the same age, from the same discipline, and who dropped out of their studies after the same number of terms. If the concrete question focuses on gender differences in the experiences and the reasons for not completing one's studies, a homogeneous group is put together comprising only female students, with male students being put into a second group. A heterogeneous group should include students of various ages, of both genders, from different disciplines (e.g., psychology and information sciences), and from different terms (e.g., dropouts from the first term and from shortly before the end of

(Continued)

(Continued)

their studies). The expectation linked to this is that the different backgrounds will lead to intensified dynamics in the discussion, which will reveal more aspects and perspectives of the phenomenon under study.

However, in a homogeneous group the members may differ in other dimensions, which were not considered as relevant for the composition of the group. In our example, this was the dimension of the students' current living situation–alone or with their own family. Another problem is that heterogeneous groups in which the members differ too much may only find a few starting points for a common discussion. If the conditions of studying the various disciplines are so different there may be little that the student dropouts can discuss in a concrete way with each other and the discussion may end up in exchanging only general statements. These considerations should make it clear that the juxtaposition of "homogeneous" and "heterogeneous" is only relative. Groups normally comprise five to ten members. Opinions about the best size of a group diverge.

This example shows how groups can be composed to meet the needs of a research question. It should also make clear that the definition of homogeneous or heterogeneous is always relative depending on the research question and the dimension that is important.

What Is the Role of the Moderator?

Another aspect that is treated differently in the various approaches is the role and function of the moderator in the discussion. In some cases, the group's own dynamic is trusted so much that moderation by researchers is abandoned altogether in order to prevent any biasing influence on the discussion in process and content that may arise as a result of their interventions. However, it is more often the case that the moderation of the discussion by a researcher is found to be necessary for pragmatic reasons. Here three forms are distinguished. *Formal direction* is limited to control of the agenda of the speakers and to fixing the beginning, course, and end of the discussion. *Topical steering* additionally comprises the introduction of new questions and steering the discussion towards a deepening and extension of specific topics and parts. Beyond this, *steering the dynamics* of the interaction ranges from reflating the discussion to using provocative questions, polarizing a slow discussion, or accommodating relations of dominance by purposively addressing members remaining rather reserved in the discussion. Another possibility is the use of texts, images, and so on to further stimulate the discussion or topics dealt with during the discussion. However, these interventions should only support the dynamics and the functioning of the group. To a large extent the discussion should find its own dynamic level. In general, the moderator's task is not to disturb the participants' own initiative but to create an open space in which the discussion keeps going first through the exchange of arguments.

If you decide to use group discussions, you will choose a combination from the alternatives available concerning the aims, the kind and composition of the group, and the function of the moderator is chosen for the particular application.

Case Study: Group Discussion with Bank Employees

Krüger (1983) has studied restrictive contexts of actions for a professional future. She conducted eight group discussions with bank employees on the lowest hierarchical level (i.e., officials in charge from specific departments of the credit business). These were real groups because the group members came from one department and knew each other. The groups were homogeneous, as she did not involve superiors in order to exclude any inhibitions. An average group included seven participants. Krüger emphasizes a nondirective style of moderating in which the moderator should always try to stimulate narrative-descriptive statements. Pointing out phenomena of the situation that have not (yet) been mentioned is suggested as a way to achieve this. The researcher gave stimuli for the discussion. A protocol of the process was made in order to be able to identify speakers in the transcript later. Krüger also underlines that it is essential for the practical conduct of a group discussion that the research question is restricted to a delimited area of experience. In terms of defining cases, she sees the text of each group discussion. This text had to undergo successive stages of interpretation.

This example shows practical issues of making a group discussion fruitful for a specific research question.

What is the Process, and What are Elements of Group Discussions?

A single scheme cannot present how you should proceed when running a group discussion. The dynamics and the composition of the group essentially influence the way a group discussion unfolds. In real or natural groups, the members already know each other and possibly have an interest in the topic of the discussion. In artificial groups, introducing members to one another and enabling members to make one another's acquaintance should be the first step. The following steps provide a rough outline of procedure:

- At the beginning, an explanation of the (formal) procedure is given. Here the expectations for the participants are formulated. Expectations can be to be involved in the discussion, maybe to argue certain topics, to manage a common task, or solve a problem together. (For example, "We would like you to openly discuss with each other the experiences you have had with your studies, and what it was that made you decide not to continue them any further").
- A short introduction of the members to one another and a phase of warming up follow to prepare the discussion. Here the moderator should emphasize the

common ground of the members in order to facilitate or to reinforce community (e.g., "As former students of psychology, you all should know the problems, the . . .").

- The actual discussion starts with a "discussion stimulus," which may consist of a provocative thesis, a short film, a lecture on a text, or the unfolding of a concrete problem for which a solution is to be found. Note some of the parallels to the focused interview (see Chapter 13 and Merton 1987). In order to stimulate discussions about the change of work and living conditions with workers, Herkommer (1979, p. 263) gave the discussion stimulus shown in Box 15.1.

- Particularly in groups with members that did not know each other in advance, phases of strangeness with, of orientation to, adaptation to, and familiarity with the group as well as conformity and the discussion drying up are gone through.

Box 15.1   Example of a Discussion Stimulus in a Group Discussion

In the following example, a group discussion in the area of research into economic crisis and the resulting uncertainty – a still very relevant issue – is stimulated as follows:

The current economic situation in Germany has become more difficult; this is indicated for example by continuously high unemployment, by problems with pensions and social security, and by tougher wage bargaining. From this, a series of problems in occupations and in workplaces has resulted for workers. In general, a decline in the working climate of factories has occurred. But there are also other problems in everyday life and in the family, e.g., in children's school education. With respect to the problems just mentioned, we would like to hear your opinion on the position: "One day our children will have a better life!" (Herkommer 1979, p. 263).

Problems in Conducting the Method

The proclaimed strength of the method compared with interviewing single persons is also the main source of the problems in applying it. The dynamics, which are determined by the individual groups, make it more difficult to formulate distinct patterns of process in discussions and also to clearly define the tasks and multiple conducts for the moderators beyond the individual group. For this reason, it is hardly possible to design relatively common conditions for the collection of data in different groups involved in a study. It is true that the opening of discussions may be shaped uniformly by a specific formulation, a concrete stimulus, and so on. But the twists and turns of the discussion during its further development can hardly be predicted. Therefore, methodological interventions for steering the group may only be planned approximately and a great deal of the decisions on data collection can only be made during the situation. Similar conditions apply to the decision about when a group has exhausted the discussion of a topic. Here no clear criteria are given, which means that the moderator has to make this decision on the spot.

Problems similar to those that occur in semi-structured interviewing emerge. The problem the researchers face in mediating between the course of the discussion and their own topical inputs is relevant here too. It becomes more serious. It is aggravated here because researchers have to accommodate the developing dynamics of the group and, at the same time, to steer the discussion in order to integrate all the participants. Thus, it remains difficult to handle the problem because of the dynamics of the situation and the group; individual members may dominate while others may refrain from entering into the discussion. In both cases, the result is that some individual members and their views are not available for the later interpretation.

Finally, the apparent economics of interviewing several persons at the same time is clearly reduced by the high organizational effort needed to make an appointment at which all members of a group can participate.

Contribution to the General Methodological Discussion

Group discussions may reveal how opinions are created and above all changed, asserted, or suppressed in social exchange. In a group discussion, you can collect verbal data in their context. Statements and expressions of opinion are made in the context of a group, and these may be commented upon and become the subject of a more or less dynamic process of discussion. A study's result of the group discussion as a method is that dynamic and social negotiations of individual views as an essential element of the social constructionist theoretical approach to reality have increasingly been taken into account in the methodological literature.

Fitting the Method into the Research Process

The theoretical background to applying the method is often structuralist models (see Chapter 6), starting from the dynamic, and from the unconscious in the generation of meanings, this manifesting in group discussions. In the more recent applications, the development of theories has been to the fore. Earlier attempts to test hypotheses with this procedure have failed owing to the lack of comparability of the data. The close link between the collection and the interpretation of data suggests a circular concept of the research process (see Chapter 8). Research questions focus on how opinions are produced and how they are distributed or shared in a group. In accessing cases and in sampling, researchers face the problem that the groups in which the individuals are assembled for the data collection become units themselves. Theoretical sampling (see Chapter 11) may focus on the characteristics of the groups to integrate (e.g., if groups of psychology students and of medical students have been involved so far, would it be better now to integrate engineering students from technical universities or from colleges?). Or it may focus on the features of the individual members. In the interpretation of the data, the individual group again is the unit to start from. Sequential analyses (e.g., objective hermeneutics–see Chapter 25) are suggested, which start from the group and the course of discussion in it. In terms of generalizing the findings, the problem arises of how to summarize the different groups.

Limitations of the Method

During the interpretation of the data, problems often arise owing to the differences in the dynamics of the groups, the difficulties of comparing the groups, and of identifying the opinions and views of the individual group members within this dynamics. As the smallest analytical unit, you should consider only the whole discussion groups or subgroups. In order to enable some comparability among the groups and among the members as cases in the whole sample, non-directed groups are now rarely used. Because of the major effort in conducting, recording, transcribing, and interpreting group discussions, their use makes sense mainly for research questions, which focus particularly on the social dynamics of generating opinions in a group. Attempts to use group discussions to economize on individual interviewing of many people at the same time have proved less effective. Often this method is combined with other methods (e.g., additional single interviews or observations).

Focus Groups

Whereas the term "group discussion" was dominant in earlier studies, especially in the German-speaking area, the method has more recently had some kind of renaissance as "focus group" in Anglo-Saxon research (for overviews see Barbour 2006; Lunt and Livingstone 1996; Merton 1987; Puchta and Potter 2004). Focus groups are used especially in marketing and media research. Again, the stress is laid on the interactive aspect of data collection. The hallmark of focus groups is the explicit use of the group interaction to produce data and insights that would be less accessible without the interaction found in a group (Morgan 1988, p. 12). Focus groups are used as a method on their own or in combination with other methods–surveys, observations, single interviews, and so on. Morgan (1988, p. 11) sees focus groups as useful for

- orienting oneself to a new field;
- generating hypotheses based on informants' insights;
- evaluating different research sites or study populations;
- developing interview schedules and questionnaires;
- getting participants' interpretations of results from earlier studies.

Box 15.2   Examples for Beginning a Focus Group

These two openings of focus groups are very typical and helpful:

Before we begin our discussion, it will be helpful for us to get acquainted with one another. Let's begin with some introductory comments about ourselves. X, why don't you start and we'll go around the table and give our names and a little about what we do for a living?

Today we're going to discuss an issue that affects all of you. Before we get into our discussion, let me make a few requests of you. First, you should know that we are tape recording the session so that I can refer back to the discussion when I write my report. If anyone is uncomfortable with being recorded please say so and, of course, you are free to leave. Do speak up and let's try to have just one person speak at a time. I will play traffic cop and try to assure that everyone gets a turn. Finally, please say exactly what you think. Don't worry about what I think or what your neighbor thinks. We're here to exchange opinions and have fun while we do it. Why don't we begin by introducing ourselves?

Source: Stewart and Shamdasani 1990, pp. 92–93

How to Conduct Focus Groups

A short overview of the literature provides some suggestions for conducting focus groups. The number of groups you should conduct depends on your research question and on the number of different population subgroups required (Morgan 1988, p. 42). It is generally suggested that it is more appropriate to work with strangers instead of groups of friends or people who know each other very well, because the level of things taken for granted, which remain implicit tends to be higher in the latter (1988, p. 48). It is also suggested that you should begin with groups as heterogeneous as possible and then run a second set of groups that are more homogeneous (1988, p. 73). In each case, it is necessary to start the group with some kind of warming up, as in the examples in Box 15.2.

According to Puchta and Potter (2004), one of the important things in running focus groups is to produce informality in the discussion. The moderators need to create a liberal climate, facilitating that the members contribute openly with their experiences and opinions. At the same time, it is important that the participants do not drift into just chatting or presenting endless anecdotes with little reference to the issue of the focus group (and the study). Puchta and Potter suggest several strategies how to balance formality and informality in the practice of focus groups.

It is suggested to use the contents of the discussions or systematic coding or content analyses as an analytic technique for focus group data. Think about the point of reference in the comparisons. You could try to take the single participants' statements and compare them across all groups. This can be difficult because of the group dynamics and the different development of each group. Therefore, the second alternative will be more adequate. This means you take the single group as a unit and compare it with the other groups you did. Comparison then focuses on the topics mentioned, the variety of attitudes towards these topics among the members in the group, the stages the discussion ran through, and the results of the discussion in each group.

What is the Contribution to the General Methodological Discussion?

Focus groups can be seen and used as simulations of everyday discourses and conversations or as a quasi-naturalistic method for studying the generation of social representations or social knowledge in general (Lunt and Livingstone 1996). The general strength of focus groups is twofold:

> First, focus groups generate discussion, and so reveal both the meanings that people read into the discussion topic and how they negotiate those meanings. Second, focus groups generate diversity and difference, either within or between groups, and so reveal what Billig (1987) has called the dilemmatic nature of everyday arguments. (1996, p. 96)

What are the Limitations of the Method?

This method faces problems similar to those already mentioned for group discussion. A specific problem is how to document the data in a way that allows the identification of individual speakers and the differentiation between statements of several parallel speakers.

How does the Method Fit into the Research Process?

Focus groups start from an interactionst point of view (see Chapter 6) and want to show how an issue is constructed and changed in a group discussing this issue. Sampling is often oriented towards diversity of the members of the various groups in a study (see Chapter 11). The analysis of data is often very pragmatic—statements rather than extensive interpretations are the focus of the analysis. A more recent development is the use of online focus groups (see Chapter 20).

Case Study: Using Focus Groups for a Feedback of Results and Member Check

In our study on health professionals' concepts of health and ageing (Flick et al. 2003, 2004), we first used episodic interviews (see Chapter 14) to collect data on these concepts, including the interviewees' ideas and experiences with prevention and health promotion. After analyzing these data, we ran focus groups with general practitioners and nurses with three goals. We wanted to give the participants feedback about our study's results. We also wanted to receive their comments on these results. And we intended to

(Continued)

(Continued)

discuss with them practical consequences of the findings for improving the day-to-day routines in home-care nursing and medicine. This improvement should be directed towards a stronger focus on health, health promotion, and prevention. In order to prevent the discussions in the groups from becoming too general and heterogeneous, we looked for a concrete sensitizing concept as an input, which opened up the overall issue. We used the results referring to the barriers against a stronger focus on prevention in their own practice that the interviewees had mentioned in the interviews. We presented the results concerning the patients' and the professionals' readiness and resistance. First, we presented an overview of the barriers that had been mentioned, then asked the participants for a ranking of their importance. Next, we asked them to discuss the results in the wider context of health in their own practice. When this discussion started to calm down, we asked them to make suggestions, how to overcome the barriers discussed before, and to discuss such suggestions. In the end, we had a list of comments and suggestions from each group, which we then compared and analyzed as a part of our study.

In this example, focus groups were used for a specific purpose. They were not used as a stand-alone method for data collection, but for a feedback and member check of first results of a study. The participants in the focus groups were the same as in the single interviews. However, not all the interviewees accepted our invitation to come and contribute again to our study. Using a stimulus–in this case, the presentation of a selection of results–was helpful to start and structure the discussion. In the end, when we compared the results, we had to use each group as a case, but ended up with comparable views and results.

Joint Narratives

In a similar direction, Hildenbrand and Jahn (1988) extend and develop the narrative approach to data collection. Their starting point was the observation in family studies that families under study jointly narrate and thus restructure and reconstruct domains of their everyday reality. Starting from this observation, the authors stimulate such joint narratives more systematically and use them as data. All the persons belonging to a household are present in the situation of data collection, which should take place at the family's home: "At the beginning of the conversation, the family members are invited to recount details and events from their former and current family life. We abandoned the use of an explicit narrative stimulus, because it produces unnecessary restrictions on the variety of topics" (1988, p. 207). In order to allow the family members to shape the conversation, the authors refrained from methodologically directed interventions. This is intended to bring the research situation as close as possible to the everyday situation of narratives in the family. Finally, by using a checklist, those social data are completed, together with the family, which have not been mentioned during the narrative. At the end, extended observational protocols are made, which refer to the context of the conversation (generative history, living conditions of the family, description of the house, and its furniture).

What is the Contribution to the General Methodological Discussion?

With this approach, the situation of the monologue of a single narrator (in the narrative interview) is extended to a collective storytelling. Analyses of the interaction are made, which refer to the realization of the narrative and to the way in which the family constructs reality for itself and the listener. This approach has been developed in the context of a specific field of research–family studies.[1] The natural structure of this field or research object is given as a particular reason for the interest in this method. It should be possible to transfer this idea of joint narratives to other forms of communality beyond families. You could imagine using the method to analyze a specific institution (e.g., a counseling service, its history, activities and conflicts, by asking the members of the teams working in it to jointly recount the history of their institution). This would not only make the narrated course of development an analytic issue but also the dynamics of the different views and presentations of the members.

How does the Method Fit into the Research Process?

The theoretical background of the method is the joint construction of reality. The aim is the development of theories grounded in these constructions (see Chapter 8). The starting point is the single case (a family in Hildenbrand and Jahn 1988), where later on other cases are included step by step (see Chapter 11). Interpretation of the material proceeds sequentially (see Chapter 25), with the aim of arriving at more general statements from the comparison of cases (see Chapter 29).

Which are Limitations of the Method?

The method has been developed in the context of a study using several other methods. Its independent use remains to be tested. A further problem is that large textual materials result from a single case. This makes interpretations of single cases very voluminous. Therefore, analyses mostly remain limited to case studies. Finally, the rather far-reaching abstinence from methodological interventions makes it more difficult to purposively apply the method to specific research questions and to direct its application in collecting data. It is possible that not only the strengths but also the problems of the narrative interview are combined with those of group discussions.

The group procedures briefly mentioned here stress different aspects of the task of going beyond interviewing individuals to data collection in a group. Sometimes it is the reduction in time spent interviewing–one group at one time instead of many individuals at different times–that is important. Group dynamics may be attributed as being a helpful or a disturbing feature in realizing the goal of receiving answers from all interviewees. In a group discussion, however, it is precisely this dynamic and the additional options of knowledge produced by the group, which are given priority. In joint narratives, it is the process of constructing reality as it occurs at this moment in this group, which is of particular interest. This process is assumed to occur in a similar form in the family's everyday life and thus also beyond the research situation. In each case, the verbal data gathered are more complex than in the single interview. The advantage of this complexity is that data are richer and more diverse in their content than in an individual interview. The problem of this complexity is that it is more difficult to locate the viewpoints of the individuals involved in this common process of meaning making than in an individual interview.

KEY POINTS

- Group interviews are seldom used compared to focus groups.
- It is suggested to use focus groups instead of single interviews only when the research question gives you a good reason. Saving time not a likely benefit of working with groups instead of interviews due to the more difficult organizational details and the work required to analyze group protocols.
- Focus groups or joint narratives can be very fruitful where the interaction and maybe the dynamics of the members can add something to the knowledge produced in the data collection situation.

Exercise 15.1

1. Look for a study in the literature using focus groups as a research method. Identify what kind of group was given in this case.
2. Try also to identify how the researcher conducted the group.
3. Think of a research issue that would be best studied by using focus groups or group discussions.

Note

1   A broader interest in collective recounting and remembering is expressed in the work of Hirst and Manier (1996) for families and in Dixon and Gould (1996) and Bruner and Feldman (1996). The method discussed here gives a concrete procedure for qualitative studies in this area of interest.

FURTHER READING

Group Interviews
Both texts deal explicitly with group interviews as a method.

Fontana, A. and Frey, J.H. (2000) "The Interview: From Structured Questions to Negotiated Text," in N. Denzin and Y.S. Lincoln (eds), *Handbook of Qualitative Research* (2nd edn). London: SAGE. pp. 645–672.
Patton, M.Q. (2002) *Qualitative Evaluation and Research Methods* (3rd edn). London: SAGE.

Group Discussions
The following text discusses methodological problems and applications of the method and links it to the discussion of focus groups.

Bohnsack, R. (2004) "Group Discussions and Focus Groups," in U. Flick, E.v. Kardorff and I. Steinke (eds), *A Companion to Qualitative Research.* London: SAGE. pp. 214–221.

Focus Groups
The first text discusses recent applications and methodological problems, whereas the other two give general overviews of the method.

Lunt, P. and Livingstone, S. (1996) "Rethinking the Focus Group in Media and Communications Research," *Journal of Communication*, 46: 79–98.
Morgan, D.L. and Krueger, R.A. (eds) (1998) *The Focus Group Kit* (6 vols). Thousand Oaks, CA: SAGE.
Puchta, C. and Potter, J. (2004) *Focus Group Practice.* London: SAGE.
Stewart, D.M. and Shamdasani, P.N. (1990) *Focus Groups: Theory and Practice.* Newbury Park, CA: SAGE.

Joint Narratives
Each text deals with a field of application of group narratives.

Bruner, J. and Feldman, C. (1996) "Group Narrative as a Cultural Context of Autobiography," in D. Rubin (ed.), *Remembering Our Past: Studies in Autobiographical Memory.* Cambridge: Cambridge University Press. pp. 291–317.
Hildenbrand, B. and Jahn, W. (1988) "Gemeinsames Erzählen und Prozesse der Wirklichkeitskonstruktion in familiengeschichtlichen Gesprächen," *Zeitschrift für Soziologie*, 17: 203–17.

16

VERBAL DATA: AN OVERVIEW

CHAPTER OBJECTIVES
After reading this chapter, you should be able to

✓ compare the different approaches to verbal data in order to make a decision about which one to use for your own research.
✓ assess your decision critically in the light of your (first) experiences with applying the method you chose.
✓ understand the method in the context of the research process and of the other stages of your research plan.

Collecting verbal data is one of the major methodological approaches in qualitative research. You can use different strategies to produce as much openness towards the object under study and the views of the interviewee, narrator, or participant in discussions as possible. At the same time, the methodological alternatives include specific elements for structuring the collection of data. Thus, you should make topics referring to the research question an issue in the interview or you should direct their treatment towards a greater depth or towards being more comprehensive. Additionally, you should introduce aspects of the research question not yet mentioned. The different methods alternate between these two goals–producing openness and producing structure. Each method orients to one or the other of these aims. In their central part, at least, narrative interviews are oriented towards openness and scope for the interviewee's presentation. The interviewer's directive interventions should be limited to the generative narrative question and to the stage of narrative enquiries at the end. In semi-structured interviews, the thematic direction is given much more preference and the interviews may be focused much more directly on certain topics. Therefore, depending on the goal of the research and on the chosen goal—openness or structuring—specific methods are recommended to a greater or lesser extent for each concrete research question. In this chapter I will outline four points of reference for such a decision between different methods for collecting verbal data.

First Point of Reference: Criteria Based Comparison of the Approaches

A comparison of the various forms of semi-structured interviews, narrative, and group methods may be taken as a first point of reference for deciding between them. As criteria for such a decision, Table 16.1 shows elements in each method for guaranteeing sufficient openness for interviewees' subjective views. Elements for producing a sufficient level of structure and depth in dealing with the thematic issue in the interview are also listed. Further features shown are each method's contribution to the development of the interview method in general and the fields of application which each was created for or is mainly used in. Finally, the problems of conducting the method and the limits mentioned in the previous chapters are noted for each approach. Thus, the field of methodological alternatives in the domain of verbal data is outlined so that the individual method may be located within it.

Second Point of Reference: The Selection of the Method and Checking its Application

The various methodological alternatives aiming at the collection and analysis of verbal data suggest that it is necessary to make a well-founded decision according to your own study, its research question, its target group, and so on. Which method do you select for collecting data? I suggest that you assess such a decision on the basis of the character of the material that you want to collect. Not all methods are appropriate to every research question: biographical processes of events may be presented in narratives rather than in the question–answer schema of the semi-structured interview. For studying processes of developing opinions, the dynamic of group discussions is instructive, whereas this feature rather obstructs the analysis of individual experiences. The research question and the issue under study are the first anchoring points for deciding for or against a concrete method. Some people are able to narrate and others are not. For some target groups, it is a highly strange procedure to reconstruct their subjective theory; others can become involved in the situation without any problem. The (potential) interviewees are the second anchoring points for methodological decisions and for assessing their appropriateness.

TABLE 16.1 Comparison of Methods for Collecting Verbal Data

Criteria	Interviews					Narratives as Data		Group Procedures		
	Focused Interview	Semi-Standardized Interview	Problem-Centered Interview	Expert Interview	Ethnographic Interview	Narrative Interview	Episodic Interview	Group Discussion	Focus Groups	Joint Narratives
Openness to the interviewee's subjective view by:	• Non-direction by unstructured questions	• Open questions	• Object and process orientation • Room for narratives	• Limited because only interested in the expert, not the person	• Descriptive questions	• Non-influencing of narratives once started	• Narratives of meaningful experiences • Selection by the interviewee	• Non-directive moderation of the discussion • Permissive climate in the discussion	• Taking the context of the group into account	• Abandonment of narrative stimulus and methodological interventions
Structuring (e.g., deepening) the issue by:	• Giving a stimulus • Structured questions • Focusing on feelings	• Hypothesis-directed questions • Confrontational questions	• Interview guide as basis for turns and ending unproductive presentations	• Interview guide as instrument for structuring	• Structural questions • Contrastive questions	• Generative narrative questions • Part of narrative questioning at the end • Balancing part	• Connection of narratives and argumentation • Suggestion of concrete situations to be recounted	• Dynamics developing in the group • Steering with a guide	• Using an interview guide to direct the discussion	• Dynamics of joint narrative • Checklist for demographic data • Observation protocol
Contribution to the general development of the interview as a method	• Four criteria for designing interviews • Analyzing the object as a second data sort	• Structuring the contents with structure-laying-technique • Suggestions for explicating implicit knowledge	• Short questionnaire • Postscript	• Highlighting of direction: limitation of the interview to the expert	• Highlighting the problem of making interview situations	• Localization of structuring the interview at the beginning and the end • Exploring narratives as research instrument systematically	• Systematic connection of narrative and argumentation as data sorts • Purposive generative narrative question	• Alternative to single interview owing to group dynamics	• Simulation of the way discourses and social representations are generated in their diversity	• Combination of narrative and interaction analyses • Stressing the constructive part in narratives
Domain of application	• Analysis of subjective meanings	• Reconstruction of subjective theories	• Socially or biographically relevant problems	• Expert knowledge in institutions	• In the framework of field research in open fields	• Biographical courses	• Change, routines, and situations in everyday life	• Opinion and attitude research	• Marketing and media research	• Family research

TABLE 16. 1 (Continued)

Criteria	Interviews				Narratives as Data			Group Procedures		
	Focused Interview	Semi-Standardized Interview	Problem-Centered Interview	Expert Interview	Ethnographic Interview	Narrative Interview	Episodic Interview	Group Discussion	Focus Groups	Joint Narratives
Problems in conducting the method	• Dilemma of combining the criteria	• Extensive methodological input • Problems of interpretation	• Unsystematic change from narrative to question–answer schema	• Role diffusion of the interviewee • Blocking by the expert	• Mediation between friendly conversation and formal interview	• Extremely unilateral interview situation • Problems of the narrator • Problematic zugzwangs	• Explication of the principle • Handling the interview guide	• Mediation between silent and talkative people • Course can hardly be planned	• How to sample groups and members	• Abandonment of topically focusing the narrative
Limitations of the method	• Assumption of knowing objective features of the object is questionable • Hardly any application in its pure form	• Introducing a structure • Need to adapt the method to the issue and the interviewee	• Problem orientation • Unsystematic combination of most diverse partial elements	• Limitation of the interpretation on expert knowledge	• Mainly sensible in combination with observation and field research	• Supposed analogy of experience and narrative • Reducing the object to what can be recounted	• Limitation on everyday knowledge	• High organizational effort • Problems of comparability	• Documentation of data • Identification of single speakers and several speakers at the same time	• Abandonment of steering • Own stand as a single method? • Extension of case analyses
References	Merton and Kendall (1946)	Groeben (1990)	Witzel (2000)	Meuser and Nagel (2002)	Heyl (2001) Spradley (1979)	Hermanns (1995) Rieman and Schütze (1987) Rosenthal (2004)	Flick (1994; 1995; 2000a)	Blumer (1969) Bohnsack (2004)	Lunt and Livingstone (1996) Merton (1987) Puchta and Potter (2004)	Bruner and Feldman (1996) Hildenbrand and Jahn (1988)

But such differences in becoming involved in specific interview situations are not only individual differences. If you take into account the research question and the level of statements your study is aiming at, then you can regard systematically the relation between method, subject(s), and issue. The criterion here is the appropriateness of the method you choose and of how you apply it. However, you should ask questions concerning this point not only at the end of your data collection, when all the interviews or discussions have been conducted, but also earlier on in the procedure after one or two trial interviews or discussions. One aspect for checking the appropriateness of the methodological choice is to examine if and how far you have applied the method in its own terms. For example, has a narrative interview really been started with a generative narrative question? Have changes of topics and new questions been introduced only after the interviewee had had enough time and scope to deal with the preceding topic in sufficient detail in a semi-structured interview?

The analysis of the initial interviews may show that it is not only the interviewees who have more problems with certain methods than with others. Interviewers may also have more problems in applying a certain method than other methods. One reason for this is that it may be over challenging the interviewer's ability to decide when and how to return to the interview guide if the interviewee deviates from the subject or to deploy the necessary active listening skills in the narrative interview. Thus, you should also check how far an interviewer and method match. If problems emerge at this level, there are two possible solutions. Careful interview training may be given (for this, see the sections on the focused and semi-standardized interview in Chapter 13 and on the narrative and episodic interviews in Chapter 14) in order to reduce these problems. If this were not sufficient, I would consider changing the method. A basis for such decisions may be provided by analyzing the interaction in the situation of collecting data for the scope allowed to the interviewee by the interviewer and for how clearly the roles of both have been defined. A final factor you should consider in choosing a method and in assessing it relates to how the data are to be interpreted later and at which level of generalization the findings will be obtained.

Suggestions for making the decision about which method of data collection to use and for assessing the appropriateness of this decision are given in the checklist in Table 16.2.[1]

Third Point of Reference: Appropriateness of the Method to the Issue

Certain procedures are considered the "ideal way" to study an issue in a practical and methodologically legitimate way during a methodological discussion. In such discussions, one central feature of qualitative research is ignored: methods

TABLE 16.2   Checklist for Selecting an Interview Type and Evaluating its Application

1   *Research question*
Can the interview type and its application address the essential aspects of the research question?

2   *Interview type*
The method must be applied according to the methodological elements and targets. There should be no jumping between interview types, except when it is grounded in the research of a question or theoretically.

3   *Interviewer*
Are the interviewers able to apply the interview type? What are the consequences of their own fears and uncertainties in the situation?

4   *Interviewee*
Is the interview type appropriate to the target group of the application? How can one take into account the fears, uncertainties, and expectations of (potential) interviewees?

5   *Scope allowed to the interviewee*
Can the interviewees present their views in the framework of the questions?
Can they assert their views against the framework of the questions?

6   *Interaction*
Have the interviewers conducted the type of interview correctly?
Have they left enough scope for the interviewee?
Did they fulfil their role? (Why not?)
Were the interviewee's role, the interviewer's role, and the situation clearly defined for the interviewee?

Could the interviewee fulfil his or her role? (Why not?)
Analyze the breaks in order to validate the interview between the first and second interview if possible.

7   *Aim of the interpretation*
Are you interested in finding and analyzing limited and clear answers or complex, multifold patterns, contexts etc.?

8   *Claim for generalization*
The level on which statements should be made:

- For the single case (the interviewed individual and his or her biography, an institution and its impact, etc.)?
- With reference to groups (about a profession, a type of institution, etc.)?
- General statements?

should be selected and evaluated according to their appropriateness to the subject under study (see Chapter 2). One exception to this is studies that explore certain methods mainly in order to obtain findings about their conduct, conductibility, and problems. Then, the object of research has only an exemplary status for answering such methodological questions. In all other cases, the decision to use a certain method should be regarded as subordinate: the issue, research question, individuals studied, and statements striven for are the anchoring points for assessing the appropriateness of concrete methods in qualitative research.

Fourth Point of Reference: Fitting the Method into the Research Process

Finally, you should check the method you selected for how it fits into the research process. The aim is to find out if the procedure for collecting data suits the procedure for interpreting them. It does not make sense to use the narrative interview during the data collection in order to allow the presentation a wide scope, if the data received then undergo a content analysis using only categories derived from the literature and paraphrases of the original text (for this see Chapter 23). It also does not make sense to want to interpret an interview that stresses the consistent treating of the topics in the interview guide with a sequential procedure (see Chapter 25), which is concerned to uncover the development of the structure of the presentation. In a similar way, you should check the compatibility of the procedure for collecting data with your method of sampling cases (see Chapter 11). And you should assess its compatibility with the theoretical background of your study (see Chapter 6) and the understanding of the research process as a whole (e.g. developing theories versus testing hypotheses: see Chapter 8) that you took as starting points.

You will find the starting points for this assessment in the paragraphs about the fitting of the method into the research process given in the sections about each method. They outline the method's inherent understanding of the research process and its elements. The next step is to check how far the design of your study and the conceptualization of the single steps are compatible with the method's inherent conceptualization.

Thus, four points of reference for deciding on a concrete method are outlined, which also can and should be applied to procedures not primarily aimed at verbal but multi-focus data (see Chapter 21) and alternatives for interpretation (see Chapter 27). In addition to the appropriateness of the methods used for the object under study (see Chapter 2), it is above all the orientation to the process of research (see Chapters 28 and 29) that becomes an essential criterion to evaluate methodological decisions.

KEY POINTS

- All methods for collecting verbal data have their strengths and weaknesses.
- They all offer ways to give the participants in the study room for presenting their experiences and so on.

- At the same time, every method structures what it studies in a specific way.
- Before and during applying a specific method for answering your research question, I suggest that you check and assess whether the method you selected is appropriate or not.

Exercise 16.1

1. Take a study from the literature, which is based on interviewing people and reflect about whether or not the applied method was appropriate for the issue under study and the people involved in the research.
2. Reflecting on your own study, what were your main reasons for using this specific method?

Note

1   For more clarity, only the term "interview" is used. If you replace it by "group discussion" or "focus group," the same questions may be asked and answers found in the same way.

FURTHER READING

Flick, U. (2000a) "Episodic Interviewing," in M. Bauer and G. Gaskell (eds), *Qualitative Researching with Text, Image and Sound: A Practical Handbook.* London: SAGE, pp. 75–92.

Hermanns, H. (2004) "Interviewing as an Activity," in U. Flick, E.v. Kardorff and I. Steinke (eds), *A Companion to Qualitative Research.* London: SAGE, pp. 209–213.

Mason, J. (2002) "Qualitative Interviewing: Asking, Listening and Interpreting," in T. May (ed.), *Qualitative Research in Action.* London: SAGE, pp. 225–241.

Puchta, C. and Potter, J. (2004) *Focus Group Practice.* London: SAGE.

Wengraf, T. (2001) *Qualitative Research Interviewing: Biographic Narrative and Semi-Structured Methods.* London: SAGE.

PART 5

MULTIFOCUS DATA

The previous part of the book presented an overview of approaches that have data on one level in common. The spoken word is central for these approaches and the data they produce. Other information beyond what participants in your study say has only limited relevance in these approaches. However, there are now methods that aim to overcome this limitation and Part 5 will make you familiar with methods going beyond words in what they produce as data. Participant and nonparticipant observation have a long tradition in qualitative research and are currently sailing under the flag of ethnography to new relevance and influence in qualitative research in general. Characteristic for such research is the use of a variety of methods and data from observation and interviews to documents and other traces of interaction and practices and this is outlined in Chapter 17. Second-hand observation–using photographs, films, or videos–has recently attracted increasing attention. Whereas the area of verbal data saw a narrative turn in the last decades, we now see other turns such as the iconic turn or the performative turn, which make extended forms of data necessary to study the research questions linked to these turns. Films and photographs are everywhere and images dominate a bigger part of our lives. So it is no big surprise that film, photographs and video have become formats to produce data as well as issues of research in qualitative studies. Chapter 18 is devoted to such forms of visual data. Qualitative research also uses mediated data as well.

The use of documents for study has a long tradition in qualitative research; for example, they can be seen as traces of personal experiences or of institutional interactions (see Chapter 19). Computer mediated communication plays a big part in our everyday life as scientists, but also for our potential study participants. E-mail, Internet, the Word Wide Web, chats, and newsgroups have become familiar ways of communicating–at least for many people. So it is no surprise that the Internet has not only been discovered as an object of research, but also as a tool for reaching people and for doing interviews and ethnographies. The promises and pitfalls of these new options and how to make such research work is outlined in Chapter 20. The final chapter in this part summarizes, and compares the different approaches to collecting multifocus data.

17

OBSERVATION AND ETHNOGRAPHY

CHAPTER OBJECTIVES

After reading this chapter, you should be able to

✓ know the different versions of observation you can use for your own study.
✓ understand the special problems of participant observation.
✓ identify ethnography as the current trend in the context of these traditions.

If you have a look at the history of qualitative research, you will find that methodological discussions about the role of observation as a sociological research method have been central to it. This is particularly so in the United States. Different conceptions of observation and of the observer's role can be found in the literature. There are studies in which the observer does not become part of the observed field (e.g., in the tradition of Goffman (1961)). These studies are complemented by approaches, which try to accomplish the goal of gaining an insider's knowledge of the field through the researcher's increasing assimilation as a participant in the observed field. Ethnography has taken over in recent years what was participant observation before.

   In general, these approaches stress that practices are only accessible through observation; interviews and narratives merely make the accounts of practices accessible instead of the practices themselves. The claim is often made for observation that it enables the researcher to find out how something factually works or occurs. Compared to that claim, presentations in interviews, are said to comprise a mixture of how something is and of how something should be, which still needs to be untangled.

NONPARTICIPANT OBSERVATION

Besides the competencies of speaking and listening used in interviews, observing is another everyday skill, which is methodologically systematized and applied in qualitative research. Practically all senses—seeing, hearing, feeling, and smelling—integrate into observations. According to different authors, we generally classify observational methods along five dimensions. You may differentiate them by asking these questions:

- Covert versus overt observation: how far is the observation revealed to those who are observed?
- Nonparticipant versus participant observation: how far does the observer have to go to become an active part of the observed field?
- Systematic versus unsystematic observation: is a more or less standardized observation scheme applied or does the observation remain flexible and responsive to the processes themselves?
- Observation in natural versus artificial situations: are observations done in the field of interest or are interactions "moved" to a special place (e.g., a laboratory) to make them observable more systematically?
- Self-observation versus observing others: mostly other people are observed, so how much attention is paid to the researcher's reflexive self-observation for further grounding the interpretation of the observed?

You can also apply this general classification to observation in qualitative research, except that here data are (in general) collected from natural situations. In this chapter, the method of nonparticipant observation is discussed first. This form refrains from interventions in the field—in contrast to interviews and participant observations. The expectations linked to this are outlined as follows: "Simple observers follow the flow of events. Behavior and interaction continue as they would without the presence of a researcher, uninterrupted by intrusion" (Adler and Adler 1998, p. 81).

Here you can take the typology of participant roles developed by Gold (1958) as a starting point to define the differences from participant observation. Gold distinguishes four types of participant roles:

- the complete participant;
- the participant-as-observer;

- the observer-as-participant;
- the complete observer.

The complete observer maintains distance from the observed events in order to avoid influencing them. You may partly accomplish this by replacing the actual observation in the situation by videotaping. Alternatively, attempts may be made to distract the attention of those under observation from the researcher in order that they become oblivious to the process of observation. In this context, covert observation is applied, in which observed persons are not informed that they are being observed. This procedure, however, is ethically contestable (see Chapter 4), especially if the field can be easily observed, and there are no practical problems in informing the observed or obtaining their consent. Often, however, this kind of observation is practiced in open spaces (e.g., in train stations or public places, in cafes with frequently changing clientele) where this agreement cannot be obtained.

Which are the Phases of Observation?

Authors such as Adler and Adler (1998), Denzin (1989b), and Spradley (1980) name the following phases of such an observation:

- the selection of a setting (i.e., where and when the interesting processes and persons can be observed);
- the definition of what is to be documented in the observation and in every case;
- the training of the observers in order to standardize such focuses;
- descriptive observations that provide an initial, general presentation of the field;
- focused observations that concentrate on aspects that are relevant to the research question;
- selective observations that are intended to purposively grasp central aspects;
- the end of the observation, when theoretical saturation has been reached, which means that further observations do not provide any further knowledge.

What are the Problems in Conducting the Method?

A main problem here is to define a role for the observers that they can take and that allows them to stay in the field or at its edge and observe it at the same time (see the discussion of participant roles in Chapter 10). The more public and unstructured the field is, the easier it will be to take a role that is not conspicuous and does not influence the field. The easier a field is to overlook, the more difficult it is to participate in it without becoming a member.

Niemann outlines how to position a researcher in the field for observing the leisure activities of adolescents at leisure sites: "The observations were covert in order to avoid influencing the behavior of the adolescents that was typical for a specific site" (1989, p. 73).

Case Study: Leisure Behavior of Adolescents

In the following example, you can see the attempt and the limitations of a study keeping strictly to nonparticipant observation. The researcher did her study in the context of education. Niemann observed adolescents "parallel at two times of measurement" in two discotheques, ice stadiums, shopping malls, summer baths, football clubs, concert halls, and so on. She selected situations randomly and documented "developmental tasks", which were specific to these situations (e.g., realizing the goal of integration in the peer group) on protocol sheets. In order to better prepare the researcher, a period of training in observational techniques was given prior to the actual research in which different and independent observations of a situation were analyzed for their correspondence with the aim of increasing the latter. An observational manual was applied in order to make the notes more uniform:

> Observations of situations in principle were given a protocol only after they finished . . . mostly based on free notes on little pieces of scrap paper, beer mats or cigarette boxes. Here, however, there was a danger of bias and imprecise representations, which would interfere with the goal of minimizing the influence on the adolescents' behaviour. (1989, p. 79)

The attempt to avoid reactivity (i.e., feedback of the procedure of observation on the observed) determines the data collection, which in this case was complemented by interviews with single juveniles.

Merkens characterizes this strategy of "nonparticipant field observation" as follows:

> The observer here tries not to disturb the persons in the field by striving to make himself as invisible as possible. His interpretations of the observed occur from his horizon . . . The observer constructs meanings for himself, which he supposes direct the actions of the actors in the way he perceives them. (1989, p. 15)

This example again demonstrates the dilemmas of a nonparticipant observation in which the researcher tries to maintain methodological standards and thus allows the methods to strongly influence and determine the issue under study.

Avoid influencing the participants' behaviors in the field. This decisively constricts the interpretation of the data, which has to be undertaken from an external perspective on the field under study.

What are the Contributions to the General Methodological Discussion?

Triangulation of observations with other sources of data and the employment of different observers increase the expressiveness of the data gathered. Gender differences are a crucial aspect also, particularly when you plan to observe in public places, the possibilities for access and moving around are much more restricted for women owing to particular dangers compared with men. Women's perceptions of such restrictions and dangers, however, are much more sensitive, which makes them observe differently and notice different things compared with male observers. This shows the "gendered nature of fieldwork" (Lofland, quoted in Adler and Adler 1998, p. 95), and this is the reason for the suggested use of mixed gender teams in observational studies. A further suggestion is the painstaking self-observation of the researcher while entering the field, during the course of the observation and when looking back on its process in order to integrate implicit impressions, apparent incidentals, and perceptions in the reflection of the process and results.

How does the Method Fit into the Research Process?

The theoretical background here is the analysis of the production of social reality from an external perspective. The goal is (at least often) the testing of theoretical concepts for certain phenomena on the basis of their occurrence and distribution (see Chapter 8). Research questions aim at descriptions of the state of certain life worlds (e.g., adolescents in Berlin). The selection of situations and persons occurs systematically according to criteria of how to have a representative sample, and random sampling therefore is applied (see Chapter 11). Data analyses are based on counting the incidence of specific activities by using procedures of categorizing (see Chapter 23).

What are the Limitations of the Method?

All in all, this form of observation is an approach to the observed field from an external perspective. Therefore, you should apply it mainly to the observation of public spaces in which the number of the members cannot be limited or defined. Furthermore, it is an attempt to observe events as they naturally occur. How far this aim can be fulfilled remains doubtful, because the act of observation influences the observed in any case. Sometimes the argument is made for the use of covert observation, which eliminates the influence of the researcher on the field; however, this is highly problematic with respect to research ethics. Furthermore the researcher's abstinence from interacting with the field leads to problems in analyzing the data and in assessing the interpretations, because of the systematic restraint on disclosing the interior perspective of the field and of the observed persons. This strategy is associated more with an understanding of methods based on quantitative and standardized research.

Participant Observation

The form of observation, which is more commonly used in qualitative research, is participant observation. Denzin gives a definition:

> Participant observation will be defined as a field strategy that simultaneously combines document analysis, interviewing of respondents and informants, direct participation and observation, and introspection. (1989b, pp. 157–158)

The main features of the method are that you as a researcher dive headlong into the field. You will observe from a member's perspective but also influence what you observe owing to your participation. The differences from nonparticipant observation and its aims, as just discussed, are elucidated in the seven features of participant observation listed by Jorgensen:

1. a special interest in human meaning and interaction as viewed from the perspective of people who are insiders or members of particular situations and settings;
2. location in the here and now of everyday life situations and settings as the foundation of inquiry and method;
3. a form of theory and theorizing stressing interpretation and understanding of human existence;
4. a logic and process of inquiry that is open-ended, flexible, opportunistic, and requires constant redefinition of what is problematic, based on facts gathered in concrete settings of human existence;
5. an in-depth, qualitative, case study approach and design;
6. the performance of a participant role or roles that involves establishing and maintaining relationships with natives in the field; and
7. the use of direct observation along with other methods of gathering information. (1989, pp. 13–14)

Openness is essential when collecting data based solely on communicating with the observed. This method is often used for studying subcultures.

What are the Phases of Participant Observation?

Participant observation should be understood as a process in two respects. First, the researcher should increasingly become a participant and gain access to the field and to persons (see below). Second, the observation should also move through a process of becoming increasingly concrete and concentrated on the aspects that are essential for the research questions. Thus, Spradley (1980, p. 34) distinguishes three phases of participant observation.

1 *descriptive observation*, at the beginning, serves to provide the researcher with an orientation to the field under study. It provides nonspecific descriptions and is used to grasp the complexity of the field as far as possible and to develop (at the same time) more concrete research questions and lines of vision;

2 *focused observation* narrows your perspective on those processes and problems, which are most essential for your research question;

3   *selective observation*, towards the end of the data collection, is focused on finding further evidence and examples for the types of practices and processes, found in the second step.

Sometimes observation sheets and schemes are used, with differing degrees of structure. More often, protocols of situations are produced (see Chapter 22), which are as detailed as possible in order to allow "thick descriptions" (Geertz 1973) of the field. Whether you prefer to use field notes to the use of structured protocol sheets, which concretely define those activities and situational features to be documented in every case, depends both on the research question and on the phase in the research process in which observations are made. The more a protocol sheet differentiates between aspects, the more those aspects integrated become voluminous and the greater is the danger that those aspects not contained in the sheet are neither perceived nor noted. Therefore, descriptive observation should refrain from using heavily structured sheets in order to prevent the observer's attention from being restricted and from limiting his or her sensitivity to the new. In selective observation, however, structured protocol sheets may be helpful for grasping fully the relevant aspects elaborated in the phase before. However, participant observations are confronted with the problem of the observer's limited observational perspective, as not all aspects of a situation can be grasped (and noted) at the same time. Bergmann holds, "We have only a very limited competence of remembering and reproducing amorphous incidents of an actual social event. The participant observers thus have no other choice than to note the social occurrences which they were witness to mainly in a typifying, resuming, fashion of reconstruction" (1985, p. 308). The question of whether to work with overt observation (where the observed know that they are observed) or with covert observation arises here as well, but less as a methodological than as an ethical question.

Case Study: Boys in White

The following example is one of the classic studies of qualitative research in the medical sociology of the 1960s. The research team included several of the pioneers of qualitative research at that time and for the following decades, among them Howard Becker, Blanche Geer and Anselm Strauss. Becker et al. (1961) studied a state medical school in order "to discover what a medical school did to students other than give them a technical education. We assumed that students left medical school with a set of ideas about medicine and medical practice that differed from the ideas they entered with . . . We did not know what perspectives a student acquired while in school" (Becker and Geer 1960, p. 269). For this purpose, over a period of one or two months, participant observations in lectures, practical exercises, dormitories, and all departments of the

(Continued)

(Continued)

hospital were carried out, which sometimes extended to the whole day. The orientations that were found were examined for the degree to which they were collectively held, which means how far they were valid for the studied groups as a whole as against only for single members.

This example is still an instructive example of using participant observation with the intention of going beyond the focus of the single member of a community and of knowledge and talk. It shows how you can study communication and the development of attitudes from observing interaction and practices.

What are the Problems in Conducting the Method?

One problem is how to delimit or select observational situations in which the problem under study becomes really "visible." According to Spradley, social situations generally may be described along nine dimensions for observational purposes:

1. *space*: the physical place or places
2. *actor*: the people involved
3. *activity*: a set of related acts people do
4. *object*: the physical things that are present
5. *act*: single actions that people do
6. *event*: a set of related activities that people carry out
7. *time*: the sequencing that takes place over time
8. *goal*: the things people are trying to accomplish
9. *feeling*: the emotions felt and expressed. (1980, p. 78)

If you cannot observe for the whole day in an institution, for example, the problem of selection arises. How can you find those situations in which the relevant actors and interesting activities can be assumed to take place? At the same time, how can you select situations which are as different from one another as possible, from the range of an average day's events, in order to increase the variation and variety of what you actually observe?

Another problem is how to access the field or the studied subculture. In order to solve this, key persons are sometimes used who introduce the researchers and make contacts for them. It is sometimes difficult, however, to find the right person for this job. However, the researchers should not leave themselves too much at the mercy of key persons. They should take care as to how far they accept the key person's perspectives uncritically and should be aware of the fact that they may only be providing the researchers with access to a specific part of the field. Finally, key persons may even make it more difficult to gain access to the field under study or to approach certain persons within it, for example, if the key persons are outsiders in the field.[1]

Going Native

In participant observation, even more than in other qualitative methods, it becomes crucial to gain as far as possible an internal perspective on the studied field and to systematize the status of the stranger at the same time. Only if you achieve the latter, will your research enable you to view the particular in what is everyday and routine in the field. To lose this critical external perspective and to unquestioningly adopt the viewpoints shared in the field is known as "going native." The process of going native, however, is discussed not only as a researcher's fault but also as an instrument for reflecting on one's own process of becoming familiar and for gaining insights into the field under study, which would be inaccessible by maintaining distance. However, the goal of the research is not limited to becoming familiar with the self-evidence of a field. This may be sufficient for a successful participation but not for a systematic observation. Researchers who seek to obtain knowledge about relations in the studied field, which transcends everyday understanding, also have to maintain the distance of the "professional stranger" (see Agar 1980). Thus, Koepping underlines the fact that, for participant observation, the researcher:

> as social figure must have exactly those features that Simmel has elaborated for the stranger: he has to dialectically fuse the two functions in himself, that of commitment and that of distance . . . [The researcher therefore tries to realize] what is outlined by the notion of participation in observation, the task of which is to understand through the eyes of the other. In participating, the researcher methodologically authenticates his theoretical premise and furthermore he makes the research subject, the other, not an object but a dialogical partner. (1987, p. 28)

Case Study: Participant Observation in Intensive Care Units

The following example is intended to show the role of preparation for a study using participant observation in a very special field and the problem of being absorbed by the field, by the members, and by the dynamics of activities in the field during observation.

Before carrying out participant observation in intensive care units, Sprenger (1989, pp. 35–36) first had to run through a basic lesson in intensive care medicine in order to become familiar with the terminology (syndromes, treatment concepts, etc.) in the field. In collecting data, observational guides were used, which were geared to the different scenarios that were to be analyzed (e.g., the doctoral round, visits by family members). During the data collection, several activities served to widen the perspective on the field under study. A weekly exchange with a professional consulting group (doctors, nurses) was the first of these. The systematic variation of the observational perspective, i.e., observations centering on physicians, nurses, or patients and scene-oriented observations

(Continued)

(Continued)

(doctoral rounds, washing, setting a catheter, etc.) was the second. Special problems (here as well) resulted from the selection of an appropriate location and the "right" moment for observing, as the following notes about the researcher's experience may clarify:

> In the room, there is a relative hurry, permanently something has to be done, and I am successfully overrun by nurse I.'s whisky business. (No minutes at the "nurses' desk".) After the end of the shift, I remark after leaving the ward that I was a quasi-trainee today. The reason is for me mainly related to the moment of my arrival in the ward. Afterwards I consider it ineffective to burst into the middle of a shift. To participate in the handing over, in the beginning of the shift, means for us as well as for the nurses the chance to adapt to each other. I did not find any time today to orient myself calmly, there was no phase of feeling or growing into the situation, which would have allowed me a certain sovereignty. So I unexpectedly slipped into the mechanisms of the little routines and constraints and before I could get rid of them, my time was gone. (1989, p. 46)

This scene elucidates two aspects. The choice of the moment or of the actual beginning of an observational sequence determines essentially what can be observed and above all how. In addition, it becomes clear here that especially in very hectic settings the observer's inundation by the events leads to her being (mis)used as "quasi-trainee" for managing the events. Such participation in activity processes can lead to observation obstacles against which Sprenger suggests a remedy:

> This problem of being inundated by the field events is virulent during the whole course of the research, but may be controlled quite well. In addition to choosing the optimal beginning for the observation, as already mentioned in the presented protocol, defining the observational goals and leaving the field intentionally as soon as the researcher's observational capacity is exhausted have proved very effective control strategies. However, this requires the researchers to learn about their own capacity limits. (1989, p. 47)

This example shows that steering and planning the observation as well as reflecting on one's own resources may reduce the danger (just outlined) of the researcher being absorbed by the field as well as the danger of "going native," and therefore, of adopting perspectives from the field inreflexively.

In terms of Gold's (1958) typology of observer roles, the role of the participant-as-observer best fits the method of participant observation. Linked to the approach of diving headlong into the field is often the experienced sense of a culture shock on the part of the observer. This is particularly obvious in ethnographic field studies in foreign cultures. But this phenomenon also occurs in observations in subcultures or generally in strange groups or in extreme situations such as intensive medicine: familiar self-evidence, norms and practices lose their normality, and the observer is confronted with strange values, self-evidence, and so on. These may seem hard to understand at first but he or she has to accept them to be able to understand them and their meaning. In particular in participant observation, the researcher's action in the field is understood not only as a disturbance but also as an additional source of or as cornerstones for knowledge: "Fortunately, the so-called 'disturbances' created by the observer's existence and activities, when properly exploited, are the cornerstones of a scientific behavioural science, and not–as is currently believed–deplorable *contretemps*, best disposed of by hurriedly sweeping them under the rug" (Devereux 1967, p. 7).

What is the Contribution to the General Methodological Discussion?

All in all, participant observation elucidates the dilemma between increasing participation in the field, from which understanding alone results, and the maintenance of a distance, from which understanding becomes merely scientific and verifiable. Furthermore, this method still comes closest to a conception of qualitative research as a process, because it assumes a longer period in the field and in contact with persons and contexts to be studied, whereas interviews mostly remain one-off encounters. Strategies like theoretical sampling (see Chapter 11) can be applied here more easily than in interview studies. If it becomes evident that a specific dimension, a particular group of persons, concrete activities, and so on is needed for completing the data and for developing the theory, the researchers are able to direct their attention to them in the next observational sequence. For interviews, this is rather unusual and needs detailed explanation if researchers want to make a second appointment. Furthermore, in participant observation, the interaction with the field and the object of research may be realized most consistently. Also, by integrating other methods, the methodical procedures of this strategy may be especially well adapted to the research issue. Methodological flexibility and appropriateness to the object under study are two main advantages of this procedure.

How does the Method Fit into the Research Process?

The use of participant observation is rooted in the theoretical backgrounds of more recent versions of symbolic interactionism (see Chapter 6). In terms of pursuing the goal of developing theories about the research object (see Chapter 8), questions of how to access the field become a decisive methodological problem (see Chapter 10). Research questions (see Chapter 9) focus on the description of the field under study and of the practices in it. In the main, step-by-step strategies of sampling (see Chapter 11) are applied. Use coding strategies to carry interpretations (see Chapters 24, 26).

TABLE 17.1 Dependability of Observations

		Volunteered	Directed by the observer	Total
Statements	To observer alone			
	To others in everyday conversations			
Activities	Individual			
	Group			
Altogether				

Source: Becker and Geer 1960, p. 287

What are the Limitations of the Method?

One problem with this method is that not all phenomena can be observed in situations. Biographical processes are difficult to observe. This also applies to comprehensive knowledge processes. Events or practices that seldom occur–although they are crucial to the research question–can be captured only with luck or if at all by a very careful selection of situations of observation. As a way of solving these problems, additional interviews of participants are integrated into the research program, which allow the reconstruction of biographical processes or stocks of knowledge that are the background of observable practices. Therefore, the researchers' knowledge in participant observation is based only in part on the observation of actions. A large part is grounded in participants' verbal statements about certain relations and facts. In order to be able to use the strengths of observation compared with interview studies and to assess how far this strength applies for the data received, Becker and Geer (1960, p. 287) suggest the scheme in Table 17.1 for locating the data.

They are interested in answering the question of how likely it is that an activity or an attitude that is found is valid for the group they studied in general or only for individual members or specific situations. They start from the notion that the group most likely shares attitudes deduced from activities in the group, because otherwise the activities would have been corrected or commented on by the other members. You can more likely see statements within the group as shared attitudes rather than a member's statements in face-to-face contact with the observer. Spontaneous activities and statements seem more reliable than those responding to an observer's intervention (e.g., a direct question). The most important thing again is to answer the question of how likely the observed activities and statements are to occur independently of the researcher's observation and participation.

Another problem arises out of the advantages of the methods that were discussed with key phrases like flexibility and appropriateness to the object of research. Participant observation can hardly be standardized and formalized beyond a general research strategy, and it does not make sense to see this as a goal for further methodological developments (Lüders 2004a). Correspondingly, the methodological discussions have stagnated in recent years. Attempts to codify participant observation in textbooks are based on the discussions of the early 1970s or else are reported from the workshop of observation.

Ethnography

In recent discussions, interest in the method of participant observation has increasingly faded into the background, while the more general strategy of ethnography, in which observation and participation are interwoven with other procedures, has attracted more attention.

> In its most characteristic form it involves the ethnographer participating, overtly or covertly, in people's daily lives for an extended period of time, watching what happens, listening to what is said, asking questions – in fact, collecting whatever data are available to throw light on the issues that are the focus of the research. (Hammersley and Atkinson 1995, p. 1)

Which are the Features of Ethnographic Research?

The concrete definition and formulation of methodological principles and steps are subordinated to practicing a general research attitude in the field, which is observed, or more generally, studied. However, in a more recent overview, Atkinson and Hammersley (1998, pp. 110–111) note several substantial features of ethnographic research as shown in Box 17.1.

Here data collection is most consistently subordinated to the research question and the circumstances in the respective field. Methods are subordinated to practice (for the plurality of methods in this context, see also Atkinson et al. 2001). Lüders (1995, pp. 320–321; 2004a) sees the central defining features of ethnography as follows:

> first [there is] the risk and the moments of the research process which cannot be planned and are situational, coincidental and individual . . . Second, the researcher's skilful activity in each situation becomes more important . . . Third, ethnography . . . transforms into a strategy of research which includes as many options of collecting data as can be imagined and are justifiable.

Box 17.1 Features of Ethnographic Research

- A strong emphasis on exploring the nature of a particular social phenomenon, rather than setting out to test hypotheses about them.
- A tendency to work primarily with "unstructured" data, that is, data that have not been coded at the point of data collection in terms of a closed set of analytic categories.
- Investigation of a small number of cases, perhaps just one case, in detail.
- Analysis of data that involves explicit interpretation of the meanings and functions of human actions, the product of which mainly takes the form of verbal descriptions and explanations, with quantification and statistical analysis playing a subordinate role at most.

Source: Atkinson and Hammersley 1998, pp. 110–111

Methodological discussions focus less on methods of data collection and interpretation than on questions of how to report findings in a field (see Chapter 30). However, methodological strategies applied in the fields under study are still very much based on observing what is going on in the field by participating in the field. Interviews and the analysis of documents are integrated into this kind of participatory research design where they hold out the promise of further knowledge.

In their recent overview of ethnography, Atkinson et al. (2001, p. 2) stated:

> Contemporary ethnographic research is characterized by fragmentation and diversity. There is certainly a carnivalesque profusion of methods, perspectives, and theoretical justifications for ethnographic work. There are multiple methods of research, analysis, and representation.

Ethnography as a research strategy (like participant observation at its outset) has been imported from anthropology into different substantial areas in other disciplines such as sociology or education. Whereas at the beginning, ethnography studied remote cultures in their unfamiliarity; current ethnography starts its research around the corner and wants to show the particular aspects of what seem familiar to us all. Small life worlds of do-it-yourselfers, members of parliaments, and body builders for example are studied and analyzed (see Honer 2004).

From a more methodological point of view, current ethnographic research is characterized by an extended participation in the field, which studied a flexible research strategy, employing all sorts of methods and focusing on writing and reporting experiences in that field (Lüders 2004a).

Smith (2002) outlines an approach called institutional ethnography in which the focus is not so much the daily practices, but how these are institutionalized in rules and general relations, in which individuals' everyday practices are embedded. In her approach, a strong link to feminist theories and topics is given, when she studies women's mothering work, for example.

> ### Case Study: Homeless Adolescents' Health Behavior
>
> In an ongoing project, I am studying the health behavior and practices of homeless adolescents. We study adolescents aged 14 to 20 years and distinguish two groups amongst them according to the time, how long they hang out on the streets, and how far they are involved in the communities of street kids. The degree of perpetuation of their homelessness is relevant here. We observe them at different locations in a big city. If adolescents are identified in participant observation as being a member of the community over time, we ask them for an interview about their experiences with health problems and services in the health system, their health concepts, and how they recount their way into homelessness. In the study, we use different methodological approaches to develop a fuller picture of of our participants' living situations.
>
> This example shows how you can use an open approach such as ethnography for studying a concrete issue (health concepts and behavior) when you use several methods addressing different levels of the issue under study, here knowledge (via interviews) and practices (via observation).

What are the Problems in Conducting the Method?

Methods define which aspects of the phenomenon are especially relevant and deserve particular attention. At the same time, they give an orientation for the researcher's practice. In ethnography, both are given up in favor of a general attitude towards the research through the use of which the researchers find their own ways in the life world under study. In this study, a pragmatic use of all sorts of methods–and data–is central. As some researchers in the field have criticized, the methodological flexibility which contemporary ethnography asks for means that researchers have to be familiar with–or even experts in–quite a variety of methods to do ethnographic studies. This requirement may sound overly-challenging, especially to novices in research.

What is the Contribution to the General Methodological Discussion?

Special attention has been attracted by ethnography in recent years due to two circumstances. First, in this context, an extensive debate about the presentation of observation has begun (Clifford and Marcus 1986), which has not been and will not be without consequences for other domains of qualitative research (see Chapter 30 for this). Second, the recent methodological discussion about qualitative methods in general in the Anglo-Saxon area (e.g., in the contributions to Denzin and Lincoln 2000a) has been strongly influenced by strategies and discussions in ethnography. Ethnography has been the most powerful influence on the transformation of qualitative research into some kind of postmodern research attitude, which is opposed to the more or less codified application of specific methods. In addition, ethnography has been rediscovered in developmental and cultural psychology (cf. the volume of Jessor et al. 1996) and has stimulated a new interest in qualitative methods in this area.[2]

How does the Method Fit into the Research Process?

Ethnography starts from the theoretical position of describing social realities and their making (see Chapter 6). It aims at developing theories (see Chapter 8). Research questions focus mainly on detailed descriptions of case studies (see Chapter 9). Entering the field has central importance for the empirical and theoretical disclosure of the field under study and is not simply a problem, which has to be solved technically (see Chapter 10). Sampling strategies generally orient to theoretical sampling or procedures based on this (see Chapter 11). Interpretations are mainly done using sequential and coding analyses (see Chapters 23 and 25). More recently, approaches like virtual ethnography have been developed (see Chapter 20) to use ethnography as a method for analyzing interactions in the cyberspace.

Which are the Limitations of the Method?

In the discussion about ethnography, data collection methods are treated as secondary. Strategies of participation in the field under study, the interpretation of data, and above all, styles of writing and the question of authority and authorship in the presentation of results (see Chapter 30 for this in greater detail) find more attention. This approach may be interpreted (in a positive way) as showing flexibility towards the subject under study but it also holds the danger of a methodological arbitrariness. The concretely applied methods make ethnography a strategy that uses the triangulation (see Chapter 29) of various methodological approaches in the framework of realizing a general research attitude.

KEY POINTS

- In qualitative research, observation can be used with different degrees of the researcher's participation in the field under study.
- In each version, the relation of methodological rigor and flexibility is different. Nonparticipant observation is characterized by keeping up distance to the field and general methodological standards.
- At the other end of the spectrum, extended participation and a methodological pragmatism oriented on adapting methods to the field and on using whatever methods lead to more insights characterize ethnography.
- Ethnography replaced participant observation, but it is a central methodological basis for any ethnographic work, ethics, and forms of going native.

Exercises 17.1

1. Look for an example of an ethnographic study in the literature. Identify which methods were used in this study, how the authors organized their participation in the field, and how they managed issues of involvement and distance in their field contacts.
2. Go to open spaces in your university (like the library or cafeterias) and do some participant observation in order to find out mechanisms and practices of integration and segregation among the people in these spaces. Are there different groups, how do they get in touch, how do they keep up the boundaries, etc.? Write down your observations in field notes (see Chapter 22). After you finish your observations, write down an account of what you saw and of what puzzled you in the field.

Notes

1   Researchers should reflect on why their key person is ready to take this role. In the literature, you will find a range of social positions from which people start to become key persons in participant observation. Most of these positions are characterized by social deficits concerning the social status of the key person in the group or in the field (e.g., the outsider, the novice, the frustrated, people needing loving care, the subordinate). That does not necessarily mean that social acceptance must be the only motive for supporting the researcher in this respect. But the consequences of the key person's motivation and role for the researcher's access and the observation should be taken into account. Thus, not only observation *by* key persons but also observation *of* key persons in the field should be integrated as a basis for such reflection.

2   However, you can find there are positions different from the dominant postmodern ethnography. For example, Shweder (1996) in his concept of "true ethnography argues against the solipsism and superficiality" of postmodern ethnography and instead makes claims for "mind reading."

FURTHER READING

Nonparticipant Observation
This text gives an overview of nonparticipant observation in qualitative research.

Adler, P.A. and Adler, P. (1998) "Observation Techniques," in N. Denzin and Y.S. Lincoln (eds), *Collecting and Interpreting Qualitative Materials.* London: SAGE. pp. 79–110.

Participant Observation
The first text is a classic example of the application of this method, whereas the others are textbooks which discuss the method in greater depth.

(Continued)

(Continued)

Becker, H.S., Geer, B., Hughes, E.C. and Strauss, A.L. (1961) *Boys in White: Student Culture in Medical School*. Chicago: University of Chicago Press.

Jorgensen, D.L. (1989) *Participant Observation: A Methodology for Human Studies*. London: SAGE.

Spradley, J.P. (1980) *Participant Observation*. New York: Holt, Rinehart and Winston.

Ethnography

The different approaches to ethnography that are characteristic of recent discussions are outlined in the textbook and the handbook chapter by the same authors and also in the reader from cultural psychology.

Atkinson, P., Coffey, A. Delamont, S., Lofland, J. and Lofland L. (eds) (2001) *Handbook of Ethnography*. London: SAGE.

Atkinson, P. and Hammersley, M. (1998) "Ethnography and Participant Observation," in N. Denzin and Y.S. Lincoln (eds), *Strategies of Qualitative Inquiry*. London: SAGE, pp. 110–136.

Hammersley, M. and Atkinson, P. (1995) *Ethnography: Principles in Practice*. (2nd edn). London: Routledge.

Jessor, R., Colby, A. and Shweder, R.A. (eds) (1996) *Ethnography and Human Development*. Chicago: University of Chicago Press.

18

VISUAL DATA: PHOTOGRAPHY, FILM, AND VIDEO

CHAPTER OBJECTIVES
After reading this chapter, you should be able to

✓ understand the opportunities to use and limits of the use of visual data methods.
✓ know that using archival photographs and taking new photographs constitute a form of data collection.
✓ comprehend the relevance of movies as a reflection of and influence on the social construction of social realities.
✓ realize the potential of using video as a source and a way of producing data with advantages and limitations.

Photos as Instrument and Object of Research

Recently, you may have noticed a certain revival of second-hand observation, both as topic and as method, which means to use visual media for research purposes. Photographs, films, and video are increasingly used as genuine forms and sources of data (see Becker 1986a; Denzin 2004a; Harper 2004; for a discussion of the use of video cameras for recording conversations or interviews see Chapter 22). Photography, in particular, has a long tradition in anthropology and ethnography. Bateson and Mead's (1942) study of the "Balinese character" is repeatedly treated as classic.

Case Study: Bateson and Mead's Study of the "Balinese Character"

Gregory Bateson and Margaret Mead were pioneers of cultural anthropology. They developed a comprehensive methodology for their study, which included the production and analysis of visual material like photos and film to document the everyday life, routines, and rituals in Bali. In their investigation of a Balinese mountain village, Bateson and Mead (1942) collected 25,000 photos, 2000 meters of film, pictures, sculptures, and children's drawings. Photos and films are especially important both as data and as an instrument of knowledge. The authors have presented the developed films to the inhabitants of the village and documented their reactions again on films. Photographs and films were understood not as mere reproductions of reality but as presentations of reality, which are influenced by certain theoretical assumptions. Bateson and Mead were aware that photographs and films–not unlike sculptures and drawings–were not mirror images of reality but only presentational forms, which remain blind without analysis. The photos and their analysis in so-called image plates are essential in the presentation of the results of the whole study. Image plates are groups of photographs together with related (textual) analyses. The images were sorted according to cultural categories assumed to be typical for Bali (such as "spatial orientation and levels," "learning," "integration and disintegration of the body," and "stages of child development"): "The images were arranged in groups that allowed several perspectives on a single subject to be presented simultaneously or in sequences that showed how a social event evolved through time" (Harper 1998, p. 132).

In this study, visual material for the complementary documentation of the analyzed culture and practices is called into play and contrasted with the presentations and interpretations in textual form in order to extend the integrated perspectives on the subject. It is already taken into account that visual material not only is accomplished against a certain theoretical background, but also is perceived and interpreted from a specific point of view.

The Camera as an Instrument for Collecting Data

A visual sociology centered on photo and film has recently been developed. Becker (1986a) inaugurated the approach. Before that Mead (1963) summarized the central purpose of using cameras in social research: they allow detailed recordings of facts as well as providing a more comprehensive and holistic presentation of lifestyles and conditions. They allow the transportation of artifacts and the presentation of them as pictures and also the transgression of borders of time and space. They can catch facts and processes that are too fast or too complex for the human eye. Cameras also allow nonreactive recordings of observations, and finally, they are less selective than observations. Photographs are available for re-analysis by others.

Following Barthes (1996), you can distinguish four types of relation between the researcher and the researched. The researcher can show photos (as demonstrator) to persons under study (as spectators) and ask them about the material (type I). The operator (who takes the photograph) can use the researched individual as a model (type II). The researchers (as spectator) may ask the subject to show them photos concerning a certain topic or period (as demonstrator) (type III). Finally, the researcher (as spectator) may observe the subjects (as operator) while they take a picture and conduct an analysis of the choice of subject matter being photographed (type IV: cf. Wuggenig 1990).

More generally, the question discussed is "how to get information on film and how to get information off film" (Hall 1986, quoted in Denzin 1989b, p. 210). One approach for example is to use the photographs in family albums to analyze the history of the family or subjects documented in them over time. Also, in family or institutional research, the integration of their self-presentation in photos and images of their members on the walls in the rooms can reveal social structures in the social field.

In general, several methodological questions have been discussed, which center on the following topics (see Denzin 1989b, pp. 213–214):

- Theoretical presumptions that determine what is photographed and when, which feature is selected from the photograph for analysis, and so on, leave their mark on the use of photographs as data or for documentation of relations.
- Cameras are incorruptible in terms of their perception and documentation of the world: they do not forget, do not get tired, and do not make mistakes. However, photographs also transform the world, which they present into a specific shape.
- Photos tell the truth: however, how far are photos also marked by the interpretation and ascription of meaning by those who take or regard them?
- Photos (and films) reveal an approach to the symbolic world of the subjects and their views.
- Photos are only expressive when they are taken at the right moment–when the interesting action occurs and the relevant persons step into the camera's field of vision.
- Not only the participant, but also the photographing observer has to find and take a role and an identity in the field.

Using Photos in the Context of Interviews

A different use of the medium of photography is outlined by Dabbs (1982). The persons under study receive cameras and are asked, "to take (or have someone else take) photographs that tell who they are" (1982, p. 55). This may be extended to a photographic diary in which people capture aspects and events of their daily lives as these unfold. The subject decides the events or aspects worthy of photographing, not the researcher. What they select and take as a picture allows the researcher to draw conclusions about the views of the subjects towards their own everyday lives. This is especially the case when comparing the perspectives of different subjects in the field expressed in their photographs and the features highlighted in them.

Wuggenig (1990, pp. 115–118) applies a similar procedure in order to study significance in the area of living. People were instructed to use a camera to document their ways of living and the interiors of their apartments typical for people like themselves in 12 photos. The instruction in Box 18.1 was given to them.

Box 18.1   Instruction for the Photo Interview

When you want to use photographs as part of data collection in the context of interviews, you should give your participants an instruction like the following one:

"What do you like most about your own room and in the flat (or house)? What do you like least about your room and in the flat (or house)? Please photograph first the three motifs you like the most in your room and then the three you like the least. Then please repeat this for the rest of the apartment. It does not matter which room you choose. All in all, you can use 12 pictures."

Source: Wuggenig 1990, p. 116

In the "photo elicitation interview" (Harper 2000, p. 725), photos from people's own lives are taken to stimulate interview partners to produce narratives or answers–first about the photo and then starting from this about their daily life. This procedure may also be seen as a way of using the focused interview (see Chapter 13) in more concrete version. Whereas here visual material is used as a support for conducting the interview, in the following example photographs are used as data in their own right.

Case Study: Analysis of Soldiers' Photos

In the following case, photos were not produced for research purposes, but existing photos were used as material for research. Haupert (1994) analyzed soldiers' photos using the method of objective hermeneutics (see Chapter 24) in order to reconstruct biographical processes. Here, photos are not produced for research purposes, but existing photos are analyzed for the general relations to the photographed period and the individual fate traced in this material. Photos here have their own special importance as genuine documents. Their analysis can be referred to other forms of data (biographical interviews). Photo analysis is explicitly understood and practiced as a form

(Continued)

(Continued)

of textual analysis. This means photos are studied here "whose textual quality in the sense of social research–although the grammar of the image for the moment remains unclear–. . . can finally be singled out by a programmatic procedure of telling grammatically correct stories which are adequate in meaning and model the contextual framework of the image" (1994, p. 286).

   This is an example of how to use existing photographic material from earlier times to support the elicitation of memories about that period so that interviews referring to it can be conducted.

In general, photos have a high iconic quality, which may help to activate people's memories or to stimulate/encourage them to make statements about complex processes and situations.

What are the Problems in the Application of the Method?

Denzin (1989b, pp. 214–215) takes up Gold's typology of observer roles (see Chapter 17) in order to describe the problems associated with finding the most appropriate role for the photographing observer. One problem is the influence of the medium. Arranging the subjects in a photo results in losing the moment's expressiveness. The same is the case if the subjects pose for the photos (self-presentation photos). The insights that photos can provide about the everyday life under study will be greatest if the photographing researchers can manage to integrate themselves with the camera in a way that attracts the least possible attention.

   Another problem is the possibility of influencing or manipulating the photographic presentation. Denzin names montage and retouch or the attempt to take artistic photos in this respect, and argues that these techniques may lead to details being left out that are relevant to the research question. Denzin also mentions various forms of censorship (by official agencies, by the photographed persons, or by the photographer) that may restrict the realization and reliability of photos as social science data (1989b, p. 220). Becker discusses this point under the heading of the photographer's control over the final image: "The choice of film, development and paper, of lens and camera, of exposures and framing, of moment and relations with subjects–all of these, directly under the photographer's control, shape the end product. . . . A second influence on the image the photographer produces, is his theory about what he is looking at, his understanding of what he is investigating" (1986a, pp. 241–242). Furthermore, Becker raises the question, "Do photographs tell the truth?", and tries to specify ways of answering it by discussing sampling questions and the problem of reactivity produced by the very act of taking the photographs. A special problem is the question of framing (what is in the picture, what is focused on, what is left out?) and how much the personal aesthetic style of the photographer determines the content of the photo.

All in all, these problems raise the question of how far the sample of the reality under study contained in the scope of the photo introduces bias into the presentation of reality, and what part the medium of photography plays in the construction of the reality under study.

How does the Method Fit into the Research Process?

The theoretical background of using photos is structuralist models such as objective hermeneutics or symbolic interactionism (see Chapter 6) in Denzin's case. Research questions focus on descriptions of aspects of reality contained in the photographs (see Chapter 9). Material is selected in a step-by-step manner (see Chapter 11). Sequential procedures are used for interpretation (see Chapter 25). The analysis of visual material is mostly triangulated with other methods and data (see Chapter 29).

What are the Limitations of the Method?

Attempts at a hermeneutic of images aim at extending the range of what counts as possible data for empirical social research into the visual domain. However, (at least up to now) procedures of interpretation familiar from analyses of verbal data have been applied to them. In this respect, such visual data are also regarded as texts. Photos tell a story; text descriptions, summaries, or transcription often accompany visual data before carrying out textual interpretation methods on visual material. Genuine analytical procedures that directly relate to images still remain to be developed.

Film Analysis as an Instrument of Research

Television and films influence everyday life. Qualitative research uses these to tell us about the social construction of reality. Denzin (1989b) analyzes Hollywood movies that contain social reflections on social experiences (such as alcoholism, corruption and so on). Such films reflect also on key moments of history (e.g., the Vietnam War), on certain institutions (e.g., hospitals), on social values (such as marriage and family) and relations, on domains of everyday life, and on emotions. These movies and the practices presented can be interpreted on different levels of meaning. Denzin distinguishes "realistic" and "subversive readings" (2004a, p. 240). Realistic readings understand a film as a truthful description of a phenomenon, whose meaning can be (completely) disclosed through a detailed analysis of the contents and the formal features of the images. The interpretation serves to validate the truth claims the film makes about reality. Subversive readings take into account that the author's ideas of reality influence the film as well as that those of the interpreter will influence its interpretation. Different interpretations influence the analysis of film material. Use various constructions of reality (see Chapter 7) to analyze and compare the interpretations.

Steps in Conducting a Film Analysis

For film analyses, Denzin (2004a, pp. 241–242) suggests four phases as a general model:

1. "Looking and feeling": The films are regarded as a whole, and impressions, questions, and patterns of meaning which are conspicuous, are noted.
2. What research question are you asking? Formulate the questions to pursue. Therefore, note key scenes.
3. "Structured microanalyses" are conducted of individual scenes and sequences, which should lead to detailed descriptions and patterns in the display (of conflicts and so on) in these excerpts.
4. When answering the research question, search for patterns in the entire film. Searching for patterns extends to the whole film in order to answer the research question. The film's realistic and subversive readings are contrasted and a final interpretation is written.

This procedure has been applied to several examples.

Case Study: Alcoholism in Hollywood Movies

Using the example of the film *Tender Mercies*, Denzin studies the presentation and treatment of problems like "alcoholism" and "families of alcoholics" in order to find out "how cultural representations form lived experiences" (1989c, p. 37). Therefore, Denzin first studied the "realistic interpretations" of the film, which he derived from reviews and film guides for their "dominant ideological meanings" (1989c, p. 40). The background assumption is that the interpretations of films and of social problems like alcoholism are often "patriarchally biased," because they are formulated from a male point of view (1989c, p. 38). Denzin contrasts this with his own "subversive reading" of the film and the problem, which he conducts from the standpoint of feminism. The focus is shifted from the main male character and his alcohol addiction to the women in his life and to the consequences that the main character's alcoholism has for the women and his family (1989c, p. 46). From this change of perspectives, an analysis of the cultural values and issues to do with the problem of alcoholism, such as family, gender relations, and the control of emotions in society is derived (1989c, p. 49). Finally, the developed readings are assessed against the interpretations of different viewers of the film. The latter are related to the viewers' subjective experiences of the problems, which are mentioned (1989c, p. 40).

(Continued)

(Continued)

The following conclusions may be drawn from this study. Use interpretation and analysis to deconstruct films. Perspective determines the central focus of the interpretation and its results. The point that Denzin seeks to make is that this is the case not only for the analyses of film reviewers–for whom that won't be news–but also for the analyses of social scientists. How far the feminist perspective Denzin takes is the most appropriate one is a question Denzin cannot and does not want to decide with respect to the multiplicity of possible interpretations he highlights.

What are the Problems in Conducting the Method?

Using films as data also leads to problems of selection (which films, which scenes are analyzed more closely?) and of interpretation (what should attention be paid to in the material?). Additionally, the question of working up the data for interpretation arises: should coding, categorization, and interpretation be done directly on the visual material or should transcriptions of dialogues and their contexts be made first thus transforming visual material into text?

What is the Contribution to the General Methodological Discussion?

Using media such as film and photographs as data in qualitative research crosses the boundaries between the various social scientific methods discussed in this book. Compared with interviews, they provide the nonverbal component of events and practices, which could otherwise only be documented in context protocols. Observed situations are ephemeral, whereas events recorded with the media allow for repeat access. This may transgress the limitations of perception and documentation that are characteristic of observation. Finally, Petermann (1995) discusses the relation between reality and the presentation of reality in scientific documentary films.

How does the Method Fit into the Research Process?

The theoretical background of using film materials is Denzin's interpretive interactionism (see Chapter 6). Research questions focus on descriptions of segments of reality contained in the film (see Chapter 9). Concrete examples of these are sampled step-by-step (see Chapter 11). Interpretation is often carried out using sequential procedures (see Chapter 25).

What are the Limitations of the Method?

Filmmakers construct versions of reality by their own choosing. But it is the viewers who interpret the material in different ways. Therefore, film analyses are rarely used as a genuine strategy but rather as an addition to or a part of other methods aimed at analyzing verbal data. Up to now there has been no method of interpretation for such material which deals directly with the visual level. Films are understood as visual texts (Denzin 1989b, p. 228), transformed into text by transcription or by recounting the stories contained in them, and then analyzed as such.

Using Video in Qualitative Research

Another way of using visual data, which goes beyond the single photograph or a series of still photographs, is to videotape aspects of a specific life world. Videotaping has become a familiar everyday technique to document experiences— like holidays or festivities. It is also present at public places, underground stations, and the like, which are subject to video camera surveillance. You can use video-taping in different ways in qualitative research. One is to use a video recorder instead of a tape recorder to document the interaction in an interview. This technical use of videotaping will be discussed in Chapter 22. But videotapes can be a source or data sort themselves.

Knoblauch (2004, p. 126) lists several data sorts, which are used in video research:

- Scientific recording of natural social situations;
- Scientific recording of experimental social situations;
- Interviews;
- Natural social situations recorded by the actors (surveillance, audio recording);
- Posed situations recorded by actors (video diaries);
- Situations recorded and edited by actors (wedding videos);
- Situations recorded by actors and edited by professionals (wedding videos, documentations).

These forms of data are discussed in this context here, as video research not only consists of analyzing video material, but also how a corpus of material is produced, which can then be analyzed. What is recorded; what is selected or cut out of the tape; which materials are selected for analyzing an issue; and what sorts of material are produced for research purposes?

Knoblauch develops a video interaction analysis as a method from using these sorts of video data, which he characterizes by three features: methodicity, order, and reflexivity. Methodicity refers to the *what* but also the *how* of the presentations of situations and actors in video material. Order focuses on sound ways of producing and interpreting the performed activities. Reflexivity or performativity means that the actors not only act, but they reflect what they do in their presentations.

Heath and Hindmarsh (2002) highlight that in their research, video recordings in naturally occurring activities are the primary data, but that the researchers have also to undertake conventional fieldwork such as becoming familiar with the setting and so on when they produce these data. If they want to use video recordings of doctor–patient interactions for example, it is crucial to do field-work, observation etc. prior to recording material. This is necessary in order to be able to decide adequately where to place the camera, what to take as the best angle or what to include of the context of the interaction and so on.

Case Study: Using Video for Studying Children in their Everyday Context

In a study of the development of egocentrism in children and changes in their per-spectives, Billmann-Mahecha (1990) used videotaping as a method to collect data in an everyday context. After an initial period of participant observation in order to get acquainted with the family, she came back and videotaped a couple of hours of an afternoon in the family and of children's play. Then she sampled appropriate episodes from the video material, transcribed them, and made her own interpretation of them. The next step was to show these episodes to the parents and to interview both about them. These interviews were also transcribed and interpreted. Both perspectives (the researcher's interpretation of the video episodes and the interpretation of the parents' answers) were triangulated on the level of the single case. Then the episodes were ana-lyzed on both levels in order to develop a typology of practices and statements of the children in the different episodes.

What are the Problems in Conducting the Method?

One problem is how to limit the technical presence of the equipment. If you use this approach you should take care that the camera and recording equipment are not dominating the social situation. Another problem is the selectivity of the camera's focus–either you will have a very narrow focus in good quality and detail but without much of the context of the situation captured on the film. Or you have a good panoramic view of the social situation, but lack the details of facial expressions, for example. What you prefer should be determined by your research questions, but this shows already the limitations of the recording. Another issue is, how to decide, when to start and when to stop recording mate-rial. Finally, you could–from a technical point of view–use recordings of surveil-lance cameras, which will give you an exhaustive overview of the activities in a place of interest. But, from an ethical point of view, you will have a lot of mate-rial, which the actors never accepted for your research (or to be recorded at all). So, avoid using this kind of material.

What is the Contribution to the General Methodological Discussion?

A video analysis extends the capacities of other approaches in several directions: compared to tape recording, they include the nonverbal parts of interaction. Compared to interviewing, they allow the recording of actions in the making instead of accounts of actions from a retrospective point of view. In addition to observation, they allow the capturing of more aspects and details than participant observers in their field notes. Videotaping allows for repeat observation of fleeting situations. Thus video analysis reduces the selectivity of several methods. However, this method produces a new selectivity due to the limits of what can be documented and filmed at a specific moment. The method highlights again the selectivity and limitations of research methods in general.

How does the Method Fit into the Research Process?

As the frequently used term of videography shows, video research is often part of an ethnographic approach to specific life worlds, such as workplace studies (Knoblauch et al. 2000). The theoretical interests linked to this research are to analyze interactions (in a form of interactionism–see Chapter 6) in such contexts and to understand the way social reality is constructed in these contexts and in or through videotapes. Concrete examples of these are sampled step-by-step (see Chapter 11). Often, video analyses are only useful in combination with other methods and other sorts of data (triangulation–see Chapter 29). The material is often analyzed against the background of ethnomethodology and conversation analysis (see Chapter 6 and 24).

What are the Limitations of the Method?

As the above examples already show, video analysis is not a stand-alone method. It is best used in combination with other methods, fieldwork in the classical sense, additional interviewing, and observation beyond the camera. The technical development of the cameras is constantly progressing, but this will not make the camera disappear from the situation that is filmed, documented, and analyzed by using it.

Photos, film, and videos have become objects of research, which means existing examples become material that can be analyzed for answering a specific research question. At the same time, they have become media for producing data–videography of social situations or settings for example. These materials as well as these media can be integrated in more comprehensive research strategies as in combination with interviews or in the context of ethnography. Seen this way, visual data methods complement verbal data methods and build up comprehensive multifocus research.

KEY POINTS

- Visual data methods make new ways of documenting the visual side of social settings and practices possible, and of making this a part of research.
- Visual data can consist of existing materials or can be produced for research purposes.
- There is still a need for developing appropriate methods for analyzing the visual parts of the data available from these methods.

Exercise 18.1

1. Find a study in the literature in which video, photos, or film was used as data. Reflect how the data were produced, whether they were used as stand-alone data or in combination with other forms of data, and how they were analyzed.
2. When you plan your own study, think about how you could use visual material in it, and which parts of your research question they could or could not refer to.

FURTHER READING

Photos
The problems of a visual sociology using photographs as data are discussed in the texts in greater detail.

Becker, H.S. (1986a) *Doing Things Together: Selected Papers*. Evanston, IL: Northwestern University Press.
Denzin, N.K. (1989b) *The Research Act* (3rd edn). Englewood Cliffs, NJ: Prentice-Hall.
Harper, D. (2004) "Photography as Social Science Data," in U. Flick, E.v. Kardorff and I. Steinke (eds), *A Companion to Qualitative Research*. London: SAGE. pp. 231–236.

Film Analysis
The approach of a visual sociology using films as data is discussed in this text in greater detail.

Denzin, N.K. (2004a) "Reading Film," in U. Flick, E.v. Kardorff and I. Steinke (eds), *A Companion to Qualitative Research*. London: SAGE. pp. 237–242.

Using Video in Qualitative Research
The use of video in the context of ethnography is outlined here:

Heath, C. and Hindmarsh, J. (2002) "Analysing Interaction: Video, Ethnography and Situated Conduct,". In T. May (ed.), *Qualitative Research in Action*. London: SAGE. pp. 99–120.

19
USING DOCUMENTS AS DATA

CHAPTER OBJECTIVES

After reading this chapter, you should be able to

✓ use documents for qualitative research.
✓ understand that documents should be analyzed in the context of their production and use in the field.
✓ comprehend that they are not just a simple representation of processes and experiences but communicative devices in constructing a version of these processes.

Our lives as individuals as well as members of a society and societal life as a whole have become subject to recording. Hardly any institutional activity–from birth to death of people–comes along without producing a record. Birth and death certificates like any other form of institutional record produce data. These data are produced for institutional purposes on the more general level in the form of statistics (how many people have married this year?) but also on a personal level (is this person married already?, can a marriage be done without a divorce?, and so on). At the same time, most people produce a lot of personal documents in their daily life, from a diary to photographs to holiday letters. In between there are biographies of people–autobiographies written by the persons themselves or biographies written about a specific person for a special occasion. Although these records and documents are not produced for research purposes, they and the information they contain can be used for research. This is the realm of analyzing documents. They can be analyzed in a quantitative way—statistics about marriages in a period and area can be analyzed for the average age of marrying or the number of migrants' compared to nonmigrants' marriages. But documents can also be analyzed in a qualitative way—how is the life history of a person constructed in the official records about this person in different institutional settings? Like other approaches in qualitative research, you can use documents and their analysis as a complementary strategy to other methods, like interviews or ethnography. Or you can use the analysis of documents as a stand-alone method. Then your research will rely on what of the reality under study is documented in this kind of data. As we have already discussed the use of photographs in the preceding chapter, I want to focus on written (textual) documents here. Even if you apply the same methods for analyzing these texts as you do for analyzing interviews for example, there is more to using documents than merely analyzing them.

What are Documents?

The following definition outlines what is generally understood as "documents":

> Documents are *standardised artefacts*, in so far as they typically occur in particular *formats*: as notes, case reports, contracts, drafts, death certificates, remarks, diaries, statistics, annual reports, certificates, judgements, letters or expert opinions. (Wolff 2004b, p. 284)

Prior gives a more dynamic, use-oriented definition:

> If we are to get to grips with the nature of documents then we have to move away from a consideration of them as stable, static and pre-defined artefacts. Instead we must consider them in terms of fields, frames and networks of action. In fact, the status of things as "documents" depends precisely on the ways which such objects are integrated into fields of action, and documents can only be defined in terms of such fields (2003, p. 2).

When you decide to do an analysis of documents, you should take two distinctions into account: either, you can use solicited documents for your research (e.g., ask people to write diaries for the next 12 months and then analyze and compare these documents); or you use unsolicited documents (e.g., the diaries people have written as part of an everyday routine). In the tradition of the research on unobstrusive methods, Webb et al. (1966) and Lee (2000) distinguish running records, which are produced to document administrative processes from episodic and private records, which are not produced continuously but occasionally. Documents are most often available as texts (in a printed form), but they can also have the form of an electronic file (a database for example).

Scott (1990, p. 14) distinguishes 12 types of documents, which are constituted by a combination of two dimensions: the authorship (who produced the document) and the access to the documents. The authorship can be distinguished into personal and official documents and the latter again into private and state documents. I can have a personal document of my birth (e.g., a photograph taken immediately afterwards). There is a birth certificate, which I possess as a private but official document. And I can be registered as born in London, for example, and this registration is an official document produced, held, and used by the state. Accessibility is the classifying term for all of these documents. Scott distinguishes four alternatives. The access can be closed (e.g., the medical records of a general practitioner are not accessible to third persons). The access can be restricted (e.g., juridical records are only accessible to specific professional groups like lawyers in a trial). The access can be open archival, which means that everyone can access the documents but (only) in a specific archive. And the access can be open published. Then the documents are published and accessible to any interested party. Combining these two dimensions–access and authorship–comprise the 12 types (see Scott 1990, pp. 14–18 for details).

Case Study: The Polish Peasant in Europe and America

The Thomas and Znaniecki (1918–1920) study is one of the earliest uses of documents. Here the authors study experiences of migration–and migration as a macro-sociological issue–by analyzing documents, which Thomas called "undesigned records." These documents were not produced for research purposes but in the everyday life of the Polish community in the United States. The main data were letters in the families and to social institutions (newspapers, emigration offices, churches, welfare institutions, and courts). These documents were analyzed for attitudes and social values documented in them and especially for the change of such attitudes and values and for the decline of solidarity among the members of the Polish community the longer they were in the United States. Therefore, some central topics were identified in these letters, like social disorganization, patterns of family interaction, individualization, and so on. The frequencies with which the issues raised and the indicators on defining the social situations by the actors in these communities changed were subject to analysis. Beyond using letters and documents, the authors only used one other form of data when they asked one individual to write down his life history.

This study is seen as a pioneering study in qualitative research and instruction for the potential and the problems of using documents as data. It has also been a pioneering study for the current biographical research.

Using Documents as Data: More than Analyzing Texts

Scott's classification can be helpful for locating the documents you want to use in your research. It can also be helpful for assessing the quality of the documents. As the dimensions already make clear, documents are not just a simple representation of facts or reality. Someone (or an institution) produces them for some (practical) purpose and for some form of use (which also includes a definition of who is meant to have access to them). When you decide to use documents in your study, you should always see them as a means for communication. You also should ask yourself, who has produced this document for which purpose and for whom? What were the personal or institutional intentions to produce and store this document or this kind of document? Therefore, documents are not only simple data you can use as a resource for your research. Once you start using them for your research you should always focus on these documents as a topic of research at the same time: what are the features of them, what are the particular conditions of their production, and so on.

Selecting Documents

For assessing the quality of documents, Scott (1990, p. 6) suggests four criteria, which you can use for deciding whether or not to employ a specific document (or set of documents) for your research.

- Authenticity. Is the evidence genuine and of unquestionable origin?
- Credibility. Is the evidence free from error and distortion?
- Representativeness. Is the evidence typical of its kind, and, if not, is the extent of its untypicality known?
- Meaning. Is the evidence clear and comprehensible? (1990 p. 6)

The first criterion addresses the question of whether the document is a primary or secondary document–is it the original report of an accident, or is it a summary of this original report by someone who did not witness the accident itself? What was omitted or misinterpreted in writing this summary? Tertiary documents are sources to find other documents, like the library catalog offers primary source documents. Looking at internal inconsistencies or by comparison with other documents, by looking at errors, and by checking whether different versions of the same document exist can assess authenticity. Credibility refers to the accurateness of the documentation, the reliability of the producer of the document, the freedom of errors. Representativeness is linked to typicality. It may be helpful to know of a specific record whether it is a typical record (which contains the information an average record contains). However, it can also be a good starting point if you know a specific document is untypical and to ask yourself what that means for your research question. Meaning can be distinguished into the intended meaning for the author of the document, the meaning for the reader of it (or for the different readers who are confronted with it) and the social meaning for someone who is the object of that document. For example, the protocol of interrogation was written by the author in order to demonstrate that this was a formally correct interrogation. For the judge at the court, the meaning of the content of the protocol is to have a basis for coming to a judgment. For the accused person, the meaning of the content of this protocol can be that he now has a conviction, which will have consequences for the rest of his life, when he tries to find a job, and so on. And for the researcher the meaning of this protocol might be that it demonstrates how crime guilt is constructed in a trial.

Constructing a Corpus

If you have decided to use documents in your research and know the sort of documents you want to use, a major step will be to construct a corpus of documents. This step is referring to issues of sampling–do you want to have a representative sample of all documents of a certain kind, or do you want to purposively select documents to reconstruct a case (see Chapter 11)? Intertextuality of documents is one problem in this context. They are linked with other documents (about the same persons referring to earlier events in their lives), but they are also virtually linked to other documents referring to other cases of a similar kind. For example, there are certain standards and routines on how to write a diagnostic report with a lot of general knowledge about a particular kind of disease, other cases, and so on in the background. So all documents refer to other documents in the way they document and construct social realities. For your research, it may be helpful to see these connections and to take them into account.

The Practicalities of Using Documents

How do you conduct an analysis using documents? Wolff (2004b) recommends that you should not start from a notion of factual reality in the documents compared to the subjective views in interviews, for example. Documents represent a specific version of realities constructed for specific purposes. It is difficult to use them for validating interview statements. They should be seen as a way of contextualizing information. Rather than using them as "information containers," they should be seen and analyzed as *methodologically created communicative turns* in constructing versions of events. Another suggestion is to take no part of any document as arbitrary, but to start from the ethnomethodological assumption of order at all points. This should also include the way a document is set up. Questions of layout or some standard or routine formulations used in a specific form of documents (for example juridical documents) are part of the communicative device "document" and should not be neglected. To see these parts of documents more clearly, it can be helpful to compare documents from different contexts–a record from juridical processes with a record from the health system, referring to the same issue or even case. What are the problems in analyzing documents? As in other research, limitations of resources may force you to be selective instead of using all the available (or necessary) documents. Sometimes the necessary documents are not available, accessible, or simply lost. Sometimes there are gatekeepers not letting you pass on to using the documents you need. In other cases, some people may block access to documents referring directly or indirectly to their person. For example, the archives of the secret services of the former East Germany were opened after the reunification of the two parts of Germany. Persons of certain public interest (like former Chancellors of West Germany) could prevent interested people (journalists, researchers, and the like) from having access to files referring to these people of public interest. Publication of these materials might have damaged the memory of these persons or produced a public outcry. Other practical problems may be that you have problems of understanding the content of the documents, because you cannot decipher the words, abbreviations, codes, or references that are used or because they are difficult to read (e.g., handwritten documents) or are damaged.

If you decide to use a certain type of documents for your research, you should always ask yourself, who has produced this document and for what purpose. Documents in institutions are meant to record institutional routines and at the same time to record information necessary for legitimizing how things are done in such routines. This becomes relevant in particular when problems, failures or mistakes have to be justified. So documents can be used, picked up, and reused in the practical context already. Garfinkel (1967) studied files and folders about patients in psychiatric contexts and found out in how many cases substantial parts of the records were missing. He found and analyzed "good" organizational reasons for "bad clinical records" (hence the title of his study). Among these reasons, time was only one–to document what you do is often secondary to doing what you do when time is short. Therefore, essential data are forgotten or omitted. Another reason is that a certain vagueness in documenting institutional practices prevents others from controlling these practices and, for example, cutting down the available time for certain routines. Thus, for researchers using such documents for their own research interest, it should also be asked: What has been left out in producing the record, by whom, and why? What are the social circumstances which may have influenced the production of the record?

Documents have a content which should be analyzed by asking what are they referenced to, what are the patterns of referencing, and what are the patterns of producing and using these documents in their mundane context?

Case Study: Analyzing Documents of Professional Training

In earlier chapters, our study on health concepts of professionals (Flick et al. 2002, 2004) was used as an example. We did not only cover interviews and focus groups about the issue, but also analyzed documents about the professional training of the doctors and nurses. We analyzed the curricula of medical training and the formation in nursing valid at the period when most of our interviewees received their training, and compared them with more recent versions of the curricula and with the statements in the interviews. We analyzed the documents in which the aims and contents of training programs, of exams and practical parts of the training are outlined for several topics: the role of health, health promotion, prevention, and ageing. The intention of analyzing these materials was to contextualize our interviewees' general statements that these topics were not part of their training but that they were confronted with them only during their later work as physicians and nurses. We could show that these issues have been given more space in more recent versions of the curricula. We also analyzed special programs of further education for doctors and nurses, which were on the market but not compulsory. They included more specialized programs referring to these issues.

What we found concerned the representation of these issues on the level of the planning of training and further education. There may be big differences between the planning and the actual training, so that you cannot refer directly from curricula (documents) to training (practice). Also, the fact that a curriculum includes a specific issue does not necessarily mean that this issue reaches the individual students during their training–they may simply have missed the lectures devoted to that issue.

This example shows different things: there may be a discrepancy between the planning of a program (in the document) and the practices in the teaching and in the reception of what is taught. Analyzing documents such as curricula can give you useful additional information, which you can relate to experiences mentioned in interviews for example. As a stand-alone method, the analysis of documents has its limitations.

In this chapter, we have concentrated on documents in a written form. As Prior (2003) shows, you can use all sorts of things as documents of practices or activities and analyze them as such. Also photos or films can be seen and analyzed as documents (see Chapter 18), and the Internet or the World Wide Web can be added as a special sort of document (see Chapter 20).

What are the Problems in Conducting the Method?

If you want to analyze documents you should take into account who produced the documents, for which purpose, who uses them in their natural context, and how to select the appropriate sample of single documents. You should avoid only focusing on the contents of documents without taking the context, the use, and function of documents into account. Documents are the means to constructing a specific version of an event or process and often, in a broader perspective, for making a specific case out of a life history or a process. Again, this should go into analyzing the documents.

What is the Contribution to the General Methodological Discussion?

Analyzing a document is often a way of using unobstrusive methods and data produced for practical purposes in the field under study. This can open a new and unfiltered perspective on the field and its processes. Therefore, documents often permit going beyond the perspectives of members in the field.

How does the Method Fit into the Research Process?

The background of much research focusing on documents is often ethnomethodology (see Chapter 6) and researchers analyze documents as communicative devices rather than as containers of contents. Depending on the specific research questions, all the methods of coding and categorizing (see Chapter 23) can be applied as well as analytic conversation approaches (see Chapter 24).

What are the Limitations of the Method?

As a stand-alone method, analyzing documents gives you a very specific and sometimes limited approach to experiences and processes. However, documents can be a very instructive addition to interviews or observations. The major problem in analyzing documents is how to conceptualize the relations between explicit content, implicit meaning and the context of functions, and use of the documents and how to take the latter into account.

KEY POINTS

- Documents can be instructive for understanding social realities in institutional contexts.
- They should be seen as communicative devices produced, used, and reused for specific practical purposes, rather than as "unobstrusive" data in the sense of bias-free data.
- They can be a fruitful addition to other forms of data if the contexts of their production and use are taken into account.

Exercise 19.1

1. Take a newspaper and a lifestyle magazine and look for the "lonely hearts" section in the advertisements. Select several of these ads from both sources and try to analyze and compare them. Try to find out who wrote and posted them and for what kind of purpose. Are there any systematic differences that you can see between the ads in the newspaper and those in the lifestyle magazine?
2. What are the limitations of such documents for analyzing an issue like individualization or the way social relations are built? How could you overcome these limitations?

FURTHER READING

These three texts give a good overview of the principles and pitfalls of analyzing documents.

Prior, L. (2003) *Using Documents in Social Research*. London: SAGE.
Scott, J. (1990) *A Matter of Record– Documentary Sources in Social Research*. Cambridge: Polity.
Wolff, S. (2004b) "Analysis of Documents and Records," in U. Flick, E.v. Kardorff and I. Steinke (eds), *A Companion to Qualitative Research*. London: SAGE. pp. 284–290.

20

QUALITATIVE ONLINE RESEARCH: USING THE INTERNET

CHAPTER OBJECTIVES
After reading this chapter, you should be able to

✓ use the Internet in qualitative research.
✓ understand the advantages of using the Internet as a support for your study.
✓ explain how qualitative research methods are used for studying the Internet.
✓ understand how basic approaches from qualitative research can be transferred into Internet-based research methods.

Qualitative research is not unaffected by the digital and technological revolutions at the beginning of the twenty-first century. Computers are used to analyze qualitative data (see Chapter 26), tape recorders, mini-disc recorders, and MP3 recorders are used for recording interviews and focus groups (see Chapter 22). You can use the Internet to find literature (see Chapter 5) and to publish your results (see Chapter 30).

But also beyond the area of research, the Internet has become a part of the everyday life of many people. Most of us are familiar with it or have an idea of the Internet and what you can do with it. Due the vast media presence of the Internet as a phenomenon and the possibilities of using and misusing it, most people have at least a rough idea about it. Due to the occasionally aggressive marketing ploys by Internet providers or telephone companies, many people have Internet access at home and a lot of professional activities and routines have integrated the use of the Internet. Finally, the number of people using e-mail as a form of communication is continually growing across social groups. Nevertheless, we should not forget that not everybody has access to the Internet or wants to have access to it. However, given the widespread use and access to this medium, it is no surprise that the Internet has been discovered as an object of research but also as a tool to use for research. In this chapter, I want to introduce you to some ways of using the Internet for qualitative research, show some advantages and possibilities of using it, but also show some limitations of research based on Internet methods.

The Internet as an Object of Research

As the rather vague formulations in the previous paragraph may have shown already, there is still a need to study who is really using the Internet and who is not. Also, there is still a need to develop knowledge about how different people use the Internet and how this varies across social groups (e.g., across age, social class, education, or gender). For such research, you can carry out traditional projects of media use and audience research. For example, you may interview potential or real users of the Internet about their experiences and practices with it. Methods can be standardized or open-ended interviews or focus groups. You can also do (participant) observations in Internet cafes to analyze how people use the computers and the Internet, or you can do conversation analyses of how people use the net collaboratively (e.g., analyzing children's talk in front of the screen in a computer class at school). Mitra and Cohen (1999) see the analysis of the numbers and experiences of users as the first approach to studying the Internet and the analysis of the text exchanged by users as the second. Common to such projects is that they use qualitative methods in a traditional way. Here, the Internet is only an object that people talk about or use in your study, but it is not in itself part of your study (as a methodological tool).

Preconditions of Qualitative Online Research

If you want to do your research online, some conditions should be given. First, you should be able to use a computer not only as a luxurious typewriter, but in a more comprehensive way. You should also have some experience using computers and software. Also you should have access to the Internet and you should enjoy being and working online and you should be (or become) familiar with the different forms of online communication like e-mail, chat rooms, mailing lists, and blogs.

I cannot give an introduction to the technical side of Internet research, but you will find easy-to-understand introductions to this special field (e.g., Mann and Stewart 2000). If these conditions are met on your side, you should consider whether your research is an issue that you can only study by using qualitative online research. For example, if you are interested in the social construction of an illness in online discussion groups, you should analyze their communication or interview the members of such groups and this can be done most easily if you address them online. Following from these two preconditions, a third becomes evident. The prospective participants of your study should have access to the Internet and they should be accessible via the Internet. If you want to study why people decide to stop using the Internet, you will have to find other ways of accessing your prospective participants and you should not plan your study as an online study. Another precondition is that you know about the methods of qualitative research independent from their online use before you transfer them to Internet research.

Transferring Qualitative Research and Methods to the Internet

Most research using the Internet is still quantitative—online surveys, Web-based questionnaires, or Internet experiments (see Hewson et al., 2003). But the use of qualitative research on the Web is expanding, too (see Mann and Stewart 2000). We can observe that researchers have transferred many qualitative methods to Internet research. We find forms of online interviewing, the use of online focus groups, participant observation, virtual ethnography (Hine 2000), and studies of interaction and traces of interaction (Bergmann and Meier 2004; Denzin 1999). Some of these methods can be transferred and applied in Internet research more easily; some of them and some of the principles of qualitative research can be transferred to the Web only with modification. In what follows, I will discuss the advantages and problems of using qualitative methods in the context of the Internet against the background of what has already been said in earlier chapters about the methods (e.g., interviewing) as such. We will end with some more general reflections on research design (see Chapter 12) and ethics (see also Chapter 4) in online research. The guiding questions will be: how can the various qualitative methods be transferred to Internet research, which modifications are necessary, and what are the benefits and costs of such a transfer (compared to their traditional offline use)?

Online Interviewing

When qualitative research is based on interviews, it is often the face-to-face kind, which allows the creation of a relationship based on verbal and nonverbal communications. In this situation, the researcher stimulates the dialogue in details and specifics. Transcribing interviews as data collection is a cost to the researchers before they analyze it. Also, you have to meet people for interviewing them, which means that they have to come to your office or you have to travel to see them. It is easier to work with a local sample. If you do your research while living in the countryside or if your interviewees are spread across the country or several countries, this can be more difficult to organize and to finance. This may reduce your sample from relevant to accessible people. Finally, there may be some people who feel uneasy to spontaneously answer a series of questions over an hour or two, which may lead them to reject participating in your research. All these—practical, sometimes technical but maybe systematic—reasons might lead you to doing interviews online if the target groups of your study are likely to be reached by e-mail or the Internet. Therefore, the guiding questions may be, what are the differences and common features of traditional and online interviewing? How can the different forms of interviewing be transferred to online research? How do you proceed in collecting and analyzing the data?

Online interviewing can be organized in a synchronous form, which means that you get in touch with your participant in a chat room where you can directly exchange questions and answers while you are both online at the same time. This comes closest to the verbal exchange in a face-to-face interview. But online interviews can also be organized in an asynchronous form, which means you send your questions to the participants and they send their answers back after some time and you are not necessarily online at the same time. The latter version is mostly done in the form of e-mail exchanges.

E-mail Interviewing

On the practical level, online interviewing will be organized differently from face-to-face interviewing. Semi-structured interviews are normally run in one meeting with the interviewee and a set of questions is prepared in advance. In an online interview, you could try to do the same by sending a set of questions to participants and asking them to send back the answers. But this comes closer to the situation of sending out a questionnaire in a survey than to the situation of a semi-structured interview. Therefore, some authors suggest that you design the collection of data more interactively by sending one or two questions, which will be answered by the participants. After that you will spend the next (one or two) questions, asking for answers and so on. Thus, the online interview is a series of e-mail exchanges.

Where do you find your participants for an e-mail interview? The easiest way is to address people whose e-mail address you already have or whose e-mail address you are able to retrieve (from their home pages or from the home pages of their institutions, such as universities). You can also use snowballing techniques, which means you ask your first participants for addresses of other potential participants for your study. You can also go into discussion groups or chat rooms and post information about your research asking people to contact you if they are interested in participating. However, you will face several problems in going these ways. First, using these ways, in some cases, will lead you into having only abbreviated information, like people's e-mail address or the nickname they use in discussion groups or chat rooms. In some cases, you will know no more about them or have to rely on the information they give you about their gender, age, location, and so on. This may raise questions of reliability of such demographic information and lead to problems of contextualizing the statements in the later interview. As Markham (2004, p. 360) holds: "What does it mean to interview someone for almost two hours before realizing (s)he is not the gender the researcher thought (s)he was?"

For example, if you want to compare statements in the context of the age of the participants, you should have reliable information about the age of every participant. These ways of access–and degrees of retaining the anonymity of the participants you accessed–may also lead to problems in sampling in your research. It is not only that traditional parameters of representativeness are difficult to apply and check in such a sample, it can also be difficult to apply strategies of theoretical or purposive sampling (see Chapter 11) here.

Once you have found a solution for how to sample and address participants for your study, you should prepare an instruction for them about what you expect from them when they participate in your study. In face-to-face research, you can explain your expectations in a direct oral exchange when recruiting people or before you start with your questions in the interview situation and respond to your participants' questions. In online interviewing you have to prepare instructions in written form, and they have to be clear and detailed, so that the participant knows what to do. At the same time, this instruction should not be too long in order to avoid confusion and neglect on the side of the interviewee.

As in face-to-face interviewing, it is necessary in online interviewing to build up a temporal relationship (rapport) with the interviewees, even if the communication may be asynchronous and responses come with some delay (even days).

Face-to-face communication (and interviewing) may be more spontaneous than online communication, but the latter allows the participants to reflect about their answers more than the former.

Mann and Stewart (2000, p. 129) following Baym (1995) see five factors as important to consider as influences on computer mediated interaction in interviews, for example:

1. What is the purpose of the interaction/interview? This will influence the interest of possible participants of whether or not to become involved in the study.
2. What is the temporal structure of the research? Are synchronous or asynchronous methods used and will there be a series of interactions in the research or not?
3. What are the possibilities and limitations coming from the software influencing the interaction?

4. What are the characteristics of the interviewer and the participants? What about the experience of and attitude to using technology? What about their knowledge of the topics, writing skills, insights, etc.? Is one-to-one interaction or researcher–group interaction planned? Has there been any interaction between researcher and participant before? How is the structure of the group addressed by the research (hierarchies, gender, age, ethnicity, social status, etc.)?
5. What is the external context of the research–inter/national culture and or communities of meaning that are involved? How do their communicative practices outside the research influence the latter?

When running the interview itself, you can send one question or a couple of questions, wait for the answers, and then probe (like in a face–to–face interview) or go on with sending the next questions. If there is a longer delay before answers come, you can send a reminder (after a few days for example). Bampton and Cowton (2002) view a decline in length and quality of responses as well as that answers are coming more slowly as a sign of fading interest on the side of the participant and for the interview to come to an end.

What are the Problems in Conducting the Method?

Online interviewing is a way to transfer face-to-face interviewing to Internet research. There is a much greater amount of anonymity for the participants, which may protect them from any detection of their person during the research and from the results. For the researchers, this makes any form of (real life) contextualization of the statements and the persons in their study much more difficult.

What is the Contribution to the General Methodological Discussion?

Online interviewing is a way of making qualitative research in the context of Internet research work. It can be very helpful if you want to integrate participants in your study, who are not easily accessible, because they live far away or because the do not want to talk to a stranger (about a possibly sensitive topic). Online research can also allow its participants to have anonymity, which can be an advantage. Online interviewing produces data, which are already available in the form of texts, so that you can skip the time-consuming step of transcribing your interviews.

How does the Method Fit into the Research Process?

Most forms of interviewing can be adapted and applied to Internet research. Sampling will have to be purposive sampling (see Chapter 11), which again has to be adapted and faces some problems if you do not get enough information about your participants. Online interviews can be analyzed quite easily by coding and categorization (see Chapter 23), whereas hermeneutic approaches have to be adapted to this sort of data.

What are the Limitations of the Method?

Online interviewing is some kind of a simulation of real-world interviewing and spontaneity of verbal exchange is replaced by the reflexivity of written exchanges. Nonverbal or paralinguistic parts of the communication are difficult to transport and integrate. Finally, the application of this approach is limited to people ready and willing to use computer-mediated communication or this kind of technology and communication in general.

Online Focus Groups

In a similar way, the approach of focus groups (see Chapter 15) has been transferred to Internet research. Here, we find similar distinctions and discussions as in the context of online interviewing. Again, you can distinguish between synchronous (or real-time) and asynchronous (non-real-time) groups. The first type of online focus group requires that all participants are online at the same time and may take part in a chat room or by using specific conferencing software. This latter version means that all participants need to have this software on their computers or that you should provide it to your participants who are supposed to load it on their computers. Besides technical problems this may cause, many people may hesitate to receive and install software for the purpose of taking part in a study. Asynchronous focus groups do not require that all participants are online at the same time (and this prevents the problems of coordinating this precondition). Like in an e-mail interview, people can take their time to respond to entries by the other participants (or to your questions or stimulus). The interventions by every participant will be addressed to a conference site and stored in a folder to which all participants have access. This type of focus group has its advantages when people from different time zones participate or when people vary in their speed in typing or responding, which might produce differences in the chance to articulate in the group.

In order to make online focus groups work, an easy access for the participants must be set up. Mann and Stewart (2000, pp. 103–105) describe in some detail the software you can use for setting up synchronous focus groups ("conferencing software"). They also describe the alternatives of how to design Web sites, whether these shall facilitate the access for those who are intended to participate and exclude others not intended to have access. The authors also discuss how the concepts of naturalness and neutrality for designing the venue of a focus group can be transferred to online settings. For example, it is important that the participants can take part in the discussions from their computers at home or at their workplace and not from a special research site. As a beginning, it is important to create a welcome message, which invites the participants, explains the procedures and what is expected from the participants, what the rules of communication among the participants should be like (e.g., "... please be polite to everyone ..."), and so on (see 2000, p. 108 for an example). The researcher should—as with any focus group—create a permissive environment.

For the recruitment of participants, you can basically use the same sources as for an online interview (see above), snowballing or looking in existing chat rooms or discussion groups for possible participants. Here again, you will face the problem that you cannot really be sure that the participants meet your criteria or that the representation they give of themselves is correct. This can become a problem if you want to set up a homogeneous group (see Chapter 15) of girls of a certain age, for example: "Unless online focus group participation combines the textual dimensions of chat rooms or conferencing with the visual dimension of digital cameras and/or voice, the researcher will be unable to be sure that the focus group really is comprised of, for example, adolescent girls" (Mann and Stewart 2000, p. 112). The number of participants in real-time focus groups should be limited as too many participants might make the discussion in the group too fast and superficial, whereas you can manage this problem more easily in asynchronous groups. Therefore, the number of participants does not have to be restricted in the latter case but should be limited in the former.

Compared to face-to-face focus groups, you can manage the issue of participant or group dynamics more easily in (especially asynchronous) online groups, but it can also become a problem. Shy participants may hesitate to intervene when they are unsure of the procedure or the issue, but the researcher has more options to intervene and work on this problem than in normal focus groups. The greater anonymity in online focus groups that is produced by the use of usernames, nicknames, and the like may facilitate topical disclosures of participants in the discussion more than in focus groups, in general. Finally, it is important that you choose a topic for the discussion, which is relevant for the group and participants in your study, so that it is attractive for them to join the group and the discussion. Or the other way around, it is important that you find groups for whom your topic is relevant in order to have fruitful discussions and interesting data.

What are the Problems in Conducting the Method?

Online focus groups can be a fruitful way to use the communication on the Internet for research purposes. Here as well, the anonymity for the participants is much greater and so may protect them from any detection of their person during the research and from the results. Again, for the researchers, this makes any form of (real life) contextualization of the statements and the persons in their study much more difficult and leads to sampling problems if you want to construct homogeneous groups, for example.

What is the Contribution to the General Methodological Discussion?

In online focus groups, you can manage problems of quiet participants more easily. You can also produce group interactions among people in anonymity and safety from being identified by the other participants or the researcher. This may lead to more disclosure than in real-world groups. The data are more easy to document and the loss of contributions due to hearing problems during transcription can be reduced.

How does the Method Fit into the Research Process?

If you receive enough information about your participants, you can adapt and apply most forms of focus groups to Internet research. Sampling will be purposive sampling (see Chapter 11). Online focus groups can be analyzed quite easily by coding and categorization (see Chapter 23), whereas hermeneutic approaches have to be adapted to this sort of data.

What are the Limitations of the Method?

Online focus groups can be affected by external influence on the participants who take part in their everyday context. This may lead to dropouts or distractions and influences on the data and their quality. This is difficult to control for the researcher. Technical problems in the online connection of one or more participants may also disturb the discussion and influence the quality of the data. Finally again, the application of this approach is limited to people ready and willing to use computer-mediated communication or this kind of technology and communication in general.

Virtual Ethnography: Interaction and Communication in the Internet

So far, we have focused on the ways and limitations of transferring verbal data methods of interviewing individuals or stimulating groups to discuss specific issues to online research. Then, the Internet becomes a *tool* to study people you could not otherwise reach, which is different and goes beyond traditional interviewing or group discussions. But you can also see the Internet as a *place* or as a *way of being* (for these three perspectives see Markham 2004). In these cases, you can study the Internet as a form of milieu or culture in which people develop specific forms of communication or, sometimes, specific identities. Both suggest a transfer of ethnographic methods to Internet research and to studying the ways of communication and self-presentation in the Internet: "Reaching understandings of participants' sense of self and of the meanings they give to their online participation requires spending time with participants to observe what they do online as well as what they say they do" (Kendall 1999, p. 62). For example, this lead Kendall in her study of a multiple users group first to observe and note the communication going on in this group and after a while to become an active participant in the group to develop a better understanding of what was going on there. This is similar to how ethnographers become participants and observers in real-world communities and cultures. The difference is that virtual ethnography is located in a technical environment instead of a natural environment. As many studies (see as an example Flick 1995, 1996) have shown, technology should not be seen as something just given and taken for granted, because its use and impact are strongly influenced by the representations and beliefs referring to it on the side of the users and nonusers. A similar approach is suggested for a virtual ethnography, which should start from research questions like the ones mentioned in Box 20.1.

Box 20.1   Research Questions for Virtual Ethnography

- How do the users of the Internet understand its capacities? What significance does its use have for them? How do they understand its capabilities as a medium of communication, and whom do they perceive their audience to be?
- How does the Internet affect the organization of social relationships in time and space? Is this different to the ways in which "real life" is organized, and if so, how do users reconcile the two?
- What are the implications of the Internet for authenticity and authority? How are identities performed and experienced, and how is authenticity judged?
- Is "the virtual" experienced as radically different from and separate from "the real"? Is there a boundary between online and offline? (Hine 2000, p. 8)

These research questions focus on representations of the virtual context on the side of the actors, on the building of virtual communities or social groups in the virtual, on identity on the Web and the links between the virtual and the real. In this context, the definition of what to understand of virtual communities may be helpful:

> Virtual communities are social aggregations that emerge from the Net when enough people carry on those public discussions long enough, with sufficient human feeling, to form webs of personal relationships in cyberspace. (Rheingold 1993, p. 5)

As in online interviews the exchange of questions and answers has to be re-conceptualized, some of the core elements of ethnography (see Chapter 17) can be transported to virtual ethnography without problems, while others have to be reformulated. This becomes evident in the ten principles of virtual ethnography suggested by Hine (2000, p. 63–65). In these principles, the author claims that sustained presence of an ethnographer in the field and the intensive engagement with the everyday life of its inhabitants is also in virtual ethnography a need for developing ethnographic knowledge. But in cyberspace, notions like the site of interaction or the field site are brought into question. What are the boundaries of the field? They cannot be defined in advance but become clear during the study. There are many links between cyberspace and "real-life," which should be taken into account. In this way, the Internet is a culture and a cultural product at the same time. Mediated communication can be spatially and temporally dislocated. You do not have to be at the same time or space to observe what's going on among members of a virtual group. You can engage in a lot of other things and then come back to your computer where your e-mails or entries in a discussion group are waiting for you and you can access them from computers placed anywhere in the world. Virtual ethnography is never holistic but always partial. You should give up the idea of studying "pre-existing, isolable and describable informants, locales and cultures," instead we find knowledge based on "ideals of strategic relevance rather than faithful representations of objective realities" (p. 65). Virtual ethnography is virtual in the sense of being disembodied and also carries a connotation of "not quite" or not strictly the real thing (p. 65).

This kind of virtual ethnography is applied to studying the contents of communications on the Internet and the textual ways in which participants communicate. Hine's own study focuses on Web pages around a trial and the way these reflected the trial, the case, and the conflicts linked to them.

Case Study: Virtual Ethnography

In her study, Hine (2000) took a widely discussed trial (the Louise Woodward case–a British au pair, who was tried for the death of a child she was responsible for in Boston) as a starting point. She wanted to find out how this case was constructed on the Internet by analyzing Web pages concerned with this issue. She also interviewed Web authors by e-mail about their intentions and experiences and analyzed the discussions in newsgroups in which ten or more interventions referring to the case had been posted. She used www.dejanews.com for finding newsgroups. At this site, all newsgroup postings are stored and can be searched by using keywords. Her search was limited to one month in 1998. Hine posted a message to several of the newsgroups, which had dealt with the issue more intensively. But different from the Web authors, the response was rather limited, an experience researchers had obviously had repeatedly (2000, p. 79). Hine also set up her own home page and mentioned it while contacting prospective participants or in posting messages about her research. She did that to make herself and her research transparent for possible participants. In summarizing her results, she had to state: "The ethnography constituted by my experiences, my materials and the writings I produce on the topic is definitely incomplete . . . In particular, the ethnography is partial in relation to its choice of particular applications of

(Continued)

(Continued)

the Internet to study. I set out to study 'the Internet,' without having made a specific decision as to which applications I intended to look at in detail" (p. 80).

Nevertheless, she produces interesting results of how people deal with the issue of the trial on the Internet and her thoughts and discussions of virtual ethnography are very instructive beyond her own study. However, they also show the limitations of transferring ethnography–or more general, qualitative research–to online research, as Bryman's critical comment illustrates: "Studies like these are clearly inviting us to consider the nature of the Internet as a domain for investigation, but they also invite us to consider the nature and the adaptiveness of our research methods" (2004, p. 473).

Going one step further, Bergmann and Meier (2004) start from a conversation analytic, ethnomethodological background, when they suggest analyzing the formal parts of interaction on the Web. Conversation analysis is more interested in the linguistic and interactive tools (like taking turns, repairing, opening up closings–see Chapter 24) people use when they communicate about an issue. In a similar way, the authors suggest that to identify the traces online communication produces and leaves is to understand how, communication is practically produced in the Web. Therefore, they use electronic process data, which means "all data that are generated in the course of computer-assisted communication processes and work activities–either automatically or on the basis of adjustments by the user" (p. 244). These data are not just simply at hand, but they must be reconstructed on the basis of a detailed and ongoing documentation of what is happening on the screen and–if possible–in front of it, when someone sends an e-mail, for example. This includes the comments of the sender while typing an e-mail, or paralinguistic aspects, like laughing and soon. It is also important to document the temporal structure of using computer-mediated communication. Here you can use special software (like Lotus Screen-Cam) that allows filming what is happening on the computer screen together with recording the interaction in front of the screen with video, for example.

What are the Problems in Conducting the Method?

Internet ethnography has to take into account how the users–individuals or communities–construct the Internet. As the example of Hine (2000, pp. 78–79) shows, it is sometimes quite difficult to receive a good response to newsgroup postings. This is seen by Bryman (2004, p. 474) as a general problem of skepticism against such cyber areas to be used by researchers. Hine concentrated on analyzing Web pages relevant for her issue more than on analyzing interactions.

What is the Contribution to the General Methodological Discussion?

The approach challenges several essentials of ethnographic research–concepts like being there, being part of an everyday life of a community or culture, and so on.

These challenges lead to interesting ways of rethinking these concepts and to adapting them to the needs of studying the virtual instead of real-world communities. It is an interesting contribution to the–after the controversies about writing and representation, authorship, and authority (see Chapters 2 and 30)–highly reflexive discussion about ethnography.

How does the Method Fit into the Research Process?

This approach has been developed against the background of the more general discussions of ethnography (see Chapter 17) and of writing and text in qualitative research (see Chapters 7 and 30). Sampling is purposive and analysis of the collected material is, like in other forms of ethnography, rather flexible.

What are the Limitations of the Method?

As the argumentation of several authors in this context shows, Internet communication is more than just communication on the Internet. To develop a comprehensive ethnography of the virtual, it would be necessary to include the links to real-world activities–in front of the screen or in the social life beyond the computer use. To find the way from virtual communities to the real life of the participants is, as has been said before, rather difficult. Therefore, the virtual ethnography remains much more partial and limited than are other forms of ethnography and than ethnographers claim as necessary for their approach.

Analyzing Internet Documents

The last approach that I want to mention here, is the transfer of analyzing documents (see Chapter 19) to the context of Internet research. The Web is full of documents like personal and institutional home pages, documents, and files you can download from these pages, online journals, advertisements, and the like. If your research question asks for analyzing such documents, you will find an endless multitude of sites and documents, often with links among them or among specific sites.

An outstanding part of the Internet is the World Wide Web and its endless variety of Web pages. These can be seen as a special form of document or text and analyzed as such. Special features characterize Web pages according to Mitra and Cohen (1999). One feature is the intertextuality of documents in the Web, organized and symbolized by (electronic) links from one text (or one page) to other texts. This kind of cross-referencing goes beyond the traditional definition and boundaries of a text and links a big number of single pages (or texts) to one big (sometimes endless) text. This explicit linking of texts is more and more supplemented by the implicit linking of texts, which becomes visible when you use a search engine and the number of links that are produced as a result of such a search.

A related feature is that texts in the Web should rather be seen as hypertexts due to the connectedness to other texts, but also due to the impermanence and infiniteness of texts in the Web. Many Web pages are permanently updated, changed, disappear, and reappear on the Web, which is why it is necessary to always mention the date you accessed a page when referring to it as a source. Furthermore, Web texts are characterized by "nonlinearity." Traditional texts have a linear structure—a beginning and an end, often a temporal structure in the content (in a narrative for example). Reading the text is normally oriented on this linearity. Web pages no longer conform to this linearity. They may have a drill-down structure, with its first page and subordinate pages. But there is no need for the user to follow the structure in the way the author—or the Web designer—planned or created the pages. Mitra and Cohen see this as a redefinition of the relation of author and reader (as writer) when Web texts are concerned. Other features of Web texts are that most of them go beyond the text as a medium and are multimedia products (including images, sounds, texts, popup pages, and so on) and that they are global. The latter is linked to the question of language; although most pages are in English, many pages are still constructed by using different language.

Some problems result from the features just discussed when you want to analyze Internet documents. First, what kind of text needs analyzing— the single homepage, an isolated Web page, or the totality of a page with its links to other related pages? Where should we begin? If you start from a notion of sequentiality (see Chapters 24 and 25), you need a beginning of a text, a more or less linear structure and an idea about the end of a text. But what is the beginning of a Web page? Or one step further: What are the criteria to select a page for your research, and what are the criteria for selecting a page for starting the analysis. A potential sequentiality could come from the main menu of a Web page and then go on to subordinate menus. But different from a written text, this is not a fixed order. The users can select which of the subordinated pages they go to next and so on.

Concerning the starting point and sampling of Web pages, you could start by using theoretical sampling (see Chapter 11). This means you can start with any page that seems interesting for your research and then decide which one(s) to include next in your sample according to the insights or unsolved questions after analyzing the first one. A search engine like Google can be helpful for finding Web pages for your topic. Here, it is important to have the adequate keywords for the search, so it can be helpful to try out several if your search is not successful at the beginning. Also you should keep in mind that all search engines cover the Web only in parts, so it could be helpful to use more than one engine for your search. As Web sites keep appearing and disappearing it can be problematic to assume that a page once found will always be accessible in the same way again. You should store copies of the most important pages for your research on your computer. At the same time, it can be fruitful to come back to Web sites during your research to check how they changed or were updated. Depending on what you want to find out exactly, you can use methods for analyzing visual material (see Chapter 18) or textual material (see Chapters 23 to 25) and also the more sophisticated QDA software (see Chapter 26) to do your study.

What are the Problems in Conducting the Method?

Web pages are somehow beyond the routines of analyzing documents in qualitative research, because it is more difficult to define their boundaries and because they are often changing and disappearing from the Web again. They have a different structure from texts and include different forms of data (images, sounds, text, links, and so on) at the same time.

What is the Contribution to the General Methodological Discussion?

At the same time, Web pages are a timely form of communication and self-presentation for individuals and organizations, and they are challenging the potential of qualitative research and methods.

How does the Method Fit into the Research Process?

Analyzing Internet documents is a way of transferring document analysis to the realm of the virtual. Depending on the concrete research question, the analytic tools of qualitative research can be selected and applied, but may have to be adapted. Sampling should be oriented on theoretical or purposeful sampling (see Chapter 11). Web pages are good examples to study and show the social construction of reality and specific issues.

What are the Limitations of the Method?

Web pages and other Internet documents represent a specific surface, a form of "presentation of self in everyday life" (Goffman 1959), which includes technical barriers to go back to what is presented here. To analyze a home page in order to make statements about the owner and creator (whether a person or institution) can be a tricky business. In such a case, I would strongly recommend a triangulation (see Chapter 29), with other methods focusing on a real-world encounter with persons or institutions.

Limits and Perspectives of Qualitative Online Research

Transferring qualitative research to the realm of the Internet is a challenge for many approaches. How do you adapt the methods and approaches? How do you adapt concepts of participation, sampling, and analysis to this field? At first sight, using the Internet for your study makes a lot of things easier. You can reach distant people with your interview without travelling, you save time and money for transcription, you can access existing groups interested in a topic, you can maintain the anonymity of your participants more easily, you can access all sorts of documents right from your desk and computer. At the same time, exchanging e-mails is different from asking questions and receiving answers face-to-face. The many people accessible on the Web do not necessarily wait to become part of your study. Problems of authenticity and contextualization result from the anonymity of participants. Web sites disappear or change and so on. Because of these technical problems, you should reflect about your issue of research and whether it really indicates using the Internet for answering your research questions. Beyond technical problems, ethical considerations (see Chapter 4) become relevant in Internet research, too. Mann and Stewart (2000, ch. 3) present an ethical framework for Internet research in greater detail. This framework refers to issues such as that you should collect data only for one specific and legitimate purpose and that they should be guarded against any form of misuse, loss, disclosure, unauthorized access, and similar risks. People should know about which personal data are stored and used and should have access to them. Informed consent in interviewing but also in ethnographic studies should be obtained, which can be difficult if your target group is not clearly defined and your contact is based on e-mail addresses and nicknames. Anonymity of the participants should be guaranteed and maintained during the research and in using the material. People should know that a researcher records their chats. This also means that simply lurking (reading and copying chat room exchanges) is not legitimate. There are several forms of "netiquettes" for the different areas of Internet use, and researchers should know them and act according to them (see Mann and Stewart 2000 for details).

If these ethical issues are taken into account, if the technical problems can be managed in a sufficient way, and if there is a good reason to use the Internet for your research project, it can be fruitful and helpful. The academic interest in the Internet as a culture and as a cultural product will lead to more development on the methodological level. The development of qualitative Internet research has only started and will continue in the future.

KEY POINTS

- Qualitative online research is a growing area, in which some of the established qualitative approaches are transferred and adapted to researching on the Internet.
- Qualitative online research offers some advantages compared to real-world research (e.g., like saving time for transcription) but faces a lot of other technical problems (like accessibility and identification of participants).
- The programmatic literature in this field is often more convincing than the examples of research, which can be found.
- Take ethical issues into account when conducting qualitative research online.

Exercise 20.1

1. Look on the Internet for an example of online research that reflects this example based on the background discussed in this chapter.
2. Take one of the methods discussed in Chapters 13 and 14 and think about ways and problems of transferring this method to online research.

FURTHER READING

Online Interviewing and Focus Groups
The first text describes e-mail interviewing in some detail, while the second refers to both areas and is a very good introduction to qualitative online research.

Bampton, R. and Cowton, C.J. (2002, May) "The E-Interview," Forum Qualitative Social Reseach, 3 (2), www.qualitative-research.net/fqs/fqs-eng.htm (date of access: 02, 22,2005).
Mann, C. and Stewart, F. (2000) *Internet Communication and Qualitative Research–A Handbook for Researching Online.* London: SAGE.

Virtual Ethnography
The first text discusses a more conversation analytic approach to Internet communication. The second discusses the use of ethnography in online research in detail.

Bergmann, J. and Meier, C. (2004) "Electronic Process Data and their Analysis," in U. Flick, E.v. Kardorff and I. Steinke (eds), *A Companion to Qualitative Research.* London: SAGE. pp. 243–247.
Hine, C. (2000) *Virtual Ethnography.* London: SAGE.

Analyzing Internet Documents
The first text outlines a framework for analyzing Internet documents on a conceptual and practical level, the second gives an example of research.

Hine, C. (2000) *Virtual Ethnography.* London: SAGE.
Mitra, A. and Cohen, E. (1999) "Analyzing the Web: Directions and Challenges," in S. Jones (ed.), *Doing Internet Research–Critical Issues and Methods for Examining the Net.* London: SAGE. pp. 179–202.

21

MULTIFOCUS DATA: AN OVERVIEW

CHAPTER OBJECTIVES
After reading this chapter, you should be able to

✓ compare the different approaches to multifocus data.
✓ evaluate your decision in the light of your (first) experiences when applying the method you choose.
✓ understand your method in the context of the research process and of the other stages of your research plan.

Multifocus data are becoming more and more relevant in qualitative research. Visual data are increasingly being rediscovered in qualitative research. Observation and ethnography are a major trend; the Internet is becoming a resource and issue for qualitative research at the same time. There are different reasons for using multifocus data instead of or in addition to verbal data. First, there is the desire on the part of the researcher to go beyond the spoken word and the report about actions in favor of analyzing the actions themselves as they naturally occur. Second, there is the advantage to be gained from the fact that some forms of observation work without the need for the researcher to make any interventions in the field under study. Finally, there is the possibility of obtaining knowledge through observing by participating and by intervening in the field and then observing consequences in the field.

Observation, in its different forms, tries to understand practices, interactions, and events, which occur in a specific context from the inside as a participant or from the outside as a mere observer. In observation, different starting points are taken to reconstruct the single case: the events in a specific setting, the activities of a specific person, the concrete interaction of several persons together. It is increasingly being taken into account that not only the observer's participation but also the mediums of film and the camera, as devices, have an influence on the events under study and their presentation for the observer. Therefore, observational procedures contribute to the construction of the very reality they seek to analyze, a reality which is already the result of processes of social construction before being observed. Observational methods provide a specific access to trace such construction processes as they occur in interaction. In the end, observational methods also lead to the production of text as empirical material. These texts range from observation protocols, to transcripts of recorded interactions, to verbal descriptions of the events in films, or the content of photographs. Other forms of documents are a fruitful way to approach everyday lives and institutional routines across the traces these lives and routines produce and leave in records, for example. Finally, the Internet has influenced many areas of everyday life and offers new ways of doing research—online interviewing, focus groups, or virtual ethnography. In the remainder of this chapter, the term "observation" will be used in a broader sense, as the use of documents, photos, video, or of communications in the Internet are forms of observing interactions and other processes, too.

First Point of Reference: Criteria-Based Comparison of the Approaches

Start by comparing multifocus data with the criteria used during the approaches to verbal data (see Chapter 16). You can also ask for recommendations as far as which procedures produce or guarantee openness in the research process. Because observations and visual material start mostly from interactions and actions, the participants' subjective perspectives are often ascertained in additional interviews. In addition to such efforts for openness, observational methods also include how to structure the data collection to garner in-depth content. The various approaches to visual data also contribute to the development of observation and the analysis of multifocus data as general methods. Furthermore, they may be characterized by the fields of applications in which they are mainly used or for which they were developed. Finally, specific problems in applying them and basic limitations are linked to each of the methods discussed here (see Table 21.1). The methods are grouped in three categories: observation and ethnography in

TABLE 21.1 Comparison of Methods for Collecting Multifocus Data

Criteria	Observation and Ethnography			Visual Data Methods			Mediated Data	
	Nonparticipant Observation	Participant Observation	Ethnography	Use of photos	Film Analysis	Video Analysis	Using Documents	Qualitative Online Research
Openness to the participants' subjective view by:	• Integration of interviews	• Integration of interviews • Empathy through participation	• Linking observation and interviewing	• Subject as photographer	• Subversive interpretations focus one protagonist's perspective	• Asking the participant to do the video recording	• Taking the context of the document into account (who produced it for which purpose?)	• Interviewees and participants have more control about what they reveal in a research situation
Openness to the process of actions and interactions by:	• Not influencing the observed field	• Distance despite participation • Most open observation	• Participation in the life world which is observed	• Documentation in photo series	• Analysis of stories and processes in films	• Comprehensive documentation of context	• Using records of processes produced for everyday purposes	• Allowing to establish interview communication without time pressure
Structuring (e.g., deepening) the analysis by:	• Increased focusing • Selective observation	• Integration of key persons • Increased focusing	• Plurality of the applied methods	• Slice and angle • Photograph at the decisive moment	• Contrasting "realistic" and "subversive" interpretations	• Focus of the camera on certain aspects	• Selection of the documents and taking their structure into account	• Better chances of probing for the researcher with more overview of what has been said
Contribution to the general development of methods for collecting multifocus data	• Refraining from interventions in the field • Elucidating the gendered nature of fieldwork • Self-observation for reflection	• Elucidating the conflicts between participation and distance	• Highlighting the appropriateness of methods • Sensitizing for problems of description and presentation	• Enriching other methods (observation, interviews)	• Fixing visual data • Documentation and detailed analysis of nonverbal components	• Extension of limits of other methods	• Ways of using data not originally produced for research purposes	• Making distant participants available for the research • Making use of an up-to-date form of communication for research

(Continued)

TABLE 21.1 (Continued)

Criteria	Observation and Ethnography			Visual Data Methods			Mediated Data	
	Nonparticipant Observation	Participant Observation	Ethnography	Use of photos	Film Analysis	Video Analysis	Using Documents	Qualitative Online Research
Area of application	• Open fields • Public places	• Delimited fields • Institutions	• Everyday life worlds	• Strange cultures • Biographic experiences	• Social problems • Cultural values	• Workplace studies • Interactions in institutional context	• Analyses of institutional or everyday processes	• Analyses of online communication in focus groups or ethnography
Problems in conducting the method	• Agreement of (unknown) people observed public places	• Going native • Problems of access • Inundation of the observer	• Unspecified research attitude instead of using specific methods	• Selectivity of the medium and its application	• Interpretation at the level of the image or at the level of the text	• How to restrict the influence of the presence of technology	• How to select and how to take contexts of documents into account	• Uncertainty about the identity of participants • Limited to users of the Internet
Limits of the method	• Covert observation as a problem of ethics	• Relation between statements and actions in the data	• Limited interest in methodological questions	• Photo analysis as text analysis	• No specific method for analyzing filmed data	• Selectivity of the camera	• Functions and purposes of the documents often can only be indirectly concluded	• Allows to approach only a very special part of everyday life (virtual communication)
References	Adler and Adler (1998)	Lüders (2004a); Spradley (1980)	Atkinson et al. (2001); Jessor et al. (1996); Lüders (2004a)	Becker (1986a); Harper (2004)	Denzin (2004b)	Heath and Hindsmarsh (2002)	Prior (2003); Scott (1990); Wolff (2004b)	Bergmann and Meier (2004);Mann and Stewart (2000)

the strict sense, visual data methods, and mediated data (e.g., documents, Internet research). The comparison in the table delimits the field of methodological alternatives in the area of using multifocus data and facilitates their positioning in this range.

Second Point of Reference: The Selection of the Method and Checking its Application

You should select the appropriate method for collecting multifocus data on the basis of your own investigation: its research question, the field that is to be observed and the persons (or materials) that are most crucial in it. You should check the method you select against the material you obtained with it. Not every method is appropriate to every research question. Events of the past may best be analyzed by using those visual materials that emerged at the time the events took place. Photos open a path in this direction. You may study how a society defines cultural values and deals with social problems in general (i.e., across various situations) by analyzing films shown in cinema and television. How such values and problems are concretely treated in situations of interaction may become clear in observing the fields and persons to whom they are relevant. But observation only has access to the actions realized in the situation, and the social and individual biographical background, knowledge, or attention can only be reconstructed in a mediated way from them. If the situation, the field, and the members can be sufficiently confined, the additional options of knowledge resulting from the researcher's participation in the field under study should be integrated. Nonparticipant observation mainly makes sense where the field cannot be delimited in a way that makes participation possible or where the actions to be observed prevent participation owing to the dangers linked to them or their illegality. Traces left in documents and on the Internet can reveal a specific part of social processes and changes.

Beyond the research question, the persons you want to study are a second consideration when you decide between methods of collecting observational visual or documentary data. Some people are more irritated and embarrassed by mere observation than by the researcher's temporary participation in their daily life, whereas others have problems with the disturbance created by the presence of the participant observer in the domain of interest. Some researchers have bigger problems in finding their way in the studied field, whereas others have more problems with the withdrawal required in mere observation. With respect to the participants in the study, it may be helpful if you clarify the situation and the researchers' procedures and check the appropriateness of the method you selected for this concrete purpose. For the observers and for solving their problems, observational training may be offered. Observed situations can be analyzed in order to find out if the relevant aspects have been taken into account or not. Field contacts should be analyzed additionally for problems in orienting and staying in the field. If this training does not solve the researcher's problems in the field, you should reconsider your choice of method or the choice of observer. The analysis of the first observation should also concentrate on the question of how far the selected method has been applied according to its rules and aims. For example, have observational sheets been applied as exactly and as flexibly as the method requires? Have the researchers maintained the necessary distance in their participation? Did the participation correspond in extension and intensity to the goals of the research? Here you should also take into account, in selecting, and assessing a method, what kind of statements you will obtain at the end and at what level of generalization. Only by taking these factors into account is it possible to specify what a good observation is (see Table 21.2).

By using the questions in Table 21.2, you can assess the appropriateness of the method and of its application from different angles. You should do the assessment this allows after the first field contacts and repeatedly in the further proceeding of the observation.

Third Point of Reference: Appropriateness of the Method to the Issue

Generally, there is no valid ideal method for collecting multifocus data. The research question and the issue under study should determine whether participant observation or a film analysis is applied. Nonparticipant observation can only provide insights that are limited to actions and interactions in concrete situations. The extension to participation in the events to be observed and to parallel conversations with the persons in the field is the more appropriate way of getting to grips with the subjective perspectives and the life world of the participants. The problem of appropriateness of methods is solved in the field of observation particularly by combining different methods in ethnographic studies.

Fourth Point of Reference: Fitting the Method into the Research Process

Locating observational methods in the research process is a fourth point of reference. You should cross-check your data collection with the method of interpretation that you will use to find out if the effort to realize openness and flexibility towards the issue under study is comparable in both cases. It does not make much sense to design the observation in the field so that it is free of methodological

TABLE 21.2   Checklist for Selecting a Multifocus Data Method and Evaluating its Application

1   *Research question*
Can the method and its application address the essential aspects of the research question?

2   *Form of data collection*
The method must be applied according to the methodological rules and goals. There should be no jumping between the forms of data collection except when it is grounded in the research question and/or theoretically.

3   *The researchers*
Are the researchers able to apply the method? What part do their own fears and uncertainties play in the situation?

4   *The participants*
Is the form of data collection appropriate to the target group?
How can the fears, uncertainties, and expectations of (potential) participants in the study be taken into account?

5   *Field*
Is the form of data collection appropriate to the field under study? How are its accessibility and reliability and ethical problems taken into account?

6   *Scope for the members*
How are the perspectives of the persons that are studied and their variability taken into account? Do the members' perspectives have a chance of asserting themselves against the methodological framework of the study (e.g., are the observational sheets flexible enough for the unexpected)?

7   *Course of the data collection*
Did the researchers realize the form of data collection? Did they leave enough scope to the members? Did he or she manage his or her roles? (Why not?)
Was the participants' role, the researcher's role, and the situation clearly defined enough for the participants? Could they fulfil their role? (Why not?)

Analyze the breaks in order to validate the data collection between the first and second field contact, if possible.

8   *Aim of the interpretation*
What are the clearly defined actions, multifold patterns, contexts, and so on?

9   *Claim for generalization*
The level on which statements should be made:
• For the single case (the participants and their actions, an institution and the relations in it, etc.)?
• Referring to groups (findings about a profession, a type of institution, etc.)?
• General statements?

restrictions and is as flexible and comprehensive as possible, if you afterwards analyze the data are exclusively with categories that you have derived from existing theories (see Chapter 23). It has proved extremely difficult to analyze data that are only documented in field notes with hermeneutic methods (see Chapter 24), like objective hermeneutics (for this problem see Lüders 2004a). Methods of interpretation located between these two poles—e.g., theoretical coding (see Chapter 22)—are more appropriate for these data. In a similar way, you should cross-check your form and design of observation with your method of sampling fields and situations and with the theoretical background of your study.

You can find starting points for this cross-checking in the considerations about fitting the method into the research process given for each method in the preceding chapters. The understanding of the research process outlined in these considerations should be compared with the understanding of the research process on which your study and its design are based.

Thus, the choice of the concrete method may be taken and assessed with respect to its appropriateness to the subject under study and to the process of research as a whole.

KEY POINTS

- All methods for collecting multifocus data have their strengths and weaknesses.
- They all offer ways to give the participants in the study room for presenting their experiences.
- At the same time, every method structures what is studied with it in a specific way.
- Before and during applying a specific method for answering your research question, I suggest that you check and assess whether the method selected is appropriate or not.

Exercise 21.1

1. Find a study from the literature which is based on using multifocus data and reflect on whether or not the method that was applied was appropriate for the issue under study and the people involved in the research.
2. For your own study reflect on what your main reasons were for using one of the multifocus data methods.

FURTHER READING

Methods for Collecting and Analyzing Multifocus Data
These texts address some of the methods for analyzing multifocus data mentioned in this part of the book.

Bergmann, J. and Meier, C. (2004) "Electronic Process Data and their Analysis," in U. Flick, E.v. Kardorff and I. Steinke (eds), *A Companion to Qualitative Research*. London: SAGE. pp. 243–247.

(Continued)

Denzin, N.K. (2004a) "Reading Film: Using Photos and Video as Social Science Material," in U. Flick, E.v. Kardorff and I. Steinke (eds), *A Companion to Qualitative Research*. London: SAGE. pp. 234–247.

Harper, D. (2004) "Photography as Social Science Data," in U. Flick, E.v. Kardorff and I. Steinke (eds), *A Companion to Qualitative Research*. London: SAGE. pp. 231–236.

Heath, C. and Hindmarsh, J. (2002) "Analysing Interaction: Video, Ethnography and Situated Conduct," In T. May (ed.), *Qualitative Research in Action*. London: SAGE. pp. 99–120.

Mann, C. and Stewart, F. (2000) *Internet Communication and Qualitative Research – A Handbook for Researching Online*. London: SAGE.

Prior, L. (2003) *Using Documents in Social Research*. London: SAGE.

PART 6

FROM TEXT TO THEORY

So far we have looked at procedures of producing data in qualitative research. Now, we will turn to the ways of analyzing data. These will include several steps again. First, you will have to document what you observed or what you have been told in order to have a basis for analyzing it. Chapter 22 on documentation introduces you to the use of field notes in observation and of transcription after interviewing and provides some suggestions on how to reflect on these – not only technical – steps in the research process. Chapter 23 then introduces you to several techniques of coding and categorizing data. The common strategy underlying these techniques is prominent in qualitative research–to analyze material by identifying relevant passages and parts and by naming and grouping these passages according to categories and types. The following chapters (24 and 25) focus on a different strategy and present methods to make it work. Here, the strategy is to understand a text – and the material – by following its internal structure and to take this strongly into account in analyzing the text and the material. Conversation and discourse analyses want to demonstrate how issues are constructed in the way that people talk about it, or discourses are produced in more general forms of communication, such as media representations and the response on the part of the recipients (Chapter 24). Hermeneutic procedures and narrative analysis need to understand a text according to the development and unfolding of the issue and its meaning (Chapter 25). Computer programs for analyzing qualitative data have been attracting a lot of attention recently. The potential and the limitations of using such programs is discussed in Chapter 26. An overview of the different analytic approaches and techniques is set out in Chapter 27.

22

DOCUMENTATION OF DATA

CHAPTER OBJECTIVES
After reading this chapter, you should be able to

✓ **understand the different ways of documenting observations.**
✓ **recognize the potential and pitfalls of transcription.**
✓ **distinguish the influences of the different ways of documentation on what is documented.**
✓ **understand the importance of this step in the research process.**

The preceding chapters have detailed the two main ways in which data are collected or produced in qualitative research. However, before you can analyze the data you may have generated in these ways, you have to document and edit your data. In the case of interview data, an important part of this editing process is that you record the spoken words and then transcribe them. For observations, the most important task is that you document actions and interactions. In both cases, a contextual enrichment of statements or activities should be a main part of the data collection. You can achieve this enrichment by documenting the process of data collection in context protocols, research diaries, or field notes. With these procedures, you transform the relations you study into texts, which are the basis for the actual analyses. In this chapter, I will discuss the methodological alternatives for documenting collected data. The data you produce as a result of this process are substituted for the studied (psychological or social) relations so that you can proceed with the next stages of the research process (i.e., interpretation and generalization). The process of documenting the data comprises mainly three steps: recording the data, editing the data (transcription), and constructing a "new" reality in and by the produced text. All in all, this process is an essential aspect in the construction of reality in the research process.

New Ways and Problems of Recording Data

The more sophisticated (acoustic and audio-visual) possibilities for recording events have had an essential influence on the renaissance and developments of qualitative research over the last 20 years. One condition for this progress was that the use of recording devices (tape, MP3, mini-disc, and video recorders) has become widespread in daily life itself as well. To some extent, their prevalence has made them lose their unfamiliarity for potential interviewees or for those people whose everyday life is to be observed and recorded by their use. It is these gadgets alone that have made possible some forms of analyses such as conversation analysis and objective hermeneutics (see Chapters 24 and 25 for more details).

Acoustic and Visual Recordings of Natural Situations

Using machines for recording makes the documentation of data independent of perspectives–those of the researcher as well as those of the subjects under study. It is argued that this achieves a naturalistic recording of events or a "natural design": interviews, everyday talk, or counseling conversations are recorded on cassettes or videotape. After informing the participants about the purpose of the recording, the researcher hopes that they will simply forget about the tape recorder and that the conversation will take place "naturally"–even at awkward points.

Presence and Influence of the Recording

This hope of making a naturalistic recording will be fulfilled above all if you restrict the presence of the recording equipment. In order to get as close as possible to the naturalness of the situation, I recommend that you restrict the use of recording technology to the collection of data necessary to the research question and the theoretical framework. Where videotaping does not document anything essential beyond that obtained with a cassette recorder, you should prefer the less obtrusive machine. In any case, the researchers should limit their recordings to what is absolutely necessary for their research question–in terms of both the amount of data that is recorded and of the thoroughness of the recording.

In research about counseling, for example, you may ask the counselors to record their conversations with clients by using a cassette recorder. In institutions where these kinds of recordings are continuously made for purposes of supervision, recording may have little influence on what is recorded. However, you should not ignore the fact that there may be some influence on the participants' statements. This influence is increased if the researchers are present in the research situation for technical reasons. The greater the effort in videotaping and the more comprehensive the insight it permits into the everyday life under study, the greater the possible skepticism and reservations on the part of participants in the study. This makes the integration of the recording procedure in the daily life under study more complicated.

Skepticism about the Naturalness of Recordings

Correspondingly, you can find thoughtful reflections on the use of recording technology in qualitative research. These forms of recording have replaced the interviewers' or observers' notes, which were the dominant medium in earlier times. For Hopf, they provide "increased options for an inter-subjective assessment of interpretations . . . for taking into account interviewer and observer effects in the interpretation . . . and for theoretical flexibility" compared with "the necessarily more selective memory protocols" (Hopf 1985, pp. 93–94). This new flexibility leads "to a new type of 'qualitative data hoarding' owing to the delays in decisions about research questions and theoretical assumptions which are now possible."

New questions concerning research ethics, changes in the studied situations caused by the form of recording,[1] and a loss of anonymity for the interviewees are linked to this. The ambivalence against the new options for recording qualitative data suggests that it is important to treat this point not as a problem of technical detail but rather in the sense of a detailed "qualitative technology assessment." Also, you should include in your considerations about the appropriate method for documentation "out-of-date" alternatives, which were displaced by the new technologies.

Field Notes

The classic medium for documentation in qualitative research has been the researcher's notes.[2] The notes taken in interviews should contain the essentials of the interviewee's answers and information about the proceeding of the interview. The participant observers repeatedly interrupt their participation to note important observations, as the description in Box 22.1 of the classic documentation technique, its problems, and the chosen solution to them makes clear.

Box 22.1   Field Notes in Practice

The following example comes from a study used as an example before, which was run by Anselm Strauss and his colleague in the 1960s in a psychiatric hospital. The example shows the authors' practices in writing field notes:

"Our usual practice was to spend limited periods of time in the field, perhaps two or three hours. When we could appropriately leave the field, we headed immediately for a typewriter or Dictaphone. If leaving was impossible, we took brief memory-refreshing notes whenever lulls occurred and recorded them fully as soon thereafter as possible. The recording of field notes presented a number of problems involving discrimination among events seen and heard, as well as an interviewer's impressions or interpretations. As professionals, all of us were mindful of the pitfalls attending recall and the all-too-easy blurring of fact and fancy. We attempted therefore to make these discriminations clearly, either by stating them unmistakably or by developing a notational system for ensuring them. Verbal material recorded within quotations signified exact recall; verbal material within apostrophes indicated a lesser degree of certainty or paraphrasing; and verbal material with no markings meant reasonable recall but not quotation. Finally, the interviewer's impressions or inferences could be separated from actual observations by the use of single or double parentheses. Although this notational system was much used, none of us was constrained always to use it."

Source: Strauss et al. 1964, pp. 28–29

Lofland and Lofland (1984) formulate as a general rule that such notes should be made as immediately as possible. The withdrawal necessary for this may introduce some artificiality in the relation to interaction partners in the field. Especially in action research when the researchers take part in the events in the field and do not merely observe them, it is additionally difficult to maintain this freedom for the researchers. An alternative is to note impressions after ending the individual field contact. Lofland and Lofland (1984, p. 64) recommend that researchers use a "cloistered rigor" in following the commandment to make notes immediately after the field contact, and furthermore that researchers estimate the same amount of time for carefully noting the observations as for spending on the observation itself. It should be ensured that (maybe much) later a distinction can still be made between what has been observed and what has been condensed by the observer in his or her interpretation or summary of events (see Chapter 28 on procedural reliability of protocols). Researchers may develop a personal style of writing notes after a while and with increasing experience.

All in all, the production of reality in texts starts with the taking of field notes. The researcher's selective perceptions and presentations have a strong influence on this production. This selectivity concerns not only the aspects that are left out but also and above all those which find their way into the notes. It is only the notation that raises a transitory occurrence out of its everyday course and makes it into an event to which the researcher, interpreter, and reader can turn their attention repeatedly. One way of reducing or at least qualifying this selectivity of the documentation is to complement the notes by diaries or day protocols written by the subjects under study in parallel with the researcher's note taking. Thus, their subjective views may be included in the data and become accessible to analysis. Such documents from the subject's point of view can be analyzed and contrasted with the researcher's notes. Another way is to add photos, drawings, maps, and other visual material to the notes. A third possibility is to use an electronic notebook, a dictating machine, or similar devices for recording the notes.

Correspondingly, Spradley (1980, pp. 69–72) suggests four forms of field notes for documentation:

- the condensed accounts in single words, sentences, quotations from conversations etc.;
- an expanded account of the impressions from interviews and field contacts;
- a fieldwork journal, which like a diary "will contain . . . experiences, ideas, fears, mistakes, confusions, breakthroughs, and problems that arise during fieldwork" (1980, p. 71);
- some notes about analysis and interpretations, which start immediately after the field contacts and extend until finishing the study.

Research Diary

Especially if more than one researcher is involved, there is a need for documentation of and reflection on the ongoing research process in order to increase the comparability of the empirical proceedings and focuses in the individual notes. One method of documentation is to use continually updated research diaries written by all participants. These should document the process of approaching a field, and the experiences and problems in the contact with the field or with interviewees and in applying the methods. Important facts and matters of minor importance or lost facts in the interpretation, generalization, assessment, or presentation of the results seen from the perspectives of the individual researcher should also be incorporated. Comparing such documentation and the different views expressed in them makes the research process more intersubjective and explicit. Furthermore, they may be used as "memos" in the sense of Strauss (1987, in particular Chapter 5) for developing a grounded theory. Strauss re-commends writing memos during the whole research process, which will contribute to the process of building a theory. Documentation of this kind is not only an end in itself or additional knowledge but also serves in the reflection on the research process.

Several methods have been outlined for "catching" the interesting events and processes, statements, and proceedings. In the noting of interventions in the everyday life under study, the researchers should be led in their decisions by the following *rule of economy*: to record only as much as is definitely necessary for answering the research question. They should avoid any "technical presence" in the situation of the data collection that is not absolutely necessary for their theoretical interests. Reducing the presence of recording equipment and informing the research partners as much as possible about the sense and purpose of the chosen form of recording, make it more likely that the researchers will truly "catch" everyday behavior in natural situations. In the case of research questions where "out-of-date" forms of documentation such as preparing a protocol of answers and observations are sufficient, I highly recommend using these forms. But you should produce these protocols as immediately and comprehensively as possible in order to mainly record impressions of the field and resulting questions.

Documentation Sheets

For interviews, I found it helpful to use sheets for documenting the context and the situation of data collection. What information they should concretely include depends on the design of the study, e.g., if several interviewers are involved or if interviews are conducted at changing locations, which supposedly might have influenced the interview. In addition, the research questions determine what you should concretely note on these sheets. The example in Box 22.2 comes from my study of technological change in everyday life, in which several interviewers conducted interviews with professionals in different work situations on the influences of technology on childhood, children's education in one's own family or in general, and so on. Therefore, the documentation sheet needed to contain explicit additional contextual information.

Transcription

If data have been recorded using technical media, their transcription is a necessary step on the way to their interpretation. Different transcription systems are available which vary in their degree of exactness (for an overview see Kowall and O'Connell 2004). A standard has not yet been established. In language analyses, the interest often focuses on attaining the maximum exactness in classifying and presenting statements, breaks, and so on. Here you can also ask about the procedure's appropriateness. These standards of exactness contribute to the natural science ideals of precision in measurement and are imported into interpretive social science through the back door. Also, the formulation of rules for transcription may tempt

---

Box 22.2 Example of a Documentation Sheet

Information about the Interview and the Interviewee

Date of the interview:

Place of the interview:

Duration of the interview:

Interviewer:

Indicator for the interviewee:

Gender of the interviewee:

Age of the interviewee:

Profession of the interviewee:

Working in this profession since:

Professional field:

Raised (countryside/city):

Number of children:

Age of the children:

Gender of the children:

Special occurrences in the interview:

....

....

....

....

....

....

....

---

one into some kind of fetishism that no longer has a reasonable relation to the question and the products of the research. Where linguistic and conversation analytic studies focus on the organization of language, this kind of exactness may be justified. For more psychological or sociological research questions, however, where linguistic exchange is a medium for studying certain contents, exaggerated standards of exactness in transcriptions are justified only in exceptional cases. It seems more reasonable to transcribe only as much and only as exactly as is required by the research question (Strauss 1987). First, precise transcription of data absorbs time and energy, which could be invested more reasonably in their interpretation instead. Second, the message and the meaning of what was transcribed are sometimes concealed rather than revealed in the differentiation of the transcription and the resulting obscurity of the protocols produced. Thus Bruce (1992, p. 145; quoted in O'Connell and Kowall 1995, p. 96) holds:

> The following very general criteria can be used as a starting point in the evaluation of a transcription system for spoken discourse: manageability (for the transcriber), readability, learnability, and interpretability (for the analyst and for the computer). It is reasonable to think that a transcription system should be easy to write, easy to read, easy to learn, and easy to search.

Beyond the clear rules of how to transcribe statements, turn taking, breaks, ends of sentences, and so on, a second check of the transcript against the recording and the anonymization of data (names, local, and temporal references) are central features of the procedure of transcription. Transcription in conversation analysis (see Chapter 24) has often been the model for transcriptions in social science. Drew (1995, p. 78) gives a "glossary of transcription conventions," which may be used after the criteria with regard to the research question mentioned above have been applied (Box 22.3).

Box 22.3 Transcription Conventions

[	Overlapping speech: the precise point at which one person begins speaking whilst the other is still talking, or at which both begin speaking simultaneously, resulting in overlapping speech.
(0.2)	Pauses: within and between speaker turns, in seconds.
'Aw:::':	Extended sounds: sound stretches shown by colons, in proportion to the length of the stretch.
Word:	Underlining shows stress or emphasis.
"fishi-":	A hyphen indicates that a word/sound is broken off.
".hhhh":	Audible intakes of breath are transcribed as ".hhhh" (the number of h's is proportional to the length of the breath).
WORD:	Increase in amplitude is shown by capital letters.
(words …):	Parentheses bound uncertain transcription, including the transcriber's "best guess."

Source: Adapted from Drew 1995, p. 78

A second version of transcribing interviews is shown in Box 22.4. I suggest using line numbers for the transcript and leaving enough space in the left and right margin for notes.

Box 22.4 Rules for Transcription and an Example

Layout	
Word processing	Word (97)
Font	Times New Roman 12
Margin	Left 2, right 5
Line numbers	5, 10, 15 etc., every page starts again
Lines	1,5
Page numbers	On top, right
Interviewer:	I: Interviewer
Interviewee:	IP: Interviewee
Transcription	
Spelling	Conventional
Interpunctation	Conventional
Breaks	Short break *; more than 1 sec *no of seconds*
incomprehensible	((incomp))
Uncertain transcription	(abc)
Loud	With Commentary
Low	With Commentary
Emphasis	With Commentary
Break off word	Abc-
Break off sentence	Abc-
Simultaneous talk	#abc#
Paralinguist utterance	With Commentary (e.g., sighs...)
Commentary	With Commentary
Verbal quote	Conventional
Abbreviations	Conventional
Anonymization	Names with°

If you use these suggestions for transcribing your interviews, transcripts like the one in Box 22.5 should result.

Box 22.5   Example from a Transcript

1

    I: Yeah the first question is, what is this for you, health? ((telephone rings)) Do you want to pick it up first?

    N: No.

    I: No? Okay.

5   N: Health is relative, I think. Someone can be healthy, too, who is old and has a handicap and can feel healthy nevertheless. Well, in earlier times, before I came to work in the community, I always said, someone is healthy if he lives in a very well ordered household, where everything is correct and super exact, and I would like to say, absolutely clean"? But I learnt better, when I started to work in the community

10   (...). I was a nurse in the Hanover Medical School before that, in intensive care and arrived here with.....

I = Interviewer; N = Nurse

In qualitative online research (see Chapter 20), the answers, statements, or narratives in interviews or focus groups come in written and electronic format, so that you can skip the step of transcription here.

Reality as Text: Text as New Reality

Recording the data, making additional notes, and the transcription of the recordings transform the interesting realities into text and tales from the field result. At the very least, the documentation of processes and the transcription of statements lead to a different version of events. Each form of documentation leads to a specific organization of what is documented. Every transcription of social realities is subject to technical conditions and limitations and produces a specific structure on the textual level, which makes accessible what was transcribed in a specific way. The documentation detaches the events from their transience. The researcher's personal style of noting things makes the field a presented field; the degree of the transcription's exactness dissolves the gestalt of the events into a multitude of specific details. The consequence of the following process of interpretation is that "Reality only presents itself to the scientist in substantiated form, as text—or in technical terms—as protocol. Beyond texts, science has lost its rights, because a scientific statement can only be formulated when and insofar as events have found a deposit or left a trace and these again have undergone an interpretation" (Garz and Kraimer 1994, p. 8).

This substantiation of reality in the form of texts is valid in two respects: as a process that opens access to a field and, as a result of this process, as a reconstruction of the reality, which has been transformed into texts. The construction of a new reality in the text has already begun at the level of the field notes and at the level of the transcript and this is the only (version of) reality available to the researchers during their following interpretations. These constructions should be taken into account in the more or less meticulous handling of the text, which is suggested by each method of interpretation.

The more or less comprehensive recording of the case, the documentation of the context of origination, and the transcription organize the material in a specific way. The epistemological principle of understanding may be realized by being able to analyze the presentations or the proceeding of situations from the inside as far as possible. Therefore, the documentation has to be exact enough to reveal structures in those materials and it has to permit approaches from different perspectives. The organization of the data has the main aim of documenting the case in its specificity and structure. This allows the researcher to reconstruct it in its gestalt and to analyze and break it down for its structure – the rules according to which it functions, the meaning underlying it, the parts that characterize it. Texts produced in this way construct the studied reality in a specific way and make it accessible as empirical material for interpretative procedures.

KEY POINTS

- The documentation of data is not only a technical step in the research process. It also has an influence on the quality of the data you can use for interpretations.
- New technologies of recording have changed the possibilities of documentation but also the characteristics of qualitative data.
- Transcription is an important step in the analysis of data, but it should not dominate the research process with too much (sometimes unnecessary) exactness.
- Field notes and research diaries can also provide precious information about the experiences in research.

Exercise 22.1

1. Record some interactions with a tape recorder and transcribe one or two pages from this recording. Then compare the recording with the written text.
2. Go to a public place and observe what is happening there. After ten minutes, find a quite spot and note what you have seen. Reflect about the problems that arise in this little exercise.

Notes

1   According to Bergmann, "an audiovisual recording of a social event is by no means the purely descriptive representation which it may seem to be at first. Owing to its time-manipulative structure it has rather a constructive moment in it" (1985, p. 317). Thus, after its recording, a conversation can be cut off from its unique, self-contained temporal course and monitored over and over again. Then it may be dissected into specific components (e.g., participants' non-verbal signals) in a way that goes beyond the everyday perceptions of the participants. This not only allows new forms of knowledge but also constructs a new version of the events. From a certain moment, the perception of these events is no longer determined by their original or natural occurrence but by their artificially detailed display.

2   You will find good overviews, reflections, and introduction in Emerson et al. (1995), Lofland and Lofland (1984) and Sanjek (1990).

FURTHER READING

The second text listed below gives an overview and some critical reflections about transcription, and the others give an orientation for how to work with field notes.

Emerson, R., Fretz, R. and Shaw, L. (1995) *Writing Ethnographic Fieldnotes.* Chicago: Chicago University Press.

Kowall, S. and O'Connell, D.C. (2004) "Transcribing Conversations," in U. Flick, E.v. Kardorff and I. Steinke (eds), *A Companion to Qualitative Research.* London: SAGE. pp. 248–252.

Lofland, J. and Lofland, L.H. (1984) *Analyzing Social Settings*, 2nd edn. Belmont, CA: Wadsworth.

Sanjek, R. (ed.) (1990) *Fieldnotes: The Making of Anthropology.* Albany, NY: State University of New York Press.

23

CODING AND CATEGORIZING

CHAPTER OBJECTIVES
After reading this chapter, you should be able to

✓ know the different approaches to coding empirical material.
✓ apply the procedures of open, axial, and selective coding as well as thematic coding to your material.
✓ understand the techniques of qualitative content analysis and the preparing step of global analysis.
✓ identify the potentials and limits of coding and categorizing approaches in general.

The interpretation of data is at the core of qualitative research, although its importance is seen differently in the various approaches. Sometimes, for example, in objective hermeneutics and conversation analysis (see Chapters 24 and 25), research refrains from using specific methods for data collection beyond making recordings of everyday situations. In these cases, the use of research methods consists of applying methods for the interpretation of text. In other approaches, it is a secondary step following more or less refined techniques of data collection. This is the case, for example, with qualitative content analysis or with some methods of handling narrative data. In Strauss's (1987) approach, the interpretation of data is the core of the empirical procedure, which, however, includes explicit methods of data collection. The interpretation of texts serves to develop the theory as well as the foundation for collecting additional data and for deciding which cases to select next. Therefore, the linear process of first collecting the data and later interpreting it is given up in favor of an interwoven procedure. Interpretation of texts may pursue two opposite goals. One is to reveal and uncover statements or to put them into their context in the text that normally leads to an augmentation of the textual material; for short passages in the original text, page-long interpretations are written sometimes. The other aims at reducing the original text by paraphrasing, summarizing, or categorizing. These two strategies are applied either alternatively or successively. In summary, we can distinguish two basic strategies in working with texts. Coding the material has the aim of categorizing and/or theory development. The more or less strictly sequential analysis of the text aims at reconstructing the structure of the text and of the case. The latter strategy will be the topic of Chapter 24 and 25.

Theoretical Coding

Theoretical coding is the procedure for analyzing data, which have been collected in order to develop a grounded theory. This procedure was introduced by Glaser and Strauss (1967) and further elaborated by Glaser (1978), Strauss (1987), and Strauss and Corbin (1990/1998). As already mentioned several times, in this approach the interpretation of data cannot be regarded independently of their collection or the sampling of the material. Interpretation is the anchoring point for making decisions about which data or cases to integrate next in the analysis and how or with which methods they should be collected. In the process of interpretation, different "procedures" for working with text can be differentiated. They are termed "open coding," "axial coding," and "selective coding." You should see these procedures neither as clearly distinguishable procedures nor as temporally separated phases in the process. Rather, they are different ways of handling textual material between which the researchers move back and forth if ne-cessary and which they combine. But the process of interpretation begins with open coding, whereas towards the end of the whole analytical process, selective coding comes more to the fore. Coding here is understood as representing the operations by which data are broken down, conceptualized, and put back together in new ways. It is the central process by which theories are built from data (Strauss and Corbin 1990/1998, p. 3).

According to this understanding, coding includes the constant comparison of phenomena, cases, concepts, and so on and the formulation of questions that are addressed to the text. Starting from the data, the process of coding leads to the development of theories through a process of abstraction. Concepts or codes are attached to the empirical material. They are formulated first as closely as possible to the text, and later more and more abstractly. Categorizing in this procedure refers to the summary of such concepts into *generic concepts* and to the elaboration of the relations between concepts and generic concepts or categories and superior concepts. The development of theory involves the formulation of *networks* of categories or concepts and the relations between them. Relations may be elaborated between superior and inferior categories (hierarchically) but also between concepts at the same level. During the whole process, impressions, associations, questions, ideas, and so on are noted in *code notes*, which complement and explain the codes that were found, or more generally, in memos.

Open Coding

Open coding aims at expressing data and phenomena in the form of concepts. For this purpose, data are first disentangled ("segmented"). Units of meaning classify expressions (single words, short sequences of words) in order to attach annotations and "concepts" (codes) to them. In Box 23.1, you will find an example in which a subjective definition of health and the first codes attached to this piece of text are presented. This example should clarify this procedure. A slash separates two sections in the interview passage from each other and

---

Box 23.1 Example of Segmentation and Open Coding

This example comes from one of my projects about health concepts of laypeople. It demonstrates how we applied the segmentation of a passage in one of the interviews in the context of open coding in order to develop codes:

Well-1[1]/link[2]/personally[3]/to health[4]/: the complete functionality[5]/ of the human organism[6]/ all[7]/ the biochemical processes[8] of the organism[9]/ included in this[10]/ all cycles[11]/ but also[12]/ the mental state[13]/ of my person[14]/ and of Man in general[15]/.

1 Starting shot, introduction.
2 Making connections.
3 Interviewee emphasizes the reference to himself, delimiting from others, local commonplace. He does not need to search first.
4 See 2, taking up the question.
5 Technical, learned, textbook expression, model of the machine, norm orientation, thinking in norms, normative claim (someone who does not fully function is ill).

Codes: functionality, normative claim

6 Distancing, general, contradiction to the introduction (announcement of a personal idea), textbook, reference to Man, but as a machine.

(Continued)

Box 23.1 (Continued)

Code: mechanistic image of Man

7   Complete, comprehensive, maximal, no differentiation, equilibrium.
8   Prison, closed system, there is something outside, passive, other directed, possibly an own dynamic of the included.
9   See 6.
10 Textbook category.
11 Comprehensive; model of the machine, circle of rules, procedure according to rules, opposite to chaos.

Code: mechanistic-somatic idea of health

12 Complement, new aspect opposite to what was said before, two (or more) different things belonging to the concept of health.

Code: multidimensionality

13 Mechanistic, negative taste, abuse, static ("what is his state?").
14 Mentions something personal, produces a distance again immediately, talks very neutrally about what concerns him, defence against too much proximity to the female interviewer and to himself.

Code: wavering between personal and general level

15 General, abstract image of Man, norm orientedness, singularity easier to overlook.

Code: distance

each superscript number indicates a section. The notes for each section are then presented: in some cases these led to the formulation of codes and in other cases they were abandoned in the further proceedings as being less suitable.

This procedure cannot be applied to the whole text of an interview or an observation protocol, but rather is used for particularly instructive or perhaps extremely unclear passages. Often the beginning of a text is the starting point. This procedure serves to elaborate a deeper understanding of the text. Charmaz suggests doing this kind of coding line-by-line, because it "also helps you to refrain from imputing your motives, fears, or unresolved personal issues to your respondents and to your collected data" (2003, p. 94). She also gives a concrete example of this procedure as in Box 23.2. You will find the codes Charmaz developed in the left column and the excerpt of the interview in the right column of the box. Cathy Charmaz is currently one of the leading researchers in the field of grounded theory.

Box 23.2   Example of Line-by-Line Coding

Shifting symptoms, having inconsistent days	If you have lupus, I mean one day it's my liver; one day it's my joints; one day it's my head, and
Interpreting images of self given by others	it's like people really think you're a hypochondriac if you keep complaining about
Avoiding disclosure	different ailments . . . It's like you don't want to say anything because people are going to start
Predicting rejection	thinking, you know, God, don't go near her, all
Keeping others unaware	she is – is complaining about this.' And I think
Seeing symptoms as connected	that's why I never say anything because I feel like everything I have is related one way or
Having others unaware	another to the lupus but most of the people don't
Anticipating disbelief	know I have lupus, and even those that do are not
Controlling others' views	going to believe that ten different ailments are the
Avoiding stigma	same thing. And I don't want anybody saying,
Assessing potential losses and risks of disclosing	you know, [that] they don't want to come around me because I complain.

Source: Charmaz 2003, p. 96

Sometimes dozens of codes result from open coding (Strauss and Corbin 1990/1998, p. 113). The next step in the procedure is to categorize these codes by grouping them around phenomena discovered in the data, which are particularly relevant to the research question. The resulting categories are again linked to codes, which are now more abstract than those used in the first step. Codes now should represent the content of a category in a striking way and above all should offer an aid to remembering the reference of the category. Possible sources for labeling codes are concepts borrowed from social science literature (*constructed* codes) or taken from interviewees' expressions (*in vivo* codes). Of the two types of code, the latter are preferred because they are closer to the studied material. The categories found in this way are then further developed. To this end the properties belonging to a category are labeled and dimensionalized (i.e., located along a continuum in order to define the category more precisely regarding its content: "To explain more precisely what we mean by properties and dimensions, we provided another example using the concept of color"). Its properties include shade, intensity, hue, and so on. Each of these properties can be dimensionalized. Thus, color can vary in shade from dark to light, in intensity from high to low, and in hue from bright to dull. Shade, intensity, and hue are what might be called general properties (1990/1998, pp. 117–118).

Open coding may be applied in various degrees of detail. A text can be coded line-by-line, sentence-by-sentence, or paragraph-by-paragraph, or a code can be linked to whole texts (a protocol, a case, etc.). Which of these alternatives you should apply depends on your research question, on your material, on your personal style as analyst, and on the stage that your research has reached. It is important not to lose touch with the aims of coding. The main goal is to break down and understand a text and to attach and develop categories and put them into an order in the course of time. Strauss and Corbin summarize open coding as follows:

> Concepts are the basic building blocks of theory. Open coding in grounded theory method is the analytic process by which concepts are identified and developed in terms of their properties and dimensions. The basic analytic procedures by which this is accomplished are: the asking of questions about the data; and the making of comparisons for similarities and differences between each incident, event and other instances of phenomena. Similar events and incidents are labelled and grouped to form categories. (1990, p. 74)

The result of open coding should be a list of the codes and categories that were attached to the text. This should be complemented by the code notes that were produced for explaining and defining the content of codes and categories, and a multitude of memos, which contain striking observations on the material and thoughts that are relevant to the development of the theory.

Not only for open coding but also for the other coding strategies, it is suggested that the researchers address the text regularly and repeatedly with the following list of so-called basic questions:

1. *What?*   What is the issue here? Which phenomenon is mentioned?
2. *Who?*   Which persons, actors are involved? Which roles do they play? How do they interact?
3. *How?*   Which aspects of the phenomenon are mentioned (or not mentioned)?
4. *When? How long? Where?*   Time, course, and location.
5. *How much? How strong?*   Aspects of intensity.
6. *Why?*   Which reasons are given or can be reconstructed?
7. *What for?*   With what intention, to which purpose?
8. *By which?*   Means, tactics, and strategies for reaching the goal.

By asking these questions, the text will be disclosed. You may address them to single passages, but also to whole cases. In addition to these questions, comparisons between the extremes of a dimension ("flip-flop technique") or with phenomena from completely different contexts and a consequent questioning of self-evidence ("waving-the-red-flag technique") are possible ways for further untangling the dimensions and contents of a category.

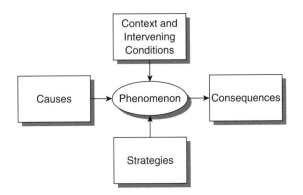

FIGURE 23.1 The Paradigm Model

Axial Coding

The next step is to refine and differentiate the categories resulting from open coding. From the multitude of categories that were originated, those are selected that seem to be most promising for a further elaboration. These axial categories are enriched by their fit with as many passages as possible. For further refining, the questions and comparisons mentioned above are employed. Finally, the relations between these and other categories are elaborated. Most importantly, relations between categories and their subcategories are clarified or established. In order to formulate such relations, Strauss and Corbin (1998, p. 127) suggest a coding paradigm model, which is symbolized in Figure 23.1.

This very simple and at the same time very general model serves to clarify the relations between a phenomenon, its causes and consequences, its context, and the strategies of those who are involved. The concepts included in each category can become a phenomenon for this category and/or the context or conditions for other categories, and for a third group of categories, they may become a consequence. It is important to note that the coding paradigm only names possible relations between phenomena and concepts and is used to facilitate the discovery or establishment of structures of relations between phenomena, between concepts, and between categories. Here as well, the questions addressed to the text and the comparative strategies mentioned above are employed once again in a complementary way. The developed relations and the categories that are treated as essential are verified over and over against the text and the data. The researcher moves continuously back and forth between inductive thinking (developing concepts, categories, and relations from the text) and deductive thinking (testing the concepts, categories, and relations against the text, especially against passages or cases that are different from those from which they were developed). Axial coding is summarized as follows:

> Axial coding is the process of relating subcategories to a category. It is a complex process of inductive and deductive thinking involving several steps. These are accomplished, as with open coding, by making comparisons and asking questions. However, in axial coding the use *of* these procedures is more focused, and geared toward discovering and relating categories in terms of the paradigm model. (Strauss and Corbin, 1990, p. 114)

In axial coding, the categories that are most relevant to the research question are selected from the developed codes and the related code notes. Many different passages in the text are then sought as evidence of these relevant codes in order to elaborate the axial category on the basis of the questions mentioned above. In order to structure the intermediate results, (means–end, cause–effect, temporal, or local) relations are elaborated between the different axial categories by using the parts of the coding paradigm mentioned above.

Coding Families

As an instrument for coding material, Glaser (1978) has suggested a list of basic codes, which he grouped as coding families. These families are sources for defining codes and at the same time and orientation for searching new codes for a set of data (see Table 23.1).

Selective Coding

The third step, selective coding, continues the axial coding at a higher level of abstraction. This step elaborates the development and integration of it in comparison to other groups.

When presented this way, you find an elaboration or formulation of the *story of the case*. At this point, Strauss and Corbin conceive the issue or the central phenomenon of the study as a case and not a person or a single interview. You should keep in mind here that the aim of this formulation is to give a short descriptive overview of the story and the case and should therefore comprise only a few sentences. The analysis goes beyond this descriptive level when the *story line* is elaborated–a concept is attached to the central phenomenon of the story and related to the other categories. In any case, the result should be *one* central category and *one* central phenomenon. The analyst must decide between equally salient phenomena and weigh them, so that one central category results together with the subcategories, which are related to it. The core category again is developed in its features and dimensions and linked to (all, if possible) other categories by using the parts and relations of the coding paradigm. The analysis and the development of the theory aim at discovering patterns in the data as well as the conditions under which these apply. Grouping the data according to the coding paradigm allocates specificity to the theory and enables the researcher to say, "Under these conditions (listing them) this happens; whereas under these conditions, this is what occurs" (1990, p. 131).

TABLE 23.1 Coding Families

Coding Families	Concepts	Examples
The Six Cs	Causes, contexts, contingencies, consequences, covariances, conditions	... of pain suffering
Process	Stages, phases, phasings, transitions, passages, careers, chains, sequences	Career of a patient with chronic pain
The Degree Family	Extent, level, intensity, range, amount, continuum, statistical average, standard deviation	Extent of pain suffering
Type Family	Types, classes, genres, prototypes, styles, kinds	Kinds of pain–sharp, piercing, throbbing, shooting, sting, gnawing, burning
The Strategy Family	Strategies, tactics, techniques, mechanisms, management	Coping with pain
Interactive Family	Interaction, mutual effects, interdependence, reciprocity, asymmetries, rituals	Interaction of pain experience and coping
Identity Self Family	Identity, self-image, self-concept, self-evaluation, social worth, transformations of self	Self-concepts of pain patients
Cutting Point Family	Boundary, critical juncture, cutting point, turning point, tolerance levels, point of no return	Start of chronification in the medical career of pain patient
Cultural Family	Social norms, social values, social beliefs	Social norms about tolerating pain, "feeling rules"
Consensus Family	Contracts, agreements, definitions of the situation, uniformity, conformity, conflict	Compliance

Source: Adapted from Glaser 1978, p. 75–82

Finally, the theory is formulated in greater detail and again checked against the data. The procedure of interpreting data, like the integration of additional material, ends at the point where *theoretical saturation* has been reached (i.e., further coding, enrichment of categories, and so on no longer provide or promise new knowledge). At the same time, the procedure is flexible enough that the researcher can re-enter the same source texts and the same codes from open coding with a different research question and aim at developing and formulating a grounded theory of a different issue.

Case Study: Awareness of Dying and Awareness Contexts

Glaser and Strauss developed and applied this method in the following study on the handling of death and dying in hospitals (Glaser and Strauss 1965a). Their research question was on what interacting with dying people depends upon and how the knowledge of a person's imminent death determines the interaction with him or her. More concretely, what they studied were the forms of interaction between the dying person and the clinical staff of the hospital, between the staff and the relatives, and between the relatives and the dying person. Which tactics are applied in the contact with dying people, and what part does the hospital as a social organization play here? The central concept at the end of the analysis was "awareness contexts." This concept expresses what each of the interactants knows about a certain state of the patient and what he or she assumes about the other interactants' awareness of his or her own knowledge. This awareness context may change owing to the patient's situation or to new information for one or all of the participants. Four types of awareness were found. *Closed awareness* means the patients do not suspect their approaching death. *Suspicion awareness* means they have a suspicion concerning this issue. *Awareness of mutual pretence* is the case when everybody knows, but nobody says it openly. *Open awareness* is given, when the patients know about their situation and speak frankly about it with all others. More generally, the analysis of awareness contexts included their description and the precondition of the social structure in each context (social relations, etc.). It also comprised resulting interactions, which included the tactics and countertactics of the participants in order to bring about changes in the awareness context and also the consequences of each form of interaction for those who are involved, for the hospital, and for further interactions. The analysis was elaborated to a theory of awareness contexts through comparisons with other situations of mutual pretence and differing awareness of those who are involved into which this typology fits. As examples, the authors mention buying and selling cars or "clowning at the circuses" (1965a, p. 277), and so on. By integrating such other fields and the grounded theories developed for them formulates a formal theory of awareness.

All in all, this is a very early research example, which allows following and understanding the steps of grounded theory development based on one central concept. The study is not only instructive from a methodological point of view but was very influential in the sociology of illness and dying and in areas such as nursing, for example.

Charmaz (2003) suggests an alternative view of the procedure in the development of grounded theory. After line-by-line coding at the beginning (see Box 23.2), she continues by exploring some of the resulting codes more deeply. In the example given in Box 23.2, these were the two codes "avoiding disclosure" and "assessing potential losses and risks of disclosing." Charmaz's second step is called focused coding.

Case Study: Unending Work and Care

Juliet Corbin and Anselm Strauss have further developed the approach of grounded theory and theoretical coding and applied it in many studies in the context of nursing and medical sociology in the 1980s and since. In one of their more recent studies, Corbin and Strauss (1988) applied their methodology to the study of how people experiencing a chronic illness and their relatives manage to deal with this serious illness and manage to conduct their personal lives. The empirical basis of this study is a number of intensive interviews with such couples at home and at work. These were undertaken to identify the problems these couples face in their personal lives in order to answer the question: How can the chronically ill be helped to manage their illnesses more effectively? (p. xi). Different from early conceptualizations of grounded theory research in which it was suggested not to develop a theoretical framework and understanding of the issue under study (e.g., in Glaser and Strauss 1967), the authors here start with an extensive presentation of the theoretical tools used in their study, which builds on previous empirical work by the same researchers. The main concept in the research is trajectory. This refers to the course of the illness as well as to the work of the people who attempt to control and shape this course. Corbin and Strauss identify several stages–trajectory phases–that are labeled as acute, comeback, stable, unstable, deteriorating, and dying stages of illness. In the theoretical framework, the authors analyze how a chronically ill member of a family changes the life plans of families and focus on biographical processes with which the victims try to manage and come to terms with the illness. In the second part of their book, the authors use this theoretical framework to analyze the various trajectory phases in greater detail.

This study is not only one of the most important studies in the field of everyday management of chronic illness. It is also very fruitful in developing and differentiating a theoretical framework for this issue, which goes beyond existing concepts of coping, adjustment, and stress. Rather, the authors develop from their empirical work a much more elaborate concept (trajectory) for analyzing the experience of their research partners. They achieve this by analyzing the different stages of trajectory by asking a set of questions. What are the different types of work? How do they get done? How do the central work processes and interactional developments enter into getting the work done? What are the biographical processes that accompany and affect those matters? (1988, p. 168). All in all, this study is a very good example of how the research strategy developed by Glaser, Strauss and Corbin in several steps can be used for analyzing a theoretically and practically relevant issue.

What is the Contribution to the General Methodological Discussion?

This method aims at a consequent breakdown of texts. The combination of open coding with increasingly focused procedures can contribute to the development of a deeper understanding of the content and meaning of the text beyond paraphrasing and summarizing it (which would be the central approaches in the qualitative content analysis which will be discussed later). The interpretation of texts here is methodologically realized and manageable. This approach allows room for maneuvering through the different techniques and flexibility in formulating rules. It differs from other methods of interpreting texts because it leaves the level of the pure texts during the interpretation in order to develop categories and relations, and thus theories. Finally, the method combines an inductive approach with an increasingly deductive handling of text and categories.

How does the Method Fit into the Research Process?

The procedure outlined here is the main part of the research process that aims at developing theories (see Chapter 8). In terms of theoretical background, symbolic interactionism has very strongly influenced this approach (see Chapter 6). The material is selected according to theoretical sampling (see Chapter 11). Research questions and the development state of the emerging theory orient the selection of data collection methods. Which methods should be used for collecting data is not determined beyond that. First, generalization aims at grounded theories, which should be related directly to the data and finally at formal theories that are valid beyond the original contexts. Integrating grounded theories developed in other contexts in the study allows the testing of formal theories.

What are the Limitations of the Method?

One problem with this approach is that the distinction between method and art becomes hazy, which makes it in some places difficult to teach as a method. Often, the extent of the advantages and strengths of the method only become clear in applying it. A further problem is the potential endlessness of options for coding and comparisons. You could apply open coding to all passages of a text, and you could further elaborate all the categories which you found, and which in most cases are very numerous. Passages and cases could be endlessly compared with each other. Theoretical sampling could endlessly integrate further cases. The method gives you few hints about what the selection of passages and cases should be oriented to and what criteria the end of coding (and sampling) should be based on. The criterion of theoretical saturation leaves it to the theory developed up to that moment, and thus to the researcher, to make such decisions of selection and ending. One consequence is that often a great many codes and potential comparisons result. One pragmatic solution for this potential infinity is to make a break, to balance what was found, and to build a list of priorities. Which codes should you definitely further elaborate, which codes seem to be less instructive, and which can you leave out with respect to your research question? The further procedure may be designed according to this list of priorities. Not only for further grounding such decisions, but also in general, it has proved helpful to analyze texts with this procedure in a group of interpreters. Then you can discuss the results among the members and to mutually check them.

Thematic Coding

I have developed this procedure on the background of Strauss (1987) for comparative studies in which the groups under study are derived from the research question and thus defined *a priori*. The research issue is the social distribution of perspectives on a phenomenon or a process. The underlying assumption is that in different social worlds or groups, differing views can be found. In order to assess this assumption and to develop a theory of such groups' specific ways of seeing and experiencing, it is necessary to modify some details of Strauss's procedure in order to increase the comparability of the empirical material. Sampling is oriented to the groups whose perspectives on the issue seem to be most instructive for analysis, and which therefore are defined in advance (see Chapter 11) and not derived from the state of interpretation, as in Strauss's procedure. Theoretical sampling is applied in each group in order to select the concrete cases to be studied. The collection of data is correspondingly conducted with a method, which seeks to guarantee comparability by defining topics, and at the same time, remaining open to the views related to them. For example, this may be achieved with the episodic interview in which topical domains are defined, concerning the situations to be recounted, which are linked to the issue of the study (see Chapter 14), or with other forms of interviews (see Chapter 13).

What is the Procedure of Thematic Coding?

In the interpretation of the material, thematic coding is applied as a multistage procedure—again, with respect to the comparability of the analyses. The first step addresses the cases involved, which are interpreted in a series of case studies. As a first orientation, you will produce a short description of each case, which you continuously recheck and modify if necessary during the further interpretation of the case. This case description includes several elements. The first is a statement, which is typical for the interview—the motto of the case. A short description should inform about the person with regard to the research question (e.g., age, profession, number of children, if these are relevant for the issue under study). Finally, the central topics mentioned by the interviewee concerning the research issue are summarized. After finishing the case analysis, this case profile forms part of the results, perhaps in a revised form. The example in Box 23.3 comes from my comparative study on everyday knowledge about technological change in different professional groups.

Box 23.3   Example of a Short Description of a Case

"For me, technology has a reassuring side"

The interviewee is a female French information technology engineer, 43 years old and with a son of 15. She has been working for about 20 years in various research institutes. At present, she works in a big institute of social science research in the computer center and is responsible for developing software, teaching, and consulting employees. Technology has to do a lot with security and clarity for her. To mistrust technology would produce problems for her professional self-awareness. To master technology is important for her self-awareness. She narrates a lot using juxtapositions of leisure, nature, feeling, and family to technology and work and repeatedly mentions the cultural benefit from technologies, especially from television.

Different from Strauss's (1987) procedure, you will carry out a deepening analysis of the single case first, which pursues several aims. It preserves the meaningful relations that the respective person deals with in the topic of the study, which is why a case study is done for all cases. It develops a system of categories for the analysis for the single case. In the further elaboration of this system of categories (similar to Strauss), first apply open coding and then selective coding. Here, selective coding aims less at developing a grounded core category across all cases than at generating thematic domains and categories for the single case first. After the first case analyzes, you will cross-check the developed categories and thematic domains linked to the single cases. A thematic structure results from this cross-check, which underlies the analysis of further cases in order to increase their comparability. The excerpts, which you find in Box 23.4 as an example (of such a thematic structure), come from the study on technological change in everyday life previously mentioned.

The structure in Box 23.4 was developed from the first cases and continuously assessed for all further cases. It is modified if new or contradictory aspects emerge. It is used to analyze all cases that are part of the interpretation. For a fine interpretation of the thematic domains, single passages of the text (e.g., narratives of situations) are analyzed in greater detail. The coding paradigm suggested by Strauss (1987, pp. 27–28) is taken as a starting point for deriving the following key questions for:

1. *Conditions*: Why? What has led to the situation? Background? Course?
2. *Interaction among the actors*: Who acted? What happened?
3. *Strategies and tactics*: Which ways of handling situations, e.g., avoidance, adaptation?
4. *Consequences*: What did change? Consequences, results?

Box 23.4 Example of the Thematic Structure of Case Analyzes in Thematic Coding

1 *First encounter with technology*
2 *Definition of technology*
3 *Computer*

   3.1 Definition
   3.2 First encounter(s) with computers
   3.3 Professional handling of computers
   3.4 Changes in communication due to computers

4 *Television*

   4.1 Definition
   4.2 First encounter(s) with television
   4.3 Present meaning

. . .

5 *Alterations due to technological change*
   5.1 Everyday life
   5.2 Household equipment

The result of this process is a case oriented display of the way it specifically deals with the issue of the study, including constant topics (e.g., strangeness of technology) that can be found in the viewpoints across different domains (e.g., work, leisure, household).

The developed thematic structure also serves for comparing cases and groups (i.e., for elaborating correspondences and differences between the various groups in the study). Thus, you analyze and assess the social distribution of perspectives on the issue under study. For example, after the case analyses have shown that the subjective definition of technology is an essential thematic domain for understanding technological change, it is then possible to compare the definitions of technology and the related coding from all cases.

Case Study: Subjective Definitions of Technology and Their Coding

Two examples of subjective definitions of technology will briefly demonstrate the results of this procedure in one thematic domain. A female information technology engineer from West Germany gave the following answer to a question regarding her definition of technology:

(Continued)

(Continued)

> Technology is for me a machine, somewhere, existing in everyday life, devices for helping people in order to somehow design life either more pleasantly or less pleasantly. What do I link to it? Yes, sometimes something positive, sometimes something negative, depending on what I have experienced with the machine, in contrast perhaps to nature, so nature and technology are in opposition.

Here, on the one hand, it becomes clear that technology equals machines and that an omnipresence of technology is seen. On the other hand, a functional understanding of technology, also a functional evaluation of technology, and finally an explicit juxtaposition of technology and nature are expressed. This definition is coded as "technology as device."

A female teacher from France answered the same question as follows:

> For me, technology is something that does not really exist in my life, because if one speaks of technology, I understand it as something scientific. Well, if I further reflect, then I say to myself, maybe it is the use of machines whose functioning needs or would need several steps.

This is coded as "technology as unfamiliar science." This aspect of unfamiliarity could be identified for the other French teachers in this study in general.

These examples show how codes are allocated to excerpts from interviews.

Coding of technology definitions include two forms of statements: definitions in a descriptive sense (e.g., "technology as . . .") and the specification of the dimensions used for classifying different technologies and machines (e.g., "professional technology versus everyday technology"). After coding the subjective definition of technology, the distribution in Table 23.2 results.

Similar codes in the individual groups are summarized and the specific topics of each (professional) group are elaborated. After the constant comparison of the cases on the basis of the developed structure, the topical range in the way the interviewees' deal with each theme can be outlined.

What is the Contribution to the General Methodological Discussion?

This procedure specifies Strauss's approach (1987) to studies, which aim at developing a theory starting from the distribution of perspectives on a certain issue or process. Group specific correspondences and differences are identified and analyzed. In contrast to Strauss's procedure, conduct case analyses in the first step. Only in the second step will you undertake group comparisons beyond the single case. By developing a thematic structure, which is grounded in the empirical material for the analysis and comparison of cases, will comparability of interpretations

TABLE 23.2 Thematic Coding of Subjective Definitions of Technology

	Information Engineers	Social Scientists	Teachers
West Germany	Technology as device Professional technology versus everyday technology	Technology as necessary means to an end Dimension "size" for typification	Technology as facility Technology as strange cold world
East Germany	Technology as device and its vulnerability Dimension "functional principle" for typification	Technology as unfamiliar device Dimension "complexity" for typification	Descriptive definitions of technology Dimension "everyday life versus profession" for typification
France	Technology as the opposite and application of science	Technology as application of science Dimension "everyday life" versus professional for typification	Technology as unfamiliar science Technology as means to an end Dimension "everyday life versus profession" for typification
Specific themes of the professions	Technology as professional device Opposition of technology and science "Functional principle" for typification	Application Technology as means to an end Typification: complexity and size	Unfamiliarity with technology "Everyday life versus profession" for typification

increase. At the same time, the procedure remains sensitive and open to the specific contents of each individual case and the social group with regard to the issue under study.

How does the Method Fit into the Research Process?

The theoretical background is the diversity of social worlds as assumed in the concept of social representations (see Chapter 6) or more generally by constructivist approaches (see Chapter 7). Research questions focus on the analysis of the variety and distribution of perspectives on issues and processes in social groups (see Chapter 9). Cases are involved for specific groups (see Chapter 11). In addition, elements of theoretical sampling are used for the selection in the groups. Data are collected with methods that combine structuring inputs and openness with regard to contents (e.g., episodic interviews: see Chapter 13). Generalization is based on comparisons of cases and groups and aims at the development of theories (see Chapter 29).

What are the Limitations of the Method?

The procedure is above all suitable for studies in which theoretically based group comparisons are to be conducted in relation to a specific issue. Therefore, the scope for a theory to be developed is more restricted than in Strauss's (1987) procedure. The analysis of texts consists of coding statements and narratives in categories, which are developed from the material. It is oriented to elaborating correspondences and differences between the groups defined in advance. These correspondences and differences are demonstrated on the basis of the distribution of codes and categories across the groups that are studied. The analysis plunges deep into text and case studies in the first step. If the intermediate step is to be conducted consequently, the procedure may become somewhat time consuming.

Qualitative Content Analysis

Content analysis is one of the classical procedures for analyzing textual material no matter where this material comes from—ranging from media products to interview data (Bauer 2000). One of its essential features is the use of categories, which are often derived from theoretical models: categories are brought to the empirical material and not necessarily developed from it, although they are repeatedly assessed against it and modified if necessary. Above all, and contrary to other approaches, the goal here is to reduce the material. Mayring (2000, 2004) has developed a procedure for a qualitative content analysis, which includes a procedural model of text analysis and different techniques for applying it.

What is the Procedure of Qualitative Content Analysis?

For Mayring, the first step is to define the material, to select the interviews or those parts that are relevant for answering the research question. The second step is to analyze the situation of data collection (how was the material generated, who was involved, who was present in the interview situation, where do the documents to be analyzed come from, and so on.). In the third step, the material is formally characterized (was the material documented with a recording or a protocol, was there an influence on the transcription of the text when it was edited, and so on). In the fourth step Mayring defines the direction of the analysis for the selected texts and "what one actually wants to interpret out of them" (1983, p. 45). The research question is further differentiated on the basis of theories in the next step. For Mayring it is important in this context that the "research question of the analysis must be clearly defined in advance, must be linked theoretically to earlier research on the issue and generally has to be differentiated in sub-questions" (1983, p. 47).

Mayring suggests defining concretely the analytic technique as one of three techniques (see below). Finally, analytic units are defined. Here, Mayring differentiates the units as the following: the "coding unit" defines what is "the smallest element of material which may be analyzed, the minimal part of the text which may fall under a category"; the "contextual unit" defines what is the largest element in the text, which may fall under a category; the "analytic unit" defines which passages "are analyzed one after the other." In the last but one step, the actual analyses are conducted before their final results are interpreted with respect to the research question and questions of validity are asked and answered.

Techniques of Qualitative Content Analysis

The concrete methodical procedure basically includes three techniques. In *summarizing content analysis*, the material is paraphrased, which means that less relevant passages and paraphrases with the same meanings are skipped (first reduction) and similar paraphrases are bundled and summarized (second reduction). This is a combination of reducing the material by skipping statements included in a generalization in the sense of summarizing the material on a higher level of abstraction. Here is an example of summarizing content analysis:

EXAMPLE: SUMMARIZING CONTENT ANALYSIS

Psychologist Philipp Mayring developed this method in a study about psychological coping with unemployment for which a great number of interviews with unemployed teachers were conducted. In an interview with an unemployed teacher, the statement "and actually, quite the reverse, I was well very–very keen on finally teaching for the first time" (Mayring 1983) results. This is paraphrased as "quite the reverse, very keen on practice" and generalized as "rather looking forward to practice." The statement "therefore, I have already waited for it, to go to a seminar school, until I finally could teach there for the first time" is paraphrased as "waited to teach finally" and generalized as "looking forward to practice." Owing to the similarity of the two generalizations, the second one then is skipped and reduced with other statements to "practice not experienced as shock but as big fun" (1983, p. 59).

Thus, you can reduce the source text by skipping those statements that overlap at the level of the generalization. The *explicative content analysis* works in the opposite way. It clarifies diffuse, ambiguous, or contradictory passages by involving context material in the analysis. Definitions taken from dictionaries or based on the grammar are used or formulated. "Narrow context analysis" picks up additional statements from the text in order to explicate the passages to be analyzed, whereas "wide context analysis" seeks information outside the text (about the author, the generative situations, from theories). On this basis an "explicating paraphrase" is formulated and tested. Here is an example of explicative content analysis:

EXAMPLE: EXPLICATIVE CONTENT ANALYSIS

In an interview, a teacher expresses her difficulties in teaching by stating that she–unlike successful colleagues– was no "entertainer type" (1983, p. 109). In order to find out what she wishes to express by using this concept, first definitions of "entertainer" are assembled from two dictionaries. Then the features of a teacher who fits this description are sought from statements made by the teacher in the interview. Further passages are consulted. Based on the descriptions of such colleagues included in these passages an "explicating paraphrase can be formulated: an entertainer type is somebody who plays the part of an extroverted, spirited, sparkling, and self-assured human being" (1983, p. 74). This explication is assessed again by applying it to the direct context in which the concept was used.

The *structuring content analysis* looks for types or formal structures in the material. Structuring is done on the formal, typifying, scaling level or as regards content:

> According to formal aspects, an internal structure can be filtered out (formal structuring); material can be extracted and condensed to certain domains of content (structuring as regards content). One can look for single salient features in the material and describe them more exactly (typifying structuring); finally, the material may be rated according to dimensions in the form of scales (scaling structuring). (Mayring 1983, pp. 53–54)

Here is an example of structuring content analysis:

EXAMPLE: STRUCTURING CONTENT ANALYSIS

One of the main questions in the project was: "Did the 'shock of the practice' influence the individual's self-confidence?" (1983, p. 88). Therefore, the concept "self-confidence" (SC) was the subject of a simple scaling, which produced four categories: "C1, high SC; C2, medium SC; C3, low SC; C4, not inferable" (1983, p. 90). For each degree, a definition is formulated (e.g., for C2: "I maneuvered through this somehow, but often it was a tightrope walk": 1983, p. 91). The next step is to formulate rules of coding. These are used to search the text for passages where statements about self-confidence can be found. These classifications finally pass a rating, which for example may aim at an analysis of frequencies of the different degrees in a category. But the fact is for this form of content analysis: "for editing the results, no general rule can be defined. It depends on the respective research question" (1983, p. 87).

What is the Contribution to the General Methodological Discussion?

Owing to the schematic elaboration of the proceedings, this procedure seems clearer, less ambiguous, and easier to handle than other methods of data analysis. This is also due to the possible reduction of the material outlined above. The many rules that are formulated underline this impression of greater clarity and unambiguity. The approach mainly suits a reductive analysis of large masses of text, which is oriented to the surface of these texts. The formalization of the procedure produces a uniform schema of categories, which facilitates the comparison of the different cases to which it is applied throughout. This is an advantage over more inductive and/or case oriented analytic procedures.

How does the method fit into the research process?

The method is not limited to a certain theoretical background. It is mainly used to analyze subjective viewpoints (see Chapters 6 and 9), collected with interviews (see Chapter 13). The selection of materials mainly follows criteria that are defined in advance, but may also proceed step-by-step (see Chapter 11).

What are the Limitations of the Method?

Often, however, the application of the rules given by Mayring proves at least as costly as in other procedures. Particularly owing to the schematization of the proceedings and to the way the single steps are tidied up, the approach is strongly marked by the ideal of a quantitative methodology. Categorization of text based on theories may obscure the view of the contents rather than facilitate analyzing the text in its depth and underlying meanings. Interpretation of the text as in other methods is done rather schematically with this method, especially when the technique of explicative content analysis is used, but without really reaching the depths of the text. Another problem is the use of paraphrases, which are used not only to explain the basic text but also to replace it–mainly in summarizing content analysis.

Global Analysis

A pragmatically oriented supplement to other analytic procedures (mainly theoretical coding or qualitative content analysis) is the global analysis suggested by Legewie (1994). Here the aim is to obtain an overview of the thematic range of the text, which is to be analyzed.

What are the Steps of Global Analysis?

As a preparatory step, a clarification of one's own background knowledge and of the research question, which is carried to the text, is suggested. When reading through the text, keywords are noted alongside the transcript and a structuring of the large passages of the text is produced. The next step refines this structure by marking central concepts or statements, and information about the communicative situation in the generation of each text is identified. Ideas are noted while reading the text. This is followed by the production of the text's table of contents, which includes the structuring keywords noted before with the numbers of the lines to which they refer. Themes (again with the line numbers) are ordered alphabetically and finally the ideas noted in the different steps are collected in a list. The final step of the global analysis is to summarize the text and to evaluate whether to include it in the actual interpretation or not. The basis for this decision is the viewpoints of the participants. You will look for indicators that the reported facts are true, complete and that the way of reporting them is appropriate to the communicative situation of the interview. Finally, you will look for indicators for things left out, biased, or distorted in the interview. The final step is that you note keywords for the entire text and formulate the consequences for working with the material or for selecting or integrating further texts, cases, and information according to theoretical sampling.

What is the Contribution to the General Methodological Discussion?

This form of editing texts before their actual interpretation may be helpful for your initial orientation to the text and for deciding whether it is worth choosing a certain interview over another one for a detailed interpretation, if the resources (e.g., of time) are limited. Combined with similar pragmatically oriented analytic procedures of qualitative content analysis, it may give you an overview of the material. In theoretical coding, this method may facilitate the finding and assignment of further passages, especially for later steps of axial and selective coding.

What are the Limitations of the Method?

This method can supplement categorizing methods but cannot replace them. Procedures like objective hermeneutics or conversation analysis, which aim at a sequential disclosure of the text (see Chapters 24 and 25) will not be compatible with this form of editing the material.

The methods discussed in this chapter have a unifying feature: analyzing textual material by its coding. Categories are mostly developed from the text but are also received from the literature. The internal (formal or meaning) structure of the analyzed text is not the (main) point of reference for the interpretation. Sooner or later, all these approaches turn to finding evidence for certain categories in the text and to assigning these to the categories. The treatment of the individual case becomes important in different ways. In thematic coding, first a case analysis is produced before the material is analyzed across cases. The other procedures take the textual material altogether as a point of reference and develop or apply a system of categories, which transcends the single case.

KEY POINTS

- Coding can start from the text in order to develop a set of categories (theoretic or thematic coding) or it can take a set of categories as a starting point (content analysis).
- Often you will find a combination of the two strategies. In theoretical coding, categories coming from the literature or from the first texts are used to code later texts, too.
- Global analysis can be a preparatory step for such coding procedures, but does not stand alone.
- Most important is the researcher's sensitiveness in coding the material for what is happening in it.
- Coding is often a combination of a very fine analysis of some parts of the text and a rough classification and summary of other parts.

Exercise 23.1

1. Look for part of an interview (maybe take the one from Exercise 22.1) and apply open coding to it. You could start from the beginning of the interview or select a part which looks very interesting to you and develop a label for this part (name a code).
2. Apply the questions suggested by Strauss and Corbin (mentioned in this chapter) to that piece of text.
3. Finally, you should apply the segmentation technique (see Box.23.1) to your piece of text.

Exercise 23.2

1. Take the same piece of text (or a different one) and apply thematic coding to it. Formulate a motto for the text. Write a short description of what is going on in the text.
2. Apply the coding paradigm mentioned above to the text.

Exercise 23.3

1. Take a piece of text and apply qualitative content analysis to it. First, try to identify similar statements and paraphrase them in order to skip identical paraphrases (summarizing content analysis).
2. Then look for unclear words or statements in the text and apply the explicative content analysis to them.

FURTHER READING

Theoretical Coding
The second text is not only a good example of the results this strategy is able to produce but also the study for which it was developed. The other texts discuss the method in its various degrees of elaboration.

Böhm, A. (2004) "Theoretical Coding," in U. Flick, E.v. Kardorff and I. Steinke (eds), *A Companion to Qualitative Research.* London: SAGE. pp. 270–275.
Glaser, B.G. and Strauss, A.L. (1965a) *Awareness of Dying.* Chicago: Aldine.
Glaser, B.G. and Strauss, A.L. (1967) *The Discovery of Grounded Theory: Strategies for Qualitative Research.* New York: Aldine.
Strauss, A.L. (1987) *Qualitative Analysis for Social Scientists.* Cambridge: Cambridge University Press.
Strauss, A.L. and Corbin, J. (1998) *Basics of Qualitative Research* (2nd edn). London: SAGE.

Thematic Coding
In these texts, some applications and the methodological background of thematic coding can be found.

Flick, U. (1994) "Social Representations and the Social Construction of Everyday Knowledge: Theoretical and Methodological Queries," *Social Science Information*, 2: 179–197.
Flick, U. (1995) "Social Representations," in R. Harré, J. Smith and L.v. Langenhove (eds), *Rethinking Psychology.* London: SAGE. pp. 70–96.
Flick, U., Fischer, C., Neuber, A., Walter, U. and Schwartz F.W. (2003). "Health in the Context of Being Old–Representations Held by Health Professionals," *Journal of Health Psychology*, 8: 539–556.

Qualitative Content Analysis
Both texts outline the method in greater detail.

Mayring, Ph. (2000) "Qualitative Content Analysis," *Forum: Qualitative Social Research,* 1 (2). qualitative-research.net/fqs
Mayring, P. (2004) "Qualitative Content Analysis," in U. Flick, E.v. Kardorff and I. Steinke (eds), *A Companion to Qualitative Research.* London: SAGE. pp. 266–269.

24

ANALYZING CONVERSATION, DISCOURSE, AND GENRES

CHAPTER OBJECTIVES
After reading this chapter, you should be able to

✓ understand the principles of conversation analysis.
✓ identify the more recent developments coming from this approach.
✓ see the different versions of discourse analysis.
✓ complete a discourse analysis.
✓ understand genre analysis.

If you want to understand and analyze statements, it is necessary to take into account the context in which they occur. Context here refers to both the discursive context and the local context in the interaction. This notion is more or less unarguable in qualitative research. For this reason in qualitative interviews open-ended questions are asked, which encourage the respondents to say more rather than less and in doing so produce enough textual material for the researcher to analyze in terms of contextual considerations. In analyzing data, coding is open for this reason, at least in the beginning. The interpretative procedures discussed in the preceding chapter increasingly strip away the gestalt of the text in the course of the rearrangement of statements into categories as a preliminary to analysis and the development of theories. As an alternative to this approach, you find approaches that pay more attention to the gestalt of the text. Therefore, these approaches "let themselves be guided by the principle of sequential analysis . . . The sequential analysis puts the idea of social order, which reproduces itself in the performance of the interaction, into methodological terms" (Bergmann 1985, p. 313). Such approaches are either guided by the assumption that order is produced turn-by-turn (conversation analysis). Or that meaning accumulates in the performance of activity (objective hermeneutics) and that contents of interviews are only presented in a reliable way if they are presented in the gestalt of a narrative (narrative analyses–see the following Chapter 25 for more details). In each case, a specific form of context sensitivity is the methodological principle.

Conversation Analysis

Conversation analysis is less interested in interpreting the content of texts, which have been explicitly produced for research purposes, for instance interview responses. Rather it is interested in the formal analysis of everyday situations. Bergmann outlines this approach, which may be considered to be the mainstream of ethnomethodological research, as follows:

> Conversation Analysis (or CA) denotes a research approach dedicated to the investigation, along strictly empirical lines, of social interaction as a continuing process of producing and securing meaningful social order. CA proceeds on the basis that in all forms of linguistic and non-linguistic, direct and indirect communication, actors are occupied with the business of analyzing the situation and the context of their actions, interpreting their utterances of their interlocutors, producing situational appropriateness, intelligibility and effectiveness in their own utterances and co-coordinating their own dealings with the dealings of others. The goal of this approach is to determine the constitutive principles and mechanisms by means of which actors, in the situational completion of their actions and in reciprocal reaction to their interlocutors, create the meaningful structures and order of a sequence of events and of the activities that constitute these events. In terms of method CA begins with the richest possible documentation – with audio-visual recording and subsequent transcription – of real and authentic social events, and breaks these down, by a comparative-systematic process of analysis, into individual structural principles of social interaction as well as the practices used to manage them by participants in an interaction (2004b, p. 296).

In this way, emphasis is placed less on the analysis of the contents of a conversation and more on the formal procedures, through which they are communicated and certain situations are produced. One starting point was the work of Sacks et al. (1974) on the organization of turn taking in conversations. Another point of departure was the work of Schegloff and Sacks (1974) in explaining closings in conversations. First, conversation analysis assumes that interaction proceeds in an orderly way and nothing in it should be regarded as random. Second, the context of interaction not only influences this interaction but also is produced and reproduced in it. And third, the decision about what is relevant in social interaction and thus for the interpretation can only be made through the interpretation and not by *ex ante* settings.

Drew (1995, pp. 70–72) has outlined a series of methodological precepts for conversation analysis (CA) shown in Box 24.1.

Box 24.1   Methodological Precepts for Conversation Analytic Studies

1   Turns at talk are treated as the product of the sequential organization of talk, of the requirement to fit a current turn, appropriately and coherently, to its prior turn.

2   In referring . . . to the observable relevance of error on the part of one of the participants . . . we mean to focus analysis on participants' analyses of one another's verbal conduct.

3   By the "design" of a turn at talk, we mean to address two distinct phenomena: (1) the selection of an activity that a turn is designed to perform; and (2) the details of the verbal construction through which the turn's activity is accomplished.

4   A principal objective of CA research is to identify those sequential organizations or patterns . . . which structure verbal conduct in interaction.

5   The recurrences and systematic basis of sequential patterns or organizations can only be demonstrated . . . through collections of cases of the phenomena under investigation.

6   Data extracts are presented in such a way as to enable the reader to assess or challenge the analysis offered.

Source: Drew 1995, pp. 70–72

Research in conversation analysis was at first limited to everyday conversation in a strict sense (i.e., telephone calls, gossip, or family conversations in which there is no specific distribution of roles). However, it is now becoming increasingly occupied with specific role distributions and asymmetries like counseling conversation, doctor–patient interactions, and trials (i.e., conversations occurring in specific institutional contexts). The approach has also been extended to include analysis of written texts, mass media, or reports i.e., text in a broader sense (Bergmann 2004a).

The Procedure of Conversation Analysis

Ten Have (1999, p. 48) suggests the following steps for research projects using conversation analysis as a method:

1.   getting or making recordings of natural interaction;
2.   transcribing the tapes, in whole or in part;
3.   analyzing selected episodes and;
4.   reporting the research.

The procedure of conversation analysis of the material itself includes the following steps. First, you identify a certain statement or series of statements in transcripts as a potential element of order in the respective type of conversation. The second step is that you assemble a collection of cases in which this element of order can be found. You will then specify how this element is used as a means for producing order in interactions and for which problem in the organization of interactions it is the answer. This is followed by an analysis of the methods with which those organizational problems are dealt with more generally. Thus, a frequent starting point for conversation analyses is to enquire into how certain conversations are opened and which linguistic practices are applied for ending these conversations in an ordered way.

Case Study: Sociopsychiatric Counselling

In my study in the field of community psychiatry, I could show for counselling conversations, how entrance into conversation is organized via "authorised starters" (Wolff 1986, p. 71), regardless of the various conditions under which the individual conversation came about. Their "task is to mark that point for all who are involved in a comprehensible way, at which organizational principles of everyday conversation (for example to be able to talk about any possible topic) only apply in a limited way which is characteristic for that specific type of activity." In the conversations analyzed, such starters may be designed rather than open-ended (e.g., "What made you come to us?" or "And, what is it about?" or "What is your desire?"). In other cases, they name the (given) topic for the counseling, or specific characteristics in the way the counseling conversation came into being. These openings, which begin the actual counseling relationship and delimit it against other forms of talk, are sometimes linked to explanations about the way the conversation came about. These explanations are specific for the situation (e.g., "So, your brother gave me a call"). I showed two achievable tasks in analyzing the ending of the first contacts in the counseling processes. A timely ending of the conversation has to be ensured. At the same time, the counselor has to guarantee the continuation of the relation (e.g., "We have . . . two communities in T-street, which have just been opened. Well, Mr S, we have to wind the whole thing up for today, we must finish it"). In the last example, the ending of the consultation is introduced with a reference to other caring services. This produces continuity in the contact with the client as well doing the work, which finishes the conversation "for today".

This analysis could show which formal steps counseling conversations ran through more or less regularly. It could also show how these steps not only built up the conversation in itself, but also were influential steps in processing the clients and their cases—regardless of the specific contents of their problems. So, the analysis was more formal than content oriented, but shows the construction of cases in the conversations.

An essential feature of conversation analytic interpretation is the strictly sequential procedure (i.e., ensuring that no later statements or interactions are consulted for explaining a certain sequence). Rather, the order of the occurrence must show itself in understanding it sequentially. The turn-by-turn production of order in the conversation is clarified by an analysis, which is oriented to this sequence of turns. Another feature is the emphasis on context. This means that the efforts in producing meaning or order in the conversation can only be analyzed as local practices i.e., only related to the concrete contexts in which they are embedded in the interaction and in which the interaction again is embedded (for example institutionally). Analyses always start from the concrete case, its embedding and its course to arrive at general statements.

Ten Have (1999, p. 104) suggests in conjunction with Schegloff's work three steps for analysis of repair in conversation, for example. Adjacency pairs mean that a specific contribution to a conversation often has to be followed by another specific reaction–a question by an answer, opening a telephone conversation by "hello" has to be followed by a greeting from the other participant, and so on. Repair means the way people start a "repair organization" in cases of comprehension problems in a conversation. According to Ten Have, you should proceed in the following steps:

1. Check the episode carefully in terms of *turn taking*: the construction of turns, pauses, overlaps, etc.; make notes of any remarkable phenomenon, especially on any "disturbances" in the fluent working of the turn-taking system.
2. Then look for *sequences* in the episode under review, especially adjacency pairs and their sequels.
3. And finally, note any phenomena of *repair*, such as repair initiators, actual repairs, etc.

What is the Contribution to the General Methodological Discussion?

Conversation analysis and the empirical results that have been obtained by applying it explain the social production of everyday conversations and specific forms of discourse. The results document the linguistic methods that are used in these discourses. Furthermore, they show the explanatory strength of the analysis of natural situations and how a strictly sequential analysis can provide findings, which accord with and take into account the compositional logic of social interaction.

How does the Method Fit into the Research Process?

The theoretical background of conversation analysis is ethnomethodology (see Chapter 6). Research questions focus on members' formal procedures for constructing social reality (see Chapter 9). Empirical material is selected as a collection of examples of a process to be studied (see Chapter 11). Research avoids using explicit methods for collecting data in favor of recording everyday interaction processes as precisely as possible (see Chapter 22).

What are the Limitations of the Method?

Formal practices of organizing interaction remain the point of reference for analyses here. Subjective meaning or the participants' intentions are not relevant to the analysis. This lack of interest in the contents of conversations in favor of analyzing how the "conversation machine" functions, which is at the forefront of many conversation analytic studies, has been repeatedly criticized (e.g., by Coulter 1983; Harré 1998). Another point of critique is that conversation analytic studies often get lost in the formal detail, i.e., they isolate smaller and smaller particles and sequences from the context of the interaction as a whole (for this see Heritage 1985, p. 8). This is enforced by the extreme exactness in producing transcripts.

Discourse Analysis

Discourse analysis has been developed from different backgrounds, one of which was conversation analysis. There are different versions of discourse analysis available now. Discursive psychology as developed by Edwards and Potter (1992), Harré (1998), and Potter and Wetherell (1998) is interested in showing how, in conversations, "participants' conversational versions of events (memories, descriptions, formulations) are constructed to do communicative interactive work" (Edwards and Potter 1992, p. 16). Although conversation analysis is named as a starting point, the empirical focus is more on the "content of talk, its subject matter and with its social rather than linguistic organisation" (1992, p. 28). This allows the analysis of psychological phenomena like memory and cognition as social, and above all, discursive phenomena. A special emphasis is on the construction of versions of the events in reports and presentations. The "interpretative repertoires", which are used in such constructions, are analyzed. Discourse analytic procedures refer not only to everyday conversations, but also to other sorts of data such as interviews (e.g., in Potter and Wetherell 1998 on the topic of racism) or media reports (in Potter and Wetherell 1998 about the construction of versions in the coverage of the Gulf War).

Willig's (2003) research process in discursive psychology first describes the steps of using naturally occurring text and talk. Then, carefully read the transcripts. This is followed by coding the material, then analyzing it. According to Potter and Wetherell (1987, p. 167), guiding questions are: Why am I reading this passage in this way? What features of the text produce this reading? The analysis focuses on context, variability, and constructions in the text and finally to the interpretative repertoires used in the texts. The last step, according to Willig, is writing up a discourse analytic research. Writing should be part of the analysis and return the researcher back to the empirical material.

Case Study: Racism in New Zealand

Jonathan Potter and Margret Wetherell are leading protagonists of discourse analysis in the context of social psychology in the United Kingdom. In one of their studies, they analyze the social construction of racism in New Zealand using the example of the white majority's treatment of the Maori culture, an indigenous minority. Interviews were conducted with over 80 representatives of the white majority population (professionals from middle-income classes like doctors, farmers, managers, teachers, and so on). Reports on parliamentary debates and informational material from the mass media were included as well. The results of the study pointed to the existence of different interpretative repertoires such as "Culture as Heritage." In this repertoire the core idea is of Maori culture as a set of traditions, rituals, and values passed down from earlier generations. Culture becomes defined in this repertoire as an archaic heritage, something to be preserved and treasured, something to be protected from the rigors of the "modern world," like great works of art or endangered species. Here is a typical example. "I'm quite, I'm certainly in favour of a bit of Maoritanga it is something uniquely New Zealand, and I guess I'm very conservation minded (yes) and in the same way as I don't like seeing a species go out of existence I don't like seeing (yes) a culture and a language (yes) and everything else fade out" (1998, p. 148). This is opposed, for example, to the repertoire of "Culture as Therapy," in which "culture is constructed as a psychological need for Maoris, particularly young Maoris who have become estranged and need to rediscover their cultural 'roots' to become 'whole' again" (p. 148).

This study shows that discourse analysts often use interview material (in difference to conversation analysts, for example) and it also can exemplify the concept of interpretative repertoires.

Note a differentiation in discourse analysis in the last few years. Parker (e.g., 2004) has developed a model of critical discourse analysis, developed on the background of Michel Foucault (e.g., 1980) which why this is also referred to as "Foucauldian Discourse Analysis" (e. g. in Willig 2003). Here issues of critique, of ideology, and of power are more in focus than in other versions of discourse analysis. Parker suggests a number of steps in the research process. The researcher should (1) turn the text to be analyzed into written form, if it is not already (2) The next step includes free association to varieties of meaning as a way of accessing cultural networks, and these should be noted down. (3) The researchers should systematically itemize the objects, usually marked by nouns, in the text or selected portion of text. (4) They should maintain a distance from the text by treating the text itself as the object of the study rather than what it seems to "refer" to. (5) Then they should systematically itemize the "subjects"–characters, persona, role positions–specified in the text, (6) reconstruct presupposed rights and responsibilities of "subjects" specified in the text, and finally (7) map the networks of relationships into patterns. These patterns in language are "discourses," and can then be located in relations of ideology, power, and institutions (see Parker 2004, p. 310).

What is the Contribution to the General Methodological Discussion?

Discourse analytic studies analyze issues, which are closer to the topics of social sciences than those of conversation analysis (see Silverman 1993 on this). They combine language analytic proceedings with analyses of processes of knowledge and constructions without restricting themselves to the formal aspects of linguistic presentations and processes.

How does the Method Fit into the Research Process?

The theoretical background of discourse analysis is social constructionism (see Chapters 6 and 7). Research questions focus on how the making of social reality can be studied in discourses about certain objects or processes (see Chapter 9). Empirical material ranges from media articles to interviews (see Chapter 11). Interpretations are based on transcripts of those interviews or the texts to be found (see Chapter 22).

What are the Limitations of the Method?

Methodological suggestions for how to carry out discourse analyses remain rather imprecise and implicit in most of the literature. Theoretical claims and empirical results are dominant in the works published up to now.

Genre Analysis

A second development coming from conversation analysis is called genre analysis (see Knoblauch and Luckmann 2004). Communicative genres are socially rooted phenomena. Communicative patterns and genres are viewed as institutions of communication, which interactants communicate with others. The methodological steps include the recording of communicative events in natural situations and their transcription. The next step is that these data are hermeneutically interpreted and subjected to a sequential analysis (see also Chapter 25) before a conversation analysis is done with the material in order to show the language's level of organization. From these two steps of analysis, structural models are set up that are then tested for their appropriateness with further cases, before in the last step, finally structural variants are considered that come about as a result of modalization (irony, pejorative forms, etc.). Examples for such communicative genres are irony, gossip, and the like. The analysis of the data is focusing first on the internal structure of communicative genres including:

- Prosody: intonation, volume, speech tempo, pauses, rhythm, accentuation, voice quality.
- Language variety: standard language, jargon, dialect, sociolect.
- Linguistic register: formal, informal, or intimate.
- Stylistic and rhetorical figures: alliteration, metaphor, rhythm, and so on.
- "Small" and "minimal forms": verbal stereotypes, idiomatic expressions, platitudes, proverbs, categorical formulations, traditional historical formulae, inscriptions and puzzles.
- Motifs, topoi, and structural markers (Knoblauch and Luckmann 2004, p. 305).

Finally, the external structure of communicative genres and the communicative economy of their use are analyzed.

What is the Contribution to the General Methodological Discussion?

Genre analytic studies analyze larger communicative patterns than conversation analysis does but use similar principles. Contrary to discourse analysis, they keep the focus on formal patterns of communication and on contents. So, they combine the methodological rigor of conversation analysis with a more content oriented approach.

How does the Method Fit into the Research Process?

The theoretical background of genre analysis again is social constructionism (see Chapters 6 and 7). Research questions focus on how the making of social reality can be studied in the patterns that are used to communicate about certain objects or processes and their function (see Chapter 9). Empirical material ranges from media articles to interviews (see Chapter 11). Interpretations are based on transcripts of those interviews or the texts to be found (see Chapter 22).

What are the Limitations of the Method?

The definition of a communicative genre is less clear than other units of qualitative analysis. The methodology is more comprehensive and more rigorous than other analytic approaches in qualitative research, but comprises several methodological approaches (hermeneutic and conversation analytic methods), which make the analysis rather complicated and time consuming.

KEY POINTS

- Conversation analysis was originally designed to study everyday interaction with a formal focus. It has been taken as a starting point for analyzing other materials.
- Discourse analysis has a broader focus concerning the material that can be analyzed, but also wants to show how communication about a specific issue is organized (as a discourse).
- Genre analysis extends this analytic attitude to bigger pieces of conversational tools, which are applied by the participants. Genre analysts want to study the use of such tools.

Exercise 24.1

1. Take your own data or find a transcript of an interaction in the literature. Analyze how this interaction is opened–how it begins, who says what, and what kind of argumentation is used.
2. Then look at the way taking turns is organized in this transcript: how does the second speaker take over from the first one, how does the first one stop talking, etc.
3. Finally, look for sequences in the transcript like question–answer, greeting-greeting back, etc.

Exercise 24.2

1. Apply the guiding questions of discourse analysis mentioned above to a piece of text from your own data or from the literature.
2. Look for interpretive repertoires in that text.

FURTHER READING

Conversation Analysis
The first three references give an overview of the theoretical and methodological background (ethnomethodology) of the research program, while the last discusses the more recent state of the art.

Bergmann, J. (2004a) "Conversation Analysis," in U. Flick, E.v. Kardorff and I. Steinke (eds), *A Companion to Qualitative Research*. London: SAGE. pp. 296–302.
Garfinkel, H. (1967) *Studies in Ethnomethodology*. Englewood Cliffs, NJ: Prentice Hall.
Sacks, H. (1992) *Lectures on Conversation*, Vols. 1, 2 (ed. G. Jefferson). Oxford: Blackwell.
Ten Have, P. (1999) *Doing Conversation Analysis: A Practical Guide*. London: SAGE.

(Continued)

Discourse Analysis
These three references give an overview of the research program.

Edwards, D. and Potter, J. (1992) *Discursive Psychology.* London: SAGE.
Parker, I. (2004) "Discourse Analysis," in U. Flick, E.v. Kardorff and I. Steinke (eds), *A Companion to Qualitative Research.* London: SAGE. pp. 308–312.
Potter, J. and Wetherell, M. (1998) "Social Representations, Discourse Analysis and Racism," in U. Flick (ed.), *Psychology of the Social.* Cambridge: Cambridge University Press. pp. 138–155.

Genre Analysis
The second text gives some explanation of the theoretical backgrounds of this approach, while the first will give you more information about how to do a genre analysis.

Knoblauch, H and Luckmann, Th. (2004) "Genre Analysis," in U. Flick, E.v. Kardorff and I. Steinke (eds), *A Companion to Qualitative Research.* London: SAGE. pp. 303–307.
Luckmann, Th. (1995) "Interaction Planning and Intersubjective Adjustment of Perspectives by Communicative Genres," in E.N. Goody (ed.), *Social Intelligence and Interaction. Expressions and Implications of the Social Bias in Human Intelligence.* Cambridge: Cambridge University Press. pp. 175–189.

25

NARRATIVE AND HERMENEUTIC ANALYSES

CHAPTER OBJECTIVES
After reading this chapter, you should be able to

✓ identify how the narrative approach is used for analyzing life histories and other forms
  of biographical data.
✓ understand the principle of sequential analysis as guiding principle of narrative and
  hermeneutic analysis.
✓ explain what objective hermeneutics means.
✓ comprehend social science hermeneutics as a further development and alternative
  approach.

Analyzing Narratives

Narrative analyses start from a specific form of sequential order. The individual
statement, which you want to interpret is first regarded in terms of whether it is
part of a narrative and then analyzed. Narratives are stimulated and collected in
the narrative interview in order to reconstruct biographical processes. More generally, life is regarded as narrative in order to analyze the narrative construction
of reality (Bruner 1987; 1991) without using a procedure of collecting data that
explicitly aims at eliciting narratives.

Analysis of Narrative Interviews for Reconstructing Events
You can find several suggestions for analyzing narrative interviews in the literature.
The "first analytic step (formal text analysis) is to eliminate all non-narrative

passages in the text and then to segment the 'purified' narrative text for its formal sections" (Schütze 1983, p. 286). A structural description of the contents follows, which specifies the different parts of narratives ("temporally limited processual structures of the life course on the basis of formal narrative connectors"–Riemann and Schütze 1987, p. 348), such as "and then" or pauses. The analytic abstraction–as a third step–moves away from the specific details of the life segments. Its intention is to elaborate "the biographical shaping *in toto,* i.e., the life historical sequence of experience-dominant processual structures in the individual life periods up to the presently dominant processual structure" (Schütze 1983, p. 286). Only after this reconstruction of patterns of process, you integrate the other non-narrative parts of the interview in the analysis. Finally, the case analyses produced in this way are compared and contrasted with each other. The aim is less to reconstruct the narrator's subjective interpretations of his or her life than to reconstruct the "interrelation of factual processual courses" (1983, p. 284).[1]

Haupert (1991) outlines a different procedure. As a preparation for the actual fine analysis, he first draws up the narrator's short biography, which includes a chronological display of the "events identified as meaningful" in the life history. This is followed by the segmentation of the interviews according to Schütze's method and by formulating headings for the single sequences. The identification of the "sequential thematic," and the attachment of quotations explaining it, is the next step. Finally, the core of the biography with the central statements of the interview is formulated. Paraphrases of statements from the text and the explication of the contexts of the interviews and the milieus lead to further abstraction. After condensing the case stories to core stories, they are classified in analytic types of processes. These types are attached to life world milieus. This procedure also reconstructs the course of the biography from the course of the narrative. Therefore, apply the sequential analysis.

This reconstruction of factual courses from biographical narratives starts from the "assumption of homology," which according to Bude, includes the following premise: "The autobiographical unprepared extempore narrative is seen . . . as a truly reproductive recapitulation of past experience" (1985, pp. 331–332). Recently, this premise has been questioned more and not only by Bude. The constructions included in narratives attract more attention.

The Analysis of Narrative Data as Life Constructions

Accordingly, Bude (1984) outlines a different view on narratives, the data contained in them, and thus, on their analysis by suggesting the "reconstruction of life constructions." Here he takes into account that narratives, like other forms of presentation, include subjective and social constructions in what is presented–life constructions in narrative interviews, for example. In a similar way, authors in psychology like Bruner (1987) understand life histories as social constructions.

In their concrete shaping, they draw on basic cultural narratives and life histories offered by the culture. The goal of analyzing narrative data is more to disclose these constructive processes and less to reconstruct factual processes. Rosenthal and Fischer-Rosenthal (2004) see the difference between a life story told in the interview and the life history, which was lived by the interviewee. They analyze narrative interviews in five steps: (1) analysis of the biographical data, (2) thematic field analysis (reconstruction of the *life story*), (3) reconstruction of the life *history*, (4) microanalysis of individual text segments, and (5) contrastive comparison of life history and life story.

Box 25.1   The Sequence of Stages in the Practical Analysis

1. Analysis of biographical data (data of events)
2. Text and thematic field analysis (sequential analysis of textual segments from the self-presentation in the interview)
3. Reconstruction of the case history (life as lived)
4. Detailed analysis of individual textual locations
5. Contrasting the life story as narrated with life as lived
6. Formation of types

Source: Rosenthal and Fischer-Rosenthal (2004)

Denzin outlines the procedure for such an interpretation as follows:

> (1) Securing the interactional text; (2) displaying the text as a unit; (3) subdividing the text into key experiential units; (4) linguistic and interpretive analysis of each unit; (5) serial unfolding and interpretation of the meanings of the text to the participants; (6) development of working interpretations of the text; (7) checking these hypotheses against the subsequent portions of the text; (8) grasping the text as a totality; and (9) displaying the multiple interpretations that occur within the text. (1989a, p. 46)

For analyzing narratives of families and the processes of constructing reality that take place in them (see Chapter 15), Hildenbrand and Jahn (1988, p. 208) suggest the following sequence analytic procedure. First, the "hard" social data of the family (birth, marriage, educational situation, stages in professional life, etc.) are reconstructed from the narrative. Then they are interpreted with respect to the room for decisions compared with the decisions actually made. Generate a hypothesis and systematically test it in the process of further interpretation on the case of the studied family. The opening sequence of the narrative in particular and the "members' self-presentation," which is evident in it are the interpretations of the sequence analytic procedure. Sampling further cases follows. The case structures elaborated in the analyses can be contrasted, compared, and generalized. The inspiration behind this procedure was the objective hermeneutics that will be discussed next.

Case Study: Example of a Case Reconstruction

Gabriele Rosenthal and Wolfram Fischer-Rosenthal have developed a practical model (see Box 25.1) for how to analyze narrative data coming from narrative interviews (see Chapter 14) and have applied it to many studies interested in biographical experiences of people in certain historical periods such as during and after World War II.

Rosenthal and Fischer-Rosenthal (2004, p. 261–264) present a detailed analysis of excerpts from a narrative interview referring to a period in a life history. Here the interviewee starts her story with the sequence: "*Nothing is as you imagined it. Everything turned out differently*" and then immediately embarks on the following report: "*The great love of my youth, met my husband at 15 and was engaged at 18 and married at 20 and at 21 had my son (laughing) that was already in '42, when there was already war then.*" The authors analyze the self-presentation in this statement on different levels – the biographical meaning of the events presented here for the interviewee and asks why the interviewee might have chosen to start her life story with this issue ("young love"). In order to understand this in greater detail, they formulate hypotheses at the level of the story of life as lived and at the level of the narrated life story. They also use further information about the life as it was lived and about the way such a life developed normally in that period. Differences from that normal life course can be analyzed as "life unlived." In the thematic field analysis, the self-presentation is reconstructed by means of complexes of topics, that is to say, by expanding thematic fields in the order of their treatment. The analysis proceeds on the basis that self-presentation cannot–or only occasionally–be intentionally controlled and that the story of experience is manifest in a piece of text production that corresponds to the uninterrupted opening narrative. In preparing this step, the interview passage is sequenced, which means segmented according to the turn taking in the interview, the text type, and the change of topic (see p. 263) and questions are formulated like: why are topics introduced at a specific point?; which topics are or are not mentioned?; why are some topics presented in greater detail and others not?; and what is the thematic field this topic fits into? In answering these questions and testing the hypotheses, the authors unfold an extensive interpretation of this case, which would then be followed by contrasting the case study with other cases from the same study or field.

This example shows how the authors develop an approach to narrative data referring to life histories, which take into account the difference between the story as it is developed and the life which is narrated in its course. The example also shows how extensive an analysis of this type can be and normally is (see Rosenthal and Fischer-Rosenthal 2004, p. 261–264 again only for an excerpt of such an analysis).

What is the Contribution to the General Methodological Discussion?

Common to all the procedures for analyzing narrative data presented here is that in the interpretation of statements they start from the gestalt of the narrative and in so doing they view the statements in the context of the proceeding of the narrative. Furthermore, they include a formal analysis of the material—which passages of the text are narrative passages, and which other sorts of text can be identified? The procedures differ in how they view the role of the narrative in the analysis of the studied relations. Schütze sees the narrative presented in the interview as a true representation of the events recounted. The other authors understand and analyze narratives as a special form of constructing events, which can also be found in everyday life and knowledge and that this special mode of construction can therefore be used for research purposes particularly well. A characteristic feature of narrative analysis is to combine a formal analysis and a sequential procedure in the interpretation of constructions of experiences in presentations.

How does the Method Fit into the Research Process?

The theoretical background is the orientation to the analysis of subjective meaning (see Chapter 6). For this purpose, narrative interviews are used for collecting data (see Chapter 14). Research questions focus on the analysis of biographical processes (see Chapter 9). Cases are mainly selected gradually (see Chapter 11), and generalizations aim at developing theories (see Chapter 8). Therefore, case analyses are contrasted with one another (see Chapter 29).

What are the Limitations of the Method?

In the main, those analyses referring to Schütze exaggerate the quality of reality in narratives as data. The influence of the presentation on what is recounted is underestimated while the possible inference from narrative to factual events in life histories is overestimated. Only in very rare examples are narrative analyses combined with other methodological approaches in order to exceed their limits. A second problem is the degree to which analyses stick to individual cases. The time and effort spent analyzing individual cases restricts studies from going beyond reconstructing and comparing a few cases. The more general theory of biographical processes that was originally aimed at and promised for quite a while has not yet been realized, although there are instructive typologies in particular domains.

Objective Hermeneutics

Objective hermeneutics was originally conceptualized for analyzing natural interactions (e.g., family conversations). Since its conception, however, the approach has been used to analyze all sorts of other documents including even works of art and photographs. Schneider (1988) has modified this approach for analyzing interviews. The general extension of the domain of (possible) objects of enquiry using objective hermeneutics is expressed by the fact that authors understand the "world as text," as indicated by the title of a volume of theoretical and methodological works in this field (Garz 1994). This approach makes a basic distinction between the subjective meaning that a statement or activity has for one or more participants and its objective meaning. The latter is understood by using the concept of a "latent structure of sense" of an activity. This structure can only be enquired into using the framework of a multistep scientific procedure of interpretation. Owing to its orientation to such structures the label "structural hermeneutics" has also been used.

What is the Procedure of Objective Hermeneutics?

In the beginning, the aim was focused on the "reconstruction of *objective* meaning structures" of texts. Analysis in objective hermeneutics were not interested in what the text producers thought, wished, hoped, or believed when they produced their text. Subjective intentions linked to text were and still are irrelevant in this context. The only relevant thing is the objective meaning structure of the text in a particular linguistic and interactive community. Later, the label "objective" was extended beyond the issue of study–the findings obtained were not only claimed to have (greater) validity but the research should, with the assistance of the procedure, achieve an objectivity of results.

Analyses in objective hermeneutics have to be "strictly sequential," which means you should follow the temporal course of the events or the text in conducting the interpretation. They should be conducted by a group of analysts working on the same text. First, the members define what is the case to be analyzed and on which level it is to be located. It could be defined as a statement or activity of a concrete person, or of someone who performs a certain role in an institutional context, or of a member of the human species. This definition is followed by a sequential *rough analysis* aimed at analyzing the external contexts in which a statement is embedded in order to take the influence of such contexts into account. The focus of this rough analysis is mainly on considerations about the nature of the concrete action problem for which the studied action or interaction offers a solution. First, case structure hypotheses, which are falsified in later steps and the rough structure of the text and of the case, are developed. The specification of the external context or the interactional embedding of the case serves to answer questions about how the data came about: "Under the heading of interactional embedding, the different layers of the external context of a protocolled action sequence must be specified with regard to possible consequences and restrictions for the concrete practice of interaction itself, including the conditions of producing the protocol as an interactional procedure" (Schneider 1985, p. 81).

The central step is the sequential *fine analysis*, which includes interpretations of interactions on nine levels as in Box 25.2 (Oevermann et al. 1979, pp. 394–402). At levels 1 and 3 of the interpretation, an attempt is made to reconstruct the objective context of a statement by constructing several possible contexts in thought experiments and by excluding them successively. Here, the analysis of the subjective meanings of statements and actions plays a minor role. Interest focuses on the structures of interactions. The procedure at level 4 is oriented to interpretations using the framework of conversation analysis, whereas at level 5 the focus is on the formal linguistic (syntactic, semantic, or pragmatic) features of the text. Levels 6 to 8 strive for an increasing generalization of the structures that have been found (e.g., an examination is made of whether the forms of communication found in the text can be repeatedly found as general forms – i.e., communicative figures – and also in other situations). These figures and structures are treated as hypotheses and are tested step-by-step against the further material and possibly falsified.

Box 25.2 Levels of Interpretation in Objective Hermeneutics

0 Explication of the context which immediately precedes an interaction.
1 Paraphrasing the meaning of an interaction according to the verbatim text of the accompanying verbalization.
2 Explication of the interacting subject's intention.
3 Explication of the objective motives of the interaction and of its objective consequences.
4 Explication of the function of the interaction for the distribution of interactional roles.
5 Characterization of the linguistic features of the interaction.
6 Exploration of the interpreted interaction for constant communicative figures.
7 Explication of general relations.
8 Independent test of the general hypotheses that were formulated at the preceding level on the basis of interaction sequences from further cases.

Source: Oevermann et al. 1979, pp. 394–402

According to Schneider (1985), the elaboration of general structures from interaction protocols can be shown in the following steps in the proceedings of sequential fine analysis. First, the objective meaning of the first interaction is reconstructed (i.e., without taking the concrete contextual conditions into account). Therefore, the research group narrates stories about as many contrasting situations, which consistently fit a statement. At the next step, it compares general structural features with the concrete contextual conditions in which the analyzed statement occurred. The meaning of an action can be reconstructed through the interplay of possible contexts in which it might have occurred and the concrete context in which it really occurred. In thought experiments, the interpreters analyze the implications of the statement first examined for the following interaction. This step shows the possible option of contrasting transparency for specifying the next statement, which *really* occurred. By increasingly excluding such alternatives of the proceeding of the interaction, the structure of the case manifests and is finally generalized by testing it against further cases.

Case Study: Counsellor–Client Interactions

Sahle (1987) has used this procedure to study the interactions of social workers with their clients. Additionally, she interviewed the social workers. She presents four case studies. In each case, the author has extensively interpreted the opening sequence of the interactions in order to elaborate the "structure formula" for the interaction, which is then tested against a passage, which was randomly sampled from the further text. She derives hypotheses about the professional self-concept of the social workers from the analyses and tests them in the interviews. In a very short comparison, Sahle relates the case studies to each other and finally discusses her results with the social workers that were involved.

More generally, Reichertz (2004, pp. 291–292) outlines three variants of text explanation in the research using objective hermeneutics:

1. The *detailed analysis* of a text at eight different levels in which the knowledge and the external context, and also the pragmatics of a type of interaction, are explained in advance and are borne in mind in the analysis.
2. The *sequential analysis* of each individual contribution to an interaction, step-by-step, without clarifying in advance the internal or external context of the utterance … This is the most demanding variant of objective hermeneutics, since it is very strongly oriented towards the methodological premises of the overall concept.
3. The full *interpretation of the objective social data* from all those who participated in an interaction before any approach is made to the text to be interpreted … This variant handles the fundamentals of a theory of hermeneutics interpretation very flexibly and uses them in a somewhat metaphorical way.

Further Developments

This procedure was developed for analyzing everyday language interactions, which are available in recorded and transcribed form as material for interpretation. The sequential analysis seeks to reconstruct the layering of social meanings from the process of the actions. Analyze from the beginning to the end when proceedings are available as recordings. Therefore, the analysis always begins with the opening sequence of the interaction. When analyzing interviews using this approach, the problem arises that interviewees do not always report events and processes in their chronological order. For example, the interviewees may recount a certain phase in their lives and then refer to them during their narrative of events, which have to be located earlier. In the narrative interview too, and particularly in the semi-structured interview, events and experiences are not recounted in chronological order. From the interviewee's statement, reconstruct the sequential order of the story (also known as the action system under study) when using this sequence. Therefore, the reported events are rearranged in the temporal order in which they occurred. The sequential analysis is then oriented to this order of occurrence and not to the temporal course in the interview: "The beginning of a sequential analysis is not the analysis of the opening of the conversation in the first interview but the analysis of those actions and events reported by the interviewee which are the earliest 'documents' of the case history" (Schneider 1988, p. 234).

Other recent developments aim at deriving a hermeneutics of images from this approach. Starting from a critique of the increasingly narrow concept of structure in Oevermann's approach, Lüders (1991) attempts to transfer the distinction between subjective and social meaning to the development of an analysis of interpretative patterns, which has also more interest for subjective viewpoints again.

What is the Contribution to the General Methodological Discussion?

A consequence of this approach is that the sequence analytical procedure has developed into a program with clearly demarcated methodological steps. A further consequence of this is that it is made clear that subjective views are only *one* form of access to social phenomena and that meaning is also produced and continued at the level of the social (on this in a different context see Silverman 2001). Finally, the idea of social sciences as textual sciences is preserved most consistently here. Another aspect is the call for doing interpretations in a group in order to increase the variation of the versions and perspectives brought to the text and in so doing to use the group to validate interpretations that have been made.

How does the Method Fit into the Research Process?

The theoretical backgrounds of this approach are structuralist models (see Chapter 6). Research questions focus on the explanation of social meanings of actions or objects (see Chapter 9). Sampling decisions are mostly taken successively (step-by-step) (see Chapter 11). Often, the researcher refrains from using explicit methods for collecting data. Instead, everyday interactions are recorded and transcribed, although interviews and occasionally field notes from observational studies are also interpreted using objective hermeneutics. Generalization in this procedure starts from case studies and is sometimes advanced using contrasting cases (see Chapter 29).

What are the Limitations of the Method?

A problem with this approach is that (because of the great effort involved in the method) it is often limited to single case studies. The leap to general statements is often made without any intermediate steps. Furthermore, the understanding of the method as art, which can hardly be transformed into didactic elaboration and mediation, makes its more general application complicated (for general skepticism see Denzin 1988). However, a relatively extensive research practice using this approach can be noted in German-speaking countries.

The common feature of the sequential methods discussed here is that they orient to the temporal-logical structure of the text and take it as a starting point for their interpretation. Thus, they remain oriented more closely to the text than do categorizing methods as discussed in Chapter 23. The relation of formal aspects and contents is shaped differently. Conversation analysis (see Chapter 24) is mainly interested in formal features of the interaction. Narrative analyses use the formal distinction between narrative and argumentative passages in interviews for deciding which ones receive interpretative attention and its contents' credibility. In interpretations using objective hermeneutics, the formal analysis of the text is a rather secondary level of interpretation. Sometimes, these methods employ hypotheses, which have been derived from passages of the text to falsify them against other ones.

Social Science Hermeneutics and Hermeneutic Sociology of Knowledge

Recent approaches have taken up basic ideas of objective hermeneutics but have developed a different understanding of hermeneutics and of the issues of research. They do not use the term "objective" any more, but focus on the social construction of knowledge more strongly. Again, non-standardized data–protocols of interaction–are preferred to interview data, for example. The researchers should approach the field under study as naively as possible and collect unstructured data. Interpretations follow a three-step procedure. First, open coding according to Strauss (1987–see Chapter 23) is applied with a focus on the sequential structure of the document (line-by-line, sometimes word-by-word). Then, researchers will look for highly aggregated meaning units and concepts that bind together the parts and units. In the third step, new data are sought with which the interpretation is falsified, modified, and extended by means of the later data collection (for more details see Reichertz 2004; Soeffner 2004).

KEY POINTS

- Narrative and hermeneutic approaches take the structure of the text into account.
- The analysis follows the structure of the text (sequentially) and sees the statements in this context.
- Biographical texts are analyzed in the context of the sequence of the events that are reported so that internal structure of the life history and the external structure of the life reported in it can be put into connection.
- Social science hermeneutics links such a sequential analysis with open coding according to grounded theory research.

Exercise 25.1

1. Take your own interview data and look for any biographical information. Identify the dates that are mentioned in them and reconstruct the case history (in the excerpts that are mentioned).
2. Analyze how the interviewee presents himself or herself in the interview in individual text locations, mainly in the beginning of the interview.
3. Apply the levels of interpretation from objective hermeneutics (see Box 25.2) to the beginning of the interview.

Note

1 The study of Hermanns (1984) has already been presented briefly in Chapter 13 as an example of a convincing application of this procedure.

FURTHER READING

Narrative Analyses
These four references give an overview of different ways of analyzing narratives in their sequential shape.

Bruner, J. (1987) "Life as Narrative," *Social Research,* 54: 11–32.
Denzin, N.K. (1988) *Interpretive Biography.* London: SAGE.
Rosenthal, G. (2004) "Biographical Research," in C. Seale, G. Gobo, J. Gubrium and D. Silverman (eds), *Qualitative Research Practice.* London: SAGE. pp. 48–65.
Rosenthal, G. and Fischer-Rosenthal, W. (2004) "The Analysis of Biographical-Narrative Interviews," in U. Flick, E.v. Kardorff and I. Steinke (eds), *A Companion to Qualitative Research.* London: SAGE. pp. 259–265.

(Continued)

Objective Hermeneutics
There are limited traces of this method in the Anglo-Saxon literature. The first two references are some exceptions, whereas the third one gives an introduction and overview.

Denzin, N.K. *(1988) Interpretive Biography.* London: SAGE.
Gerhardt, U. (1988) "Qualitative Sociology in the Federal Republic of Germany," *Qualitative Sociology,* 11, pp. 29–43.
Reichertz, J. (2004) "Objective Hermeneutics and Hermeneutic Sociology of Knowledge," in U. Flick, E.v. Kardorff and I. Steinke (eds), *A Companion to Qualitative Research*. London: SAGE. pp. 290–295.

Social Science Hermeneutics and Hermeneutic Sociology of Knowledge
These two chapters describe this recent development.

Reichertz, J. (2004) "Objective Hermeneutics and Hermeneutic Sociology of Knowledge," in U. Flick, E.v. Kardorff and I. Steinke (eds), *A Companion to Qualitative Research*. London: SAGE. pp. 290–295.
Soeffner, H.G. (2004) "Social Science Hermeneutics," in U. Flick, E.v. Kardorff and I. Steinke (eds), *A Companion to Qualitative Research*. London: SAGE. pp. 95–100.

26

USING COMPUTERS IN QUALITATIVE ANALYSIS

CHAPTER OBJECTIVES
After reading this chapter, you should be able to

✓ identify what computers contribute to making qualitative research easier.
✓ understand the role of computers in their main domain in qualitative research–supporting the analysis of material.
✓ comprehend that software neither does the analysis nor replaces the use of a method for analyzing material, but only offers some tools for making it more comfortable.
✓ select a program for your study and for finding the right one.

New Technologies: Hopes, Fears, and Fantasies

Qualitative research is undergoing a technological change and this change is influencing the essential character of qualitative research. For example, see Chapter 22 for the discussion about new technologies of recording and the new forms of data they have made possible for the first time. Since the mid-1980s, a potential and maybe far-reaching technological change started in the analysis of data, which is linked to the introduction of computers in qualitative research. Here, note the general changes in working patterns in the social sciences brought about by the personal computer and word processing. However, it is also important to see the specific developments in and for qualitative research. If these developments become more established than they have up to now, considerable impacts on qualitative research and its practices will probably result. Now, quite a range of software programs is available, mostly focused on the area of qualitative data analysis. Therefore, the programs are sometimes referred to as QDA (qualitative data analysis) software or as CAQDAS (computer-aided qualitative data analysis software).

In general, the introduction of computers in this field has produced mixed feelings: some researchers have high hopes about the advantages of using them, whereas others have concerns and fears about how the use of computers will change or even distort qualitative research practice. Some of these hopes may be right, some of these fears may have a kernel of truth, but some parts of both are more fantasy than anything else. For both parts it should be emphasized that there is a crucial difference between this kind of software and programs for statistical analysis (like SFSS). QDA software does not *do* qualitative analysis itself or in an *automatic* way like SPSS can do a statistical operation or a factor analysis. QDA software is more like a word processor, which does not write your text but makes it somewhat easier for you to write a text (although there is a long-running debate about how writing in general has changed due to the use of word processors). In a similar way, QDA supports qualitative research but does not automate it or do it, although this support may have an impact on the research. As it is still the author who writes by using the word processor, it is still the researcher who does the coding and so on by using QDA.

In the last few years, overviews of the perpetually developing market have been published. Some of them have been written from the program developer's point of view (e.g., Richards and Richards 1998) and some from that of the user (Kelle 2004; Seale 2000; Weitzman 2000; Weitzman and Miles 1995) or based on users' experiences. Fielding and Lee (1998) often refer to an empirical study of their own based on focus groups with users of such software. As the progress in the software development permanently leads to the improvement of existing programs and updated versions and the appearance of new programs, all of these overviews are partly outdated as soon as or shortly after they are available.

Ways of Using Computers in Qualitative Research

Although most of the software and computers in qualitative research are used for analyzing data, there are also other steps in the qualitative research process for which computers can be employed. In general, the following ways of using computers and software in the context of qualitative research are mentioned:

1. making notes in the field;
2. writing or transcribing field notes;

3. editing–correcting, extending, or revising field notes;
4. coding–attaching keywords or tags to segments of text to permit later retrieval;
5. storage–keeping text in an organized database;
6. search and retrieval–locating relevant segments of text and making them available for inspection;
7. data "linking"–connecting relevant data segments to each other, forming categories, clusters, or networks of information;
8. memo writing–writing reflective commentaries on some aspect of the data, as a basis for deeper analysis;
9. content analysis–counting frequencies, sequence, or locations of words and phrases;
10. data display–placing selected or reduced data in a condensed, organized format, such as a matrix or network, for inspection;
11. conclusion drawing and verification–aiding the analyst to interpret displayed data and to test or confirm findings;
12. theory building–developing systematic, conceptually coherent explanations of findings; testing hypotheses;
13. graphic mapping–creating diagrams that depict findings or theories;
14. report writing–interim and final reports (Miles and Huberman 1994, p. 44; Weitzman 2000, p. 806).

Some other aspects could be added to this list; most notably, the transcription of interviews, the writing of a research diary, the communication with other researchers through computer networks, e-mail, using the Internet, and writing articles about one's own research or its methods and so on. Most of these activities in the above list can be more or less comfortably carried out with the usual word processors (see points 1, 2, 3, 8, 14, and with the skillful use of luxurious programs also points 4, 6, 9, cf. Weitzman and Miles 1995, p. 5). Thus, the first way of using computers has been outlined–the simple and straightforward use of word processors and/or the creative use of their programs to perform specific functions. But, as Seale (2000, pp. 162–163) points out, the use of word processors for such purposes is much more time consuming than applying special software. Some of the more developed QDA software is able to manage, store, and display audio and visual material–photos, films, recorded texts, and video material– and to include these into analytic procedures, which definitely goes beyond what word processors are able to do.

Why Use Software for Analyzing Qualitative Data: Hopes and Expectancies

In the literature, several expectations are mentioned as "real hopes" (Weitzman 2000, p. 806). The first one is *speed* in handling, managing, searching, and displaying data and related items like codes, or memos, in links to the data. But you should take into account the time necessary for deciding on a program, installing it, and learning to use it (or even the computer). Therefore, the real gain of time will be worth the effort in the long run and with bigger projects and bigger data sets rather than in the short run and with smaller amounts of data.

The second expectancy is the *increase of quality* in qualitative research by using computers or that it becomes easier to demonstrate quality. Here, the gain of consistency in analytic procedures is mentioned or the extra rigor in analysis. Kelle and Laurie (1995) link the use of QDA software to a surplus of validity in qualitative research. Finally, the transparency of the research process can be increased and using computers can facilitate the communication in a research team and by analyzing the way links between texts and codes were developed, for example. Weitzman also mentions a consolidation of the research as the computer allows the researcher to have all research documents (from initial field notes to final displays, tables and writings about the findings) in one place–the computer's hard disk. Seale (2000) discusses *a facilitation of sampling* decisions based on the state of data analysis so far (according to theoretical sampling, see Chapter 11) due to using a computer program.

A major expectancy is that *data management* becomes easier with computers. Kelle (e.g., 2004 p. 278) lists a series of data management techniques supported by QDA computer programs:

- the definition of pointers containing index words together with the "addresses" of text passages, which can be used to retrieve indexed text segments;
- the construction of electronic cross-references with the help of so-called "hyperlinks," which can be used to "jump" between linked text passages;
- facilities for storing the researchers' comments ("memos"), which can be linked to index words or text segments;
- features for defining linkages between index words;
- the use of variables and filters so that the search for text segments can be restricted by certain limitations;
- facilities for the retrieval of text segments with specified formal relations to each other (e.g., text segments that appear with a certain specified maximum distance of each other);
- facilities for the retrieval of quantitative attributes of the database.

QDA computer programs (but not word processors or standard database systems) offer the first two, whereas the other five are only offered by more elaborate software packages for qualitative research. Better QDA programs facilitate the *representation* of data, of structures in the data, and of findings in graphic maps and other forms of displays to immediately import into word processors for writings about research and findings. Finally, no technological development is safe from being "misused" for other purposes than what they were created for. Some people use programs like NUD•IST as a reference manager in their personal library or ATLAS•ti (see below) to do the project planning in their jobs.

This list of expectancies and hopes includes quite a variety. None of the programs available so far can fulfill each of these and definitely not in the same way. Similar to the earlier days of word processing, the decision to use one of the software alternatives makes it more complicated to switch from one to another. There are problems of compatibility and data export. There is still no standard, which allows taking data and codes from one package to another one, for example. Thus, the decision for one or the other software package should be well considered and carefully taken. And finally, the potential user should keep in mind, "There is still no one best program" (Weitzman 2000, p. 803).

Types of Software for Analyzing Qualitative Data

The programs available at the moment can be summarized in various types[1]:

- Word processors, which allow one not only to write but also to edit texts, to search for words, or word sequences at least in a limited way.
- Text retrieval programs, which specifically allow one to search, summarize, list, and so on certain word sequences.
- Text-base managers for administering, searching, sorting, and ordering text passages.
- Code-and-retrieve-programs for splitting the text into segments, to which codes are assigned and for retrieving or listing all segments of the text, which were marked with each code; marking, ordering, sorting and linking texts and codes are supported and both (text and code) are presented and administered together.
- Code-based theory building. Additionally, these programs support theory building by supporting steps and operations at the level of the text (attachment of one or more passages to a code) but also at the conceptual level (relations between codes, superior and subcategories, networks of categories), always going back to the attached text passages. In some programs, more or less luxurious graphic editors are included and it is possible to integrate video data.
- Conceptual networking is possible in the last group, which offer extensive options for developing and presenting conceptual networks, networks of categories, and various ways to visualize relations among the various parts of the network.

Software for Analyzing Qualitative Data: How to Choose?

If word processor performances are not sufficient for your research purpose, you should turn to existing software for specific ends or even write your own program. Many of the programs available today have been created in this way–starting from specific needs and necessities in a concrete research project. Some programs have had their range of options extended in a way, which allows them to be used for other research questions and data sorts as originally intended.

As a result, more than 25 programs are now available, which have been developed especially for analyzing qualitative data. However, this has been accompanied by a lack of clarity as to the exact nature of the supplies/range of products available on the market. Additionally, all these programs are subject to specific limitations resulting from their original developmental context and purpose and the accents of the program. The advantages and disadvantages of single programs compared to other programs can be clarified in three ways: First, formulate and apply general questions to the single program. Second, researchers need to ask themselves some key questions when deciding on special software. And finally, more empirical research focusing the users' experiences with QDA-software might be helpful (Fielding and Lee 1998; Weitzman 2000).

Guiding Questions for Analyzing and Comparing Programs

For a very early stocktaking of the programs available at that time, I used the guiding questions (Box 26.1) for assessing computer programs for qualitative research in the early 1990s. Although more developed programs have become available, you should still ask these questions before using a program. More recent reviews have been provided by Weitzman (2000) and Weitzman and Miles (1995) who give some hints for the decision for or against the use of computers for the assistance of qualitative analyses and for specific programs; they also provide a criteria based test and comparison of 24 programs.

Box 26.1   Guiding Questions for Analyzing and Comparing Computer Programs in Qualitative Research

---

- Data-related questions: For which kind of data was the program conceived? For which data can it be used beyond these original data? For which data should it not be used?
- Activity-related questions: Which activities can be carried out with this program? Which should not be carried out with it?
- Process-related questions: How did the program influence the handling of data and the part played by the researcher or interpreter according to experiences had up to now? Which new options did it open? What has become more difficult or laborious in the process of interpretation due to the program?
- Technical questions: What are the necessary conditions in the hardware (type of computer, Ram, hard disk, graphic card, screen . . .) or in the software (systems software, other programs needed) and networking options to other programs (SPSS, word processors, databases . . .)?
- Competence related questions: Which specific technical skills does the program require from the user (programming skills, maybe in specific programming languages, etc.)?

Key Questions Before Deciding on a Software

Authors like Weitzman (2000, pp. 811–815) or Weitzman and Miles (1995, pp. 7–9) suggest that potential users ask themselves a series of key questions before deciding on a program or for using computers generally. These key questions have been complemented by some other questions:

- What kind of computer user are you? Here, four levels of computer use are distinguished. The beginner (level 1) is new to the computer and engaged with learning the computer's functions and how to use software at all. These users are likely to be challenged by more elaborate CAQDAS-software and should reserve some extra time for learning the software before analyzing their texts. A user at level 2 has some experience with software and hardware and is comfortable learning and exploring new programs. The user at level 3 has a real interest in exploring the features and capacities of computer programs, whereas level 4 (the hacker) is something between an expert and an addict. Additionally, the question arises, which kind of computer and operating system shall be used or are already used (IBM-DOS/Windows, UNIX, or Apple)? Finally, the question of your own experience with qualitative research should be considered. Beginners in qualitative research as well as beginners in using computers are usually over challenged by the more demanding programs, the options they make, and by the decision about which program to use.
- Do you make the decision for using a program for a concrete research project or for general research use over the coming years? Three questions are linked to this point. First, what is the balance of the costs in training with the program (i.e., compare the data preparation against time savings when using the computer), especially if only a very limited amount of data is to be analyzed with the computer? Second, how far is the program selected according to the current conditions (the kind of data, the research question, etc.) and how far, with respect to later, maybe more complex studies? Third, what is the stage of the current project? If you are close to the end of funding and the motivation to choose a computer is to speed up the last steps of analyzing the data, it is more likely that the extra time needed to get the computer, software, and computer aided analysis going will actually hamper the research project rather than help due to the equipment and program learning curves.
- What kind of data and project is given (one or more data sources, case or comparative study; structured or open data; uniform or various inputs of data; size of the databases)? Is it only text or are you using video or photos, acoustic data or moving images, or e-mail and Internet traces (Bergmann and Meier 2004)? Not all software is ready to work with these forms of data. Are there several data sources for each case or only one sort of data, are you running a case study or do you work with several cases? Are the records you want to use fixed in

their format (e.g., the exactness of transcription) from the beginning to the end or might the format be changed (e.g., refined) during the progress of the project? Are the data structured (e.g., by an interview guide applied in every case) or free format (e.g., a narrative of the individual life course without any external structuring)? Finally, consider the database's size and limits when making a selection.

- What kind of analysis do you plan? Exploratory or confirming, predefined coding scheme or one to be developed, multiple or simple coding, one round through the data or multistep analysis, delicacy of the analyses, interest in the context of the data, how the data is to be presented and, only qualitative or also numeric analyses? Is a fixed coding system or an evolving set of categories used? Some programs were explicitly designed to allow testing hypotheses (see the contributions to Kelle 1995), others more for developing theories. How important is it to leave the data in their context or to have the context of a statement available? Is it necessary to be able to attach several codes to one element of text? Are several researchers working and coding the same text at the same time or in a sequence?
- How important is the proximity of the data in the process of analyzing them? Should the text which is interpreted always be accessible (on the screen) or only the categories, etc?
- Limits of costs: Can you afford to buy the program and the computers needed for using it?
- How fine is the analysis? For example, conversation analysts work very intensely with very small parts of their data (e.g., a turn in a conversation). Paul ten Have (1999) informs about ways of using computers for this kind of analysis.

Examples: ATLAS•ti, NUD•IST, and MAXqda

ATLAS•ti

Muhr (1991, 1994) developed ATLAS•ti in a research project at the Technical University of Berlin. The software is based on the approach of grounded theory and theoretical coding according to Strauss (1987; see Chapter 23). Technical preconditions of the current version (release 5.0) are: IBM-compatible PC (Processor Pentium/AMD 133 MHz recommended: Pentium/AMD 900 MHz or faster) with 128 MB (better: 256 MB or more) RAM, VGA-graphic card Video 800×600, True Color 1024×768 or better, True Color), DOS 3.0 and higher, mouse, hard disk (Available Disk Space 25 MB free 45 MB), CD-Rom. Windows 98SE, Windows ME, Windows NT 4.0 SP6, Windows 2000 SP3, Windows XP, Windows 2003 W2000 and XP. The program can work with different sorts of text documents: Plain text with soft line breaks, Rich Text with embedded objects (Excel tables, Powerpoint, etc), direct access to Word documents. Its more recent versions are not only able to process texts but also images, graphics, and sound. Most authors file this program in the category of "conceptual network builders" (e.g., Weitzman 2000, p. 809), but mainly in the group of the "code based theory builders." It supports operations on the textual and the conceptual level. A "hermeneutic unit" is formed on the screen that unifies the primary text (e.g., the interview to interpret) and the interpretations or coding related to it. The program shows the primary text with all codes attached to it and comments in different windows on the screen. It offers some functions, which are present on the screen in the form of symbols (retrieval, copy, cut, coding, networking, etc.).

Apart from the retrieval of sequences of words in the text and the attachment of codes, the presentation of codes and categories in conceptual networks is helpful. The relation to the passage to which the categories and super categories are linked, is maintained and can be presented immediately on the screen. Codes can be listed on the screen or printed. Interfaces to SPSS and other programs are integrated. Furthermore, it is possible for different authors to work on the same text on different computers. One limitation is that it only can be used with PCs and not with Apple MacIntosh computers. If ATLAS.ti is to be used on Mac, a PC emulation software has to be installed. For a good performance, this requires one of the newer G4 or G5 Mac processors. There is quite good support from the author and a very active electronic list of users. For more information about the program and contact with other users, see the author's home page on the Internet: www.atlasti.com.

NUD•IST

Richards and Richards (e.g., 1998) developed NUD•IST originally as a Mac program but then transferred to PC versions as well, but it still runs on both computer systems. The latest version (N6), however, is only available for PCs and the Mac user is referred to PC-emulation as well. Technical specifications: The PC should have an Intel Pentium Processor with 100MHz or better, an available RAM of 64–128 MB preferred, 25 MB of hard disk space for the program and a virtual memory of 16 MB, run on Microsoft Windows 95, 98 or Microsoft Windows NT 3.51 or 4.0, Windows, 2000 and XP as operating systems. The program is filed by Weitzman (2000, p. 809) as code-based theory builder. The latest version includes a full command language for automating coding and searching and allows the merging analytic files from two or more research projects initially run separately.

This program was distributed commercially very early and promoted very actively by the authors. Some features like "system closure" (i.e., memo or search results can be added to the original data) or the display of codes on the screen ("indexing") in a hierarchical tree structure are rather typical features of the program. Information and support can be found on the Internet at www.qsrinternational.com.

MAXqda

Developed by Kuckartz (1995), MAXqda is the successor product of winMAX, a program that has a history since 1989. With MAXqda you can create and import texts in Rich Text Format (rtf) from anywhere on your hard disk and from the Internet by drag and drop. Objects, like photos, Excel tables, PowerPoint sheets, etc., may be imported as embedded objects of a .rtf-file. The program has a hierarchical code system with up to ten levels. Codings are visualized in 11 different colored strips. Memos are visualized by little "post-it" icons; they can be attached at any line right beside the text or at the codes (to give e.g. code definitions). Eleven different icons can freely be assigned to a memo to indicate different types. A Code-Matrix Browser and a Code-Relations Browser visualize the distribution of codes over all texts, respectively the intersections of codes. The values can be exported to SPSS or Excel. Also you can automatically code search results and import attributes from SPSS, or any other quantitative package, as well as export them to MAXqda. A project in MAXqda is just one file. A special strength is the teamwork functions and the features to merge qualitative and quantitative analyses. MAXqda offers a fully integrated add-on module, MAXdictio, which allows an analysis of the word frequencies or even to perform a quantitative content analysis. MAXqda requires as a processor: Pentium 2 or better with an available RAM of 64MB (minimum). The operating systems are Microsoft Windows 98, Windows ME, Windows NT 4.0 or Windows 2000. The monitor is recommended to have a 1024×768 resolution. More information can be found at www.maxqda.com.

These three programs (earlier versions of them are described in detail in Weitzman and Miles 1995) were just examples of the continually developing range of available programs and versions. More information about the field and other programs (links to producers, reference to newer literature, etc.) can be found on the home page of the CAQDAS project at Surrey University, UK at www.soc.surrey.ac.uk/caqdas.

How to Use Software in Qualitative Research

In an overview of using computers in qualitative research, Kelle (2000, pp. 295–296) outlines two possible strategies of using software in qualitative research. The first one is rather typical for using computers in grounded theory oriented research (see Chapter 23), starting from developing codes from the empirical material, i.e., the texts:

Step 1:   formatting textual data
Step 2:   coding data with ad hoc codes (open coding)
Step 3:   writing memos and attaching them to text segments

Step 4: comparing text segments to which the same codes have been attached
Step 5: integrating codes and attaching memos to codes
Step 6: developing a core category (Kelle 2000, p. 295)

The second strategy is much more formalized, developing a code scheme in the beginning and a numerical data matrix. Here, the use of computers is planned with a strong interest of linking the qualitative analysis to a more quantitative analysis in the later step.

Step 1: formatting textual data
Step 2: defining a code scheme
Step 3: coding data with the predefined code scheme
Step 4: linking memos to the codes (not to text segments) while coding
Step 5: comparing text segments to which the same codes have been attached
Step 6: developing subcategories from this comparison
Step 7: recode the data with these subcategories
Step 8: producing a numerical data matrix, whereby the rows represent the text documents, the columns the categories (codes), and the values of the categories the subcategories
Step 9: analyzing this data matrix with SPSS (Kelle 2000, p. 296).

These two strategies should only be seen as suggestions about how to proceed. As a user of CAQDAS programs, you should develop your own strategy against the background of the aims and research questions as well as the sorts of data and resources in the project.

Case Study: Social Representation of Aids Among Zambian Adolescents

In their study, Joffe and Bettega (2003) used ATLAS.ti for analyzing interviews with adolescents in Zambia about AIDS. They did 60 semi-structured, depth interviews with Zambian adolescents aged 15 to 20. The interviews and results focused on representations of (1) the origin of HIV/AIDS; (2) the spread of HIV/AIDS; and (3) of the personal risk of HIV/AIDS. With ATLAS.ti, the authors created thematic networks like the one in Figure 26.1, which represents the ideas about the origin of HIV/AIDS mentioned by the participants of the study:

This example shows how you can use software like Atlas.ti to structure your categories and your results. The interesting thing about using such software is the link between category and the original texts (statements, stories) it is linked to.

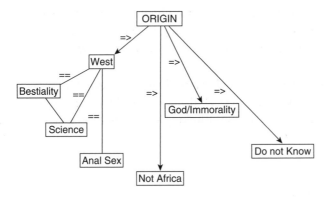

Key: => Caused by
         = = Associated with (reproduced from Joffe and Battega 2003)

FIGURE 26.1   Origin of AIDS Represented in a Thematic Network Produced with Atlas•ti

Source: Joffe and Bcttega

Software's Impact on Qualitative Research: Examples

A discussion about the impact of software on qualitative research has started right from the beginning of the development of the first programs. You find different concerns. First of all, some of the leading programs were developed on the background of a specific approach–coding according to grounded theory–and are more difficult to apply to other approaches. If software does not fit a more sequential interpretation of data, is it just ignored by those researchers using this approach? Or does it change the way of analyzing data? Or does it lead to some kind of common approach, a gold standard of qualitative research (Coffey et al. 1996) in qualitative research? Fielding and Lee (1998) found in their empirical study on software use that two thirds of the projects they interviewed did not use grounded theory but used CAQDAS programs. This shows that the link between software and grounded theory is not as close as some authors suspect. Ten Have (1999) shows how this software can be applied to conversation analysis. Another concern is that software implicitly forces its logical and display structure upon the data and the researcher's analysis. For example, NUD•IST supports developing a hierarchical tree structure of coding. Among its users, a certain inflation of tree structured coding systems can be found. Seale (2000) gives a nice illustration of this problem when he applies NUD•IST and ATLAS.ti to a grounded theory developed by Glaser and Strauss and shows how different the display and the structure of this theory looks in both programs. Finally, there is a fear that the attention attracted by the computer and the software will distract the researcher from the real analytic work–reading, understanding, and contemplating the texts, and so on (e.g., Lee and Fielding 1991). Similarly, Richards and Richards, developers of one of the leading programs (NUD•IST), state: "The computer method can have dramatic implications for the research process and outcomes, from unacceptable restrictions on analysis to unexpected opening out of possibilities" (1998, p. 211). But in the end, it depends on the users and their ways of making the computer and the software useful for the ongoing research and how they reflect what they are doing. Thus, computers and software are pragmatic tools that support qualitative research. Their users should reflect the technologies; impact on the research itself. Neither should they be overloaded with hopes and expectancies, nor should they be demonized. The further development in this field should be watched with interest, but a technological revolution of qualitative research due to PCs and CAQDAS programs in general has not happened so far.

What is the Contribution to the General Methodological Discussion?

The use of computer programs has made the use of analytic techniques like theoretic coding more explicit and transparent. Using computer programs leads to more transparency about how the researcher has developed categories from the analyzed text and applied them to it. This can be documented and communicated among the researchers in the team as well as to readers of the research report, for example. Some authors see an increase of validity in such a form of transparency. Furthermore, such software allows new forms of administrating codes and texts and the links between both and supports new forms of display. It also supports linking textual/verbal and nontextual/visual data in an analysis.

How does the Method Fit into the Research Process?

Software best fits into a grounded theory research in which theoretical coding is applied to develop categories from the material. The limitations of the forms of data that can be used with this software are less restricted. Although other forms of data analysis are compatible with using QDA software, their link to coding and categorizing is the closest.

What are the Limitations of the Method?

One problem with using QDA software is that it is only a tool for facilitating analysis and interpretation, which needs a method to be used. Often you find in articles or other reports about qualitative research the statement of the authors that they used for example Atlas.ti. When this is the only explanation of how the data were analyzed, I sometimes have the impression that the role of the software was misunderstood. In such case, a program is confused with a method instead seeing it as a tool. The incompatibilities with certain approaches in qualitative research are another limitation.

KEY POINTS

- Computer programs for analyzing texts can be helpful, if you decide early enough in the research process to use them and have the time to prepare their use.
- The available programs develop fast, but as in other areas develop fast towards similar features and capacities. Selecting one has to do with availability and personal preferences in the end.
- They do not do the analysis and their impact on the way their users do their research is more limited than critics sometimes see. However, it is crucial to reflect about the way you use the software and how you subordinate it to your style of analysis (and not the other way around).

Exercise 26.1

1. Go to one of the Internet links mentioned in this chapter and download a demonstration version of one (or more) of the programs (e.g., ATLAS•ti or MAXqda). Explore the programs to understand their capabilities.
2. Think of how you could use the program in your study to make your analysis a bit more transparent.
3. How could you use the program to save time or make your work easier?
4. Look for a study that was done without such software. How could software have improved the study you found? What would have been the impact of the software on the analysis?

Note

1   See Richards and Richards (1998); Seale (2000); Weitzman (2000); Weitzman and Miles (1995).

FURTHER READING

These texts give concrete suggestions for using computers in qualitative research and also address problems associated with their use.

Fielding, N. and Lee, R.M. (1998) *Computer Analysis and Qualitative Research*. London: SAGE.
Kelle, U. (2000) "Computer Assisted Analysis: Coding and Indexing," in M. Bauer and G. Gaskell (eds), *Qualitative Researching with Text, Image and Sound*. London: SAGE. pp. 282–298.
Kelle, U. (2004) "Computer Assisted Analysis of Qualitative Data," in U. Flick, E.v. Kardorff and I. Steinke (eds), *A Companion to Qualitative Research*. London: SAGE. pp. 276–283.
Weitzman, E.A. (2000) "Software and Qualitative Research," in N. Denzin and Y.S. Lincoln (eds), *Handbook of Qualitative Research* (2nd edn). London: SAGE. pp. 803–820.
To remain updated with the fast developments in this area, I suggest that you visit: www.soc.surrey.ac.uk/caqdas.

27

TEXT INTERPRETATION: AN OVERVIEW

CHAPTER OBJECTIVES
After reading this chapter, you should be able to

✓ compare the ways of analyzing your data.
✓ identify the strengths and weaknesses of methods of qualitative data analysis in context.
✓ understand your method of data analysis in the context of the research process and of the other stages of your research plan.

Sooner or later in qualitative research texts become the basis of interpretative work and of inferences made from the empirical material as a whole. The starting point is the interpretative understanding of a text, i.e., an interview, a narrative, an observation as these may appear both in a transcribed form and in the form of other documents. In general, the aim is to understand and comprehend each case. However, different attention is paid to the reconstruction of the individual case. In content analysis, you work mainly in relation to categories rather than to cases. For example, the approach adopted by Strauss does not make a principle of a thoroughgoing case analysis. In a similar fashion conversation analyses restrict their focus to the particular socio-linguistic phenomenon under study and dedicate their attention to collecting and analyzing instances of this phenomenon as opposed to attempting analysis of complete cases.

In thematic coding, in the analysis of narrative interviews and in objective hermeneutics, the focus is on conducting case studies and only at a later stage is attention turned to comparing and contrasting cases. Global analysis aims at a rough editing of texts to prepare them for later case-oriented and case-comparing analyses. The understanding of the case in the different interpretative procedures can be located at various points in the range from a consequent idiographic approach to a quasi-nomothetic approach. The first alternative takes the case as case and infers directly from the individual case (an excerpt of a conversation, a biography or a subjective theory) to general structures or regularities expressed in this case. A particularly good example of this approach is objective hermeneutics and other related approaches of case reconstruction. In the second alternative, several examples are collected and–hence, "quasi-nomothetic"–the single statement is at least partly taken out of its context (the case or the process) and its specific structure in favor of the inherent general structure.

The procedures of text interpretation presented and discussed in detail in the preceding chapters may be appropriate to your own research question. As an orientation for a decision for or against a specific procedure, four points of reference can again be outlined.

First Point of Reference: Criteria-Based Comparison of Approaches

The different alternatives for coding and sequential interpretation of texts may be compared (see Table 27.1). The criteria I suggest for this comparison are as follows. The first is the degree to which precautions are taken in each method to guarantee sufficient openness to the specificity of the individual text with regard to both its formal aspects and its content. A second criterion is the degree to which precautions are taken to guarantee a sufficient level of structural and depth analysis in dealing with the text and the degree to which such structures are made explicit. Further criteria for a comparison are each method's contribution to developing the method of text interpretation in general and the main fields of application they were created for or are used in. The problems in applying each method and each method's limitations mentioned in the preceding chapters are again noted for each approach at the end. This display of the field of methodological alternatives of text interpretation allows the reader to locate the individual methods in it.

Second Point of Reference: The Selection of the Method and Checking its Application

As with collecting data, not every method of interpretation is appropriate in each case. Your decision between the methodological alternatives discussed here should be grounded in your own study, its research question, and aims and in the data

TABLE 27.1 Comparison of Methods for the Interpretation of Data

Criteria	Coding and Categorizing		Qualitative Content Analysis	Global Analysis	Conversation and Discourse Analysis		Narrative and Hermeneutic Analysis		Computers CAQDAS – software like ATLAS/ti
	Theoretical Coding	Thematic Coding			Conversation Analysis	Discourse Analysis	Narrative Analysis	Objective Hermeneutics	
Openness to each text by:	• Open coding	• Principle of case analysis • Short characterization of the case	• Explicating content analysis	• Case-oriented edition of texts	• Sequential analysis of the "talk-in-interaction"	• Reconstructing participants' versions	• Sequential analysis of the case	• Sequential analysis of the case	• Allowing open coding of material
Structuring (e.g., deepening) the issue by:	• Axial coding • Selective coding • Basic questions • Constant comparison	• Elaboration of a thematic structure for case analysis • Core and social distribution of perspectives	• Summarizing content analysis • Structuring content analysis	• Overview supports orientation in the search for additional evidence	• Comparative analysis of a collection of cases	• Integration of other forms of texts	• Assessing formal qualities of the text (narrative versus argumentative)	• Group of interpreters • Consulting context • Falsification of hypotheses against the text	• Supporting specific structures of categories (e.g., tree structures in N6)
Contribution to the general development of interpretation as a method	• Combination of induction and deduction • Combination of openness and structuring	• Comparison of groups in relation to the issue after case analysis	• Strongly rule based procedure for reducing large amounts of data	• Complementary suggestion for orienting in texts in coding interpretation	• Formal analysis of natural interaction shows how conversation and talk work	• Reorientation of discourse analysis to contents and social science topics	• Concrete model for interpreting narratives	• Transgressing subjective perspectives • Elaboration of a methodology of text-interpretation	• Making coding more explicit and documentation of coding
Domain of application	• Theory building in all possible domains	• Group comparisons	• Large amounts of data from different domains	• Preparation for other procedures	• Formal analysis of everyday and institutional talk	• Analysis of the contents of everyday and other discourses	• Biographical research	• All sorts of texts and images	• All sorts of texts and images

(Continued)

TABLE 27. 1 (Continued)

| Criteria | Coding and Categorizing | | Qualitative Content Analysis | Global Analysis | Conversation and Discourse Analysis | | Narrative and Hermeneutic Analysis | | Computers CAQDAS – software like ATLAS/ti |
	Theoretical Coding	Thematic Coding			Conversation Analysis	Discourse Analysis	Narrative Analysis	Objective Hermeneutics	
Problems in application	• Fuzzy criteria for when to stop coding	• Time consuming due to case analysis as intermediate step	• Applying the schematic rules often proves difficult	• Fast overview of the text does not replace and may even impede its fine analysis	• Limitation to formal order and to minimal sequences in conversations	• Hardly developed genuine methodology	• Analyses stick to the case which makes generalization difficult	• Transition from the single case to general statements	• Compatibility with sequential methods
Limits of the method	• Flexibility of methodological rules can be learned mainly through practical experience	• Limited to studies to pre-defined comparative groups	• Strongly oriented to quantitative methodology	• Compatibility with sequential analyzes is uncertain	• Limited focus on social science relevant contents	• No concrete definition of the concept of discourse	• Assumption of homology between narrative and reality (in the case of Schütze)	• Concept of structure • Art instead of method	• Not a method, only a tool • Not enough for making an analysis explicit.
References	Böhm (2004); Strauss (1987); Strauss and Corbin (1990/1998)	Flick (1994; 1995); Flick et al. (2003)	Mayring (2000; 2004)	Legewie (1994)	Bergmann (2004b); Drew (1995)	Harré (1998); Potter and Wetherell (1998)	Rosenthal (2004); Rosenthal and Fischer-Rosenhtal (2004)	Reichertz (2004)	www.soc. surrey.ac.uk/ caqdas

that you collected. You should review your decision against the material to be analyzed. Evaluation of an interpretative method and checking its application should be done as early as possible in the process of interpretation–in case analyses no later than after finishing the interpretation of the first case. A central feature of this evaluation is whether the procedure in itself was applied correctly, e.g., whether the principle of strict sequential interpretation was kept to or whether the rules on content analysis were applied. The specific problems the individual interpreter has with the attitude of interpretation demanded by the method should be taken into account. If any problems arise at this level, it makes sense that you, in a group of interpreters, reflect on them and the way you work with the text. If it is impossible to remedy the problems in this way, you should also consider changing the method. Another point of reference for assessing the appropriateness of an interpretative procedure is the level at which you seek results. If you have to analyze large amounts of text with regard to ensuring that your results are representative on the basis of many interviews, approaches like objective hermeneutics may make the attainment of this goal more difficult or even obstruct it. Qualitative content analysis, which would be a more appropriate method for this type of analysis, would not be recommended for deeper case analyses.

Suggestions for deciding on a method of interpretation and for checking the appropriateness of this decision are given in the checklist in Table 27.2.

Third Point of Reference: Appropriateness of the Method to the Issue

The interpretation of data is often the decisive factor in determining what statements you can make about the data and which conclusions you can draw from the empirical material regardless of how it was collected. Here, as with other procedures in qualitative research–despite all the rhetoric surrounding certain approaches–no procedure is appropriate in every case. Procedures like objective hermeneutics were originally developed for the analysis of a specific domain of issues (interaction in families viewed from the perspective of socialization theory). Over time their field of application has been increasingly extended both in terms of materials used for analysis (interviews, images, art, television programs, etc.) and in terms of issues and topics analyzed. Similarly, the approach of Strauss and Corbin (1998) is marked by a claim for more and more general applicability as made clear by the formulation of a very general "coding paradigm" (see Chapter 23). If the postulated applicability of approaches is extended like this, the criterion of appropriateness to the issue will again need to be taken into account. You should reflect on it in two respects. It should be clarified not only to which issues each method of interpretation is appropriate, but also to

TABLE 27.2   Checklist for Selecting a Method of Interpretation and Evaluating its Application

1 *Research question*

Can the method of interpretation and its application address the essential aspects of the research question?

2 *Interpretative procedure*

The method must be applied according to the methodological precautions and targets. There should be no jumping between forms of interpretation, except when this is based on the research question or theoretically.

3 *Interpreter*

Are the interpreters able to apply the type of interpretation? What is the effect of their personal fears and uncertainties in the situation?

4 *Text(s)*

Is the form of interpretation appropriate to the text or the texts? How is their structure, clarity, complexity, and so on taken into account?

5 *Form of data collection*

Does the form of interpretation fit the collected material and the method of data collection?

6 *Scope for the case*

Is there room for the case and its specificity in the framework of the interpretation? Can this specificity become clear also against the framework of the interpretation?

7 *Process of the interpretation*

Did the interpreters apply the form of interpretation correctly? Did they leave enough scope for the material?
Did they manage their roles? (Why not?)
Was the way of handling the text clearly defined? (Why not?)

Analyze the breaks in order to validate the interpretation(s) between the first and second case if possible!

8 *Aim of the interpretation*

Are you looking for delimited and clear answers in their frequency and distribution or complex, multifold patterns, contexts, etc.?
Or do you want to develop a theory or distribution of viewpoints in social groups?

9 *Claim for generalization*

The level on which you want to make statements:
- For the single cases (the interviewed individuals and their biography, an institution, and its impact etc.)?
- Referring to groups (about a profession, a type of institution etc.)?
- General statements?

which it is *not* appropriate, in order to derive the concrete use of the method in a grounded way.

Fourth Point of Reference: Fitting the Method into the Research Process

Finally, you should assess the method you choose for its compatibility with other aspects of the research process. Here you should clarify whether the procedure of interpreting data works well with the strategy of data collection you used. If, when conducting an interview, you paid great attention to the gestalt of the narrative in the interviewee's presentation, it does not make much sense to apply a content analysis on the data in which only a few categories are used which were defined in advance. Attempts to sequentially analyze field notes with objective hermeneutics have proved impractical and unfruitful. Similarly, it needs to be examined whether the method of interpreting data works well with the method of selecting the material (see Chapter 11). Also you should consider whether the theoretical framework of your study corresponds to the theoretical background of the interpretative method (see Chapters 6, 7) and whether both understandings of the research process (see Chapter 8) correspond. If the research process is conceptualized in the classical linear way, much is determined at the beginning of the interpretation– above all which material was collected and how. In this case, you should answer the question of selecting and evaluating an interpretative procedure with regard to these parameters to which it should correspond. In a research process, which is conceptualized in a more circular way, the method of interpretation may determine the decisions made about procedure in the other steps. Here, the collection of data is oriented to the sampling and the method to the needs, which result from the type and the state of interpretation of data (see Chapter 8). At this point, it is clear that you should make the evaluation of methodological alternatives and the decision between them with consideration to the process of the research. Suggestions for answering these questions are provided by the paragraphs about fitting the individual method into the research process, and the research questions and the goals of the concrete empirical application.

KEY POINTS

- None of the methods for analyzing data is the one and only method. Each of them has strengths and weaknesses, which makes them helpful for your own study.
- You should carefully reflect, which method best fits your kind of data and your research question.

- Each method produces a specific structure in the way it suggests and allows you to work with the data.
- Before and during applying a specific method for answering your research question, I suggest that you check and assess whether the method you selected is appropriate or not.

Exercise 27.1

1. Take a study from the literature, which is based on analyzing textual material and consider whether or not the method that was applied was appropriate for the issue under study and the texts involved in the research.
2. Reflect for your own study what your main reasons are why you decided to use this specific method.

FURTHER READING

Methods for Analyzing Texts in Qualitative Research
These resources give you a comparative overview of analytic methods in qualitative research by presenting methods in more detail.

Flick, U., Kardorff, E.v. and Steinke, I. (eds) (2004) *A Companion to Qualitative Research*. London: SAGE (especially chapters 5.10–5.21).
Gibbs, G. (forthcoming) *How To Analyze Data* (book six of the Qualitative Research Kit). London: SAGE.
Silverman, D. (2001) *Interpreting Qualitative Data: Methods for Analyzing Talk, Text and Interaction* (2nd edn). London: SAGE.
Strauss, A.L (1987) *Qualitative Analysis for Social Scientists*. Cambridge: Cambridge University Press.

PART 7

GROUNDING AND WRITING QUALITATIVE RESEARCH

In this final part, we address two major questions: how to evaluate qualitative research, and how to present results and the ways that you produced these results to your audience? The first question becomes increasingly relevant the more that qualitative research becomes established, wants to be taken seriously, and competes with quantitative research in the social sciences or with research in natural sciences for reputation, funding, and legitimacy. In answering this question, you can go two ways. Either, you orient on the discussions about quality criteria and about which ones to use; you will find quite a variety of suggestions for criteria in qualitative research, and you will also find a lot of argumentation criticizing these attempts. Chapter 28 gives an overview of the various criteria and the discussions linked to them. Or, you try to assess the quality of qualitative research beyond criteria, in which case you will use strategies like triangulation or analytic induction to extend the credibility of your research and results. Then you should also answer the question of indication and think about quality management as an alternative way of assessment. In general, it is more the research process as a whole, which becomes relevant for checking the quality of research, rather than the single step, which you would apply a criterion to. Chapter 29 describes such process-oriented strategies of quality management in research. Lastly, Chapter 30 addresses the issue of how to present your research. You can either see this as a technical problem—what are the best ways to write about your research? But this can also be seen as a fundamental problem—how do the researchers' act of writing and their style cover the act of research, the realities in the field, and the perspective of the people that were studied. Then the problem of writing becomes an issue of legitimacy and the problems linked to this issue may drive qualitative research back into the tension between art and method. This will raise questions about the future of qualitative research and its development.

28

QUALITY CRITERIA IN QUALITATIVE RESEARCH

CHAPTER OBJECTIVES
After reading this chapter, you should be able to

✓ understand the problems when you try to apply the standard criteria from quantitative research to qualitative studies.
✓ identify the alternative ways of reformulating traditional criteria.
✓ learn about alternative criteria coming from qualitative researchers.
✓ recognize the general problems linked to the idea of using criteria in qualitative research.

The problem of how to assess qualitative research has not yet been solved. It is repeatedly taken up as an argument in order to raise general questions about the legitimacy of this kind of research. Should qualitative research be assessed with the same criteria and concepts as quantitative research or are there any specific ways of how to assess qualitative research? Are there any generally accepted criteria or strategies for assessing qualitative research and its results? Can research be "valid" and "reliable" without being subject to the traditional ways of assessing validity and reliability? Such questions have dominated the discussions about the value of qualitative research as a specific approach or as part of a wider concept of empirical research.

Selective Plausibilization

One critique often expressed is that the interpretations in and results of qualitative research are made transparent and comprehensible for the reader only by the interweaving of "illustrative" quotations from interviews or observation protocols. Especially where the researchers use this as "the only instrument for documenting their statements," Bühler-Niederberger (1985, p. 475) critically holds that "the credibility passed on by this is not sufficient." Why this is the case is clarified by Girtler, although involuntarily, in a very illustrative way:

> If I now prepare the publication about my research . . . I finally present what is characteristic. In order to make vivid and provable these characteristics or the characteristic rules from which I "understand" the social practice to be studied or which I use to explain it, I quote the corresponding passages from my observational protocols or interviews. Of course, I quote only those passages which I believe illustrate the characteristics of the everyday world under study. (1984, p. 146)

This procedure, which may also be labeled "selective plausibilization," cannot solve the problem of comprehensibility in an adequate way. Above all, it remains unclear how the researchers handle cases and passages, which they "believe" are not so illustrative of the characteristics, or cases and passages that may even be deviant or contradictory.

The different facets of the problem mentioned here could be summarized as "grounding qualitative research." Essentially, four topics fall under this heading:

1. Which criteria should be used to assess the procedure and results of qualitative research in an appropriate way?
2. What degree of generalization of the results can be obtained each time, and how can one guarantee generalization (see Chapter 29)?
3. Are there other ways to address the question of quality in qualitative research more adequately (see Chapter 29)?
4. How do you present procedures and results of qualitative research (see Chapter 30)?

Concerning the criteria for assessing the procedure and results of qualitative research, the following alternatives are discussed in the literature. The first is to apply classical criteria like validity and reliability to qualitative research or to reformulate them in an adequate way for this purpose. The second is to develop new, "method-appropriate criteria," which do justice to the specificity of qualitative research because they have been developed from one of its specific theoretical backgrounds and take the peculiarity of the qualitative research process into account. A third version engages with the discussion about how is it still possible at all to ask about validity, given the crises of representation and legitimation mentioned by Denzin and Lincoln (2000b, p. 17). This last version surely will neither contribute to further establishing the credibility of qualitative research nor contribute to its results being considered as relevant in any way to the community. Therefore, attention will be given here to the first two ways. In terms of the use of classical criteria, the discussion concentrates on reliability and validity.

Reliability

In order to specify the sense of reliability as a criterion for assessing qualitative research, Kirk and Miller (1986) discuss three forms. They see *quixotic reliability* as the attempt to specify how far a particular method can continuously lead to the same measurements or results. The authors reject this form of specifying reliability as trivial and misleading. Especially in the field research, you should view statements or observations, which are stereotypically repeated as an indicator for a purposively shaped version of the event rather than as a clue for how it "really" was. Kirk and Miller discuss *diachronic reliability* as the stability of measurements or observations in their temporal course. What becomes problematic here is the precondition that the phenomenon under study in itself may not undergo any changes, so that this criterion is effective. Qualitative studies are seldom engaged in such unchanging objects. *Synchronic reliability* is the constancy or consistency of results obtained at the same moment but by using different instruments. Kirk and Miller emphasize that this criterion is most instructive when it is *not* fulfilled. The question then follows as to why this is the case and also raises questions concerning the different perspectives on the issue resulting from different methods applied by several researchers.

Procedural Reliability

Reliability receives its importance as a criterion for assessing qualitative research only against the background of a specific theory of the issue under study and about the use of methods. But researchers can go different ways in order to increase the reliability of data and interpretations. In ethnographic research, in terms of which Kirk and Miller discuss these criteria, the quality of recording and documenting data becomes a central basis for assessing their reliability and that of succeeding interpretations. One starting point for examining this is the field notes in which researchers document their observations. Standardization of notes increases the reliability of such data if several observers collect the data. The four forms of field notes that have already been discussed in Chapter 22 on documentation (see also Spradley 1979) are one approach to this structuring. For increasing their reliability, Kirk and Miller (1986, p. 57) suggest conventions for note taking, which are further developed by Silverman (1993, p. 147). These are shown in Box 28.1.

The underlying idea is that the conventions for how to write notes increase the comparability of the perspectives, which have led to the corresponding data. In particular, the separation of concepts of the observed from those of the observers in the notes makes reinterpretation and assessment by different analysts possible. Transcription rules that clarify procedures for transcribing conversations have a similar function to conventions for writing notes in such a way.

Box 28.1   Conventions for Field Notes

Sign	Convention	Use
" "	Double quotation marks	Verbatim quotes
' '	Single quotation marks	Paraphrases
( )	Parentheses	Contextual data or fieldworker's interpretations
< >	Angled brackets	Emic concepts (of the member)
/ /	Slash	Etic concepts (of the researcher)
_____	Solid line	Beginning or end of a segment

Source: adapted from Kirk and Miller 1986; Silverman 1993

For interview data, reliability can be increased by interview training for the interviewers and by checking the interview guides or generative questions in test interviews or after the first interview (see Chapter 16). For observations, the requirement to train the observers before they enter the field and to regularly evaluate the observing can be added. In the interpretation of data, training, and reflexive exchange about the interpretative procedures and about the methods of coding can increase the reliability. From analyzing the opening sequence of a narrative, a hypothesis about the case structure can be derived and falsified against following sequences. This is another way to arrive at reliable interpretations. Assessing categories developed in open coding with other passages has a similar function in grounded theory research. In each of these examples, the attempt is made to check the reliability of an interpretation by testing it concretely against other passages in the same text or against other texts.

In general, the discussion about reliability in qualitative research comes down to the need for explication in two respects. First, the genesis of the data needs to be explicated in a way that makes it possible to check what is a statement of the subject and where the researcher's interpretation begins. Second, procedures in the field or interview and with the text need to be made explicit in training and rechecking in order to improve the comparability of different interviewers or observers' conduct. Finally, the reliability of the whole process will be better the more detailed the research process is documented as a whole. Thus, the criterion of reliability is reformulated in the direction of checking the dependability of data and procedures, which can be grounded in the specificity of the various qualitative methods. Reject other understandings of reliability, such as frequently repeated data collection leading to the same data and results. If this form of reliability is used it may be more convenient to mistrust rather than to trust the dependability of the data.

Validity

In the discussions about grounding qualitative research, validity receives more attention than reliability.[1] The question of validity can be summarized as a question of whether the researchers see what they think they see. Basically, three errors may occur: to see a relation, a principle, and so on where they are not correct (type 1 error); to reject them where they are indeed correct (type 2 error); and finally to ask the wrong questions (type 3 error) (Kirk and Miller 1986, pp. 29–30).

A basic problem in assessing the validity of qualitative research is how to specify the link between the relations that are studied and the version of them provided by the researcher. In other words: what would these relations look like if they were not issues of empirical research at that moment? And is the researcher's version grounded in the versions in the field, in the interviewee's biography, etc., and hence, in the issue?

This implies less that the assumption is made of a reality existing independently of social constructions (i.e., perceptions, interpretations, and presentations) than that the question should be asked as to how far the researcher's specific constructions are empirically grounded in those of the members. In this context, Hammersley (1992, pp. 50–52) outlines the position of a "subtle realism." This position starts from three premises. (1) The validity of knowledge cannot be assessed with certainty. Judge assumptions based their plausibility and credibility. (2) Phenomena also exist independently of our claims concerning them. Our assumptions about them can only more or less approximate these phenomena. (3) Reality becomes accessible across the (different) perspectives on phenomena. Research aims at presenting reality not reproducing it.

If one starts from this position, the question of the validity of qualitative research turns into a different question. How far the researchers' constructions are grounded in the constructions of those whom they studied (cf. Schütz 1962) and how far this grounding is transparent for others (see Chapter 7 on this) are issues. Thus, the production of the data becomes one starting point for judging their validity and the presentation of phenomena and of the inferences drawn from them becomes another one.

Analyzing the Interview Situation

One approach for specifying the validity of interviews is to check formally if it was possible to guarantee the degree of authenticity, which was aimed at during the interview. In the framework of biographical research, this is realized by answering the question of whether the respondent's presentation is a narrative or not. This is an attempt to answer the question of the validity of the statements received in this way by equating an unimpeded narrative (e.g., free of any interventions by the researcher) with a valid depiction. Various authors criticize this approach on the grounds that it only addresses a very limited part of the problem of validity (see Chapter 25).

Legewie (1987, p. 141) made more differentiated suggestions for judging the validity of interview data and especially biographical self-presentations. According to this author, claims for validity made by a speaker in an interview have to be differentiated (and that means having to be judged separately in terms of the following considerations): "(a) That the contents of what is said is correct, (b) that what is said is socially appropriate in its relational aspect . . . and (c) that what is said is sincere in terms of the self-presentation" of the speaker. The point of departure for validating biographical statements is to analyze the interview situation for how far "the conditions of non-strategic communication" were given and whether "goals and particularities of the interview . . . - are negotiated in the form of a more or less explicit . . . "working contract." (1987, pp. 145–149)

The main question here is whether the interviewees were given any cause to consciously or unconsciously construct a specific (i.e., biased) version of their experiences which does not or does not only correspond with their views in a limited way. Analyze the interview situation for any signs of such deformations. This should provide a basis for finding out which systematic deformations or deceptions in the text are a result of the interview situation and how far and how exactly they have to be taken into account in the interpretation. You can further extend such reflections on the side of the researcher by involving the interviewee.

Communicative Validation

Another version of specifying validity aims at involving the actors (subjects or groups) in the research process a little further. One way is to introduce communicative validation at a second meeting after the interview and its transcription (for concrete suggestions see Chapter 13 here). The promise of further authenticity made here is twofold. The interviewees' agreement with the contents of their statements is obtained after the interview. The interviewees develop a structure of their own statements in terms of the complex relations the researcher is looking for (e.g., a subjective theory of trust as a form of everyday knowledge that is relevant for counseling: see Chapter 13 for an example). For a more general application of such strategies, however, two questions remain to be satisfactorily answered. First, how can you design the methodological procedure of communicative validation in such a way that it really does justice to the issues under study and to the interviewees' views? Second, how can the question of grounding data and its results provide answers beyond the subjects' agreement? One way of proceeding here is to attempt a general validation of the reconstruction in a more traditional way.

Reformulating the Concept of Validity

Mishler (1990) goes one step further in reformulating the concept of validity. He starts from the process of validating (instead of from the state of validity) and defines "validation as the social construction of knowledge" (1990, p. 417) by which we "evaluate the 'trustworthiness' of reported observations, interpretations, and generalizations" (1990, p. 419). Finally, "reformulating validation as the social discourse through which trustworthiness is established elides such familiar shibboleths as reliability, falsifiability, and objectivity" (1990, p. 420). As an empirical basis for this discourse and the construction of credibility, Mishler discusses the use of examples from narrative studies.

Lather (1993) picks up several postmodernist and poststructuralist theories. However, she does not reject the question of legitimation and thus the validation of scientific knowledge as a whole, but derives updated concepts of validity, which she sets in four frameworks:

- From Baudrillard she derives the idea of an "ironic validity." The background assumption is that more and more simulacra, as copies without originals, have replaced representations as copies of real objects (1993, p. 677). The consequence for the concept of validity is: "Contrary to dominant validity practices where the rhetorical nature of scientific claims is masked with methodological assurance, a strategy of ironic validity proliferates forms, recognizing that they are rhetorical and without foundation, post-epistemic, lacking in epistemological support."
- From Lyotard (1984) she derives the idea of a "paralogic/neo-pragmatic validity": scientific knowledge does not aim at corresponding with the reality, but aims at discovering differences and at leaving contradictions in their tension. You can specify the validity of knowledge by answering the question of how far these goals have been reached.
- From Deleuze and Guattari (1976) and Derrida (1990), Lather takes the idea of "rhizomatic validity."
- She suggests, as a fourth framework, sensual validity or situated validity. Here the question of the genderedness of knowledge and in looking at scientific knowledge is asked.

How far these concepts contribute anything substantial to answering the question of whether qualitative data and results, or the research, which produced them, manifest a minimum of credibility, remains an open matter.[2] Their main importance is that recent theoretical movements are taken up in order to outline ways to reformulate the concept of validity in the framework of a constructivist understanding of research.

Procedural Validity

For the research process in ethnography, Wolcott suggests nine points, which need to be realized in order to guarantee validity:

> (1) The researcher should refrain from talking in the field but rather should listen as much as possible. He or she should (2) produce notes that are as exact as possible, (3) begin to write early, and in a way (4) which allows readers of his or her notes and reports to see for themselves. This means providing enough data for readers to make their own inferences and follow those of the researcher. The report should be as complete (5) and candid (6) as possible. The researcher should seek feedback on his or her findings and presentations in the field or from his or her colleagues (7). Presentations should be characterized by a balance (8) between the various aspects and (9) by accuracy in writing. (1990a, pp. 127–128)

These steps for guaranteeing validity in the research process can be summarized as an attempt to act sensitively in the field, and above all, as the transferral of the problem of validity in the research to the domain of writing about research (for this see the next chapter). Finally, Altheide and Johnson formulate the concept of "validity as reflexive accounting," which creates a relation between researcher, issues, and the process of making sense and locates validity in the process of research and the different relationships at work in it:

1. the relationship between what is observed (behaviors, rituals, meanings) and the larger cultural, historical, and organizational contexts within which the observations are made (the substance);
2. the relationship among the observer, the observed, and the setting (the observer);
3. the issue of perspective (or point of view), whether the observer's or the members', used to render an interpretation of the ethnographic data (the interpretation);
4. the role of the reader in the final product (the audience);
5. the issue of representational, rhetorical, or authorial style used by the author(s) to render the description and/or interpretation (the style). (1998, pp. 291–292)

In the above suggestions, validation is discussed within the framework of the total research process and the factors involved. These suggestions, however, remain at the programmatic level rather than at the level at which concrete criteria or starting points are formulated, in terms of which individual studies or parts of them may be assessed. All in all, attempts at using or reformulating validity and validation face several problems. Formal analyses of the way the data were produced, for example in the interview situation, do not tell us anything about the contents of these interviews and whether they have been appropriately treated in the further proceeding of the research. The concepts of communicative validation or member check face a special problem. The subjects' consent becomes problematic as a criterion where the research systematically goes beyond the subject's viewpoint, for example in interpretations, which want to permeate into social or psychological unconsciousness or which derive from the distinctiveness of various subjective viewpoints.[3]

The attempts to reformulate the concept of validity that were discussed here are marked by a certain fuzziness, which does not necessarily offer a solution for the problem of grounding qualitative research but rather provides questioning and programmatic statements. As a general tendency, a shift from validity to validation and from assessing the individual step or part of the research towards increasing the transparency of the research process as a whole may be stated (see Chapter 29 for this).

Objectivity

The third classical criterion in empirical research, objectivity, is seldom taken up in discussion about how to evaluate qualitative research. One of the few exceptions is a paper by Maddill, Jordan, and Shirley (2000). They discuss issues of objectivity and reliability in qualitative research for three epistemological backgrounds (realist, contextualist, and radical constructionist epistemologies). The authors show that objectivity, as a criterion, is only appropriate to a realist framework. In such a case, objectivity is interpreted as consistency of meaning, when two or more independent researchers analyze the same data or material. Arriving at the same conclusions surmises them as as objective and reliable. The basic strategy employed here is to triangulate results from different researchers working independently. The authors stress the need for researchers to make their epistemological position clear in order to make an appropriate evaluation of the research and its results possible. This paper is an attempt to discuss objectivity as a criterion for qualitative research rather than a satisfying suggestion of how to use it.

Whether it makes sense or not to apply classical criteria to qualitative research is questioned, because "the 'notion of reality' in both streams of research is too heterogeneous" (Lüders and Reichertz 1986, p. 97). A similar reservation can already be found in Glaser and Strauss: they

> raise doubts as to the applicability of the canons of quantitative research as criteria for judging the credibility of substantive theory based on qualitative research. They suggest rather that criteria of judgement be based on generic elements of qualitative methods for

collecting, analyzing and presenting data and for the way in which people read qualitative analyses. (1965b, p. 5)

From this skepticism, a series of attempts have been made over time to develop "method-appropriate criteria" in order to replace criteria, like validity and reliability.

Alternative Criteria

Since the middle of the 1980s, various attempts to develop alternative criteria for assessing qualitative research can be noted.

Trustworthiness, Credibility, Dependability

Lincoln and Guba (1985) suggest trustworthiness, credibility, dependability, transferability, and confirmability as criteria for qualitative research. The first of these criteria is considered to be the main one. They outline five strategies for increasing the credibility of qualitative research:

- activities for increasing the likelihood that credible results will be produced by a "prolonged engagement" and "persistent observation" in the field and the triangulation of different methods, researchers, and data;
- "peer debriefing": regular meetings with other people who are not involved in the research in order to disclose one's own blind spots and to discuss working hypotheses and results with them;
- the analysis of negative cases in the sense of analytic induction;
- appropriateness of the terms of reference of interpretations and their assessment;
- "member checks" in the sense of communicative validation of data and interpretations with members of the fields under study.

Procedural Dependability: Auditing

Dependability is checked through a process of auditing, based on the procedure of audits in the domain of financing. Thus, an auditing trail is outlined in order to check procedural dependability in the following areas (see also Schwandt and Halpern 1988):

- the raw data, their collection and recording;
- data reduction and results of syntheses by summarizing, theoretical notes, memos, and so on, summaries, short descriptions of cases, etc.;
- reconstruction of data and results of syntheses according to the structure of developed and used categories (themes, definitions, relationships), findings

(interpretations and inferences), and the reports produced with their integration of concepts and links to the existing literature;

- process notes (i.e., methodological notes and decisions concerning the production of trustworthiness and credibility of findings);
- materials concerning intentions and dispositions like the concepts of research, personal notes, and expectations of the participants;
- information about the development of the instruments including the pilot version and preliminary plans (see Lincoln and Guba 1985, pp. 320–327, 382–384).

This concept of auditing is discussed more generally in the framework of quality management (see Chapter 29 for this). Thus, a series of starting points for producing and assessing the procedural rationality in the qualitative research process are outlined. In this way, proceedings and developments in the process of research can be revealed and assessed. In terms of the findings that have already been produced in a particular piece of research, the questions answered through the use of such an assessment procedure can more generally be summarized as follows, according to Huberman and Miles:

- Are findings grounded in the data? (Is sampling appropriate? Are data weighed correctly?)
- Are inferences logical? (Are analytic strategies applied correctly? Are alternative explanations accounted for?)
- Is the category structure appropriate?
- Can inquiry decisions and methodological shifts be justified? (Were sampling decisions linked to working hypotheses?)
- What is the degree of researcher bias (premature closure, unexplored data in the field notes, lack of search for negative cases, feelings of empathy)?
- What strategies were used for increasing credibility (second readers, feedback to informants, peer review, adequate time in the field)? (1998, p. 202)

Although the findings are the starting point for evaluating the research, an attempt is made to do this by combining a result-oriented view with a process-oriented procedure.

Criteria for Evaluating the Building of Theories

The connection of outcome and process-oriented considerations about qualitative research becomes relevant when the development of a grounded theory is the general aim of qualitative research. Corbin and Strauss (1990, p. 16) mention four points of departure for judging empirically grounded theories and the procedures that led to them. According to their suggestion, you should critically assess:

1. the validity, reliability, and credibility of the data,
2. the plausibility, and the value of the theory itself,
3. the adequacy of the research process which has generated, elaborated, or tested the theory, and
4. the empirical grounding of the research findings.

For evaluating the research process itself, they suggest seven criteria:

Criterion 1   How was the original sampling selected? On what grounds (selective sampling)?

Criterion 2   What major categories emerged?

Criterion 3   What were some of the events, incidents, actions, and so on that indicated some of these major categories?

Criterion 4   On the basis of what categories did theoretical sampling proceed? That is, how did theoretical formulations guide some of the data collection? After the theoretical sampling was carried out, how representative did these categories prove to be?

Criterion 5   What were some of the hypotheses pertaining to relations among categories? On what grounds were they formulated and tested?

Criterion 6   Were there instances when hypotheses did not hold up against what was actually seen? How were the discrepancies accounted for? How did they affect the hypotheses?

Criterion 7   How and why was the core category selected? Was the selection sudden or gradual, difficult or easy? On what grounds were the final analytic decisions made? How did extensive "explanatory power" in relation to the phenomenon under study and "relevance" . . . figure in decisions? (1990, p. 17).

Evaluating theory development ends up by answering the question of how far the concepts of the approach of Strauss–like theoretical sampling and the different forms of coding–were applied and whether this application corresponds with the methodological ideas of the authors. Thus, efforts for evaluating proceedings and findings remain within the framework of their own system. A central role is given to the question of whether the findings and the theory are grounded in the empirical relations and data–if it is a grounded theory (building) or not. For an evaluation of the realization of this aim, Corbin and Strauss suggest criteria for answering the question of the empirical grounding of findings and theories:

Criterion 1   Are concepts generated? . . .

Criterion 2   Are the concepts systematically related? . . .

Criterion 3   Are there many conceptual linkages and are the categories well developed? Do the categories have conceptual density? . . .

Criterion 4   Is there much variation built into the theory? . . .

Criterion 5   Are broader conditions that affect the phenomenon under study built into its explanation? . . .

Criterion 6   Has "process" been taken into account? . . .

Criterion 7   Do the theoretical findings seem significant and to what extent? (1990, pp. 17–18)

The point of reference, here again, is the procedure formulated by the authors and whether it has been applied or not. Thus, the methodology of Strauss becomes more formalized. Its evaluation becomes more a formal one: were the concepts applied correctly? The authors see this danger and therefore they included the seventh criterion of relevance in their list. They emphasize that a formal application of the procedures of grounded theory building does not necessarily make for "good research." Points of reference like the originality of the results from the viewpoint of a potential reader, the relevance of the question, and the relevance of the findings for the fields under study, or even for different fields, do not play any role here.[4]

Such aspects, however, are included in the criteria suggested by Hammersley (1992, p. 64) as a synopsis of various approaches for evaluating theories developed from empirical field studies (Box 28.2). These criteria are specific to the evaluation of qualitative research and its procedures, methods and results, and they start from theory building as one feature of qualitative research. The procedure that led to the theory–the degree of development of the theory which is the result of this process, and finally the transferability of the theory to other fields and back into the studied context–become central aspects of evaluating all research.

Box 28.2   Criteria for Theory Development in Qualitative Research

1 The degree to which generic/formal theory is produced.
2 The degree of development of the theory.
3 The novelty of the claims made.
4 The consistency of the claims with empirical observations and the inclusion of representative examples of the latter in the report.
5 The credibility of the account to readers and/or those studied.
6 The extent to which findings are transferable to other settings.
7 The reflexivity of the account: the degree to which the effects on the findings of the researcher and of the research settings employed are assessed and/or the amount of information about the research process that is provided to readers.

Source: Hammersley 1992, p. 64

Traditional or Alternative Criteria: New Answers to Old Questions?

The approaches to grounding qualitative research discussed here provide a methodical approach to analyzing understanding as an epistemological principle. Criteria are defined which serve to judge the appropriateness of the procedures, which were applied. Central questions are how appropriately each case (whether a subject or a field) has been reconstructed, with how much openness it was approached, and what controls have been installed in the research process in order to assess this openness. One starting point is to reflect upon the construction of social realities in the field under study and in the research process. The decisive question, however, is whose constructions were addressed and were successful in the process of knowledge production and in the formulation of the results–those of the researcher, or those met in the studied field. Then the problem of grounding qualitative research is made concrete with three questions: How far are the researchers' findings based on the constructions in the field? How are the translation and documentation of these constructions in the field into the texts, which are the empirical material, made? How did the researcher proceed from the case study to the developed theory or to the general patterns found? Grounding qualitative research becomes a question of analyzing the research as process. After discussing the alternatives mentioned, the impression remains that both strategies–the application of traditional criteria and the development of alternative, specific criteria–have featured in recent discussions and that neither has yet given a really satisfactory answer to the problem of grounding qualitative research.

The equation or connection of alternative and traditional criteria by Miles and Huberman (1994, p. 278) outlines an interesting perspective for structuring this field:

- objectivity/confirmability;
- reliability/dependability/auditability;
- internal validity/credibility/authenticity;
- external validity/transferability/fittingness;
- utilization/application/action orientation.

But at the same time, this equation makes clear that attempts to reformulate criteria for qualitative research did not really lead to new solutions. Rather, the problems with traditional criteria derived from different backgrounds have to be discussed for alternative criteria as well.

Quality Assessment as a Challenge for Qualitative Research

Nevertheless, the question of how to assess the quality of qualitative research is currently raised in three respects. First, by the researchers who want to check and secure their proceeding and their results. Second, by the consumers of qualitative research–the readers of publications or the funding agencies, who want to assess what has been presented to them; and finally in the evaluation of research in reviewing research proposals and in peer reviews of manuscripts submitted to journals. In the latter context, you will find a growing number of guidelines for evaluating research papers (articles, proposals, etc.) Seale (1999, p. 189–192) presents a criteria catalog of the British Sociological Association Medical Sociology, which includes a set of questions referring to 20 areas from research questions to sampling, collection and analysis of data, or presentations and ethics. The guiding questions are helpful, but it you want to answer them, you are drawn back to your own–maybe implicit–criteria. For example, when you want an answer in area 19 ("Are the results credible and appropriate?"), the question "Do they address the research question(s)?" (p. 192) is suggested.

Another catalog has been presented by the National Institutes of Health, Office of Behavioral and Social Sciences (NIH 2001) for the field of Public Health. Here, especially questions of design have been emphasized. Analysis and interpretations are summarized under design as well as the combination of qualitative and quantitative research. A checklist complements the catalog with items like "Data collection procedures are fully explained" (p. 16).

Elliot, Fischer, and Rennie (1999) have developed a catalog of guidelines for publishing qualitative research, with two parts. One can be applied both to quantitative and qualitative research; the second part is focused on the special character of qualitative research and includes concepts like member checks, peer debriefing, triangulation, etc. But as the strong reaction of Reicher (2000) shows, that despite these guidelines' rather general formulation, they are not consensual for different forms of qualitative research.

Quality Criteria or Strategies of Quality Assurance?

These catalogs show basically one thing: Qualitative research will be confronted with issues of quality from the outside, even if it does not answer such questions internally. If criteria are set up, shall they be applied to any form of qualitative research or do we need specific criteria for the single approach? Can we set up criteria, which include a benchmark for deciding the question of good and bad research? How much authenticity is necessary, and what is a nonsufficient authenticity? In quantitative research, criteria like reliability come with benchmarks of enough and not enough reliability, which makes the decision between good and bad research simple. Therefore, another distinction may become relevant for qualitative research. Do we look for criteria or do we need strategies of quality assessment? Maybe it is very difficult to frame the "real" qualities of qualitative research in criteria. How can you evaluate in an exploratory study, what this study really produced as new knowledge? How can you evaluate whether or not methods were appropriate to the field and the research question? How can you judge the originality in approaching the field and in creating or using methods? How can you evaluate creativity in collecting and analyzing empirical material? Yardley (2000) discusses "dilemmas in qualitative research" in this context. So in the end, perhaps thinking about strategies, which will be discussed in the following chapter, will be the more promising way than formulating criteria.

KEY POINTS

- Traditional criteria often miss the specific features of qualitative research and data.
- There are many suggestions for alternative criteria, but none of them solves the problem of adequate quality assessment.
- One issue is whether to develop criteria for qualitative research as a whole or for specific approaches in qualitative research.
- Criteria can focus on formal aspects (was the method applied correctly?) or on the quality of the insights produced by the research (what's new?).
- Quality assessment is a challenge, which qualitative research is confronted with from outside entities (funding agencies, customers of qualitative research, and results).

Exercise 28.1

1. Take several articles reporting qualitative research. Identify how the authors assess the quality of their research and which criteria did they use.
2. Take your own research and ask the question: Why did I take these cases, and why did I take these examples, excerpts, and so on for presenting my results?
3. Why are my results valid? And for what?

Notes

1 For example in Hammersley (1990; 1992), (Kvale 1989) and Wolcott (1990a).
2 For a while, communicative validation was also discussed for the interpretation of texts. Not only due to the ethical problems that arise in the confrontation of interviewees with interpretations of their statements (see Köckeis-Stangl 1982), this notion of communicative validation has lost its importance.
3 One problem in approaches like Lather's is that questions and concepts of postmodernity are picked up with great enthusiasm. However, second-hand quotations predominate and the treatment of the concepts remains more or less oriented to the shells of the words. This impression is also given in several of the contributions to Denzin and Lincoln (2000a), especially about the grounding of qualitative research. Thus, more questions are raised than ways are mapped for treating problems linked to specifying validity.
4 This question is addressed less to Strauss's concept of research than to the attempts of evaluating it in Corbin and Strauss (1990).

FURTHER READING

Reliability
These texts give good overviews of the problematics of reliability in qualitative research.

Kirk, J.L. and Miller, M. (1986) *Reliability and Validity in Qualitative Research.* Beverly Hills, CA: SAGE.
Silverman, D. (1993/2001) *Interpreting Qualitative Data: Methods For Analyzing Talk, Text and Interaction.* London: SAGE.

Validity
These texts give good overviews of the problematics of validity in qualitative research.

Hammersley, M. (1990) *Reading Ethnographic Research: A Critical Guide.* London: Longman.
Hammersley, M. (1992) *What's Wrong with Ethnography?* London: Routledge.
Kvale, S. (ed.) (1989) *Issues of Validity in Qualitative Research.* Lund: Studentlitteratur.

Alternative Criteria
In these texts, the authors most consistently try to develop alternative criteria for qualitative research.

Lincoln, Y.S. and Guba, E.G., (1985*) Naturalistic Inquiry.* London: SAGE.
Seale, C. (1999) *The Quality of Qualitative Research.* London: SAGE.

Theory Evaluation
These two references give a good overview of how to evaluate theories grounded in and resulting from qualitative research.

Corbin, J. and Strauss, A. (1990) "Grounded Theory Research: Procedures, Canons and Evaluative Criteria," *Qualitative Sociology,* 13: 3–21.
Hammersley, M. (1992*) What's Wrong with Ethnography?* London: Routledge.

General Overview
Flick, U. (2006a) *How To Evaluate Qualitative Research* (Book eight of the Qualitative Research Kit). London: SAGE.

29

THE QUALITY OF QUALITATIVE RESEARCH: BEYOND CRITERIA

CHAPTER OBJECTIVES

After reading this chapter, you should be able to

- ✓ understand the ways of addressing the issue of quality in qualitative research beyond criteria.
- ✓ identify the potential and problem of answering the question of indication of methods.
- ✓ recognize the strategies of triangulation and analytic induction and their contribution to answering the question of quality.
- ✓ distinguish the problems and ways of generalization in qualitative research.
- ✓ understand the potential of process evaluation and quality management in research.

In this chapter some issues of enhancing and ensuring the quality of qualitative research will be discussed, which go beyond the idea of quality criteria (see Chapter 28 for this). The idea behind this chapter is that quality in qualitative research cannot be reduced to formulating criteria and benchmarks for deciding about good and bad use of methods. Instead, the issue of quality in qualitative research is located on the level of research planning–from indication of research designs and methods to quality management–on the level of process evaluation, research training, and the relation of attitude and technology–or art and method–in research (see also Chapter 30). Thus, the focus of this chapter will be on when to use qualitative research and when to use which kind of qualitative research and on how to manage quality in the research as approaches to describe (good) qualitative research.

Indication of Qualitative Research

From a methodological point of view, one of the interesting questions in qualitative research is: What makes us decide to use a specific method in our research? Is it habit? Is it a tradition of research? Is it the researcher's experience with this method? Or is it the issue under study, which drives the decision for or against certain methods?

Transferring the Idea of Indication from Therapy to Research

Not only in the field of qualitative research, but also in empirical research in general, textbooks of methodology hardly give any help with deciding to select a specific method for a study. Most books treat the single method or research design separately and describe their features and problems. In most cases, they do not arrive at a comparative presentation of the different methodological alternatives or at giving starting points for how to select a specific method (and not a different one) for a research issue. Thus, one need for qualitative research is to further clarify the question of indication. In medicine or psychotherapy, the appropriateness of a certain treatment for specific problems and groups of people is checked. This is named as indication. The answer to this question is whether or not a specific treatment is appropriate (indicated) for a specific problem in a specific case. If transferred to qualitative research, the relevant questions are, when are certain qualitative methods appropriate and also appropriate for which issue? Which research question? Which group of people (population) or fields to be studied? And so on. When are quantitative methods or a combination of both indicated? (See Table 29.1.)

How to Choose Appropriate Methods?

The checklist in Table 29.2 includes orienting questions that should be helpful for deciding which research design and/or method to select for a concrete study. Questions 1 and 2 should be answered by checking the literature about the issue of the study. If there is little knowledge and a need for or an explicit interest in exploring field and issue, the researcher should select methods that approach the issue, participants' views, or social processes in a very open way (e.g., ethnography or narrative rather than semi-structured interviews). For selecting methods with more openness the information in the categories are as follows: "openness to the interviewee's subjective view by" (Table 16.1), "openness to the observed person's subjective view by" or "openness to the process of actions and interactions by" (Table 21.1), and "openness to each text" (Table 27.1) can be used. Questions 2, 5, and 7 in Table 29.2 refer to the way theory and method match in the study.

TABLE 29.1 Indication of Qualitative Research Methods

Psychotherapy and Medicine			Qualitative Research		
Which disease, symptoms, diagnosis, population	**indicate**	which treatment or therapy?	Which issue, population, research question, knowledge of issue and population When is a particular method appropriate and indicated? How do you make a rational decision for or against certain methods?	**indicate**	which method or methods?
			1 When is a particular method appropriate and indicated? 2 How do you make a rational decision for or against certain methods?		

TABLE 29.2 Checklist for Selecting a Qualitative Research Method

1	What do I know about the issue of my study, or how detailed is my knowledge already?
2	How developed is the theoretical or empirical knowledge in the literature about the issue?
3	Am I more interested in exploring the field and the issue of my study?
4	What is the theoretical background of my study, and which methods fit this background?
5	What is it that I want to get close to in my study–personal experiences of (a group) of certain people or social processes in the making? Or am I more interested in reconstructing the underlying structures of my issue?
6	Do I start with a very focused research question right away, or do I start from a rather unfocused approach in order to develop the more focused questions underway in the process of my project?
7	What is the aggregate I want to study–personal experiences, interactions or situations, or bigger entities like organizations or discourse?
8	Is it more the single case (e.g., of a personal illness experience or of a certain institution) I am interested in or the comparison of various cases?
9	What are resources (time, money, wo/manpower, skills . . .) available to run my study?
10	What are the characteristics of the field I want to study and of the people in it? What can you request of them and what not?
11	What is the claim of generalization of my study?

You can also refer to Table 2.2 in Chapter 2 for an overview of the research perspectives and theoretical positions discussed in Chapters 6 and 7; it also allocates the methods of data collection and interpretation to them, which are also discussed in Chapters 13 to 25.

Question 6 in Table 29.2 refers to the information given in the categories "structuring the issue by" (Tables 16.1 and 21.1) and "structuring the analysis by" (Table 27.1). Here, information is given as to what kind of structure the single method provides or supports. Questions 7 and 8 in Table 29.2 refer to the decision for methods that are case sensitive (e.g., narrative interviews or objective hermeneutics) or for those that are more oriented to immediately comparing cases (e.g., semi-structured interviews or coding and categorizing methods). This alternative is also alluded to in question 9 as case sensitive methods are rather demanding in the resources (time and wo/man power in particular) needed.

The preceding chapters of this book have dealt with the major steps of the qualitative research process and with the different methods available and used in qualitative research. They, and especially the overview chapters (16, 21 and 27), give starting points for allocating methods to the answers to the questions in Table 29.2. Not only should the decision be prepared by using this information, but also the decisions taken in this process should be reflected for their consequences and impact on the data and the knowledge to be obtained.

Rules of Thumb and Key Questions for Reflecting Research Steps and Methods

There is no one right method to use in qualitative research. This form of commitment is not appropriate to qualitative research. But there are some other forms of commitment necessary in qualitative research. Research should be methodologically planned and based on principles and reflection. Notions like fixed and well-defined paradigms rather obstruct the way to the issue under study than they open new and appropriate ways to it. Take and reflect upon decisions for theory and method in qualitative research in a knowledge-based way. Table 29.3 gives some rules of thumb about how to make decisions during the research process and some key questions to reflect what has been decided and applied in the ongoing research process.

Taking these rules of thumb seriously and asking these questions should help qualitative researchers evaluate their decisions on a background of consideration and reflection. They will prevent qualitative researchers from sticking to methods not appropriate to the concrete case of their research and from being trapped in fundamentalist trench fights of qualitative versus quantitative research, as well as those fights among research paradigms in qualitative research (see also Chapter 3).

To think about the question of indication of qualitative research methods and approaches is a way of arriving at methodological decisions. These decisions then will be driven by the idea of appropriateness of methods and approaches to the

TABLE 29.3 Rules of Thumb and Key Questions for Reflecting on Research Steps and Methods

1	Decide and reflect on whether to select qualitative or quantitative research. Why qualitative research? Which reasons do you have for the one or the other? What are your expectations to the (qualitative) research that you plan?
2	Reflect on the theoretical background of your knowledge interest. What is the impact of your setting on the research? How open and how closed is your access to what you want to study?
3	Carefully plan your study, but allow for reconsidering the steps and modifying them according to the state of the study. What are the resources available for the study? How realistic are the aims of your research in relation to the available resources? What are necessary and appropriate shortcuts?
4	Carefully plan your sampling. What are your cases? What do they stand for?
5	Think about whom in the field you should contact and inform about your research. Reflect about the relation to establish to field subjects. What can you learn about your research field and issues from the way you get into the field or are rejected?
6	Think about why you chose the special method of collecting data. Was it a decision for a pet method (the one you or your colleagues have always used) due to habitual reasons? What could or would alternative methods provide? What are the impacts of the methods you use on your data and your knowledge?
7	Plan how to document your data and research experiences. How exactly should you write your notes? What do you need as information to document systematically? What are the influences of the documentation on your research and on your field subjects? What are the impacts of the documentation on your methods of collection and analysis?
8	Think about the aims of your data analysis. Was it a decision for a pet method (the one you or your colleagues have always used) due to habitual reasons? What could or would alternative methods provide? What are the impacts of the methods you use on your data and your knowledge?
9	Think about the way you want to present what you have experienced in the field and found in your research. What are the target audiences of your writing? What is it you want to convince them about your research? What is the impact of the format of your writing on your research and its findings?

(Continued)

TABLE 29.3   (Continued)

10	Plan how to establish the quality of your research. What are the quality criteria your research should meet? How shall these criteria be realized? What is their impact on your research and your field subjects or relationships?
11	Think carefully whether or not you want to use computers and software in the research. Which computers or software do you want to use? What are your expectancies and aims in using them? Why do you use them? What is their impact on your research and your field subjects or relationships?

issue under study, to the research question you want to answer, and to the fields and people addressed by the research. It is the first step in ensuring and enhancing the quality of qualitative research, which should be followed by strategies to enhance the quality of research. New ways of research evaluation are necessary. In the next step, we will discuss two strategies, which are alternatives to the idea of criteria for evaluating qualitative research.

Triangulation

This keyword is used to name the combination of different methods, study groups, local and temporal settings, and different theoretical perspectives in dealing with a phenomenon. Denzin (1989b, pp. 237–241) distinguishes four types of triangulation. *Data triangulation* refers to the use of different data sources, which should be distinguished from the use of different methods for producing data. As "subtypes of data triangulation," Denzin makes a distinction between time, space, and persons and suggests studying phenomena at different dates and places and from different persons. Thus, he comes close to Glaser and Strauss's strategy of theoretical sampling. In both cases, the starting point is to involve purposively and systematically persons, and study groups, local and temporal settings in the study.

As a second type of triangulation, Denzin names *investigator triangulation*. Different observers or interviewers are employed to detect or minimize biases resulting from the researcher as a person. This does not mean a simple division of labor or delegation of routine activities to assistants but rather a systematic comparison of different researchers' influences on the issue and the results of the research.

Theory triangulation is the third type in Denzin's systematology. The starting point is "approaching data with multiple perspectives and hypotheses in mind . . . Various theoretical points of view could be placed side by side to assess their utility and power" (1989b, pp. 239–240). However, the purpose of the exercise is to extend the possibilities for producing knowledge.

As a fourth type, Denzin mentions *methodological triangulation*. Here again, two subtypes should be differentiated: within-method and between-method triangulation. An example for the first strategy is to use different subscales for measuring an item in a questionnaire, whereas an example for the second is to combine the questionnaire with a semi-structured interview.

Triangulation was first conceptualized as a strategy for validating results obtained with the individual methods. The focus, however, has shifted increasingly towards further enriching and completing knowledge and towards transgressing the (always limited) epistemological potentials of the individual method. Thus, Denzin now emphasizes that the "triangulation of method, investigator, theory, and data remains the soundest strategy of theory construction" (1989b, p. 236).

An extension of this approach is the systematic triangulation of the several theoretical perspectives (Flick 1992) linked to the various qualitative methods. For example, conducting interviews for reconstructing a subjective theory (e.g., about trust in counseling) and using conversation analysis to study how the subjective theory is mobilized and trust is invoked during counseling conversations. Thus, the orientation to the subject's point of view is linked to the perspective of producing social realities (see Chapter 6).

Triangulation may be used as an approach for further grounding the knowledge obtained with qualitative methods. Grounding here does not mean to assess results but to systematically extend and complete the possibilities of knowledge production. Triangulation is less a strategy for validating results and procedures than an alternative to validation (cf. Denzin and Lincoln 2000b; Flick 1992; 2004a,c), which increases scope, depth, and consistency in methodological proceedings.

Analytic Induction

Florian Znaniecki (1934) introduced analytic induction. This strategy explicitly starts from a specific case. According to Bühler-Niederberger it can be characterized as follows:

> Analytic induction is a method of systematic interpretation of events, which includes the process of generating hypotheses as well as testing them. Its decisive instrument is to analyze the exception, the case, which is deviant to the hypothesis. (1985, p. 476)

This procedure of looking for and analyzing deviant cases is applied after a preliminary theory (hypothesis pattern or model, etc.) has been developed. Analytic induction is oriented to examining theories and knowledge by analyzing or integrating negative cases. The procedure of analytic induction includes the steps in Box 29.1.

Box 29.1   Steps of Analytic Induction

1 A rough definition of the phenomenon to be explained is formulated.
2 A hypothetical explanation of the phenomenon is formulated.
3 A case is studied in the light of this hypothesis to find out whether the hypothesis corresponds to the facts in this case.
4 If the hypothesis is not correct, either the hypothesis is reformulated or the phenomenon to be explained is redefined in a way that excludes this case.
5 Practical certainty can be obtained after a small number of cases have been studied, but the discovery of each individual negative case by the researcher or another researcher refutes the explanation and calls for its reformulation.
6 Further cases are studied, the phenomenon is redefined and the hypotheses are reformulated until a universal relation is established; each negative case calls for redefinition or reformulation.

Source: adapted from Bühler-Niederberger 1985, p. 478

Lincoln and Guba (1985) took up the concept of the "analysis of negative cases." There are links to questions of generalization of case studies (see below), but analytic induction has its own importance as a procedure for assessing analyses. Both of these approaches can be seen as strategies to increase the quality of qualitative research going beyond the use of quality criteria.

Generalization in Qualitative Research

The generalization of concepts and relations found from analysis is another strategy of grounding qualitative research. At the same time, if the question is asked as to which considerations and steps have been applied in order to specify these domains, this is a starting point for the evaluation of such concepts. This is discussed as generalization. The central points to consider in such an evaluation are first the analyses, and second the steps taken to arrive at more or less general statements. The problem of generalization in qualitative research is that its statements are often made for a certain context or specific cases and based on analyses of relations, conditions, processes, and so on in them. This attachment to contexts often allows qualitative research a specific expressiveness. However, when attempts are made at generalizing the findings, this context link has to be given up in order to find out whether the findings are valid independently of and outside specific contexts. In highlighting this dilemma, Lincoln and Guba (1985) discuss this problem under the heading of "the only generalization is: there is no generalization." But in terms of the "transferability of findings from one context to another" and "fittingness as to the degree of comparability of different contexts," they outline criteria and ways for judging the generalization of findings beyond a given context.

Correspondingly, various possibilities are discussed for mapping out the path from the case to the theory in a way that will allow you to reach at least a certain generalization. A first step is to clarify which degree of generalization you aim at and is possible to obtain with the concrete study in order to derive appropriate claims for generalization. A second step is the cautious integration of different cases and contexts in which the relations under study are empirically analyzed. The generalizability of the results is often closely linked to the way the sampling is done. Theoretical sampling, for example, offers a way of designing the variation of the conditions under which a phenomenon is studied as broadly as possible. The third step is the systematic comparison of the collected material. Here again, the procedures for developing grounded theories can be drawn on.

The Constant Comparative Method

In the process of developing theories, and additional to the method of "theoretical sampling" (see Chapter 11), Glaser (1969) suggests the "constant comparative method" as a procedure for interpreting texts. It basically consists of four stages: "(1) comparing incidents applicable to each category, (2) integrating categories and their properties, (3) delimiting the theory, and (4) writing the theory" (1969, p. 220). For Glaser, the systematic circularity of this process is an essential feature:

> Although this method is a continuous growth process—each stage after a time transforms itself into the next—previous stages remain in operation throughout the analysis and provide continuous development to the following stage until the analysis is terminated (1969, p. 220).

This procedure becomes a method of *constant* comparison when interpreters take care that they compare coding over and over again with codes and classifications that have already been made. Material, which has already been coded, is not finished with after its classification but is continually integrated into the further process of comparison.

Contrasting Cases and Ideal Type Analysis

The constant comparison is further developed and systematized in strategies of contrasting cases. Gerhardt (1988) had made the most consistent suggestions based on the construction of ideal types, going back to Max Weber (1949). This strategy includes several steps. After reconstructing and contrasting the cases with one another, types are constructed. Then "pure" cases are tracked down. Compared with these ideal types of processes, the understanding of the individual case can be made more systematic. After constructing further types, this process comes to an end by structure understanding (i.e., the understanding of relationships pointing beyond the individual case). The main instruments are the *minimal* comparison of cases that are as similar as possible, and the *maximal* comparison of cases that are as different as possible. They are compared for differences and correspondences. The comparisons become more and more concrete with respect to the range of issues included in the empirical material. The endpoints of this range receive special attention in the maximal comparison, whereas its center is focused in the minimal comparison. In a similar way, Rosenthal (1993) suggests the minimal and maximal contrasting of individual cases for a comparative interpretation of narrative interviews. Haupert (1991) structures the cases according to "reconstructive criteria" in order to develop a typology from such interviews. Biographies with maximal similarities are classified in groups, which are labeled as empirical types in the further proceedings. For each type, specific everyday situations are distilled from the material and analyzed across the individual cases.

Generalization in qualitative research is the gradual transfer of findings from case studies and their context to more general and abstract relations, for example a typology. The expressiveness of such patterns can then be specified for how far different theoretical and methodological perspectives on the issue–if possible by different researchers–have been triangulated and how negative cases were handled. The degree of generalization striven for in individual studies should also be taken into consideration. Then, the question of whether the intended level of generalization has been reached becomes a further criterion for evaluating results of qualitative research and of the process, which led to them.

Process Evaluation and Quality Management

The question of grounding qualitative research has not yet been answered in a definite way (see Chapter 28). Starting from this observation is the need to try new ways of evaluation and of specifying quality in qualitative research. One starting point comes from the process character of qualitative research (see Chapter 8) as well as from procedural specifications of reliability and of the evaluation of theory building (see Chapter 28): to specify and even more to produce the grounding of qualitative research in relation to the research process.

Process Evaluation

Qualitative research is embedded in a process in a special way. It does not make sense to ask and answer questions of sampling or concerning special methods in an isolated way. Whether a sampling is appropriate can only be answered with regards to the research question, to the results, and to the generalizations that are aimed at and to the methods used. Abstract measures like the representativeness of a sample, which can be judged generally, do not have any benefit here. A central starting point for answering such questions is the sounding of the research process, which means whether the sampling that was applied harmonizes with the concrete research question and with the concrete process. Activities for optimizing qualitative research in the concrete case have to start from the stages of the qualitative research process. Correspondingly, note a shift in the accent of evaluating qualitative methods and their use from a mere evaluation of the application to a process evaluation.

This kind of process evaluation has been realized first at the Berlin research association "Public Health," in which 23 research projects worked with qualitative and/or quantitative methods on various health-related questions. For example, questions of networking among social services and programs, ways of how to design an everyday life outside hospital, citizen's participation in health relevant urban planning and administration, and the organization of preventative interventions were studied. The different projects use narrative and semi-structured interviews, participant observations, conversation analysis, or theoretical coding among other methods. I directed a cross-sectional project called "Qualitative Methods in Health Sciences" in that context, which served as a methodological support and process evaluation. Starting from a process-oriented understanding of qualitative research, a continuous program of project consultations, colloquia, and workshops was established. In this program, the different projects in this association were consulted and evaluated according to the stages of the qualitative research process (formulation and circumscription of the research question, sampling, collection and interpretation of data, grounding, and generalization of results). This program serves to define a framework for a discussion of methodological questions of operationalization of the research question and the application of methods across projects. This means a shift in emphasis from an evaluation that views methods and their application in isolation to a process evaluation, which takes the specific character of research process and issue into account. The *leitmotiv* of this shift is that the application of qualitative methods should be judged for its soundness with regard to its embedding in the process of research and to the issue of the study and less for its own sake.

Thus, the aspect of grounding is shifted to the level of the research process. The aim of this shift is also to underscore a different understanding of quality in qualitative research and to relate it to a concrete project.

Quality Management
Impulses for further developments can be provided by the general discussion about quality management (Kamiske and Brauer 1995), which is led mainly in the areas of industrial production but also of public services (Murphy 1994). This discussion surely cannot be transferred to qualitative research without restrictions.

But some of the concepts and strategies used in this discussion may be adopted to promote a discussion about quality in research, which is appropriate to the issues and research concepts. The concept of auditing is discussed in both areas (see Chapter 28; Lincoln and Guba 1985). It provides first intersections: "An audit is understood as a systematic, independent examination of an activity and its results, by which the existence and appropriate application of specified demands are evaluated and documented" (Kamiske and Brauer 1995, p. 5).

In particular the "procedural audit" is interesting for qualitative research. It should guarantee that "the pre-defined demands are fulfilled and are useful for the respective application . . . Priority is always given to an enduring remedy of causes of mistakes, not only a simple detection of mistakes" (Kamiske and Brauer 1995, p. 8). Such specifications of quality are not conducted abstractly–for certain methods *per se,* but with regards to the client-orientation (pp. 95–96) and the co-workers' orientation (pp. 110–111).

On the first point ask who are the clients of qualitative research. Quality management differentiates between internal and external clients. Whereas the latter are the consumers of the product, the former are those who are involved in its production in a broader sense (e.g., employees in other departments). For qualitative research, this distinction may be translated as follows. External clients are those outside the project for whom its results are produced (overseers, reviewers, and so on as external clients). Then, internal clients are those for and with whom one attempts to obtain the result (interviewees, institutions under study, etc.). Concepts like "member checks" or communicative validation (see Chapter 28) explicitly take this orientation into account. Designing the research process and proceeding in a way, which gives enough room to those who are studied, realizes this orientation implicitly. For an evaluation, both aspects may be analyzed explicitly: how far did the study proceed in a way that it answered its research question (orientation on external clients) and did it give enough room to the perspectives of those who were involved as interviewees (orientation on internal clients)?

Box 29.2   Principles of Quality Management in the Qualitative Research Process

- Make sure a definition of the goals and the standards of the project are as clear as possible; and that all researchers and co-workers integrate themselves in this definition.
- Define how these goals and standards, and more generally, the quality is obtained; and finally, a consensus about the way to apply certain methods (perhaps through joint interview training) and its analysis is a precondition for quality in the research process.
- Provide a clear definition of the responsibilities for obtaining quality in the research process.
- Allow the transparency of the judgement and the assessment and quality in the process.

The co-worker orientation wants to take into account that "quality arises from applying suitable techniques but on the basis of a corresponding mentality" (Kamiske and Brauer 1995, p. 110). Transferred to qualitative research, this underlines that not only the application of methods essentially determine its quality, but also the attitude, with which the research is conducted. Another point of departure here is "to give responsibility (for quality) to the co-workers by introducing self-assessments instead of outside control" (Kamiske and Brauer 1995, p. 111). Quality in the qualitative research process can be realized, like elsewhere, if it is produced and assessed together with the researchers involved. First, they define together what should be and what is understood as quality in this context. Quality management then includes "activities . . . defining the quality policy, the goals and the responsibilities and realizing these by means of quality planning, quality steering, quality assessment/quality management, and quality improvement" (ISO 9004, quoted in Kamiske and Brauer 1995, p. 149).

These guiding principles of quality management are summarized in Box 29.2. They can be realized by defining the goals, documenting process and problems, and by regularly reflecting jointly about process and problems. Joint process evaluation in connection with consultation, training, and retraining, as outlined above, can be an instrument for realizing quality management in qualitative research. Other strategies will follow and advance the discussion about the appropriate realization and evaluation of qualitative research. A definition of quality in research, and how to realize and guarantee it in the process which is appropriate to the issue, and the experience that quality can only be produced through a combination of methods and a corresponding attitude, are links to the discussion about quality management.

KEY POINTS

- The quality of qualitative research often lies beyond what you can assess by applying criteria.
- A crucial and often neglected point is to answer the question of indication: Why this method, why qualitative research, and so on in this specific research?
- Strategies like triangulation and analytic induction can sometimes contribute more and give more additional insights about the quality of qualitative research than criteria.
- Generalization in qualitative research means to ask two questions: To which social entities can I generalize or transfer my findings? And what are the limitations of my findings?
- Process evaluation and quality management extend the issue of quality to assessing the whole research process.

Exercise 29.1

1. Take your own research and decide how to generalize your results.
2. Think about the forms of triangulation that could have extended your findings and what extra insights they offer.
3. Are there any negative cases (which your results do not fit to) in your study? How did you deal with them?
4. Apply the principles of quality management (Box 29.2) to your own research.

FURTHER READING

The following text outlines indication, process evaluation, and quality management of qualitative research.

Flick, U. (2006b) *Qualitative Research in Psychology: A Textbook.* London: SAGE.

Triangulation
These texts discuss the strategy of triangulation in qualitative research.

Denzin, N.K. (1989b) *The Research Act* (3rd edn). Englewood Cliffs, NJ: Prentice Hall.
Flick, U. (1992) "Triangulation Revisited: Strategy of or Alternative to Validation of Qualitative Data," *Journal for the Theory of Social Behavior*, 22: 175–97.
Flick, U. (2004a) "Triangulation in Qualitative Research," in U. Flick, E.v. Kardorff and I. Steinke, (eds), *A Companion to Qualitative Research.* London: SAGE. pp. 178–183.

Generalization
This is still the classic text on generalization in qualitative research.

Glaser, B.G. (1969) "The Constant Comparative Method of Qualitative Analysis," in G.J. McCall and J.L. Simmons (eds), *Issues in Participant Observation.* Reading, MA: Addison-Wesley.

30

WRITING AND THE FUTURE OF QUALITATIVE RESEARCH – ART OR METHOD?

CHAPTER OBJECTIVES
After reading this chapter, you should be able to

✓ understand different ways of how to present your research.
✓ comprehend the problems linked to writing about others and about one's own research experience.
✓ identify the basic problems touched with these discussions.
✓ explain what that might mean for the further development of qualitative research as a whole.

The question of how to display research findings and proceedings has come to the fore in qualitative research—especially in ethnography—since the middle of the 1980s. In the social sciences, text is not only an instrument for documenting data and a basis for interpretation and thus an epistemological instrument, but also and an instrument of mediating and communicating findings and knowledge. Sometimes writing is even seen as the core of social science:

> To do social science means mainly to produce texts ... Research experiences have to be transformed into texts and to be understood on the basis of texts. A research process has findings only when and as far as these can be found in a report, no matter whether and which experiences were made by those who were involved in the research. The

observability and practical objectivity of social science phenomena is constituted in texts and nowhere else. (Wolff 1987, p. 333)

In this context, writing becomes relevant in qualitative research in three respects:

- for presenting the findings of a project;
- as a starting point for evaluating the proceedings which led to them and thus the results themselves;
- and finally as a point of departure for reflexive considerations about the overall status of research altogether.

Pragmatic Function of Writing: Presentation of Results

You can locate the various alternatives for how to present findings of your research between two poles. At one end, you may locate the aim of developing a theory from the data and interpretations according to the model of Strauss (1987). At the other end, you find the "tales from the field" (van Maanen 1988), which are intended to illustrate the relations the researcher met.

Theories as a Form of Presentation

In Chapter 28, criteria for judging theories in the sense of Strauss (1987) were discussed. The presentation of such a theory requires, according to Strauss and Corbin:

> (1) A clear analytic story. (2) Writing on a conceptual level, with description kept secondary. (3) The clear specification of relationships among categories, with levels of conceptualization also kept clear. (4) The specification of variations and their relevant conditions, consequences, and so forth, including the broader ones. (1990, p. 229)

In order to attain these goals, the authors suggest as a first step that the researcher outlines a logical draft of the theory. In this draft, you should develop the analytic logic of the story and note the contours of the theory. A clear summary of the central outline of the theory should be the first part of this draft. As a third step, the authors suggest that you make a visual presentation of the "architecture" of the central draft (1990, pp. 230–231). Thus, they lay the main stress in the presentation on clarifying the central concepts and lines of the developed theory. A visualization in the form of concept networks, trajectories, and so on is a way of presenting the theory in a concise form. In order to avoid falling into the trap of wanting to write the perfect manuscript (which is never finished), Strauss and Corbin suggest letting things go at the right moment and accepting a certain degree of imperfection in the theory and presentation (1990, pp. 235–236).

Finally, they suggest taking the potential readership of the manuscript into account and formulating the text for the target readership. The suggestions of Lofland (1974) for presenting findings in the form of theories head in a similar direction. He mentions as criteria for writing the same criteria for evaluating such reports, namely ensuring that:

> (1) The report was organized by means of a *generic* conceptual framework; (2) the generic framework employed was *novel*; (3) the framework was *elaborated* or developed in and through the report; (4) the framework was *eventful* in the sense of being abundantly documented with qualitative data; (5) the framework was interpenetrated with the empirical materials. (1974, p. 102)

Tales from the Field

Van Maanen (1988) distinguishes three basic forms of presenting research findings and processes in ethnographic studies, which can be transferred to other forms of qualitative research. *Realist tales* are characterized by four conventions. First, the author is absent from the text: observations are reported as facts or documented by using quotations from statements or interviews. Interpretations are not formulated as subjective formulations. Second, emphasis in the presentation is laid on the typical forms of what is studied. Therefore, many details are analyzed and presented. Third, the viewpoints of the members of a field or of interviewees are emphasized in the presentation: how did they experience their own life in its course? What is health for the interviewees? Finally, presentations may seek to give the impression of "interpretive omnipotence" (1988, p. 51). The interpretation does not stop at subjective viewpoints but goes beyond them by various and far-reaching interpretations. The author demonstrates that he or she is able to provide a grounded interpretation. Transfer the subject's statements to a general level using "experience-distant concepts" (Geertz) taken from social science literature for expressing relations. One example of this form of interpretive omnipotence is the presentation of findings after applying objective hermeneutics (see Chapter 25) in which the real causes for activities are sought in the elaborated structures far beyond the acting subject. Van Maanen characterizes *confessional tales* by a personalized authorship and authority. Here, the authors express the role that they played in what was observed, in their interpretations, and also in the formulations that are used. The authors' viewpoints are treated as an issue in the presentation as well as problems, breakdowns, mistakes, etc. (van Maanen 1988, p. 79) in the field. Nevertheless, it is attempted to present one's own findings as grounded in the issue that was studied. Naturalness in the presentation is one means of creating the impression of "a fieldworker and a culture finding each other and, despite some initial spats and misunderstandings, in the end making a match" (1988, p. 79). The result is a mixture of descriptions of the studied object and the experiences made in studying it. An example of this form of presentation is the description of entering the field as a learning process or descriptions of failing to successfully enter the field (see Wolff 2004a).

Impressionist tales are written in the form of dramatic recall:

> Events are recounted roughly in the order in which they are said to have occurred and carry with them all the odds and ends that are associated with the remembered events. The idea is to draw an audience into an unfamiliar story world and to allow it, as far as possible, to see, hear, and feel as the fieldworker saw, heard, and felt. Such tales seek to imaginatively place the audience in the fieldwork situation. (van Maanen 1988, p. 103)

The knowledge in the report is presented step-by-step in a fragmentary way. Narratives are often chosen as a form of presentation. The aim is to maintain the tension for the readers and to convey consistency and credibility. But impressionist reports are never completely finished. Their meaning is further elaborated in the contact with the reader (1988, p. 120). A good example is the presentation of the Balinese cockfight of Geertz (1973).

Other forms are the *critical stories*, which seek to bring social issues to the reader's attention and *formal stories*, which aim rather at the presentation of theoretical relationships. In these forms of reports, different emphases are placed on findings and processes. Sometimes, these forms of reports complement each other (e.g., initially a realistic tale is given and only in a second publication is provided a version of the field contact that is designed more as a confession). Conventions of writing ethnographic reports have changed, as van Maanen documents for his own styles of writing: today fewer realist and more impressionist or confessional tales are published. This change has occurred in two respects: more works are not only written in these styles, but also accepted for publication. There is a shift from realist tales to confessions and also an increasing awareness that there exists neither the perfect theory nor the perfect report about it. Thus, the dimension of partial failure and the limits of one's own knowledge should be taken into account as elements of the findings, which are worthy of presentation.[1]

The Ability to Write and How to Learn It

With regard to the presentation of findings–whether as theory or as story–give attention to the question of writing and writing competencies in the context of qualitative research. Where findings cannot be briefly reduced to numbers, to a statistical distribution, or to tables, considerations like Becker's (1986b) about writing as an (in)competence of social scientists become particularly relevant. Howard Becker is one of the pioneers in qualitative research in the United State and has a long experience with research and writing about it. The background of Becker's considerations is his own experience with seminars on writing aimed especially for social scientists. Becker notes a certain fear in social scientists of taking their position that for him is one reason for the limited persuasiveness of texts in social sciences: "We write that way because we fear that others will catch us in obvious error if we do anything else, and laugh at us. Better to say something innocuous but safe than something bold you might not be able defend against criticism" (1986b, pp. 8–9).

Considerations about grounding social science findings coming from qualitative research by systematically integrating negative cases and by contrasting extremely different cases (see the previous chapters) are particularly helpful here. They inspire a more positive handling of findings and results, which encourages the researcher to write and to present them more unambiguously and concretely.

> Bullshit qualifications, making your statements fuzzy, ignore the philosophical and methodological tradition, which holds that making generalizations in a strong universal form identifies negative evidence which can be used to improve them (1986b, p. 10).

According to Becker, the fact that the mode of presentation attracts more attention in every form of scientific knowledge production should lead to considering the potential reader as a central focus in the design of the text in which the research is presented. Findings and results never exist in pure form and are never communicable in this form, but are at least influenced by the leadership they are written for. Therefore, another suggestion that Becker makes (not only for the participants in his writing seminars), is to use this orientation actively as a resource in shaping social science texts:

> Making your work clearer involves considerations of audience, who is it supposed to be clearer to? Who will read what you write? What do they have to know so that they will not misread or find what you say obscure or unintelligible? You will write one way for the people you work with closely on a joint project, another way for professional colleagues in other specialities and disciplines, and differently yet for the "intelligent layman." (1986b, p. 18)

Questions of how to present findings and processes will increasingly influence methodological discussions in qualitative research, if the trend towards a textual science continues. Texts (including those in social sciences) seek to and indeed do design a certain version of the world and seek to persuade with this version other scientists in particular and (potential) readers more generally. This persuasion will indeed be achieved not only by the "how" of the presentation but also by the "what" in that presented. However, the function and effect of social science texts depend on taking the following experience into account: "We talked about scientific writing as a form of rhetoric, meant to persuade, and which forms of persuasion the scientific community considered okay and which illegitimate" (Becker 1986b, p. 15). Correspondingly, it is not only the technique of writing which has attracted more attention recently. Both the constructive and interpretative processes in producing and empirically reworking texts, and the questions of grounding which have to be directed to text and construction, version and interpretation, findings and results, have come to the fore.[2]

New Outlets for Writing about Qualitative Research

During the development of qualitative research, the medium of written–and printed–text has always been the main format for publishing results and ways of obtaining these results. Sometimes the amount of material produced in a qualitative study and often necessary to make the concrete procedures transparent, go beyond what can be published in a journal article, and sometimes also exceed the format of a book. The new media can be an alternative here. Publishing on the Internet does not only make publications faster, but also is a way to go beyond such limitations in space and costs. Publications on the Internet may come with more material like interview excerpts, but also photos and videos that were used as empirical material and would have lost a lot of their significance when printed in excerpts in black and white in a book. Using CDs or DVDs as formats to publish the proceeding and results of qualitative research as a stand-alone medium or as a supplement to more conventional media like books can be a way to transferring richer material and analyses. These forms of publishing are new options for transporting the insights from the research to its audience. However, they come along with new questions of how to protect the privacy of the participants–whether it is more text (and context) from the empirical material that is provided with a publication or whether it is the rich and contextual image or series of images (see also Chapter 4). As with all technological progress in this area, we should see the positive and the negative sides of such developments.

Legitimizing Function of Writing

That the communication of social science knowledge is essentially dependent on the forms in which it is presented has been neglected for a long time. Recently, however, this issue has been brought to the foreground in methodological discussions within different areas of the social sciences, as Bude makes clear:

> One is made aware that scientific knowledge is always presented scientific knowledge. And the consequence is that a "logic of presentation" has to be considered as well as a "logic of research." How researchers' constitution of experiences is linked to the way those experiences are saved in presentations has only begun to become an issue for reflection and research. (1989, p. 527).

As mentioned above, the background to these considerations is the methodological discussion in different areas of the social sciences: considerations in historical sciences and the thoughts of Clifford Geertz (1988) about the role of the "anthropologist as author." Clifford Geertz himself is one of the most influential researcher is cultural anthropology and his considerations about the anthropologist as author come from his own experience of researching, writing, and analyzing the writings of his colleagues. The anthropologist as author provides less an image of the studied culture *per se* than a specific presentation of this culture, which is clearly marked by his or her style of writing. Thus, Geertz deals with four classic researchers in anthropology (Malinowski, Evans-Pritchard, Levi-Strauss, Benedict) as four classic authors of anthropological texts and regards their texts from a literary viewpoint. In his considerations, the discussion that takes place in modern anthropology about the "crisis of ethnographic representation" plays a central role.[3] In this discussion, the problems with traditional understandings of representation, which were mentioned in Chapter 7, are taken up and focused on the problem of the representation of the other (i.e., here, the other culture): "The turn towards the text discloses a dimension in the scientific process of knowledge, which remained underexposed up to now. Where knowledge is thematized as the production of text, as the transcription of discourse and practice, the conditions of possibility for discussing ethnographic practices of representation are created" (Fuchs and Berg 1993, p. 64). In the ethnography of foreign and faraway cultures and the attempt to make them understandable to readers who do not have direct experience of them, the problem of presentation may be evident. However, in researchers' attempts to make a certain everyday life, a biography, an institutional milieu from their own cultural context comprehensible to readers, the problem of presentation, though less obvious, is equally relevant: "Ethnography always has to struggle with the mis-relation of limited personal experience, on which the process of knowledge is based, and the claim for an authoritative knowledge about a whole culture, which it makes with its product, i.e., the texts" (1993, p. 73).

As soon as social science adopts this critical re-examination of the conditions of the production of scientific texts and of their significance for what is described, explained, or narrated in these texts,[4] the discussion about the appropriate form of displaying its findings is entered into. Writing then is not only a part of the research process[5] but also a method of research (Richardson 2000) that like other methods is subject to the changes in historical and scientific contexts. Postmodernity has especially influenced scientific writing in the field of qualitative research in a lasting way and has questioned it in its self-evidence. Special importance is attributed to writing in the research process, because the "new criteria" for assessing qualitative research as a whole (discussed in the previous chapters) begin from the ways in which processes and results are displayed. Where trustworthiness and credibility replace reliability and validity of data and findings as the central criteria (e.g., in Lincoln and Guba 1985), the problem of grounding is transferred to the level of the writing and reporting.

> The research report with its presentation of and reflection on the methodological proceedings, with all its narratives about access to and the activities in the field, with its

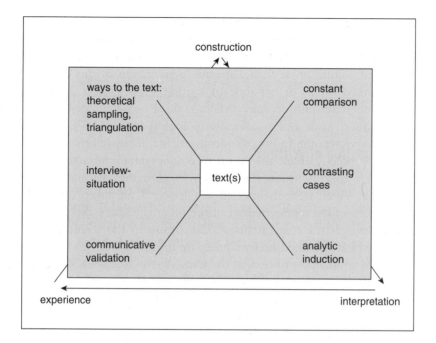

FIGURE 30.1   Grounding the Text

documentation of various materials, with its transcribed observations and conversations, interpretations and theoretical inferences is the only basis for answering the question of the quality of the investigation. (Lüders 1995, p. 325)

Thus, if the findings and procedures of scientific research are mainly judged according to their presentation and to the stylistic and other qualities of the report or article, the border between science and (fine) literature becomes blurred. In each case, the text is brought to the foreground of the discussion about the grounding of qualitative research. In addition to the discussions in Chapter 7 (see Figure 7.2), the text becomes the central element for judging the translation of experiences into constructions and interpretations. The credibility of the presentation can be specified in the suggestions for realizing the criteria for grounding qualitative research, which were treated in the previous chapters. The following approaches ground the interpretation (see Figure 30.1): communicative validation, the analysis of the interview situation, a consequent application of theoretical sampling and of triangulation of methods, and perspectives to the methodological starting points for generalization of findings by the constant comparison and contrasting of cases and the analysis of negative cases.

Reichertz (1992) goes one step beyond a text-centered treatment of credibility. He makes it clear that this form of persuasion concerning credibility is produced not only in the text but also in the interaction of author, text, and reader:

> The decisive point, however, is the attitude which is expressed in the text, with which the ethnographer turns toward his own interpretations and those of his colleagues in order to relate them to each other according to the needs of the individual case. It is not the way of accounting claimed for in the writing, which is relevant for the reader, but the attitude of accounting, which is shown in the text, which of course always has to use semiotic means, and these are means which are sensitive to cheating. (1992, p. 346)

Reflexive Function of Writing

Research, then, includes not only the interaction between the researcher and the issue, but also the interaction between the researchers and their potential readers, for whom they finally write their presentations. This relationship—as well as the text produced for this purpose and the writing linked to it—is determined in multiple ways: "contextually . . . rhetorically … institutionally … generically … politically … historically" (Clifford 1986, p. 6).

More generally, such considerations push the relationship between author, text, and readers and the conditions of producing scientific texts to the front of the relationship between researcher and issue, which is only documented in the text in summary form. A similar reflection can be noted for the production of research in (natural) science (see Knorr-Cetina 1981). In this case, social science (as it always did) is dealing with the "other" (i.e., concretely the (natural) scientists and their laboratories and the practices involved in the manufacturing of knowledge). The discussion about writing in ethnography and more generally in qualitative research, however, has led to self-reflection in social science research. Here, the role and the self-awareness of the qualitative researcher are increasingly questioned: "The qualitative researcher is not an objective, authoritative, politically neutral observer standing outside and above the text" (Bruner 1993, quoted in Lincoln and Denzin 2000, p. 1049).

This leads to the question of what validity can be claimed for what is presented, given that the form of presentation used by the author essentially determines what is presented and how. This question is discussed under the heading of the authority of the text:

> By the *authority of the text,* we reference the claim any text makes to being accurate, true, and complete . . . Is a text, that is, faithful to the context and the individuals it is supposed to represent? Does the text have the right to assert that it is a report to the larger world that addresses not only the researcher's interests, but also the interests of those studied? (Lincoln and Denzin 2000, p. 1052)

Here, questions about the claims of qualitative research arise—claims for an appropriate analysis and presentation of the contexts and persons that were studied and their legitimacy. The questioning of the authority of the text leads to a questioning of the authority and legitimacy of the research altogether. But, in such discussions, the original motive for the research–to produce knowledge about contexts of living and subjective points of view and their contexts–is in danger of getting lost in an endless discourse of self-referentiality.[6]

Dissolution of Science into Styles of Writing?

It is ironic that just as qualitative research has–(with difficulties but successfully)– achieved its place amongst the sciences, it now faces the danger of getting lost in endless debates about the role and problems of writing. Perhaps it does make sense to consider the writing styles of established ethnographers as authors (Geertz 1988 on Levi-Strauss and others; Wolff 1992 again on Geertz) in order to differentiate the style of writing in ethnography from that in other genres. Nevertheless, the claim made by qualitative research–for doing science, for specifying the borders with other genres of presentation, but also for marking the borders of a good, successful study from another, less successful or even failed study–should not be given up. In favoring the discussion about writing in the research, one must neither give up the discussion about quality in research and not only that of a good and credible text–nor reduce the emphasis on research practice.

The Future of Qualitative Research: Art or Method?

The other side of the coin is the overemphasis on the part played by art in qualitative research. For several methods it is explicitly claimed that they are art and to be taught as art (e.g., for the objective hermeneutics). For other methods, sometimes the impression is given that their applications by those who have developed them are the best measure for assessing their potential. Other theoretical and methodological presentations and applications fall clearly behind the creator's claims for the insights they can give into process and procedures. Furthermore, Denzin and Lincoln's handbook (2000a) gives the impression of qualitative research as art in many passages. A whole section is entitled, "The art and practices of interpretation, evaluation, and representation" and then provides relatively little concrete advice on how to do an interpretation or evaluation. It is more the art than the practices or even the methods that are outlined. The description of the state of the art of qualitative research, Denzin and Lincoln (2000b) provide as an introduction underlines this impression. They give the impression that questions of methods and how to apply them are strongly pushed to the back or filed as being outdated and in the "modernist phase" of earlier times in favor of the crises of representation and legitimation that they discuss. This may be linked to the strong orientation on ethnography, which characterizes the presentation of qualitative research in this handbook. According to Hammersley and Atkinson (1983) or Lüders (2004a), it is characteristic for ethnography that single methods are integrated in a pragmatic-pluralistic attitude or vanish behind such an attitude. The big attention that is attracted by the question of writing qualitative research and the crises and problems linked to it in this context will definitely neither accelerate the development of methods nor the application of the developed methods and will not necessarily lead to more and better research. Whether or not the more recent expectation of Lincoln and Denzin (2000, p. 1052), that the future of qualitative research lies in a "sacred epistemology," will lead a way out of the tension of art and method or lead back into another tension of earlier times (science or religion), has to be awaited.

Perhaps qualitative research should be understood as art *and* method. Progress should rather be expected from the combination of methodological developments and their successful and reflected application in as many fields and research questions as possible. Clifford Geertz underlined in his considerations about the "world in pieces" that the need for this kind of research is increasing:

> The same dissolution of settled groupings and familiar divisions, that has rendered the political world so angular and hard to fathom, has made the analysis *of* culture, of how it is people see things, respond to them, imagine them, judge them, deal with them, a far more awkward enterprise than it was when we knew, or rather thought that we knew what went with what and what did not . . . What we need are ways of thinking that are responsible to particularities, to individualities, oddities, discontinuities, contrasts, and singularities, responsive to what Charles Taylor has called "deep diversity" – a plurality of ways of belonging and being, and that yet can draw from them – from it – a sense of connectedness, a connectedness that is neither comprehensive nor uniform, primal nor changeless, but nonetheless real . . . But if what we are in fact faced with is a world of pressed-together dissimilarities variously arranged . . . there is nothing for it but to get down to cases, whatever the cost to generality, certainty or intellectual equilibrium. (2000, pp. 223–226).

KEY POINTS

- The discussion about writing qualitative research goes beyond the question in which formal mode you want to present what you have found.
- Fundamental issues like representation, legitimacy, authority, and the like have made this discussion a key discussion in qualitative research (for a while at least).
- The danger with such a fundamental discussion is that it might prevent people from doing research and finding interesting insights (and presenting them) and lead them to end up in endless reflexives loops.
- Nevertheless, it is the way how we write about what we experienced in the field that shapes how and what of it we can transfer to our audiences.

Exercise 30.1

1. Take an example from the qualitative research literature. After reading it, ask yourself whether or not it was transparent for you, how the researchers found their access to the field and the people in it, how they collected their data and analyzed them, etc.

2. Look at it again and think about how much you heard the voices from the field in the version the authors presented. And whether this would have been necessary or helpful.

3. Look at any of your own papers about your research. What kind of presentation did you select? How far do the discussions about writing qualitative research meet your paper? Try to answer these questions.

Notes

1   How far Bude's (1989) suggestion of using "the essay as a form of presenting social science knowledge" may map a path in this context awaits further clarification. The same is the case for the profit and specialty of sociological narratives discussed by the same author in a different context (Bude 1993).

2   This impression results not only from the publications about ethnography, but more generally in reading the handbook edited by Denzin and Lincoln (2000a) which is very strongly marked by the ongoing discussions about writing ethnographies and culture in times of postmodernity.

3   This discussion is documented in great detail in Clifford and Marcus (1986).

4   That it should do this has been stated more generally by René König: "The ideas of the 'foreign' or of the 'foreign distance,' which are fundamental for the ethnographer's work are relevant for the sociologists as well as who study their own reality. Because the idea that they as members of the given social reality have a substantial 'preliminary knowledge' at hand, which can be elaborated by the corresponding presentation as scientific knowledge, is nowadays everything other than the case" (1984, p. 23).

5   For this aspect, beyond Becker (1986b), see also Wolcott (1990b) and Richardson (1990).

6   Lincoln and Denzin see a similar danger: "Endless self-referential criticisms by poststructuralists can produce mountains of texts with few referents to concrete human experience" (2000, p. 1050).

FURTHER READING

Writing Research
These texts go further into the details of the problems mentioned here concerning the different functions of writing in qualitative research.

Becker, H.S. (1986b) *Writing for Social Scientists*. Chicago: University of Chicago Press.
Clifford, J. and Marcus, G.E. (eds) (1986) *Writing Culture: The Poetics and Politics of Ethnography*. Berkeley, CA: University of California Press.

(Continued)

(Continued)

Geertz, C. (1988) The *Anthropologist as Author*. Stanford, CA: Stanford University Press.
Van Maanen, J. (1988) *Tales of the Field: On Writing Ethnography*. Chicago: University of Chicago Press.

The Future of Qualitative Research: Art or Method
In their outlook, the authors make the tension of art and method evident in a specific way.

Lincoln, Y.S. and Denzin, N.K. (2000) "The Seventh Moment," in N. Denzin and Y.S. Lincoln (eds), *Handbook of Qualitative Research* (2nd edn). London: SAGE. pp. 1047–165.

REFERENCES

Adler, P.A. and Adler, P. (1987) *Membership Roles in Field Research.* Beverly Hills, CA: SAGE.

Adler, P.A. and Adler, P. (1998) "Observational Techniques," in N. Denzin and Y.S. Lincoln (eds), *Collecting and Interpreting Qualitative Materials.* London: SAGE. pp. 79–110.

Agar, M.H. (1980) *The Professional Stranger.* New York: Academic Press.

Allmark, P. (2002) "The Ethics of Research with Children," *Nurse Researcher,* 10: 7–19.

Altheide, D.L. and Johnson, J.M. (1998) "Criteria for Assessing Interpretive Validity in Qualitative Research," in N. Denzin and Y.S. Lincoln (eds), *Collecting and Interpreting Qualitative Materials.* London: SAGE. pp. 293–312.

Atkinson, P. and Hammersley, M. (1998) "Ethnography and Participant Observation," in N. Denzin and Y.S. Lincoln (eds), *Strategies of Qualitative Inquiry.* London: SAGE. pp. 110–136.

Atkinson, P., Coffey, A., Delamont, S., Lofland, J. and Lofland L. (eds) (2001) *Handbook of Ethnography.* London: SAGE.

Atteslander, P. (1996) "Auf dem Wege zur lokalen Kultur. Einführende Gedanken," in W.F. Whyte, *Die Street Corner Society. Die Sozialstruktur eines Italienerviertels.* Berlin, N.Y.: de Gruyter. pp. IX–XIV.

Bampton, R. and Cowton, C.J. (2002, May) "The E-Interview," Forum Qualitative Social Reseach, 3 (2), www.qualitative-research.net/fqs/fqs-eng.htm (date of access: 02, 22,2005).

Barthes, R. (1996) *Camera Lucida. Reflections on Photography.* New York: Hill and Wang.

Barton, A.H. and Lazarsfeld, P.F. (1955) "Some Functions of Qualitative Analysis in Social Research," *Frankfurter Beiträge zur Soziologie.* I. Frankfurt a. M.: Europäische Verlagsanstalt. pp. 321–361.

Banister, P., Burman, E., Parker, I., Taylor, M. and Tindall, C. (1994) *Qualitative Methods in Psychology: A Research Guide.* Buckingham: Open University Press.

Barbour, R. (2006) *Producing Data Using Focus Groups.* (Book five of the Qualitative Research Kit). London: SAGE.

Bateson, G. and Mead, M. (1942) *Balinese Character: A Photographic Analysis*, vol. 2. New York: New York Academy of Sciences.

Bauer, M. (2000) "Classical Content Analysis: A Review," in M. Bauer and G. Gaskell (eds), *Qualitative Researching with Text, Image and Sound–A Handbook.* London, Thousand Oaks, New Delhi: SAGE. pp. 131–150.

Bauer, M. and Gaskell, G. (2000) (eds) *Qualitative Researching with Text, Image, and Sound.* London: SAGE.

Baum, F. (1995) "Researching Public Health: Behind the Qualitative-Quantitative Methodological Debate," *Social Science and Medicine,* (40): 459–468.

Baym, N.K. (1995) "The Emergence of Community in Computer-Mediated Communication," in S. Jones (ed.), *Cybersociety–Computer-Mediated Communication and Community.* London: SAGE. pp. 138–163.

Beck, U. (1992) *Risk-Society.* London: SAGE.

Beck, U. and Bonß, W. (eds) (1989) *Weder Sozialtechnologie noch Aufklälarung? Analysen zur Verwendung sozialwissenschaftlichen Wissens.* Frankfurt: Suhrkamp.

Becker, H.S. (1986a) *Doing Things Together. Selected Papers.* Evanston, IL: Northwestern University Press.

Becker, H.S. (1986b) *Writing for Social Scientists.* Chicago: The University of Chicago Press.

Becker, H.S. (1996) "The Epistemology of Qualitative Research," in R. Jessor, A. Colby and R.A. Shweder (eds), *Ethnography and Human Development.* Chicago: The University of Chicago Press. pp. 53–72.

Becker, H.S., Geer, B., Hughes, E.C. and Strauss, A.L. (1961) *Boys in White: Student Culture in Medical School.* Chicago: University of Chicago Press.

Becker, H. and Geer, B.S. (1960) "Participant Observation: Analysis of Qualitative Data," in R.N. Adams and J.J. Preiss (eds), *Human Organization Research.* Homewood, IL: The Dorsey Press. pp. 267–289.

Berger, P. L. and Luckmann, T. (1966). *The Social Construction of Reality.* Garden City, NY: Double Day.

Bergmann, J.R. (1980) "Interaktion and Exploration: Eine konversationsanalytische Studie zur sozialen Organisation der Eröffnungsphase von psychiatrischen Aufnahmegesprächen." Konstanz. Dissertation.

Bergmann, J.R. (1985) "Flüchtigkeit und methodische Fixierung sozialer Wirklichkeit. Aufzeichnungen als Daten der interpretativen Soziologie," in W. Bonß and H. Hartmann (eds), *Entzauberte Wissenschaft–Zur Realität und Geltung soziologischer Forschung.* Göttingen: Schwartz. pp. 299–320.

Bergmann, J. (2004a) "Conversation Analysis," in U. Flick, E.v. Kardorff and I. Steinke (eds), *A Companion to Qualitative Research.* London: SAGE. pp. 296–302.

Bergmann, J. (2004b) "Ethnomethodology," in U. Flick, E.v. Kardorff and I. Steinke (eds), *A Companion to Qualitative Research.* London: SAGE. pp. 72–80.

Bergmann, J. and Meier, C. (2004) "Electronic Process Data and Their Analysis," in U. Flick, E.v. Kardorff and I. Steinke (eds), *A Companion to Qualitative Research.* London: SAGE. pp. 243–247.

Bertaux, D. (ed.) (1981) *Biography and History: The Life History Approach in Social Sciences.* Beverly Hills, CA: SAGE.

Billig, M. (1987) *Arguing and Thinking: A Rhetorical Approach to Social Psychology.* Cambridge: Cambridge University Press.

Billman-Mahecha, E. (1990) *Egozentrismus und Perspektivenwechsel.* Göttingen: Hogrefe.

Blumer, H. (1938) "Social Psychology," in E. Schmidt (ed.), *Man and Society.* New York: Prentice Hall. pp. 144–198.

Blumer, H. (1969) *Symbolic Interactionism: Perspective and Method.* Berkeley and Los Angeles: University of California.

Böhm, A. (2004) "Theoretical Coding," in U. Flick, E.v. Kardorff and I. Steinke (eds), *A Companion to Qualitative Research.* London: SAGE. pp. 270–275.

Bohnsack, R. (2004) "Group Discussions and Focus Groups," in U Flick, E.v Kardorff and I. Steinke (eds), *A Companion to Qualitative Research.* London: SAGE. 214–220.

Bonß, W. (1982) *Die Einübung des Tatsachenblicks. Zur Struktur und Veränderung empirischer Sozialforschung.* Frankfurt. Suhrkamp.

Bonß, W. (1995) "Soziologie," in U. Flick, E.v. Kardorff, H. Keupp, L.v. Rosenstiel and S. Wolff (eds), *Handbuch Qualitative Sozialforschung* (2nd edn). Munich: Psychologie Verlags Union. pp. 36–39.

Bonß, W. and Hartmann, H. (1985) "Konstruierte Gesellschaft, rationale Deutung – Zum Wirklichkeitscharakter soziologischer Diskurse," in W. Bonß and H. Hartmann (eds), *Entzauberte Wissenschaft: Zur Realität und Geltung soziologischer Forschung.* Göttingen: Schwartz. pp. 9–48.

Borman, K.M., LeCompte, M. and Goetz, J.P. (1986) "Ethnographic Research and Qualitative Research Design and Why it Doesn"t Work," *American Behavioral Scientist,* 30: 42–57.

Bourdieu, P. (1996) "Understanding," *Theory, Culture and Society,* 13 (2): 17–37.

Bruce, G. (1992) "Comments," in J. Svartvik, (ed.), *Directions in Corpus Linguistics: Proceedings of the Nobel Symposium 82, Stockholm,* August 4–8, 1991. Berlin: de Gruyter. pp. 145–147.

Bruner, E.M. (1993) "Introduction: The Ethnographic Self and the Personal Self," in P. Benson (ed.), *Anthropology and Literature.* Urbana: University of Illinois Press. pp. 1–26.

Bruner, J. (1987) "Life as Narrative," *Social Research,* 54: 11–32.

Bruner, J. (1990) *Acts of Meaning.* Cambridge, MA: Harvard University Press.

Bruner, J. (1991) "The Narrative Construction of Reality," *Critical Inquiry,* 18: 1–21.

Bruner, J. and Feldman, C. (1996) "Group Narrative as a Cultural Context of Autobiography," in D. Rubin (ed.), *Remembering our Past: Studies in Autobiographical Memory.* Cambridge: Cambridge University Press. pp. 291–317.

Bryman, A. (1992) "Quantitative and Qualitative Research: Further Reflections on their Integration," in J. Brannen (ed.), *Mixing Methods: Quantitative and Qualitative Research.* Aldershot: Avebury. pp. 57–80.

Bryman, A. (2004) *Social Research Methods* (2nd edn). Oxford: Oxford University Press.

Bude, H. (1984) "Rekonstruktion von Lebenskonstruktionen: eine Antwort auf die Frage, was die Biograpnieforschung bringt," in M. Kohli and G. Robert (eds), *Biographie und soziale Wirklichkeit. Neuere Beiträge und Forschungsperspektiven.* Stuttgart: Metzler. pp. 7–28.

Bude, H. (1985) "Der Sozialforscher als Narrationsanimateur. Kritische Anmerkungen zu einer erzähltheoretischen Fundierung der interpretativen Socialforshung," *Kölner Zeitschrift und Socialpsychologie,* 37: 327–336.

Bude, H. (1989) "Der Essay als Form der Darstellung sozialwissenschaftlicher Erkenntnisse. *Kölner Zeitschrift für Soziologie und Sozialpsychologie,* 41: 526–539.

Bude, H. (1993) "Die soziologische Erzählung," in T. Jung and S. Müller-Doohm (eds), *"Wirklichkeit" im Deutungsprozeß. Verstehen und Methoden in den Kultur- und Sozialwissenschaften.* Frankfurt: Suhrkamp. pp. 409–429.

Bude, H. (2004) "Qualitative Generation Research," in U. Flick, E.v. Kardorff and I. Steinke (eds), *A Companion to Qualitative Research.* London: SAGE. pp. 108–112.

Bühler-Niederberger, D. (1985) "Analytische Induktion als Verfahren qualitativer Methodologie," *Zeitschrift für Soziologie,* 14: 475–485.

Chamberlain, K. (1999) "Using Grounded Theory in Health Psychology," in M. Murray and K. Chamberlain (eds), *Qualitative Health Psychology–Theories and Methods.* London. SAGE. pp. 183–201.

Charmaz, K. (2003) "Grounded Theory," in J.A. Smith (ed.), *Qualitative Psychology–A Practical Guide to Research Methods.* London. SAGE. pp. 81–110.

Cicourel, A.V. (1964) *Method and Measurement in Sociology.* New York: Free Press.

Cicourel, A.V. (1981) "Notes on the Integration of Micro- and Macrolevels of Analysis," in K. Knorr-Cetina and A.V. Cicourel (eds), *Advances in Social Theory and Methodolog: Towards an Integration of Micro- and Macro-Sociologies*. London. Routledge and Kegan Paul. pp. 51–80.

Clifford, J. (1986) "Introduction. Partial Truths," in J. Clifford and G.E. Marcus (eds), *Writing Culture: The Poetics and Politics of Ethnography*. Berkeley, CA: The University of California Press. pp. 1–26.

Clifford, J. and Marcus, G.E. (eds) (1986) *Writing Culture: The Poetics and Politics of Ethnography*. Berkeley, CA: The University of California Press.

Coffey, A., Holbrook, B. and Atkinson, P. (1996) "Qualitative Data Analysis: Technologies and Representations," *Sociological Research Online*, 1. (www.socresonline.org.uk/socresonline/1/1/4html)

Corbin, J. and Strauss, A. (1988) *Unending Work and Care–Managing Chronic Illness at Home*. San Francisco: Jossey Bass.

Corbin, J. and Strauss, A. (1990) "Grounded Theory Research: Procedures, Canons and Evaluative Criteria," *Qualitative Sociology*, 13: 3–21.

Coulter, J. (1983) *Rethinking Cognitive Theory*. London: Macmillan.

Creswell, J.W. (2003) *Research Design–Qualitative, Quantitative, and Mixed Methods Approaches*. Thousand Oaks, CA: SAGE.

D'Andrade, R.G. (1987) "A Folk Model of the Mind," in D. Holland and N. Quinn (eds), *Cultural Models in Language and Thought*. Cambridge: Cambridge University Press. pp. 112–149.

Dabbs, J.M. (1982) "Making Things Visible," in J. Van Maanen, J.M. Dabbs and R. Faulkner (eds), *Varieties of Qualitative Research*. London: SAGE. pp. 31–64.

Dann, H.D. (1990) "Subjective Theories: A New Approach to Psychological Research and Educational Practice," in G.R. Semin and K.J. Gergen (eds), *Everyday Understanding: Social and Scientific Implications*. London: SAGE. pp. 204–226.

Deleuze, G. and Guattari, F. (1976) *Rhizome: Introduction*. Paris: Les éditions de Minuit.

Denzin, N.K. (1988) *Interpretive Biography*. London: SAGE.

Denzin, N.K. (1989a) *Interpretive Interactionism*. London: SAGE.

Denzin, N.K. (1989b) *The Research Act* (3rd edn). Englewood Cliffs, NJ: Prentice Hall.

Denzin, N.K. (1989c) "Reading *Tender Mercies*: Two Interpretations," *Sociological Quarterly*, 30: 1–19.

Denzin, N.K. (ed.) (1993) *Studies in Symbolic Interactionism*, Vol. 15. Greenwich, CT: JAI Press.

Denzin, N.K. (1997) *Interpretive Ethnography: Ethnographic Practices for the 21st Century*. Thousand Oaks, CA: SAGE.

Denzin, N.K. (1999) "Cybertalk and the Method of Instances," in S. Jones (ed.), *Doing Internet Research–Critical Issues and Methods for Examining the Net*. London: SAGE, pp.107–126.

Denzin, N.K. (2000) "The Practices and Politics of Interpretation," in N. Denzin and Y.S. Lincoln (eds), *Handbook of Qualitative Research* (2nd edn). London: SAGE. pp. 897–922.

Denzin, N.K. (2004a) "Reading Film: Using Photos and Video as Social Science Material," in U. Flick, E.v. Kardorff and I. Steinke (eds), *A Companion to Qualitative Research*. London: SAGE. pp. 234–247.

Denzin, N.K. (2004b) "Symbolic Interactionism," in U. Flick, E.v. Kardorff and I. Steinke (eds), *A Companion to Qualitative Research*. London: SAGE. pp. 81–87.

Denzin, N. and Lincoln, Y.S. (eds) (2000a) *Handbook of Qualitative Research* (2nd edn). London: SAGE.

Denzin, N. and Lincoln, Y.S. (2000b) "Introduction: The Discipline and Practice of Qualitative Research," in N. Denzin and Y.S. Lincoln (eds), *Handbook of Qualitative Research* (2nd edn). London: SAGE. pp. 1–29.

Department of Health (2001) *Research Governance Framework for Health and Social Care*. London: Department of Health.

Derrida, J. (1990) *Writing and Difference*. London: Routledge (original: *L"ecriture et la difference*, Paris: Editions du Seuil, 1967).

Devereux, G. (1967) *From Anxiety to Methods in the Behavioral Sciences*. The Hague, Paris: Mouton.

Dixon, R.A. and Gould, O.N. (1996) "Adults Telling and Retelling Stories Collaboratively," in P.B. Baltes and U. Staudinger (eds), *Interactive Minds: Lifespan Perspectives on the Social Foundation of Cognition*. Cambridge: Cambridge University Press. pp. 221–241.

Douglas, J.D. (1976) *Investigative Social Research*. Beverly Hills, CA: SAGE.

Drew, P. (1995) "Conversation Analysis," in J.A. Smith, R. Harré and L.v. Langenhove (eds), *Rethinking Methods in Psychology*. London: SAGE. pp. 64–79.

Edwards, D. and Potter, J. (1992) *Discursive Psychology*. London: SAGE.

Elliot R., Fischer C.T. and Rennie D.L. (1999) "Evolving Guidelines for Publication of Qualitative Research Studies in Psychology and Related Fields." *British Journal of Clinical Psychology*, 38: 215–229.

Emerson, R., Fretz, R. and Shaw, L. (1995) *Writing Ethnographic Fieldnotes*. Chicago: Chicago University Press.

Erdheim, M. (1984) *Die gesellschaftliche Produktion von Unbewußtheit*. Frankfurt/M: Suhrkamp.

"Ethik-Kodex der Deutschen Gesellschaft für Soziologie und des Berufsverbandes Deutscher Soziologen." *DGS-Informationen*, 1/93: 13–19.

Fielding, N.G. and Fielding, J.L. (1986) *Linking Data*. Beverly Hills, CA: SAGE.

Fielding, N.G. and Lee, R.M. (eds) (1991) *Using Computers in Qualitative Research*. London: SAGE.

Fielding, N. and Lee, R.M. (1998) *Computer Analysis and Qualitative Research*. London: SAGE.

Fleck, L., Trenn, T.J. and Merton, R.K. (1979) *Genesis and Development of a Scientific Fact*. Chicago: Chicago University Press.

Flick, U. (1992) "Triangulation Revisited. Strategy of or Alternative to Validation of Qualitative Data," *Journal for the Theory of Social Behavior*, 22: 175–197.

Flick, U. (1994) "Social Representations and the Social Construction of Everyday Knowledge: Theoretical and Methodological Queries," *Social Science Information*, 2: 179–197.

Flick, U. (1995) "Social Representations," in R. Harré, J. Smith and L. Van Langenhove (eds), *Rethinking Psychology*. London: SAGE. pp. 70–96.

Flick, U. (1996) *Psychologie des technisierten Alltags*. Opladen: Westdeutscher Verlag.

Flick, U. (ed.) (1998) *Psychology of the Social: Representations in Knowledge and Language*. Cambridge: Cambridge University Press.

Flick, U. (2000a) "Episodic Interviewing," in M. Bauer and G. Gaskell (eds), *Qualitative Researching with Text, Image and Sound: A Practical Handbook*. London: SAGE. pp. 75–92.

Flick, U. (2000b). "Qualitative Inquiries into Social Representations of Health," *Journal of Health Psychology*, (5): 309–318.

Flick, U. (2003) (ed.) "Health Concepts in Different Contexts" (Special Issue). *Journal of Health Psychology*, 8 (5).

Flick, U. (2004a) "Triangulation in Qualitative Research," in U. Flick, E.v. Kardorff and I. Steinke, (eds), *A Companion to Qualitative Research*. London: SAGE. pp. 178–183.

Flick, U. (2004b) "Constructivism," in U. Flick, E.v. Kardorff and I. Steinke, (eds), *A Companion to Qualitative Research*. London: SAGE. pp. 88–94.

Flick, U. (2004c) *Triangulation-eine Einführung*. Wiesbaden: Verlag für Sozialwissenschaften.

Flick, U (2006a) *How To Evaluate Qualitative Research* (Book eight of the Qualitative Research Kit). London: SAGE.

Flick, U. (2006b) *Qualitative Research in Psychology: A Textbook*. London: SAGE.

Flick, U. and Bauer, M. (2004) "Teaching Qualitative Research," in U. Flick, E.v. Kardorff and I. Steinke (eds), *A Companion to Qualitative Research*. London: SAGE. pp. 340–348.

Flick, U. Fischer, C., Walter, U., and Schwartz, F.W. (2002) Social Representations of Health Held by Health Professionals–The Case of General Practitioners and Home Care Nurses," *Social Science Information*, 41/4: 581–602.

Flick, U., Fischer, C., Neuber, A., Walter, U. and Schwartz, F.W. (2003) "Health in the Context of Being Old–Representations Held by Health Professionals," *Journal of Health Psychology*, 8/5: 539–556.

Flick, U., Kardorff, E.v. and Steinke, I. (eds) (2004) *A Companion to Qualitative Research*. London: SAGE.

Flick, U., Walter, U., Fischer, C., Neuber, A. and Schwartz, F.W. (2004) *Gesundheit als Leitidee? – Gesundheitsvorstellungen von Ärzten und Pflegekräften*. Bern: Huber.

Fontana, A. and Frey, J.H. (2000) "The Interview: From Structured Questions to Negotiated Text," in N. Denzin and Y.S. Lincoln (eds), *Handbook of Qualitative Research* (2nd edn). London: SAGE. pp. 645–72.

Foucault, M. (1980) *Power/Knowledge: Selected Interviews and Other Writings 1972–1977*. Hassocks, Sussex: Harvester.

Freud, S. (1912/1958) "Recommendations to Physicians Practising Psychoanalysis," in *The Standard Edition of the Complete Psychological Work of Sigmund Freud*, Vol. XII (trans. J. Strachey). London: The Hogarth Press. pp. 109–120.

Fuchs, W. (1984) *Biographische Forschung: Eine Einführung in Praxis und Methoden*. Opladen: Westdeutscher Verlag.

Fuchs, M. and Berg, E. (1993) "Phänomenologie der Differenz. Reflexionsstufen ethnographischer Repräsentation," in E. Berg and M. Fuchs (eds), *Kultur, soziale Praxis, Text: Die Krise der ethnographischen Repräsentation*. Frankfurt: Suhrkamp. pp. 11–108.

Garfinkel, H. (1967) *Studies in Ethnomethodology*. Englewood Cliffs, NJ: Prentice Hall.

Garfinkel, H. (1986) *Ethnomethodological Studies of Work*. London. Routledge and Kegan Paul.

Garfinkel, H. and Sacks, H. (1970) "On Formal Structures of Practical Actions," in J. McKinney and E. Tiryyakian (eds), *Theoretical Sociology*. New York: Appleton.

Garz, D. (ed.) (1994) *Die Welt als Text*. Frankfurt: Suhrkamp.

Garz, D. and Kraimer, K. (1994) "Die Welt als Text. Zum Projekt einer hermeneutisch-rekonstruktiven Sozialwissenschaft," in D. Garz (ed.), *Die Welt als Text*. Frankfurt: Suhrkamp. pp. 7–21.

Gaskell, G. and Bauer, M. (2000) "Towards Public Accountability: Beyond Sampling, Reliability and Validity," in M. Bauer and G. Gaskell (eds), *Qualitative Researching with Text, Image, and Sound–A Handbook*. London Thousand Oaks, New Delhi: SAGE. pp. 336–350.

Gebauer, G. and Wulf, C. (1995) *Mimesis: Culture, Art, Society*. Berkeley, CA: University of California Press.

Geertz, C. (1973) *The Interpretation of Cultures: Selected Essays*. New York: Basic Books.

Geertz, C. (1983) *Local Knowledge: Further Essays in Interpretative Anthropology*. New York: Basic Books.

Geertz, C. (1988) *The Anthropologist as Author*. Stanford, CA: Stanford University Press.

Geertz, C. (2000) *Available Light: Anthropological Reflections on Philosophical Topics.* Princeton, NJ: Princeton University Press.

Gerdes, K. (ed.) (1979) *Explorative Sozialforschung. Einführende Beiträge aus "Natural Sociology" und Feldforschung in den USA.* Stuttgart: Enke.

Gergen, K.J. (1985) "The Social Constructionist Movement in Modern Psychology," *American Psychologist,* 40: 266–275.

Gergen, K.J. (1994) *Realities and Relationship: Soundings in Social Construction.* Cambridge, MA: Harvard University Press.

Gergen, K.J. (1999) *An Invitation to Social Construction.* London, Thousand Oaks, New Dehli: SAGE.

Gerhardt, U. (1986) *Patientenkarrieren. Eine medizinsoziologische Studie.* Frankfurt: Suhrkamp.

Gerhardt, U. (1988) "Qualitative Sociology in the Federal Republic of Germany," *Qualitative Sociology,* 11: 29–43.

Gibbs, G. (forthcoming) *How to Analyse Qualitative Data* (Book Six of the Qualitative Data Research Kit). London: Sage.

Gildemeister, R. (2004*)* "Gender Studies," in U. Flick, E.v. Kardorff and I. Steinke (eds), *A Companion to Qualitative Research.* London: SAGE. pp. 123–128.

Girtler, R. (1984) *Methoden der qualitativen Sozialforschung.* Wien: Böhlau.

Glaser, B.G. (1969) "The Constant Comparative Method of Qualitative Analysis," in G.J. McCall and J.L. Simmons (eds), *Issues in Participant Observation.* Reading, MA: Addison-Wesley.

Glaser, B.G. (1978) *Theoretical Sensitivity.* Mill Valley: University of California.

Glaser, B.G. (1992) *Basics of Grounded Theory Analysis: Emergence vs. Forcing.* Mill Valley, CA: Sociology Press.

Glaser, B.G. and Strauss, A.L. (1965a) *Awareness of Dying.* Chicago: Aldine.

Glaser, B. and Strauss, A. (1965b) "Discovery of Substantive Theory: A Basic Strategy Underlying Qualitative Research," *The American Behavioral Scientist,* 8: 5–12.

Glaser, B.G. and Strauss, A.L. (1967) *The Discovery of Grounded Theory: Strategies for Qualitative Research.* New York: Aldine.

Glasersfeld, E.v. (1992) "Aspekte des Konstruktivsimus: Vico, Berkeley, Piaget," in G. Rusch and S.J. Schmidt (eds), *Konstruktivismus: Geschichte und Anwendung.* Frankfurt a. M.: Suhrkamp. pp. 20–33.

Glasersfeld, E.v. (1995) *Radical Constructivism: A Way of Knowing and Learning.* London: The Falmer Press.

Goffman, E. (1959) *The Presentation of Self in Everyday Life.* New York: Doubleday.

Goffman, E. (1961) *Asylums: Essays on the Social Situation of Mental Patients and Other Inmates.* New York: Anchor Doubleday.

Gold, R.L. (1958) "Roles in Sociological Field Observations," *Social Forces,* 36: 217–223.

Goodman, N. (1978) *Ways of Worldmaking.* Indianapolis: Hackett.

Grathoff, R. (1978) "Alltag und Lebenswelt als Gegenstand der phänomenologischen Sozialtheorie," in K. Hammerich and M. Klein (eds), *Kölner Zeitschrift für Soziologie und Sozialpsychologie* Sonderheft 20: *Materialien zur Soziologie des Alltags.* pp. 67–85.

Groeben, N. (1990) "Subjective Theories and the Explanation of Human Action," in G.R. Semin and K.J. Gergen (eds), *Everyday Understanding: Social and Scientific Implications.* London: SAGE. pp. 19–44.

Guba, E.G. (ed.) (1990) *The Paradigm Dialog.* Newbury Park, CA: SAGE.

Guba, E.G. and Lincoln, Y.S. (1998) "Competing Paradigms in Qualitative Research," in N. Denzin and Y.S. Lincoln (eds), *The Landscape of Qualitative Research: Theories and Issues.* London: SAGE. pp. 195–220.

Gubrium, J.F. and Holstein, J. A. (1995) *The Active Interview.* Qualitative Research Methods. Series, 37. Thousand Oaks, London, New Dehli: SAGE.

Gubrium, J.F. and Holstein, J.A. (eds) (2001) *Handbook of Interviewing Research.* Thousand Oaks, London, New Dehli: SAGE.

Habermas, J. (1967) *Zur Logik der Sozialwissenschaften.* Tübingen: Mohr.

Habermas, J. (1996) *The Habermas Reader.* Cambridge: Polity Press.

Hall, E.T. (1986) "Foreword," in J. Collier Jr. and M. Collier (eds), *Visual Anthropology: Photography as a Research Method.* Albuquerque: University of New Mexico Press. pp. xii–xvii.

Hammersley, M. (1990) *Reading Ethnographic Research: A Critical Guide.* London: Longman.

Hammersley, M. (1992) *Whats Wrong with Ethnography?* London: Routledge.

Hammersley, M. (1995) *The Politics of Social Research.* London: SAGE.

Hammersley, M. and Atkinson, P. (1995) *Ethnography–Principles in Practice* (2nd edn). London, New York: Routledge.

Hammersley, M. and Atkinson, P. (1983) *Ethnography: Principles in Practice.* London: Tavistock.

Harper, D. (1998) "On the Authority of the Image: Visual Methods at the Crossroads," in N. Denzin and Y.S. Lincoln (eds), *Collecting and Interpreting Qualitative Materials.* London: SAGE. pp. 130–149.

Harper, D. (2000) "Reimagining Visual Methods: Galileo to Neuromancer," in N. Denzin and Y.S. Lincoln (eds), *Handbook of Qualitative Research* (2nd edn). London: SAGE. pp. 717–732.

Harper, D. (2004) "Photography as Social Science Data," in U. Flick, E.v. Kardorff and I. Steinke (eds), *A Companion to Qualitative Research.* London: SAGE. pp. 231–236.

Harré, R. (1998) "The Epistemology of Social Representations," in U. Flick (ed.), *Psychology of the Social: Representations in Knowledge and Language.* Cambridge: Cambridge University Press. pp. 129–137.

Hart, C. (1998) *Doing a Literature Review.* London: SAGE.

Hart, C. (2001) *Doing a Literature Search.* London: SAGE.

Haupert, B. (1991) "Vom narrativen Interview zur biographischen Typenbildung," in D. Garz and K. Kraimer (eds), *Qualitativ-empirische Sozialforschung.* Opladen: Westdeutscher Verlag. pp. 213–254.

Haupert, B. (1994) "Objektiv-hermeneutische Fotoanalyse am Beispiel von Soldatenfotos aus dem zweiten Weltkrieg," in D. Garz (ed.), *Die Welt als Text.* Frankfurt: Suhrkamp. pp. 281–314.

Have, P. Ten (1999) *Doing Conversation Analysis: A Practical Guide.* London: SAGE.

Heath, C. and Hindmarsh, J. (2002) "Analysing Interaction: Video, Ethnography, and Situated Conduct," in T. May (ed.), *Qualitative Research in Action.* London: SAGE. pp. 99–120.

Heritage, J. (1985) "Recent Developments in Conversation Analysis," *Sociolinguistics,* 15: 1–17.

Herkommer, S. (1979) *Gesellschaftsbewußtsein und Gewerkschaften.* Hamburg: VSA.

Hermanns, H. (1984) "Ingenieurleben – Der Berufsverlauf von Ingenieuren in biographischer Perspektive," in M. Kolbi and G. Roberts (eds), *Biographie und soziale Wirklichkeit. Neuere Beiträge und Forschungsperspektiven.* Stuttgart: Metzler. pp. 164–191.

Hermanns, H. (1995) "Narratives Interview," in U. Flick, E.v. Kardorff, H. Keupp, L.v. Rosenstiel and S. Wolff (eds), *Handbuch Qualitative Sozialforschung* (2nd edn). Munich: Psychologie Verlags Union. pp. 182–185.

Hermanns, H. (2004) "Interviewing as an Activity," in U. Flick, E.v. Kardorff and I. Steinke (ed.), *A Companion to Qualitative Research*. London: SAGE. pp. 203–208.

Heyl, B.S. (2001) "Ethnographic Interviewing," in P. Atkinson, A. Coffey, S. Delamont, J. Lofland, and L. Lofland (eds) *Handbook of Ethnography*. London: SAGE. pp. 369–383.

Hewson, C., Yule, P., Laurent, D. and Vogel, C. (2003) *Internet Research Methods–A Practical Guide for the Social and Behavioural Sciences*. London: SAGE.

Hildenbrand, B. (1987) "Wer soll bemerken, daß Bernhard krank wird? Familiale Wirklichkeitskonstruktionsprozesse bei der Erstmanifestation einer schizophrenen Psychose," in J.B. Bergold and U. Flick (eds), *Ein-Sichten: Zugänge zur Sicht des Subjekts mittels qualitativer Forschung*. Tübingen: DGVT-Verlag. pp. 151–162.

Hildenbrand, B. (1995) "Fallrekonstruktive Forschung," in U. Flick, E.v. Kardorff, H. Keupp, L.v. Rosenstiel and S. Wolff (eds), *Handbuch Qualitative Sozialforschung* (2nd edn). Munich: Psychologie Verlags Union pp. 256–260.

Hildenbrand, B. and Jahn, W. (1988) "Gemeinsames Erzlihien und Prozesse der Wirklichkeitskonstruktion in familiengeschichtlichen Gesprachen," *Zeitschrift für Soziologie*, 17: 203–217.

Hine, C. (2000) *Virtual Ethnography*. London: SAGE.

Hirst, W. and Manier, D. (1996) "Remembering as Communication: A Family Recounts its Past," in D. Rubin (ed.), *Remembering Our Past: Studies in Autobiographical Memory*. Cambridge: Cambridge University Press. pp. 271–290.

Hitzler, R. and Eberle, T.S. (2004) "Phenomenological Analysis of Lifeworlds," in U. Flick, E.v. Kardorff and I. Steinke (eds), *A Companion to Qualitative Research*. London: SAGE. pp. 67–71.

Hoffmann-Riem, C. (1980) "Die Sozialforschung einer interpretativen Soziologie: Der Datengewinn," *Kölner Zeitschrift für Soziologie und Sozialpsychologie*, 32: 339–372.

Hollingshead, A.B. and Redlich, F. (1958) *Social Class and Mental Illness*. New York: Wiley.

Hopf, C. (1982) "Norm und Interpretation," *Zeitschrift für Soziologie*, 11: 309–327.

Hopf, C. (1982) "Norm und Interpretation," *Zeitschrift für Soziologie*, 7: 97–115.

Honer, A. (2004) "Life-World Analysis in Ethnography," in U. Flick, E.v. Kardorff and I. Steinke (eds), *A Companion to Qualitative Research*. London: SAGE, pp. 113–117.

Hopf, C. (1978) "Die Pseudo-Exploration: Überlegungen zur Technik qualitativer Interviews in der Sozialforschung," *Zeitschrift für Soziologie*, 7: 97–115.

Hopf, C. (1985) "Nichtstandardisierte Erhebungsverfahren in der Sozialforschung. Überlegungen zum Forschungsstand," in M. Kaase and M. Kuchler (eds), *Herausforderungen der empirischen Sozialforschung*. Mannheim. ZUMA. pp. 86–108.

Hopf, C. (2004a) "Qualitative Interviews: An Overview," in U. Flick, E.v. Kardorff and I. Steinke (eds), *A Companion to Qualitative Research*. London: SAGE. pp. 203–208.

Hopf, C. (2004b) "Research Ethics and Qualitative Research: An Overview," in U. Flick, E.v. Kardorff and I. Steinke (eds), *A Companion to Qualitative Research*. London. SAGE. pp. 334–339.

Huberman, A.M. and Miles, M.B. (1998) "Data Management and Analysis Methods," in N. Denzin and Y.S. Lincoln (eds), *Collecting and Interpreting Qualitative Materials*. London: SAGE. pp. 179–211.

Humphreys, L. (1973) "Toilettengeschäfte," in J. Friedrichs (ed.), *Teilnehmende Beobachtung abweichenden Verhaltens*. Stuttgart: Enke. pp. 254–287.

Humphreys, L. (1975) *Tearoom Trade: Impersonal Sex in Public Places* (enlarged edn). New York: Aldine.

Iser, W. (1993) *The Fictive and the Imaginary: Charting Literary Anthropology*. Baltimore: Johns Hopkins University Press.

Jacob, E. (1987) "Qualitative Research Traditions: A Review," *Review of Educational Research*, 57: 1–50.

Jessor, R., Colby, A., and Shweder, R.A. (eds) (1996) *Ethnography and Human Development*. Chicago: Chicago University Press.

Jick, T. (1983) "Mixing Qualitative and Quantitative Methods: Triangulation in Action," in J.v. Maanen (ed.), *Qualitative Methodology*. London: SAGE. pp. 135–148.

Joas, H. (1987) "Symbolic Interactionism," in A. Giddens and J.H. Turner (eds), *Social Theory Today*. Cambridge: Polity Press. pp. 82–115.

Joffe, H. and Bettega, N. (2003) "Social Representations of AIDS among Zambian Adolescents," *Journal of Health Psychology*, 8: 616–631.

Jorgensen, D.L. (1989) *Participant Observation: A Methodology for Human Studies*. London: SAGE.

Kamiske, G.F. and Brauer, J.P. (1995) *Qualitätsmanagement von A bis Z: Erläuterungen moderner Begriffe des Qualitätsmanagements* (2nd edn). Munich: Carl Hanser Verlag.

Kelle, U. (ed.) (1995) *Computer-aided Qualitative Data Analysis: Theory, Methods, and Practice*. London: SAGE.

Kelle, U. (2000) "Computer Assisted Analysis: Coding and Indexing," in M. Bauer and G. Gaskell (eds), *Qualitative Researching with Text, Image, and Sound*. London: SAGE. pp. 282–298.

Kelle, U. (2004) "Computer Assisted Analysis of Qualitative Data," in U. Flick, E.v. Kardorff and I. Steinke (eds), *A Companion to Qualitative Research*. London: SAGE. pp. 276–283.

Kelle, U. and Erzberger, C. (2004) "Quantitative and Qualitative Methods: No Confrontation," in U. Flick, E.v. Kardorff and I. Steinke (eds), *A Companion to Qualitative Research*. London: SAGE. pp. 172–177.

Kendall, L. (1999) "Recontextualising Cyberspace: Methodological Considerations for On-Line Research," in S. Jones (ed.), *Doing Internet Research–Critical Issues and Methods for Examining the Net*. London: SAGE. pp. 57–74.

Kelle, U. and Laurie, H. (1995) "Computer Use in Qualitative Research and Issues of Validity," in U. Kelle (ed.), *Computer-aided Qualitative Data Analysis: Theory, Methods, and Practice*. London: SAGE. pp. 19–28.

Kirk, J.L. and Miller, M. (1986) *Reliability and Validity in Qualitative Research*. Beverly Hills, CA: SAGE.

Kitzinger, C. (2004) "The Internet as Research Context Research," in C. Seale, G. Gobo, J. Gubrium and D. Silverman (eds), *Qualitative Research Practice*. London: SAGE. pp. 125–140.

Kleining, G. (1982) "Umriss zu einer Methodologie qualitativer Sozialforschung," *Kölner Zeitschrift für Soziologie und Sozialpsychologie*, 34: 224–53.

Knoblauch, H. (2004) "The Future Prospects of Qualitative Research," in U. Flick, E.v. Kardorff and I. Steinke (eds), *A Companion to Qualitative Research*. London: SAGE. pp. 354–358.

Knoblauch, H., Heath, C. and Luff, P. (2000) "Technology and Social Interaction: The Emergence of Workplace Studies," *British Journal of Sociology*, 51, 2: 299–320.

Knoblauch, H. and Luckmann, Th. (2004) "Genre Analysis," in U. Flick, E.v. Kardorff and I. Steinke (eds)*, A Companion to Qualitative Research*. London: SAGE. pp. 303–307.

Knorr-Cetina, K. (1981) *The Manufacture of Knowledge: An Essay on the Constructivist and Contextual Nature of Science*. Oxford: Pergamon Press.

Knorr-Cetina, K. and Mulkay, M. (eds) (1983) *Science Observed: Perspectives on the Social Studies of Science*. London: SAGE.

Köckeis-Stangl, E. (1982) "Methoden der Sozialisationsforschung," in K. Hurrelmann and D. Ulich (eds), *Handbuch der Sozialisationsforschung.* Weinheim: Beltz. pp. 321–370.

König, R. (1984) "Soziologie und Ethnologie," *Kölner Zeitschrift für Soziologie und Sozialpsychologie,* Sonderheft 26: *Ethnologie als Sozialwissenschaft:* 17–35.

König, H.D. (2004) "Deep Structure Hermeneutics," in U. Flick, E.v. Kardorff and I. Steinke (eds), *A Companion to Qualitative Research.* London: SAGE. pp. 313–320.

Koepping, K.P. (1987) "Authentizitat als Selbstfindung durch den anderen: Ethnologie zwischen Engagement und Reflexion, zwischen Leben und Wissenschaft, in H.P. Duerr (ed.), *Authentizität und Betrug in der Ethnologie.* Frankfurt. Suhrkamp. pp. 7–37.

Kowall, S. and O'Connell, D.C. (2004) "Transcribing Conversations," in U. Flick, E.v. Kardorff and I. Steinke (eds), *A Companion to Qualitative Research.* London: SAGE. pp. 248–252.

Krüger, H. (1983) "Gruppendiskussionen: Überlegungen zur Rekonstruktion sozialer Wirklichkeit aus der Sicht der Betroffenen," *Soziale Welt,* 34: 90–109.

Kuckartz, U. (1995) "Case-oriented Quantification," in U. Kelle (ed.), *Computer-aided Qualitative Data Analysis.* London: SAGE. pp. 158–166.

Kvale, S. (ed.) (1989) *Issues of Validity in Qualitative Research.* Lund: Studentlitteratur.

Kvale, S. (1996) *Interviews: An Introduction to Qualitative Research Interviewing.* London: SAGE.

Lather, P. (1993) "Fertile Obsession: Validity after Post-structuralism," *Sociological Quarterly,* 35: 673–693.

Lau, T. and Wolff, S. (1983) "Der Einstieg in das Untersuchungsfeld als soziologischer Lernprozeß," *Kölner Zeitschrift für Soziologie und Sozialpsychologie,* 35: 417–37.

Lee, R.M. (2000) *Unobstrusive Methods in Social Research.* Buckingham: Open University Press.

Lee, R.M. and Fielding, N. (1991) "Computing for Qualitative Research: Options, Problems and Potential," in N. Fielding and R.M. Lee (eds), *Using Computers in Qualitative Research.* London. SAGE. pp. 1–14.

Legewie, H. (1987) "Interpretation und Validierung biographischer Interviews," in G. Jüttemann and H. Thomae (eds), *Biographie und Psychologie.* Berlin: Springer. pp. 138–150.

Legewie, H. (1994) "Globalauswertung," in A. Böhm, T. Muhr and A. Mengel (eds), *Texte verstehen: Konzepte, Methoden, Werkzeuge.* Konstanz: Universitätsverlag. pp. 100–114.

Lincoln, Y.S. and Denzin, N.K. (2000) "The Seventh Moment," in N. Denzin and Y.S. Lincoln (eds), *Handbook of Qualitative Research* (2nd edn). London: SAGE. pp. 1047–1065.

Lincoln, Y.S. and Guba, E.G. (1985) *Naturalistic Inquiry.* London: SAGE.

Livingston, E. (1986) *The Ethnomethodological Foundations of Mathematics.* London: Routledge and Kegan Paul.

Lofland, J.H. (1974) "Styles of Reporting Qualitative Field Research," *American Sociologist,* 9: 101–111.

Lofland, J. and Lofland, L.H. (1984) *Analyzing Social Settings* (2nd edn). Belmont, CA: Wadsworth.

Luckmann, Th. (1995) "Interaction Planning and Intersubjective Adjustment of Perspectives by Communicative Genres," in E.N. Goody (ed.), *Social Intelligence and Interaction. Expressions and Implications of the Social Bias in Human Intelligence.* Cambridge: Cambridge University Press. pp. 175–189.

Lüders, C. (1991) "Deutungsmusteranalyse: Annäherungen an ein risikoreiches Konzept," in D. Garz and K. Kraimer (eds), *Qualitativ-empirische Sozialforschung.* Opladen: Westdeutscher Verlag. pp. 377–408.

Lüders, C. (1995) "Von der Teilnehmenden Beobachtung zur ethnographischen Beschreiibung –
Ein Literaturbericht," in E. König and P. Zedler (eds), *Bilanz qualitativer Forschung,* Vol. 1.
Weinheim: Deutscher Studienverlag. pp. 311–342.

Lüders, C. (2004a) "Field Observation and Ethnography," in U. Flick, E.v. Kardorff and I. Steinke
(eds), *A Companion to Qualitative Research.* London: SAGE. pp. 222–230.

Lüders, C. (2004b) "The Challenges of Qualitative Research," in U. Flick, E.v. Kardorff and I. Steinke
(eds), *A Companion to Qualitative Research.* London: SAGE. pp. 359–364.

Lüders, C. and Reichertz, J. (1986) "Wissenschaftliche Praxis ist, wenn alles funktioniert und keiner
weiß warum: Bemerkungen zur Entwicklung qualitativer Sozialforschung," *Sozialwissenschaftliche
Literaturrundschau,* 12: 90–102.

Lunt, P. and Livingstone, S. (1996) "Rethinking the Focus Group in Media and Communications
Research," *Journal of Communication,* 46: 79–98.

Lyotard, J.-F. (1984) *The Postmodern Condition: A Report on Knowledge.* Manchester: Manchester
University Press.

Madill, A., Jordan, A. and Shirley, C. (2000) "Objectivity and Reliability in Qualitative Analysis:
Realist, Contextualist, and Radical Constructionist Epistemologies," *British Journal of
Psychology*, 91: 1–20.

Maijalla, H., Astedt-Kurki, P. and Paavilainen, E. (2002) "Interaction as an Ethically Sensitive
Subject of Research," *Nurse Researcher*, 10: 20–37.

Malinowski, B. (1916) *Magic, Science, and Religion and Other Essays.* New York: Natural History
Press, 1948.

Mangold, W. (1973) "Gruppendiskussionen," in R. König (ed.), *Handbuch der empirischen
Sozialforschung.* Stuttgart: Enke. pp. 228–259.

Mann, C. and Stewart, F. (2000) *Internet Communication and Qualitative Research–A Handbook for
Researching Online.* London: SAGE.

Markham, A. M. (2004) "The Internet as Research Context Research," in C. Seale, G. Gobo,
J. Gubrium and D. Silverman (eds), *Qualitative Research Practice.* London: SAGE. pp. 358–374.

Marshall, C. and Rossman, G. B. (1995) *Designing Qualitative Research* (2nd edn). Thousand Oaks,
London, New Dehli: SAGE.

Mason, J. (2002) "Qualitative Interviewing: Asking, Listening, and Interpreting," in T. May (ed.),
Qualitative Research in Action. London: SAGE. pp. 225–241.

Mauthner, M., Birch, M., Jessop, J. and Miller, T. (eds) (2002) *Ethics in Qualitative Research.*
London, Thousand Oaks, New Dehli: SAGE.

Maxwell, J.A. (1996) *Qualitative Research Design–An Interactive Approach.* Thousand Oaks,
London, New Dehli: SAGE.

Maynard, M. (1998) "Feminists' Knowledge and the Knowledge of Feminisms: Epistemology,
Theory Methodology, and Method," in T. May and M. Williams (eds), *Knowing the Social World.
Buckingham:* Open University Press.

Mayring, P. (1983) *Qualitative Inhaltsanalyse. Grundlagen und Techniken* (7th edn. 1997).
Weinheim: Deutscher Studien Verlag.

Mayring, Ph. (2000) "Qualitative Content Analysis," *Forum: Qualitative Social Research,* 1 (2). qual-
itative-research.net/fqs.

Mayring, P. (2004) "Qualitative Content Analysis," in U. Flick, E.v. Kardorff and I. Steinke (eds), *A
Companion to Qualitative Research.* London: SAGE. pp. 266–269.

McKinlay, J.B. (1993) "The Promotion of Health through Planned Sociopolitical Change: Challenges
for Reserach and Policy," *Social Science and Medicine*, 38: 109–117.

McKinlay, J.B. (1995) "Towards Appropriate Levels: Research Methods and Healthy Public Policies," in I. Guggenmoos-Holzmann, K. Bloomfield, H. Brenner and U. Flick (eds), *Quality of Life and Health: Concepts, Methods, and Applications.* Berlin: Basil Blackwell. pp. 161–182.

Mead, M. (1963) "Anthropology and the Camera," in W.D. Morgan (ed.), *The Encyclopedia of Photography,* Vol. I. New York: Greystone. pp. 163–184.

Merkens, H. (1989) "Einleitung," in R. Aster, H. Merkens and M. Repp (eds), *Teilnehmende Beobachtung: Werkstattberichte und methodologische Reflexionen.* Frankfurt: Campus. pp. 9–18.

Merkens, H. (2004) "Selection Procedures, Sampling, Case Construction," in U. Flick, E.v. Kardorff and I. Steinke (eds), *A Companion to Qualitative Research.* London, SAGE. pp. 165–171.

Merton, R.K. (1987) "The Focused Interview and Focus Groups: Continuities and Discontinuities," *Public Opinion Quarterly,* 51: 550–56.

Merton, R.K. and Kendall, P.L. (1946) "The Focused Interview," *American Journal of Sociology,* 51: 541–57.

Merton, R.K., Fiske, M. and Kendall, P.L. (1956) *The Focused Interview.* Glenoe, IL: Free Press.

Meuser, M. and Nagel, U. (2002) "ExpertInneninterviews – vielfach erprobt, wenig bedacht. Ein Beitrag zur qualitativen Methodendiskussion," in A. Bogner, B. Littig and W. Menz (eds), *Das Experteninterview.* Opladen: Leske & Budrich. pp. 71–95.

Mies, M. (1983) "Towards a Methodology for Feminist Research," in G. Bowles and R. Duelli Klein (eds), *Theories of Womens's Studies.* London: Routledge. pp. 120–130.

Miles, M.B. and Huberman, A.M. (1994) *Qualitative Data Analysis: A Sourcebook of New Methods* (2nd edn). Newbury Park, CA: SAGE.

Mishler, E.G. (1986) "The Analysis of Interview-Narratives," in T.R. Sarbin (ed.), *Narrative Psychology.* New York: Praeger. pp. 233–255.

Mishler, E.G. (1990) "Validation in Inquiry-Guided Research: The Role of Exemplars in Narrative Studies," *Harvard Educational Review,* 60: 415–442.

Mitra, A. and Cohen, E. (1999) "Analyzing the Web: Directions and Challenges," in S. Jones (ed.), *Doing Internet Research–Critical Issues and Methods for Examining the Net.* London: SAGE, pp. 179–202.

Morgan, D.L. (1988). *Focus Groups as Qualitative Research.* Newbury Park, CA: SAGE.

Morgan, D.L. and Krueger, R.A. (eds) (1998) *The Focus Group Kit* (6 vols). Thousand Oaks, CA: SAGE.

Morse, J.M. (1998) "Designing Funded Qualitative Research," in N. Denzin and Y.S. Lincoln (eds), *Strategies of Qualitative Research.* London: SAGE. pp. 56–85.

Moscovici, S. (1973) "Foreword," in C. Herzlich, *Health and Illness: A Social Psychological Analysis.* London: Academic Press.

Muhr, T. (1991) "ATLAS•ti: A Prototype for the Support of Textinterpretation," *Qualitative Sociology,* 14: 349–371.

Muhr, T. (1994) "ATLAS•ti: Ein Werkzeug für die Textinterpretation," in A. Böhm, T. Muhr and A. Mengel (eds), *Texte verstehen: Konzepte, Methoden, Werkzeuge.* Konstanz: Universitätsverlag. pp. 317–324.

Murphy, J.A. (1994) *Dienstleistungsqualität in der Praxis.* Munich: Carl Hanser Verlag.

Murphy, E. and Dingwall, R. (2001) "The Ethics of Ethnography," in P. Atkinson, A. Coffey, S. Delamont, J. Lofland, and L. Lofland (eds), *Handbook of Ethnography.* London: SAGE. pp. 339–351.

Murray, M. (2000) "Levels of Narrative Analysis in Health Psychology," *Journal of Health Psychology,* 5: 337–349.

Niemann, M. (1989) "Felduntersuchungen an Freizeitorten Berliner Jugendlicher," in R. Aster, H. Merkens and M. Repp (eds), *Teilnehmende Beobachtung: Werkstattberichte und methodologische Reflexionen.* Frankfurt. Campus. pp. 71–83.

NIH (Office of Behavioral and Social Sciences Research) (ed.) (2001) *Qualitative Methods in Health Research: Opportunities and Considerations in Application and Review*. No. 02–5046, December. Washington.

Northway, R. (2002) "Commentary," *Nurse Researcher*, 10: 4–7.

Oakley, A. (1999) "People's Ways of Knowing: Gender and Methodology," in S. Hood, B. Mayall and S. Olivier (eds), *Critical Issues in Social Research: Power and Prejudice*. Buckingham: Open University Press. pp. 154–170.

O'Connell, D. and Kowall, S. (1995) "Basic Principles of Transcription," in J. A. Smith, R. Harré and L.v. Langenhove (eds), *Rethinking Methods in Psychology*. London, Thousand Oaks, New Dehli: SAGE. pp. 93–104.

Oerter, R. (1995) "Persons Conception of Human Nature: A Cross-Cultural Comparison," in J. Valsiner (ed.), *Comparative Cultural and Constructivist Perspectives. Vol. III, Child Development within Culturally Structured Environments*. Norwood, NJ: Ablex. pp. 210–242.

Oerter, R., Oerter, R., Agostiani, H., Kim, H.O. and Wibowo, S. (1996) "The Concept of Human Nature in East Asia: Etic and Emic Characteristics," *Culture & Psychology*, 2: 9–51.

Oevermann, U., Allert, T., Konau, E., and Krambeck, J. (1979) "Die Methodologie einer 'objektiven Hermeneutik' und ihre allgemeine forschungslogische Bedeutung in den Sozialwissenschaften," in H.G. Soeffner (ed.), *Interpretative Verfahren in den Sozial- und Textwissenschaften*. Stuttgart: Metzler. pp. 352–433.

Parker, I. (2004) "Discourse Analysis," in U. Flick, E.v. Kardorff and I. Steinke (eds), *A Companion to Qualitative Research*. London: SAGE. pp. 308–312.

Parsons, T. and Shils, E. A. (1951) *Towards a General Theory of Action*. Harward, MA: Harvard University.

Patton, M.Q. (2002) *Qualitative Evaluation and Research Methods* (3rd edn). London: SAGE.

Petermann, W. (1995) "Fotografie- und Filmanalyse," in U. Flick, E.v. Kardorff, H. Keupp, L.v. Rosenstiel and S. Wolff (eds), Handbuch Qualitative Sozialforschung (2nd edn), München: Psychologie Verlags Union. pp. 228–231.

Pollock, F. (1955) *Gruppenexperiment: Ein Studienbericht*. Frankfurt: Europäische Verlagsanstalt.

Potter, J. and Wetherell, M. (1987) *Discourse and Social Psychology: Beyond Attitudes and Behaviour*. London: SAGE.

Potter, J. and Wetherell, M. (1998) "Social Representations, Discourse Analysis, and Racism," in U. Flick (ed.), *Psychology of the Social: Representations in Knowledge and Language*. Cambridge: Cambridge University Press. pp. 177–200.

Prior, L. (2003) *Using Documents in Social Research*. London: SAGE.

Puchta, C. and Potter, J. (2004) *Focus Group Practice*. London: SAGE.

Ragin, C.C. (1994) *Constructing Social Research*. Thousand Oaks, London, New Dehli: Pine Forge Press.

Ragin, C.C. and Becker, H.S. (eds) (1992) *What Is a Case? Exploring the Foundations of Social Inquiry*. Cambridge: Cambridge University Press.

Reicher, S. (2000) "Against Methodolatry: Some Comments on Elliot, Fischer, and Rennie," *British Journal of Clinical Psychology*, 39: 11–26.

Reichertz, J. (1992) "Beschreiben oder Zeigen: Über das Verfassen ethnographischer Berichte," *Soziale Welt*, 43: 331–350.

Reichertz, J. (2004) "Objective Hermeneutics and Hermeneutic Sociology of Knowledge," in U. Flick, E.v. Kardorff and I. Steinke (eds), *A Companion to Qualitative Research*. London: SAGE. pp. 290–295.

Rheingold, H. (1993) *The Virtual Community: Homesteading on the Electronic Frontier.* Reading, MA: Addison-Wesley.

Richards, T.J. and Richards, L. (1998) "Using Computers in Qualitative Research," in N. Denzin and Y.S. Lincoln (eds), *Collecting and Interpreting Qualitative Materials.* London: SAGE. pp. 211–245.

Richardson, L. (1990) *Writing Strategies, Reaching Diverse Audiences.* London. SAGE.

Richardson, L. (2000) "Writing: A Method of Inquiry," in N. Denzin and Y.S. Lincoln (eds), *Handbook of Qualitative Research* (2nd edn). London: SAGE. pp. 923–948.

Ricoeur, P. (1981) "Mimesis and Representation," *Annals of Scholarship,* 2: 15–32.

Ricoeur, P. (1984) *Time and Narrative,* Vol. 1. Chicago. The University of Chicago Press.

Riemann, G. (1987) *Das Fremdwerden der eigenen Biographie: Narrative Interviews mit psychia- trischen Patienten.* Munich: Fink.

Riemann, G. and Schütze, F. (1987) "Trajectory as a Basic Theoretical Concept for Analyzing Suffering and Disorderly Social Processes," in D. Maines (ed.), *Social Organization and Social Process: Essays in Honor of Anselm Strauss.* New York: Aldine de Gruyter. pp. 333–357.

Roller, E., Mathes, R. and Eckert, T. (1995) "Hermeneutic-Classificatory Content Analysis," in U. Kelle (ed.), *Computer-aided Qualitative Data Analysis.* London: SAGE. pp. 167–176.

Rosenthal, G. (1993) "Reconstruction of Life Stories: Principles of Selection in Generating Stories for Narrative Biographical Interviews," *The Narrative Study of Lives,* 1 (1): 59–81.

Rosenthal, G. (2004) "Biographical Research," in C. Seale, G. Gobo, J. Gubrium, and D. Silverman (eds), *Qualitative Research Practice.* London: SAGE. pp. 48–65.

Rosenthal, G. and Fischer-Rosenthal, W. (2004) "The Analysis of Biographical-Narrative Interviews," in U. Flick, E.v. Kardorff and I. Steinke (eds), *A Companion to Qualitative Research.* London: SAGE. pp. 259–265.

Ruff, F.M. (1990) *Ökologische Krise und Umweltbewußtsein: zur psychischen Verarbeitung von Umweltbelastungen.* Wiesbaden: Deutscher Universitatsverlag.

Ruff, F.M. (1998) "Gesundheitsgefährdungen durch Umweltbelastungen: Ein neues Deutungsmuster," in U. Flick (ed.), *Wann fühlen wir uns gesund?* Weinheim: Juventa. pp. 285–300.

Sacks, H. (1992) *Lectures on Conversation,* Vols 1, 2 (ed. by G. Jefferson). Oxford: Blackwell.

Sacks, H., Schegloff, E. and Jefferson, G. (1974) "A Simplest Systematics for the Organization of Turntaking for Conversation," *Language,* 4: 696–735.

Sahle, R. (1987) *Gabe, Almosen, Hilfe.* Opladen: Westdeutscher Verlag.

Sanjek, R. (ed.) (1990) *Fieldnotes: The Making of Anthropology.* Albany: State University of New York Press.

Sarbin, T.R. (ed.) (1986) *Narrative Psychology: The Storied Nature of Human Conduct.* New York: Praeger.

Schatzmann, L. and Strauss, A.L. (1973) *Field Research.* Englewood Cliffs, NJ: Prentice Hall.

Scheele, B. and Groeben, N. (1988) *Dialog-Konsens-Methoden zur Rekonstruktion Subjektiver Theorien.* Tübingen: Francke.

Schegloff, E. and Sacks, H. (1974) "Opening up Closings," in R. Turner (ed.), *Ethnomethodology.* Harmondsworth: Penguin. pp. 233–264.

Schneider, G. (1985) "Strukturkonzept und Interpretationspraxis der objektiven Hermeneutik," in G. Jüttemann (ed.), *Qualitative Forschung in der Psychologie.* Weinheim: Beltz. pp. 71–91.

Schneider, G. (1988) "Hermeneutische Strukturanalyse von qualitativen Interviews," *Kölner Zeitschrift für Soziologie und Sozialpsychologie,* 40: 223–244.

Schönberger, Ch. and Kardorff, E.v. (2004) *Mit dem kranken Partner leben.* Opladen: Leske & Budrich.

Schütz, A. (1962) *Collected Papers,* Vols I, II. Den Haag. Nijhoff.

Schutze, F. (1976) "Zur Hervorlockung und Analyse von Erzählungen thematisch relevanter Geschichten im Rahmen soziologischer Feldforschung," in Arbeitsgruppe Bielefelder Soziologen (eds), *Kommunikative Sozialforschung.* Munich: Fink. pp. 159–260.

Schütze, F. (1977) "Die Technik des narrativen Interviews in Interaktionsfeldstudien, dargestellt an einem Projekt zur Erforschung von kommunalen Machtstrukturen." Manuskript der Universität Bielefeld, Fakultät für Soziologie.

Schütze F. (1983) "Biographieforschung und Narratives Interview," *Neue Praxis,* 3: 283–93.

Schwandt, T.A. and Halpern, E.S. (1988) *Linking Auditing and Metaevaluation: Enhancing Quality in Applied Research.* Thousand Oaks, CA: Sage.

Scott, J. (1990) *A Matter of Record–Documentary Sources in Social Research.* Cambridge: Polity.

Seale, C. (1999) *The Quality of Qualitative Research.* London: SAGE.

Seale, C. (2000) "Using Computers to Analyse Qualitative Data," in D. Silverman (ed.), *Doing Qualitative Research: A Practical Handbook.* London: SAGE. pp. 154–174.

Shweder, R.A. (1996) "True Ethnography: The Lore, the Law, and the Lure," in R. Jessor, A. Colby and R.A. Shweder (eds), *Ethnography and Human Development.* Chicago: Chicago University Press. pp. 15–32.

Silverman, D. (1985) *Qualitative Methodology and Sociology.* Aldershot: Gower.

Silverman, D. (1993/2001) *Interpreting Qualitative Data: Methods for Analyzing Talk, Text and Interaction* (2nd edn). London: SAGE.

Skeggs, B. (2001) "Feminist Ethnography," in P. Atkinson, A. Coffey, S. Delamont, J. Lofland, and L. Lofland (eds), *Handbook of Ethnography.* London: SAGE. pp. 426–442.

Smith, D. (2002) "Institutional Ethnography," in T. May (ed.), *Qualitative Research in Action.* London: SAGE. pp. 17–52.

Smith, J.A. (1995) "Semi-structured Interview and Qualitative Analysis," in J.A. Smith, R. Harré and L.v. Langenhove (eds), *Rethinking Methods in Psychology.* London: SAGE. pp. 9–26.

Soeffner, H.G. (2004) "Social Science Hermeneutics," in U. Flick, E.v. Kardorff and I. Steinke (eds), *A Companion to Qualitative Research.* London: SAGE, pp. 95–100.

Spradley, J.P. (1979) *The Ethnographic Interview.* New York: Holt, Rinehart and Winston.

Spradley, J.P. (1980) *Participant Observation.* New York: Rinehart and Winston.

Sprenger, A. (1989) "Teilnehmende Beobachtung in prekären Handlungssituationen: Das Beispiel Intensivstation," in R. Aster, H. Merkens and M. Repp (eds), *Teilnehmende Beobachtung: Werkstattberichte und methodologische Reflexionen.* Frankfurt: Campus. pp. 35–56.

Stewart, D.M. and Shamdasani, P.N. (1990) *Focus Groups: Theory and Practice.* Newbury Park, CA: SAGE.

Strauss, A.L. (1987) *Qualitative Analysis for Social Scientists.* Cambridge: Cambridge University Press.

Strauss, A.L. and Corbin, J. (1990/1998) *Basics of Qualitative Research* (2nd edn 1998). London: SAGE.

Strauss, A.L., Schatzmann, L., Bucher, R., Ehrlich, D. and Sabshin, M. (1964) *Psychiatric Ideologies and Institutions.* New York: Free Press.

Stryker, S. (1976) "Die Theorie des Symbolischen Interaktionismus," in M. Auwärter, E. Kirsch and K. Schröter (eds), *Seminar. Kommunikation, Interaktion, Identität.* Frankfurt. Suhrkamp. pp. 257–274.

Tashakkori, A. and Teddlie, Ch. (eds) (2003a) *Handbook of Mixed Methods in Social & Behavioral Research*. Thousand Oaks, CA: SAGE.

Tashakkori, A. and Teddlie, Ch. (2003b) "Major Issues and Controversies in the Use of Mixed Methods in Social and Behavioral Research," in A. Tashakkori and Ch. Teddlie (eds), *Handbook of Mixed Methods in Social & Behavioral Research*. Thousand Oaks, CA: SAGE. pp. 3–50.

Thomas, W.I. and Znaniecki, F. (1918–1920) *The Polish Peasant in Europe and America*, Vols 1–2. New York. Knopf.

Toulmin, S. (1990) *Cosmopolis: The Hidden Agenda of Modernity*. New York: The Free Press.

Ulrich, C.G. (1999) "Deutungsmusteranalyse und diskursives Interview," *Zeitschrift für Soziologie*, 28: 429–447.

Ussher, J. (1999) "Feminist Approaches to Qualitative Health Research," in M. Murray and K. Chamberlain (eds), *Qualitative Health Psychology–Theories and Methods*. London. SAGE. pp. 98–110.

Van Maanen, J. (1988) *Tales of the Field: On Writing Ethnography*. Chicago: University of Chicago Press.

Webb, E.J., Campbell, D.T., Schwartz, R.D. and Sechrest, L. (1966) *Unobstrusive Measures: Nonreactive Research in the Social Sciences*. Chicago: Rand McNally.

Weber, M. (1919) "Wissenschaft als Beruf," in J. Winkelmann (ed.), (1988) *Max Weber: Gesammelte Aufsätze zur Wissenschaftslehre*. Tübingen: Mohr. pp. 582–613.

Weber, M. (1949) *The Methodology of the Social Sciences* (trans and edited by Edward A. Shils and Henry A. Finch). New York: Free Press.

Weitzman, E.A. (2000) "Software and Qualitative Research," in N. Denzin and Y.S. Lincoln (eds), *Handbook of Qualitative Research* (2nd edn). London: SAGE. pp. 803–820.

Weitzman, E. and Miles, M.B. (1995) *Computerprograms for Qualitative Data Analysis: A Software Sourcebook*. London: SAGE.

Wengraf, T. (2001) *Qualitative Research Interviewing: Biographic Narrative and Semi-Structured Methods*. London: SAGE.

West, C. and Zimmerman, D.H. (1991) "Doing Gender," in J. Lorber and S.A. Farrell (eds), *The Social Construction of Gender*. Newbury Park, CA: SAGE. pp. 13–37.

Whyte, W.F. (1955) *Street Corner Society*. Enlarged Edition. Chicago: The University of Chicago Press.

Wiedemann, P.M. (1995) "Gegenstandsnahe Theoriebildung," in U. Flick, E.v. Kardorff, H. Keupp, L.v. Rosenstiel and S. Wolff (eds), *Handbuch Qualitative Sozialforschung* (2nd edn). Munich: Psychologie Verlags Union. pp. 440–445.

Wilkinson, S. (1999) "Focus Groups–A Feminist Method," *Psychology of Women Quarterly*, 23: 221–244.

Williamson, G. and Prosser, S. (2002) "Illustrating the Ethical Dimensions of Action Research," *Nurse Researcher*, 10: 38–49.

Willig, C. (2003) *Introducing Qualitative Research in Psychology–Adventures in Theory and Method*. Buckinghamshire: Open University.

Wilson, T.P. (1982) "Quantitative 'oder' qualitative Methoden in der Sozialforschung," *Kölner Zeitschrift für Soziologie und Sozialpsychologie*, 34: 487–508.

Winograd, T. and Flores, F. (1986) *Understanding Computers and Cognition*. Reading, MA: Addison-Wesley.

Winter, R. (2004) "Cultural Studies," in U. Flick, E.v. Kardorff and I. Steinke (eds), *A Companion to Qualitative Research*. London: SAGE. pp. 118–122.

Witzel, A. (1985) "Das problemzentrierte Interview," in G. Jüttemann (ed.), *Qualitative Forschung in der Psychologie.* Weinheim: Beltz. pp. 227–255.

Witzel, Andreas (2000, January). The Problem-Centered Interview [27 paragraphs]. Forum Qualitative Sozialforschung / Forum: Qualitative Social Research [Online Journal], 1(1). www.qualitative-research.net/fqs-texte/1–00/1–00witzel-e.htm [Date of Access: Dec., 10th, 2004].

Wolcott, H.F. (1990a) "On Seeking and Rejecting: Validity in Qualitative Research," in W. Eisner and A. Peshkin (eds), *Qualitative Inquiry in Education: The Continuing Debate.* New York: Teachers College Press. pp. 121–152.

Wolcott, H.F. (1990b) *Writing up Qualitative Research.* London: SAGE.

Wolff, S. (1986) "Das Gespräch als Handlungsinstrument: Konversationsanalytische Aspekte sozialer Arbeit," *Kölner Zeitschrift für Soziologie und Sozialpsychologie,* 38: 55–84.

Wolff, S. (1987) "Rapport und Report. Über einige Probleme bei der Erstellung plausibler ethnographischer Texte," in W. v. d. Ohe (ed.), *Kulturanthropologie: Beiträge zum Neubeginn einer Disziplin.* Berlin. Reimer. pp. 333–364.

Wolff, S. (1992) "Die Anatomie der Dichten Beschreibung: Clifford Geertz als Autor," in J. Matthes (ed.), *Zwischen den Kulturen? Sozialwissenschaften vor dem Problem des Kulturvergleichs.* Soziale Welt Sonderband 8. Göttingen: Schwartz. pp. 339–361.

Wolff, S. (2004a) "Ways into the Field and Their Variants," in U. Flick, E.v. Kardorff and I. Steinke (eds), *A Companion to Qualitative Research.* London. SAGE. pp. 195–202.

Wolff, S. (2004b) "Analysis of Documents and Records," in U. Flick, E.v. Kardorff and I. Steinke (eds), *A Companion to Qualitative Research.* London. SAGE. pp. 284–290.

Wolff, S., Knauth, B. and Leichtl, G. (1988) "Kontaktbereich Beratung. Eine konversationsanalytische Untersuchung zur Verwendungsforschung". Projektbericht, Hildesheim. MS.

Wuggenig, U. (1990) "Die Photobefragung als projektives Verfahren," *Angewandte Sozialforschung,* 16: 109–131.

Wundt, W. (1928) *Elements of Folk Psychology.* London: Allen and Unwin.

Yardley, L. (2000) "Dilemmas in Qualitative Health Research," *Psychology and Health,* 15: 215–228.

Znaniecki, F. (1934) *The Method of Sociology.* New York: Farrar and Rinehart.

NAME INDEX

SUBJECT INDEX

Indexed by Caroline Eley

ABOUT THE AUTHOR

Uwe Flick is trained as a psychologist and sociologist. He is Professor of Qualitative Research in Social Work, Nursing and Gerontology at Alice Salomon University of Applied Sciences in Berlin, Germany. Previously, he was Adjunct Professor at the Memorial University of Newfoundland at St. John's Canada and has been a Lecturer at the Free University of Berlin in Research Methodology, a Reader and Assistant Professor at the Technical University of Berlin in Qualitative Methods and Evaluation; and Associate Professor and Head of the Department of Medical Sociology at the Hannover Medical School. He has held visiting appoinments at the London School of Economics, the Ecole des Hautes Etudes en Sciences Sociales in Paris, at Cambridge University (UK), Memorial University of St. John's (Canada), University of Lisbon (Portugal), in Italy and Sweden, and at the School of Psychology at Massey University, Auckland (NZ). His main research interests are qualitative methods, social representations in the fields of individual and public health, and technological change in everyday life. He is editor or co-editor of *A Companion to Qualitative Research* (London: Sage 2004), *Psychology of the Social* (Cambridge: Cambridge University Press, 1998), *Quality of Life and Health*: Concepts, Methods and Applications (Berlin: Blackwell Science, 1995), and *La perception quotidienne de la Santé et la Maladie: Théories subjectives et Représentations sociales* (Paris: L'Harmattan, 1993).